# Handbook of Winning Football

# Handbook of

# Winning Football

GEORGE ALLEN

with  Don Weiskopf

**Allyn and Bacon, Inc.**
*Boston • London • Sydney*

**Library of Congress Cataloging in Publication Data**

*Allen, George Herbert (date)*
    *Handbook of winning football.*

    *Includes index.*
        *1.  Football.    2.  Football coaching.    I.  Weis-*
*kopf, Don.    II.  Title.*
*GU951.A684        796.33'2077        75-28135*

**ISBN (*hardbound*):  0-205-05426-9**

**ISBN (*paperbound*):  0-205-04880-3**

To my loving wife, Etty,
and family,
Bruce, Jennifer, George, Jr., and Gregory.

They have provided me with appreciation in victory and support in defeat.

Without their support, consideration, and sacrifice, success would have been impossible.

# Contents

## PART 1  Fundamental Skills

**Chapter 1    The Quarterback**    3

Qualifications / Taking the Snap / Pivots / Hand-off / Faking / Running / The Pitchout / Drills

**Chapter 2    Passing**    23

Basic Qualities / Setting Up the Pass / Passing Technique / Types of Passes / Correct Mental Attitude / Split Vision / Faking / Drills

**Chapter 3    Pass Receiving**    39

Qualifications / Stance / Mental Attitude / Releases / Holding Up Receivers / Getting Open / Running under Control / Pass Patterns / The Long Bomb / Adjusting a Pattern / Primary Receivers / The Goal Line Pass / Catching the Ball / Putting the Ball Away / Drills

# Foreword

Ara Parseghian
*University of Notre Dame*

George Allen is one of the most successful and most respected coaches in football today. While numerous qualities have characterized his coaching success, perhaps the key to his brilliant career is his ability to motivate. He has a method of building a togetherness, a team feeling. To some people, the word "togetherness" may sound trite, but I have learned early in my career that a coach has to have it, if he wants to win.

George Allen and his collaborator, Don Weiskopf, have created a book that will undoubtedly rank as an all-time football classic on playing techniques, game strategy, team organization, and training—emphasizing his theory that no detail is too small.

Allen uses a simple, basic approach in developing outstanding football teams. A tough, aggressive defense is the trademark of George Allen–coached teams. He wants his players to *attack* the offense and manhandle it!

A well-organized program of practice and training is typical of George Allen's operation. He is a sound believer in fundamentals, physical conditioning, and purposeful drill. George seems to be the happiest when he is teaching football on the practice field or at squad meetings.

Organization and pre-planning are so essential to the success of a football team, and George has proven quite convincingly that he is one of football's great planners and organizers. A strongly dedicated and demanding coach, he will accept from his players and staff nothing but the best.

George has always been able to get the most out of his football players. One reason, perhaps, is that he takes time to work individually with players. He listens to their problems. When you have the regular workload of preparing for a game, it is difficult to give that individual attention. But George does it!

George Allen is an excellent psychologist.

He has a way of being aware of each player on the team and knowing what makes him tick. Throughout his coaching career, he has given his players a thorough understanding of their responsibilities.

George Allen is a tremendous competitor. His own motivation to win seems to motivate everyone else around him to work just as hard to achieve that goal. And winning is the story of George's coaching career. His winning percentage is an impressive .750, making him the winningest coach in the National Football Conference.

*South Bend, Indiana*

However, when his teams lose, George is reluctant to blame anybody but himself. A defeat becomes a challenge to him. More determined to do a better job, he will prepare a new program, designed to bring victory next time.

Having for many years enjoyed a friendship with George, I am pleased to be able to introduce for him his newest book on football. In my judgment, George Allen's *Handbook of Winning Football* deserves a prominent place in the literature of football.

**Ara Parseghian**
**Former Head Football Coach**
**University of Notre Dame**

# Preface

*Handbook of Winning Football* is, as the title suggests, a very practical guide for winning in football. It is designed for football coaches at all levels—Pop Warner, interscholastic, collegiate, and professional—as well as students of the game who aspire to be the coaches of tomorrow. Described in great detail here are the fundamentals, drills, training, strategy, and tactics used by my teams in Los Angeles and Washington, teams that have enjoyed winning records. This information will help coaches perform their duties with greater skill, confidence, and efficiency so that they may achieve success. It will also be a help to the athlete and serious fan who want to better understand and appreciate the game of football.

*Handbook of Winning Football* shows how to begin with a well-organized pre-season training program and consistently build championship teams—teams with a winning attitude, perfected fundamentals, attacking defenses, explosive offenses that can put points on the board, and special teams that make things happen. It presents a fresh and dynamic approach to today's highly sophisticated offenses and defenses.

Part one, "Fundamental Skills," covers all aspects of individual play, both offensive and defensive, with specific drills for each position. Part two, the extremely thorough section on team play, includes in-depth chapters on team offense, team defense, and special teams. Part three covers the organizational

and training aspects of the football program, including a year-round program of weight training and conditioning. Chapter 17, "Motivating the Team," provides a stimulating approach to team motivation. What more could be asked of a book on football?

Chapter 13, "Special Teams," is perhaps the most detailed and absorbing study of the kicking game ever published. While in Los Angeles, I was the first to hire a special teams coach. The kicking game has unquestionably become an increasingly vital area of football. Just this past year, I saw the need to hire a full-time weight training coach . . . perhaps starting another trend.

The impressive array of photographs in this book includes appealing game-action shots of recent Redskins games, featuring many star players of the National Football League. The text offers exclusive pictures and analysis of the Redskins' game-day organization, including pre-game talks, sideline organization, half-time briefings, and post-game procedures.

I would like to extend my appreciation to the members of my coaching staffs at Los Angeles and Washington for the valuable contributions they made in the writing of the book, and to my players on the Washington Redskins and other NFL teams for their excellent demonstrations of the basic techniques of the game and their commentary on how they play their positions.

I am indebted to George S. Halas, owner

and former head coach of the Chicago Bears, with whom I had a long association, and Edward Bennett Williams, president of the Washington Redskins, for his assistance and cooperation.

Special thanks go to the following: Joe Blair, director of public relations for the Washington Redskins; Bill Hickman, my administrative assistant, who drew many of the diagrams and illustrations; and my personal secretary, Shirley Krystek.

I would also like to express my gratitude to Nate Fine, the official photographer of the Redskins, his son, Paul, and Dick Gentile for their excellent photographs used throughout the book. Nate's dedication to the project and his many services are particularly appreciated. Paul and Dick performed much of the camera work, providing excellent photographs that clarify and complement the text visually. Another strong member of the photographic team was Dave Drennan, who printed many of the photographs and handled a couple of camera assignments. John Griffith, publisher of *Athletic Journal,* provided excellent sequence series on the soccer style of place-kicking, in addition to his overall support of the text. Dave Boss of NFL Properties, Inc., was very kind to take the much-appreciated photo of the Allen family that appears on the dedication page. I would also like to acknowledge the use of the photo laboratory at American River College, with special assistance from Howard Sweezey.

Mrs. Annegrete Weiskopf is deserving of special praise for her long hours of dedicated service in typing the manuscript and handling a variety of important assignments.

The many college and high school coaches across the nation who made significant contributions have my warmest regards and respect, particularly John McKay, University of Southern California; Ara Parseghian, Notre Dame University; Vic Rowen, San Francisco State University; Ray Schultz, American River College (Sacramento); Don Brown, Mira Loma High School (Sacramento); Gary Kenworthy, El Dorado High School (Placerville, California); Ron Marciniak, University of Dayton; Darrell Royal, University of Texas; Bill Yeoman, University of Houston; and John Ralston, former Stanford University head coach, now head coach of the Denver Broncos of the National Football League.

Sincere thanks must go to John Gilman, Dr. Arthur Miller, Paul Solaqua, and Sheryl Avruch for their fine editorial assistance and cooperation, to Amato Prudente, the designer, and the entire production staff of Allyn and Bacon, Inc.

And I would like to express my appreciation to my longtime friend Don Weiskopf of Sacramento for his able assistance in planning, writing, and editing this publication. Don is the author of many books and articles on sports and was responsible for coordinating the excellent photography in this book.

George Allen

# The George Allen Story

From his job as defensive coach for the Chicago Bears, head coach of the Los Angeles Rams, to his present position as head coach and general manager of the Washington Redskins, George Allen's career has been capped with ever-increasing success. Allen played right end at Alma College in 1943 and at Marquette University in 1944. He was a nine-letter winner in high school, competing in football, basketball, and track. George graduated from the University of Michigan with B.A. and M.A. degrees. While at Ann Arbor, he worked with the 150-pound team for two years under H. O. "Fritz" Crisler and Bennie Oosterbaan and tied for the Big Ten championship.

Allen's professional coaching career began in Los Angeles with the Rams in 1957 after nine years of college coaching success at Morningside (Iowa) and Whittier (California). Following the 1957 campaign, Allen left the Rams and joined the staff of the Chicago Bears as a defensive specialist under head coach George Halas. Quickly he became a most valued assistant to Halas. In addition, he was in charge of the Bears' player personnel department.

With the Bears, Allen was instrumental in developing some of the toughest defensive units in the National Football League. He built the Bears' powerful defensive unit that led the league in 10 of 18 defensive categories and finished second in seven others.

His defensive unit crushed the highly potent passing attack of Y. A. Tittle and the New York Giants in the 1963 NFL championship game. For his leadership and teaching, he became the first assistant coach to be awarded the game ball from a championship game.

The spectacular rise of the Los Angeles Rams from perennial loser to title contender in only two years under Allen's tutelage earned George the coveted NFL "Coach of the Year" award by *The St. Louis Sporting News*. When owner Daniel F. Reeves signed him in 1966, the Rams' record over the previous seven years was 65 defeats, 25 wins, and 4 ties. Since 1958, they had failed to produce a winning season or finish better than fifth. Under Coach Allen's direction, they moved up to third place in 1966 with an 8-6-0 record. The following year, the Rams compiled an 11-1-2 season and won the Coastal Division Championship by beating the Green Bay Packers and the Baltimore Colts on consecutive weekends. In 1968, although their record was an impressive 10-3-1, the Rams could not overtake the Colts in a tight race that went down to the final week of play.

The 1969 season proved to be another successful campaign in the remarkable career of Coach Allen. In taking their first 11 league games, Los Angeles made a runaway of the Coastal Division race.

In five years with the Rams, Coach Allen

had a road record of 27 wins, 7 losses, and 2 ties—the best in the NFL and modern football. In the five years prior to Allen's arrival, the Rams' road record was 6 wins, 28 losses, and 2 ties.

When Allen left the Rams to take over the floundering Washington Redskins (whose five-year record was a poor 30-35-5), he made the statement, *"The future is now."* And he commented later: "Foremost in my mind was getting a team on the field capable of being a contender. Washington had been down for so many years that I was certain that we had to do something immediately, not wait and go through a rebuilding process that might take years."

With remarkable genius and trading instinct, Allen put together overnight what has become known as the "Over the Hill Gang." He blended some of the new players into an offense that has been highly effective, but he added most of the newcomers to his revamped defensive unit, with startling results.

"Improving our defense had to be the No. 1 goal," said Allen. "Washington had a fine offense. Then we wanted to improve the kicking, help the offense a bit by getting one more wide receiver, and aid the offensive line by getting one topflight guard."

In his first year in the nation's capital, Coach Allen led the Redskins to the play-offs for the first time in over a quarter of a century. Once again, he had taken a previous perennial loser, changed its image, personnel, and outlook, and produced a winner.

The Redskins went 9-4-1 for their best record in 29 years, they earned their first play-off berth since 1945, and Coach Allen was selected coach of the year. The Redskins allowed only 190 points, the second fewest in

the NFC. Pass protection was the best in their long history, as the quarterbacks were sacked only 17 times.

Then in 1972, Allen took his team to a Super Bowl slot by winning 13 of 16 games, before losing to the Miami Dolphins 14-7. For the second year, he was selected the NFL and NFC "Coach of the Year" by his peers. The 1973 Redskins again made the play-offs with a fine 10-4-0 record. "While we were defeated in the play-offs, we did some good things," said George. "We led all 26 teams in defense against the rush with a 3.3-yard average, which will be hard to improve upon. We had 53 sacks, a team record that also will be hard to match, and led the NFC with 27 interceptions."

Despite a slow start, which could be attributed to the players' strike and a rash of injuries, Allen's 1974 Redskins made the play-offs for the fourth consecutive year. Their 10-4-0 mark earned them a tie with the St. Louis Cardinals for the National Conference Eastern Division title. Although they beat the Rams earlier in the month, the Redskins lost a hard-fought opening play-off game in Los Angeles 19-10.

In summing up the success of his teams, Coach Allen says, "It is a matter of a lot of dedicated people working together . . . the players, the front office, and the people in the community. When we came to Washington, we said we wouldn't let our fans down. We set out to win for them and we did. This team had been a loser for so long, but once we started winning, the fans never let down. They've given us everything . . . standing ovations when we've needed them. Their loyalty has been instrumental in our success."

**Don Weiskopf**

# Profile of a Winning Football Coach

"A winning organization" should be the number 1 objective of every football coach; he can reach this objective only when everyone is going in the same direction—and that is toward a championship. The coach has to develop a winning program and believe in it. Then he must sell the program to his players, the student body, and the community.

*Dedication.* Today's brand of winning football requires total commitment. I do not believe you can win by working only from nine to five. I think anyone who is a nine-to-five type of person is not dedicated enough. You have to take work home and think about your job off the field.

In all the study and review—the training films, the playbooks, the pages of scouting reports—there should be something to give a team the edge. The coaching staff and players must be willing to work to get that edge.

You have to want to win so badly that everyone else around you will work just as hard to win. The head coach himself has to put in the time.

The more setbacks I have, the more I am determined to overcome them. I think every setback can be an asset for you, can strengthen you, bring you closer together, and make you more determined to do a better job.

When you lose, the world does not stop; you do not panic when you lose a game. You simply have to look ahead and work harder. There are no rewards for an easy job.

*Preparation.* A winner is a man who consciously does everything he can think of to prepare himself as completely as possible. A loser is a man who is not prepared and who does not know he is unprepared.

Winning is the science of being totally prepared. Preparing a team to win is what football coaching is all about. My definition of preparation can be stated in only three words: leave nothing undone. That is what 17-hour workdays and 110 percent effort are all about.

I am very fortunate in having a wonderful wife, Etty, who understands me and who is patient. Without such a partner I do not

if you are not willing to pay the price. The tougher the job, the greater the reward.

No task should be too big or too small; no detail is too big or too small. I think of *what* has to be done, not of *whether* it can be done.

You do not win with gimmicks. There are no shortcuts to success. You win with hard work and good football players—players who can hit and those who can run.

An easy-paced training camp might win a coach a popularity contest with his players, but it will not lead him to a championship.

*Pride in Accomplishments.*   I strongly believe that no man is truly alive unless he is accomplishing something. Furthermore, you have to take pride in your accomplishments in order to accomplish fully. I want football players who set achievable goals, who so dedicate themselves that they cannot be swerved from their objective, and who, when they get there, take great pride in having reached the goal.

A winning coach takes pride in what he does, and he is always striving to be the best. He sets goals and he sets them high.

Good things do not just happen to most men. You have to make them happen. Nothing is impossible to those who are willing to pay the price!

think I could succeed completely. In order to do all the things that I want to do with my work, I have to have a wife like mine who will put up with my being away from home so much.

*Striving for Perfection.*   A stickler for detail, the winning coach strives for perfection. The late Vince Lombardi was a perfectionist, and he demanded perfection from everyone. Attention to detail was one of his great attributes. He would make the Packers execute the same plays over and over, one hundred times if necessary, until they would do every little thing right automatically. The Packers practiced technique over and over—but they won!

One of the great qualities in coaching is thoroughness. For example, I want our players to learn all they can about an opponent. I would rather have them "overlearn" than underlearn. There is always something new that will help us know more about the team we are playing and give us an advantage.

*Work.*   Work is simply a synonym for effort. As I tell my players, a 100 percent effort is not enough. The world belongs to those who aim for 110 percent. You cannot win

*Team Play.* Every player must have a strong belief in the total success of the team. Victory can come only if a group of players will go to work together, as a team. Along with the coaching staff, each player must have the same purpose and goal, and it is this kind of group feeling or team spirit that wins games.

A coach must strive to build a togetherness, a team feeling. The team is all-important.

*Motivation.* A coach's success depends on his ability to stimulate players into playing well, on getting them to react with enthusiasm. He must know how to handle and motivate men. Players must be emotionally inspired to play to the best of their ability.

Football is played by people, not by machines. Because each player is unique, each is motivated by something different. The problem that *every* coach has is to get his players properly motivated to execute the fundamentals correctly. Yet, I do not believe a coach should scream at his players. Instead, he should think about teaching, motivation, team spirit, and morale.

In other words, I do not believe in tearing people down. Yelling and screaming is not my style. I do not believe in tearing down. I believe in building up!

*Attaining Goals.* We give all of our units goals to shoot for, something we know they can attain. We set up charts in the meeting room so the players can be reminded at all times of just what they are shooting for. For example, leading the NFL in interceptions was a big achievement to come off our 1971 defensive chart. I told the defensive unit if they intercepted two passes a game, they would be winners. That meant 28 for the season and we had 29. We gave them something to shoot for and they proved to themselves they could do it.

Experience over the years will help the coach know what goals to set. We have done a complete study of how teams who won got to that point. For instance, if you hold your opponents under 200 points for the season, then you should win the title.

The key to a goal system is not to allow a team to forget what it is striving to achieve. I go over it with our team all the time so they won't forget. I try to make them aware of the goals constantly so they won't let down. When they walk into the meeting room, the players see those charts on the wall. They see what they must do, what they have already done, and how it has affected the outcome of each game.

*Communication.* One of the most important jobs of a coach is to communicate with his players. He must have the ability to relate to his players, to establish the rapport necessary for a harmonious coach-player relationship.

While a coach can be tough, he should also be human. Players recognize and appreciate that. The players must respect the coach's authority, but they also must know he will be fair with them.

While the coach has a responsibility to criticize, he should be ready to praise as well.

*Solving Problems.* Football coaching consists of an unending series of problems. A problem is only a problem when you cannot solve it. The winning coach is a successful problem-licker. When I talk about total preparation, I mean overcoming every problem.

The coach should take time to work individually with players and listen to their problems. Normally, with the regular workload of preparing for a game, it is difficult for the coach to give that individual attention. But if he can do it, he will be much closer to his players.

*A Balanced Attack.* A sound running game is the basis for establishing a balanced attack. The majority of coaches today stress ball control and a strong defense. To establish a good ball control offense, a strong ground game is necessary. An effective passing game, however, must complement inside running power and quick outside pitchouts, roll-outs, and sweeps.

The running game, of course, sets up the passing attack. If the defense feels it can rush our passer without fear of the run we are in trouble! Having a two-dimensional offense enables us to do a much better job in attacking the defense.

As for the front line, I cannot overemphasize the importance of producing strong lines, offensively and defensively. Sharp, effective blocking is an absolute must for both the run and the pass. The team that controls the line of scrimmage wins the game.

*A Strong Defense.* Without a strong defense, a good offense can lose its effectiveness by working against mounting resistance, often from poor field position. Furthermore, if you cannot stop your opponents, you do not get the football. Every man on the defensive unit must believe that he is going to make a big play on every play. If he does, he *will* be ready.

Very seldom have I seen a football game won by a team that did not play good defense—that did not block and tackle. To have a good defense, the players have to be good enough to stop the run. If you cannot stop a simple run on first and 10, you have got to start wondering.

*Execution.* Execution of the fundamentals—not new formations—wins football games. The team that plays basic football and executes well will win its share of games. What the coach puts in the playbook is not worth much if it cannot be done on the playing field.

Football is a team game, a sport of precision and unit cohesion.

*Aggressiveness.* An aggressive attitude is absolutely necessary in winning football games—both on offense and defense. Therefore, a team must be given a lot of aggressive, physical work to properly prepare for a ball game. By game time, they must be ready to pay whatever price it takes to be physical and aggressive.

Football is a physical game: the team that hits hardest wins. A football player may be big, fast, and have all the moves, but the key question his coaches want to determine is: "Will he hit?"

Coaching football is the greatest profession in the world and I would not trade it for anything.

George Allen

# GEORGE ALLEN'S TEN COMMANDMENTS

1. Football comes first.
2. The greatest feeling in life is to take an ordinary job and accomplish something with it.
3. If you can accept defeat and open your pay envelope without feeling guilty, then you are stealing.
4. Everyone, the head coach especially, must give 110 percent.
5. Leisure time is that five or six hours when you sleep at night.
6. No detail is too small. No task is too small, or too big.
7. You must accomplish things in life; otherwise, you are like the paper on the wall.
8. A person without problems is dead.
9. We win and lose as a team.
10. My prayer is that each man will be allowed to play to the best of his ability.

# Series Foreword

## The Allyn and Bacon Sports Education Series
### Arthur G. Miller, *Consulting Editor*

Sports play a major role in the lives of practically everyone—the players, the coaches, the officials, and the spectators! Interest in sports is the result of several factors.

There is increased emphasis on *personal physical fitness.* Formal exercises or calisthenics, while worthwhile, are not as popular nor as motivating to the promotion of fitness as participation in sports. Through *sports participation,* children and adults gain fitness but also develop skills, group and personal satisfactions, and enjoyment.

Another factor in the growing interest in sports is the increase in television and radio broadcasts of sporting events. Team sports such as baseball, football, basketball, soccer, and hockey are seasonally covered by practically all channels. The lifetime sports including bowling, golf, tennis, and skiing are also receiving more air time. Activities such as gymnastics, swimming, and other aquatic sports have, and will continue to receive, more expanded coverage. The analysis of skills and strategy within each sport by knowledgeable commentators using instant video replay and stop-action techniques, makes the game or activity more interesting to the viewer.

The Allyn and Bacon Sports Education Series has been created to meet the need for players, coaches, and spectators to be informed about the basic and advanced skills, techniques, tactics, and strategies of sports. Each book in the Series is designed to pro-vide an in-depth treatment of a selected sport or activity. Players find the individual skills and accompanying picture sequences very valuable. Coaches gain basic and advanced knowledge of individual and team play along with techniques of coaching. Sports fans are provided information about the activities and are thus able to become more knowledgeable about and appreciative of the basic and finer aspects of sports.

The authors of the Sports Education Series have been carefully selected. They include experienced teachers, coaches, and managers of college and professional teams. Some books represent the combined effort of two or more authors, each with a different background and each contributing particular strengths to the text. For other books, a single author has been selected, whose background offers a breadth of knowledge and experience in the sport being covered.

Among the authors and titles of some of the team-sport books is George Allen, successful coach of the Washington Redskins, who collaborated with Don Weiskopf on the informative book *Handbook of Winning Football.* Weiskopf also wrote with Walter Alston, of the Los Angeles Dodgers, *The Complete Baseball Handbook,* and *The Baseball Handbook.* The book *Basketball—Concepts and Techniques,* by Bob Cousy and Frank Power, presents the game for men. *Women's Basketball,* by Mildred Barnes of Central Missouri State

University, covers the "new" five-player game for girls and women. Dr. Barnes also wrote the book *Field Hockey. The Challenge of Soccer* is by Hubert Vogelsinger, coach of the Boston Minutemen, and the book *Winning Volleyball* was written by Allen Scates of UCLA. A group of authors including General Managers Jack Kelley of the New England Whalers and Milt Schmidt of the Washington Capitals collaborated on the book *Hockey— Bantam to Pro.*

Individual sports included in the series are: *Advantage Tennis: Racket Work, Tactics, and Logic* by Jack Barnaby of Harvard University, *Modern Track and Field for Girls and Women* by Donnis Thompson of the University of Hawaii, *Track and Field* by Jim Bush and Don Weiskopf, and *Women's Gymnastics* by Kitty Kjeldsen, formerly of the University of Massachusetts.

Dr. Thomas Tutko and Jack Richards collaborated on the meaningful book, *Psychology of Coaching,* and Patsy Neal of Bre-vard College also collaborated with Dr. Tutko on *Coaching Girls and Women: Psychological Perspectives.*

This sports series enables readers to experience the thrills of the sport from the point of view of participants and coaches, to learn some of the reasons for success and causes of failure, and to receive basic information about teaching and coaching techniques.

Each volume in the series reflects the philosophy of the authors, but a common theme runs through all: the desire to instill in the reader a knowledge and appreciation of sports and physical activity which will carry over throughout his life as a participant or a spectator. Pictures, drawings, and diagrams are used throughout each book to clarify and illustrate the discussion.

The reader, whether a beginner or one experienced in sports, will gain much from each book in this Allyn and Bacon Sports Education Series.

Arthur G. Miller
**Chairman, Department of Human Movement and Health Education Boston University**

# Part One

# FUNDAMENTAL SKILLS

# 1

# The Quarterback

The T-formation quarterback is the key man in today's wide-open, Pro-style formations. He has to be proficient at many tasks. He must be a passer, a general, and, on occasion, a runner. Moreover, he has to be a clever ball handler, an expert faker, and a skillful coordinator and director of the offense.

No other position in sports demands such rigid conformity to the fundamentals. From Pop Warner to pro, the better he learns the fundamentals, the better the quarterback will perform. Therefore, a coach spends more time with his quarterback and his backup man than he does with any of the other players.

Quarterbacks in the NFL are rated in five departments:

- Leadership
- Reaction under pressure
- Setup speed
- Throwing ability
- Ability to read defenses

A top quarterback must have a strong and quick arm, durability, and good vision. In addition to reading the defense, he must be able to hit his receiver at the right time—to hit him on the break. What makes an outstanding passer is the ability to hit the receiver on the break.

The quarterback has the responsibility to lead and direct his team toward the goal line. This calls for the proper selection of plays, which demands a sound understanding of offensive football and—above all—defensive football. The signal caller must have the ability to detect defensive weaknesses and take advantage of what the opposition is doing.

**A**

**B**

FIGURE 1-2. The complete quarterback, exemplified by Sonny Jurgensen (A), Joe Theismann (B), and Bill Kilmer (C). The quarterback is a real asset to a ball club if he can pass well, run, and be a good ball handler. He has to provide able leadership.

**C**

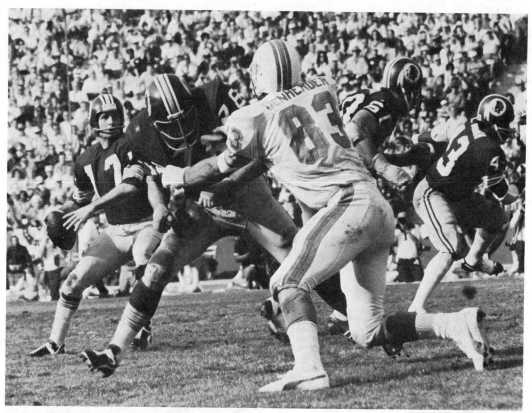

FIGURE 1-3. *The quarterback has to be a passer. He must be disciplined to stay in the pocket and throw. Above, Bill Kilmer (17) has time to get set on his back foot and is ready to step up into the pocket to throw the ball. By staying in the pocket, the quarterback gives his receivers time to get open. Against tough coverage, the receivers must have those last steps to get open. However, the quarterback should be capable of getting out of the pocket and scrambling when necessary.*

## QUALIFICATIONS

First of all, the quarterback has to be a passer. He must be able to make long and short passes accurately and with a minimum of arm action. Some coaches place more stress on the running ability of the quarterback, believing it is easier to teach a player how to pass a football than it is to teach him how to run.

In recent years, the quarterback's ability to run has gained more prominence. The very popular run-pass option play has been a prime factor in the success of many of the top collegiate elevens.

The quarterback should have good size. The tall quarterback has a tremendous advantage because he is able to see more of the action.

The quarterback must be quick with his hands. He must release the football quickly on both short and deep passes. Quick and sure hands are also used to advantage in handing off or faking to the remaining backs in the backfield.

But right along with his physical attributes, the quarterback has to be a strong leader. He should act the part. If he has confidence in himself, his teammates will very likely take their cue from him. For the signal caller to be a leader, it helps to be a high-caliber individual, with good character. To lead his team effectively, the quarterback must be respected by his teammates. If a quarterback has the respect of his teammates, his judgment will not likely be questioned in a clutch situation. He can gain their respect by every act he performs on and off the playing field.

Coolness under fire is one of the great attributes of a quarterback. No matter how difficult the game situation may be, he has to remain outwardly calm and confident, even though he may have some doubts and indecision within.

One other quality that a top quarterback must possess is toughness. To be successful, he has to be tough. He should be able to take some physical punishment, since he is going to get knocked down often.

*I like to have a quarterback who is dedicated, because a coach lives or dies with his quarterback. The two have to get along and understand each other. And if they don't, their team is not going to win.*

The quarterback must develop a mas-

FIGURE 1-4. *Directing the attack. The quarterback must be a leader. Bill Kilmer exemplifies the feeling of confidence as he barks out the signals loud and clear.*

tery of mechanical details, such as the exchange from the center, various pivots, ball handling and fakes, and perfection of passing and running techniques. He must be able to keep the ball moving. Therefore, in order to lead his team effectively, he must learn to study the opposing defense. To call the correct play, he must use the knowledge of his team's strengths and the opponent's weaknesses. In short, he has to be a student of the game. He has to be able to work and study motion pictures; if he doesn't, he is not going to be prepared. *There is no easy way.*

The quarterback should have a clear, crisp voice. It gives a team needed self-confidence when the signal caller comes to the line of scrimmage and really belts out those signals—the letters, colors, and code words—loud and clear!

As he scans the defense, his head is up and his eyes shift from different players, up and down his own line. Besides checking things out, he can call his signals with the necessary authority.

By all means, the quarterback must establish a consistent method of calling cadence, so his team will become confident with it and will respond by firing off the line of scrimmage on that count.

The quarterback should follow the game plan. When he is getting in trouble with the game plan, because the defense is doing something differently, he will be able to read what the defense is doing to him and use that portion of the game plan to defeat a specific area of the defense.

When Roman Gabriel played for me with the Rams, he said, "I try to think at least two plays ahead when I call a first-down play. I've got to think what I'm going to come back to for a second and long situation, or second and short."

In choosing his plays intelligently, the quarterback must have a thorough knowledge of defensive football. Along with its

FIGURE 1-5. *Before taking the field, quarterbacks Sonny Jurgensen and Bill Kilmer go over the game plan with offensive coach Ted Marchibroda. The signal callers must have a thorough understanding of the game plan.*

strengths and weaknesses, he must know the theory of the defense. He must learn how to take advantage of defensive tactics, like audiblizing at the line of scrimmage to counter different alignments. This calls for a complete knowledge of the blocking assignments of every man on every play, against every type of defense.

Therefore, the signal caller must be able to recognize quickly the various defensive formations that confront his team. So, the modern pro quarterback must pass, run, and above all, *THINK!*

### The Correct Play

The successful quarterback has the ability to call the correct play at the correct time. His offense simply will not work if the defense is ready for his play, no matter how well he can throw the ball or how well his backs carry the ball. It's very simple to evaluate a quarter-

FIGURE 1-6. *The quarterback should follow the game plan. If the defense starts out to do something differently, he will anticipate and "read" what tactics the defense is attempting to execute.*

*Here, Bill Kilmer goes to the sideline to discuss strategy with Coach Allen.*

back . . . the ability to "read" the defense and call an effective play is a prime asset of any outstanding quarterback at any level of competition. The test is whether there is one man on the squad who can do this, regardless of how he performs.

The weaknesses of the defense must be hit! Naturally, the specific game plan will change from one week to the next, according to the strengths and weaknesses of the opponents. Whether the quarterback passes or runs on a particular play may depend on the defense he "reads" when he approaches the line of scrimmage.

The signal caller must mix up his play and use a varied attack. In setting up the defense for a long pass or run, the element of surprise is so very important. It takes generalship, as well as talent, to win a football game.

It is the quarterback's job to know what the situation is at all times. He should be busy thinking about what plays work against the team he is playing. He must consider the down, the yardage he needs, the score, and the prevailing weather conditions.

Most of the NFL quarterbacks are "reactive thinkers." Their strategy is built on what they believe the opposition thinks they are going to do, and what they expect the defense to do. Therefore, they try to disrupt and confuse the defense.

## A Typical Call

When the quarterback goes back in the huddle, he calls the formation. After the formation, he calls the ball carrier, then the hole number, the type of blocking, and the style of play. Then he gives the snap count. For example, to call an end run, he would say: "Red right, 29 on 3."

Should the quarterback listen to suggestions from his teammates? I think that as the season progresses, the quarterback will get to know his players. While he has to listen to them, he has to insist on a "unity of command," rather than let other individuals control him. Only sparingly should he accept information from his teammates. Having one leader in command can eliminate confusion and enable the team to play more efficiently. However, his teammates can tell him what backs are coming up fast for the short passes, and what linemen can be trapped or "suckered."

Before he calls the signals, the quarterback must get into a comfortable position, so that he is able to take the ball properly. The play cannot start or be executed properly unless he gets the ball. First, we have the quarterback call the defense, by number; he might give an audible call or a dummy call,

*The successful quarterback has the ability to call the correct play at the correct time.*

**A**                    **B**

*FIGURE 1-7. Bill Kilmer demonstrates taking the snap. The quarterback and the center must spend a great amount of time perfecting the exchange so that it becomes automatic.*

then a number following it. Then, he goes into a normal cadence call. It might be, for example, "46-2-26, set, hut one, hut two."

### Audibles

Modern football has been marked by shifting defenses, in which the offense is often faced with the possibility that the play it called in the huddle will run into a stone wall. Therefore, the signal caller tries to counter the defense and to come up with a better play. Thus, he goes to an audible. On an automatic, most teams will pass or go to quick-hitting runs or trap-type plays. The quarterback should be positive that he has a good idea and that it is going to work. He shouldn't be guessing.

## TAKING THE SNAP

The quarterback, as he takes the snap, must receive the ball comfortably and accurately. The placement of the hands is so vital in getting off a good snap. This is why the center and quarterback must spend a considerable amount of time perfecting the exchange (Figure 1-7).

### Stance

The quarterback's stance should be as natural as possible. His feet should be spread approximately shoulder-width apart, with the toes parallel to the line. The weight is equally distributed over the feet, with a little more

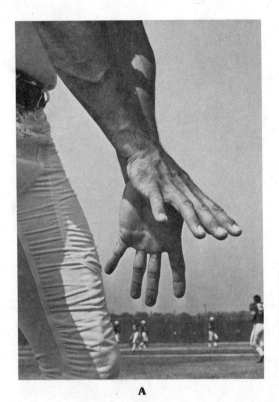

A

B

*FIGURE 1-8. Position of the hands. The quarterback places his right hand under the seat of the center. The fingers are spread slightly and the hands are relaxed.*

weight on the toes. The back is straight, the knees are bent slightly, and the hands are under the center to a point almost up to his wrist. There is a bend in the elbow so that he is able to give with the center's forward charge in the event that he has to.

We have the quarterback place the right foot forward a bit. When he takes the first step back with the right foot, it will bring him back a little farther than if the feet were parallel. Some coaches like to employ the strictly parallel stance, though.

The right-handed thrower puts his right hand under the buttocks of the center. The thumb of the other hand is placed in the groove of the right thumb; the thumbs are not parallel. This tends to keep the hands together more and also gives the quarterback

a little more of the ball. He must make sure he exerts enough pressure to let the center feel his hands. This gives the center a target to shoot for. The fingers are spread slightly and the hands are in a relaxed position (Figure 1-8). The type of cadence will determine the snap of the ball. A team might use a cadence in which the ball is snapped on the first, second, or third sound, for example, "hut one, hut two, hut three." In this case, the center might start the snap on the "hut" part of the count. Both the ball and the line are moving on the "hut" count.

### Exchange

We have the center bring the ball up in a quarter snap or turn of the ball. We feel we are getting the ball as quickly as we can from the center with this quarter turn. Also, the quarter turn allows the quarterback to get a good portion of the ball. If he allows the center to snap it naturally, the ball will make about a quarter of a turn, and it will fit perfectly into his hands. It will hit his hand with the laces against his fingertips. It should hit his hand hard, with a good "pop." Because it comes straight up against his palm, the ball would fall straight down if it were dropped.

Once he has control of the ball, the quarterback should bring it in to his stomach and work from his stomach, parallel to the ground. He keeps his hands on the ball at all times, prior to giving it to the back. The hand closest to the back should be removed, and the hand farthest away from the back should follow on through the direction the back is going.

The quarterback should get into the habit of riding with the center's motion. His hand has to go with the center, who must move forward and sometimes laterally as he

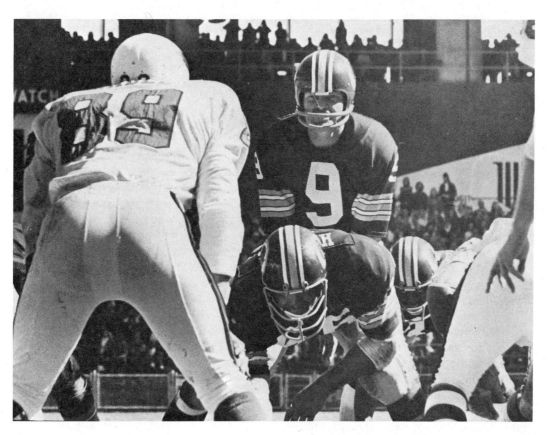

FIGURE 1-9. *Reading the defense is one of the most difficult tasks of the quarterback (Sonny Jurgensen). By using the audible system, the quarterback can make any necessary changes prior to the snap. If he feels the defense is lined up to stop a particular play, he can audible to another play. He should know how to cope with attacking, stunting, or jumping defenses.*

| A | B | C |

FIGURE 1-10. *The open pivot is a basic pivot in which the quarterback just hands the ball to the back hitting into the hole. We tell the quarterback to step first with the foot closest to the hole, parallel to the line of scrimmage. On the second step, he hands off the ball to the offensive back. The quarterback (here, Sonny Jurgensen) must open up toward the back (Larry Brown), turn, and hand him the ball. For protection, he keeps both hands on the ball until he actually hands off.*

snaps the ball. The quarterback doesn't want to be pulling away as the center moves forward.

## PIVOTS

In handing the ball off to a back, the quarterback must be able to execute the following pivots: open, inside, reverse, drop-back.

### Open Pivot

The open, or front, pivot (Figure 1-10) is perhaps the most natural pivot and is easiest to teach and perform. We use it in conjunction with what we call the Dive series, when the halfback or fullback is hitting straight into the line. The quarterback comes down along the line of scrimmage and just hands the ball to the back hitting into the hole. This is very basic and fundamental; the quarterback has nothing to do but hand the ball off to the back.

In Figure 1-10, Sonny Jurgensen is shown starting to lead-step toward Larry Brown, the ball carrier—a short move, approximately one foot. His head immediately looks for the target. He has the ball in the area of his stomach, with his elbows in. Notice that his weight shifts to his left foot as he extends his arms and places the ball in the pocket. Observe that the distance is slightly less than an arm's length between the quarterback and the back. This helps our faking as well as the effectiveness of the hand-off and helps prevent fumbling caused by two players bumping into each other.

### Inside Pivot

The inside pivot (Figure 1-11) is used on the inside power play and the fullback dive play, since it provides better deception. It enables the offense to have other backs lead the ball carrier.

In Figure 1-11, Sonny Jurgensen, the quarterback, pivots on the left toe and swings the right leg through on the inside.

He becomes balanced as the weight shifts to the left foot. The quarterback is now ready for the hand-off.

The quarterback, by keeping the elbows in close to the body, will do a better job of concealing the ball. The ball carrier can do his part by providing a wide pocket. The close elbows are the secret to hiding the ball from the defense.

### Reverse Pivot

The reverse pivot is just the opposite of the open pivot. The quarterback, instead of opening up toward the back, opens up away from the back, more or less from the blind side. This is the pivot used basically for the power sweep or off-tackle play, where the quarterback flips the ball to a halfback. The pivot also is effective for some fake off-tackle and roll-out passes.

The quarterback's hand will follow the center's movement forward, although the quarterback's body is starting backward. The weight shifts to the right toe, as the pivot is performed off that toe.

Next, the quarterback brings his elbows in to conceal the ball from the defense. The left leg follows naturally and ends up directly behind the right foot. The feet are approximately 18 inches apart. The quarterback then naturally moves in the direction of the roll-out.

### Drop-back Pivot

The drop-back pivot (Figure 1-12) is used by most quarterbacks who throw from the Pro-type pocket. As he gets the snap, the quarterback lets his hands follow the center's move forward, but begins moving his body backward.

Perhaps the most important step is a hard push-off from the left foot. Actually, we tell our quarterbacks to spring off the left foot. The quarterback should sprint backward with his body facing that direction, but with his head turned toward the defense. Notice that his eyes never leave the defense, as the ball is brought up to the area of the shoulders with both hands holding it firmly.

Because of the time element, the quarterback moves backward as fast as possible in getting to the desired depth. We like our

FIGURE 1-11. *The inside pivot provides better deception than the open pivot. Here, Sonny Jurgensen pivots on the left toe and swings the right leg through on the inside. He becomes balanced as the weight shifts to the left foot. He then hands off to the running back, Moses Denson. By keeping the elbows in close to the body, the quarterback can do a better job of hiding the ball. The runner does his part by providing a wide pocket.*

C           B           A

**C**          **B**          **A**

**D**          **E**

FIGURE 1-12.  *Drop-back action. As he receives the snap, the quarterback (Bill Kilmer) lets his hands follow the center's move forward, but he begins moving his body backward. The most important step is a hard push-off from the left foot. He sprints backward with his body facing in that direction. However, his head is turned toward the defense as he looks over his left shoulder. Meanwhile, the ball is brought up into throwing position. The quarterback must continually strive to improve his quickness in setting up.*

quarterback to take a little jump so he can get set off his back foot and be ready to deliver the pass. He must make sure he gets set on his back foot and is ready to step up into the pocket to throw the ball.

## HAND-OFF

The first thing the quarterback must do, after receiving the ball from center, is bring the ball into his stomach and work parallel with the line of scrimmage at all times. In handing off to the ball carrier he keeps both hands on the ball until he actually hands off. The responsibility for a good hand-off is primarily with the quarterback because the back must have his eyes on the hole in front of him (Figure 1-13).

In Figure 1-11, as Jurgensen takes the ball from center, he immediately brings it close in to his body. His hands come quickly back toward his stomach, his elbows in close, his hands grasping the ball tightly.

The quarterback can help conceal the play by hiding the ball with his body. As he moves with short, sliding steps, he should pick up the back and focus in on the target area where he will place the ball.

He should place the ball into his pocket firmly, not necessarily hard. When he receives it, the back should have good control over it.

The moment that he places the ball in the pocket, the quarterback removes the hand closest to the ball carrier, as he follows through with the hand farthest away. After handing off, he must make sure he doesn't look at the ball carrier, thus tipping off the direction of the play.

If the hand-off is to the right, the quarterback gives with the left hand, his hand moving quickly from left to right into the stomach of the back.

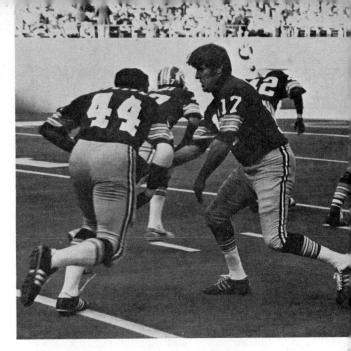

FIGURE 1-13. Hand-off. The running back receives the ball with the outside foot ahead of the inside foot. This provides a good pocket for the quarterback and helps prevent the possibility of a runner knocking the ball out of the quarterback's hands. The distance between the quarterback and the halfback is such that they are just brushing shoulders. Although in this picture Bill Kilmer is still an arm's distance away from the ball carrier, Moses Denson, they will eventually brush shoulders.

There are a number of reasons for a fumble occurring on the hand-off. Occasionally, the quarterback won't work from his stomach. He may put the ball down a little too low, where it hits the runner's knees. His legs are coming up, and they just kick it out of there. And sometimes, we find that the backs do not give the quarterback a proper target or pocket to place the ball into.

## FAKING

Faking plays an important part in a good hand-off and helps create more deception in the offensive backfield. The hand-off and fake to a running back are perhaps the most difficult skills for a quarterback to perfect. His chief concern is trying to fool the linebackers. He has to make the three linebackers think either pass or run.

We tell our quarterback to have actual contact with the back. For example, if he is faking to the fullback, we tell him to make sure that he is touching at least the stomach of the back and placing the ball there. The back tries to come in and fake like he is getting the ball and moving into the line.

Most faking should be done with both hands kept on the ball until the moment it is given to the back or pulled away and given to another back. Then the quarterback may employ a shoulder dip, keeping the ball tucked away and dipping with his shoulder as the faking back comes by.

The pivot man should put the ball in there and then take it out because at that instant a defensive lineman might have seen it go in. Then, because he may have been obscured by an offensive lineman, he might not see the ball come out. So, the big thing here is making contact on any fake that he has.

A good fake at times can be executed in dropping straight back, but it is a little more difficult when moving off to the side or at a 45-degree angle. The quarterback should hide the ball even after the fake, in case he has to throw. In addition, the back to whom he is faking also assumes a responsibility for faking and deceiving the opposition.

## RUNNING

All our Redskin quarterbacks go through exactly the same running drills as our backs do. This running practice is designated to improve their running skill, even though the quarterbacks are primarily throwers.

In the roll-out pass the passer rolls out to the same side as the intended receiver with the idea of placing pressure on the defense. This maneuver forces the defender either to drop back and cover the receiver or to move up to rush the passer. The result is that one or the other is left open.

One of the biggest offensive threats in football is the quarterback who can smoothly execute the roll-out option run or pass. More than any other play, this one play pressures the defense. If the defender pressures him, the quarterback must throw, usually on the run. If the opponent loosens up, the quarterback should run, quickly and deceptively. Speed is the key—how quickly he can get to the option run or pass area. Then he must execute this pivot in flawless fashion.

### Roll-out Right

At the snap, the quarterback's weight shifts from both feet to the right toe. He spins on the right toe and then springs off his right toe. This enables him to get away quickly. (See Figure 1-14.)

When the defense starts to exert pressure on him, he prepares to throw the ball. We remind the quarterback to turn the shoulder square to the target. After cocking the ball, he is ready to throw, raising the throwing arm overhead and throwing with a direct, over-the-head motion.

### Roll-out Left

This pivot and pass is very difficult for a right-handed quarterback. As the quarterback starts his pivot, the left heel is off the ground, enabling the pivot to be executed quickly on the left toe. As he rolls out to his left, his eyes are focused on the defensive man to his outside, and he starts to turn the shoulders square toward the target as he brings the ball into a throwing position.

**A**

FIGURE 1-14. *Roll-out right. While he rolls out, the quarterback (Sonny Jurgensen) brings the ball up to the throwing position. He keeps both hands on the ball until ready to throw. He should keep his eyes continuously on the defensive area to his right.*

**B**

**C**

**D**

The right-handed quarterback must throw with a sidearm motion when running to his left, which is a difficult maneuver. The elbow is straight out and the ball is held away from the body.

On the roll-out, we tell our quarterback to take off to an assigned depth, so that the proper blocking can take place up front. As he rolls out to this depth, he wants to key his defender, one way or the other. This is the way we use the option. Once he has keyed the defender, he must make up his mind either to throw the ball or run it.

### The Quarterback Sneak

The sneak is a surprise maneuver employed by the quarterback. It is one of the safest ways of picking up a yard or so, especially if the quarterback is big and strong. With the offensive line wedging in toward the center, he can go straight ahead behind this wedge.

### The Quarterback Draw

This play is nothing more than a typical draw play, with the quarterback doing the running. The quarterback goes back as if to pass, but instead of throwing, he moves forward, keying his blockers, and runs into a lane opened up by his blockers. This is similar to a draw play executed by a fullback or a halfback.

Successful execution of the draw play demands a big, strong type of runner, one capable of breaking an arm tackle, or two. Most quarterbacks like to take the time to make a pump before starting forward. Bill Wade was effective on this type of play.

### The Bootleg

The bootleg play can be a powerful weapon for the quarterback who is a running threat. A big part of the success of a bootleg depends on the acting ability of the other backs. Therefore, we tell our backs to hit in there just as if they had the ball.

On the bootleg, the quarterback tries to get outside of the defensive end, while he is working against the offensive blocker. After he gets outside the end, he hides the ball from the linebackers and the halfbacks by holding it on his hip. Then he can decide whether to throw or to run by the manner in which they react to the situation.

Since it is easier for a right-handed passer to throw while running to his right, most bootlegs go to the right.

## THE PITCHOUT

We like to have our quarterback execute a pitchout by keeping both hands on the ball. If he calls for the pitchout, we want him to take the ball away from the back hitting into the line, pull it into the stomach, and then throw it with both hands out to the receiver. With two hands, the quarterback has a good grip on the ball and good control.

The back who will receive the pitchout is instructed to run with his hands in a natural running position, then take the ball with both hands at hip level. Again, the quarterback should use two hands to prevent a lineman from coming through and hitting him when he has one hand on the ball.

By keeping his rear low on the spin, the quarterback can hide the ball better from the defense.

## DRILLS

The key to success of the T-formation is the quarterback! For success, the quarterback therefore has to spend many hours learning to handle the ball and learning to fake. He literally has to live with a football. He must learn how to take the ball from center until it becomes automatic. He should practice doing it on the count. In addition, a full-length mirror comes in handy when practicing faking and pivoting.

Most coaches like their quarterbacks to go through a 10-minute warm-up drill. In improving his grip on the ball, the quarterback should drop and catch the ball with one hand, then the other. Another effective routine is passing the ball behind the back and between the legs.

We use a daily technique period for our quarterbacks. This session is devoted to fundamentals, such as setting up quickly to pass, throwing, follow-through, looking-off, and all the other basic skills that are sometimes overlooked. In the set drill, the quarterback works on getting set to pass. In performing this, the passer should learn to set up at three, five, seven, and nine steps. He also works on reading the defense and having a key in each defense he throws against. In addition, our quarterbacks spend considerable time studying films and utilizing the self-improvement chart.

1. *Stance*   The quarterback lines up facing the coach and assumes a parallel stance, flexing at the knees. The quarterback should extend his hands as if a center were in front of him.

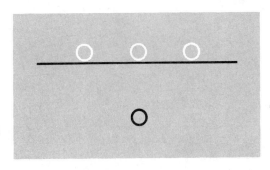

DIAGRAM 1-1.   *Stance.*

2. *Exchange*   The quarterback must practice taking the ball from center until it becomes automatic. He should practice doing it on the count. This drill is similar to the stance drill, but a center with a football is added. The quarterback places his "take" hand firmly against the center's crotch.

A full-length mirror is useful for practicing faking and pivoting.

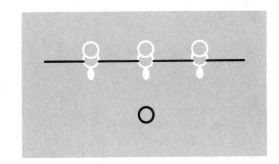

DIAGRAM 1-2.   *Exchange.*

3. *Hand-offs*   This drill features all the steps and pivots necessary for a well-rounded offense. Markers (such as helmets, tires, even towels) can be placed on the ground so that the quarterback must take the proper steps.

The following maneuvers should be performed in the sequence listed:

(a) Hike and take
(b) Lateral lead step
(c) Opposite foot step
(d) Inside hand forward with ball

(e) Second lead step
(f) Second follow foot step
(g) Hop and set
(h) Fake setup for pass

4. *Faking*   With managers or assistants across the line of scrimmage in defensive positions, the quarterback and offensive running backs should execute the plays that involve faking or hiding the ball.

5. *Drop-back*   In this drill, the quarterback works

on getting set to pass. In performing the drop-back, the passer should learn to set up at three, five, seven, and nine steps. A stopwatch should be used daily to chart the quarterback's drop-back times (see Chart 11-1 in chapter 11).

6. *Pull-up and sprint-out drills* In addition to performing full sprint-out plays, the quarterback should be instructed to fake a sprint-out and pull up or stop. This moves the pocket over about 5 or 6 yards. The sprint-out requires precision and timing, which, of course, must be developed during the practice work-outs.

7. *Recognition* The most effective method to teach the quarterback to recognize defensive sets is to set a full defensive perimeter in front of him. The two areas that receive emphasis are keys before the snap and keys after the snap. The quarterback must be trained to know what offensive plays are best suited to run against the various formations.

# 2

# Passing

*To win, a team must have an effective passing attack.*

**George Allen**

A strong passing attack keeps the defense from bunching up. Therefore, the passing attack should feature a variety of name pass patterns, and individual pass cuts to keep the defensive unit off balance and out of position. The running game must be established first; then, it will be much easier to get the passing game rolling. In addition, the play-action passing game must be coordinated with the offense.

The pro's, of course, have emphasized the passing game for years. The college game now has more passing. This emphasis on passing has been felt in high school play as well.

Being able to hit a receiver on the break is a major attribute of an outstanding passer. Some passers never develop this quality. If he can hit his man on the break, especially if the pattern calls for it, a passer will not get intercepted so much.

The ability to run is another dimension that contributes to the effectiveness of a quarterback, particularly against defenses designed to pressure the drop-back passer. Indeed, the passer who has the quickness and agility to get out of the pocket and scramble when necessary can be a continual threat to the defense.

Developing the art of faking should be a prime concern of every quarterback. With little feints of his hands, arms, and body, he can make defenders move in the wrong direction.

Using his blockers to the best advantage is still another attribute that can provide the passer with the strong protection he needs until his receivers can get open.

I favor a precision type of passing, in which the receiver goes to a prescribed depth and then breaks. The ball must be thrown *before* the man makes his break. Then, the defense doesn't have as much chance to break it up. We have a stopwatch at every practice. When the timing is off, it is someone's fault and we want to know why.

Perfection in the passing game is a matter of timing and practice. There is no substitute for hard work and practice, and timing will come only through practice. It can't be done on a blackboard but requires hours of drilling against a defense, such as our 7-on-7 period provides. Too much emphasis is put on blackboard passing.

We call it 7-on-7 because seven offensive players are matched against seven defenders. For 25 to 30 minutes each day—even more if necessary—we move up and down the field and try to create tactical situations so the players will get used to playing the hash marks. We do everything we can to make our passing game realistic.

## BASIC QUALITIES

Ability is the No. 1 point in becoming a top-notch passer. A passer has to have ability to throw the football. The best passers have a strong arm, the quick release, and the deadly accuracy over a full season.

Second, he has to be physically strong, because the quarterback takes quite a beating from those huge defensive linemen. Quarterbacks, generally, are all superbly coordinated athletes.

An outstanding passer has good depth perception. He is able to pick out his receivers even in heavy traffic and when he has to go to an alternate receiver. *This is the big test.*

## SETTING UP THE PASS

The passer must get back to the pocket as quickly as possible. This is one of the most important points in successful passing. The sooner the quarterback can get back, the more time he has to set up to throw the ball. The defense can go after opposing passers who do not get back quickly enough. We work almost every day in training camp on increasing our speed in setting up the pass. As a yardstick, for the seven-step drop-back, we have our quarterbacks strive for 1.75 seconds in getting back. For the five-step, it is 1.3 seconds.

Our quarterbacks have a specific number of steps for a certain pattern, and this is the way we operate our passing game throughout the season. However, when a breakdown occurs, the quarterback must be ready to unload the ball, when and if this is necessary. There can be numerous false steps in quarterbacking, in dropping back for the pass. You will find that a player often takes a step forward upon receiving the snap from center. To eliminate this, have him take his first step backward on the right foot; you want him back as quickly as possible. He should not work from a parallel stance: have him place his right foot slightly ahead of the left, prior to the snap.

The quarterback *must execute quickness in going back.* Although his hands remain in contact with the center, the quarterback's body is just starting to leave right before the snap. This gives him a little edge in getting back more quickly.

If the right foot is slightly forward on the initial stance, the first backward step of the quarterback will give him an additional 6 to 8 inches. The quarterback's feet should point toward the goal line so that his hips are free to move.

As he drops back, the quarterback is glancing over his shoulder, looking downfield as much as he can. He takes short, quick, jabbing steps as he goes backward. He is actually working hard to set up quickly. He is running in "modified" form. He looks

FIGURE 2-2. If a quarterback has time to throw, any defense is in trouble. Here, quarterback Bill Kilmer is given good protection by the Redskins' offensive line.

directly at the intended receiver, but sees the entire field with his peripheral vision. He hits his maximum depth and then readies himself on his last two steps. The quarterback should throw with his weight on the back foot. Many quarterbacks take a little jump after a set action. The important thing is for him to get set on his back foot and be ready to step up into the pocket to deliver the ball.

Balance is the key to the drop-back action. Many inaccurate passes are a result of the quarterback's being off-balance at the deepest point. Usually, this occurs when the quarterback overstrides when taking his jump step. This ends in a poorly thrown pass.

Again, we like the quarterback to work out of the pocket. While the scrambling quarterback is an exciting quarterback, we don't like to get in situations where it is second and 19, or third and 18. Basically we want him to drop back, stay in that pocket, and execute from there. Unless the quarterback is forced out of the pocket, he should stay there. Teams have not become great using quarterbacks who try to prove they can run.

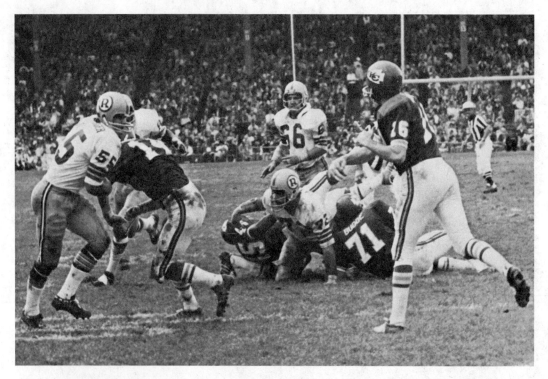

FIGURE 2-3. *Passing from the pocket. Quarterback Len Dawson of the Kansas City Chiefs, behind a well-formed pocket, delivers a long one against the Redskins. In all pocket passing, it is wise to have a prescribed depth for the quarterback to throw from, even though he may be forced to release the ball earlier. Len is concentrating on his receiver and is not concerned with the rush, a characteristic of a good, courageous quarterback. Note the good follow-through.*

## PASSING TECHNIQUE

The actual passing delivery is a smooth overhand motion with a good follow-through. During our workouts, we place considerable emphasis on the proper follow-through, which we feel is essential for better direction and distance.

The short passes are thrown with a snap of the wrist and often hard and right at the receiver. The long pass is usually a "soft" throw and should lead the receiver. The passer aims the ball so the receiver will just reach it while running at full speed.

Once the passer is back in the pocket and decides to throw, he should use the minimum amount of motion in throwing the ball. Long arm-action delivery is undesirable; it destroys timing and assists the defense.

### Grip

The passer must first have a good grip on the ball. This means a grip that enables him to be comfortable when throwing. Some individuals stress seeing daylight between the ball and the palm. Others who palm it have been equally successful.

Our passers grip the ball with the thumb

A                    B

*FIGURE 2-4. The passer should use a firm, comfortable grip. Joe Theismann likes to grip the ball with the thumb underneath the three fingers on the lacing, well spread out and slightly behind the center of the ball. Looking over the field, he holds the ball in a cocked position at shoulder level, allowing for a quick release. The passer should grip the ball firmly, since palming it tends to inhibit a smooth passing delivery. The fingertips should feel the pebble grain of the football. The passer should always have both hands on the ball prior to the release.*

underneath and the fingers on the lacing, well spread out and slightly behind the center of the ball. We tell them not to squeeze the ball, but to have a firm enough grasp to keep the ball from slipping.

### Stance

The passer should assume a stance that is natural for him when he arrives back in the pocket. His feet are spread, and his body is balanced as he faces the target. His weight rests on the ball of each foot so that he can shift quickly in any direction.

When he first gets back in the pocket, his weight basically is resting on the back foot. This foot is dug in, ready to push off for the start of the throw. The other foot is planted in the direction he intends to throw the ball.

The quarterback should hold the ball at shoulder level or a little above. The ball should be held with both hands. I have no-

A          B          C

*FIGURE 2-5. The passing delivery requires the coordination of the shoulders, arm, and feet. Using the wrist primarily, the short, quick pass is thrown more overhand past the ear. The ball is cocked; the wrist motion is the same as that used to crack a whip, assuring proper timing, and thereby increasing the speed of delivery. The arm will be extended almost straight up as the delivery nears completion. A good follow-through assures accuracy and the necessary velocity. On all quick passes, the ball should be held at shoulder height to eliminate unnecessary movement of the ball. (Bill Kilmer is shown here.)*

ticed that some young passers hold the ball too low. This can cause fumbling because the defense can slap the ball away.

### The Delivery

In delivering the football, the passer should step with his lead foot directly at the receiver. It is essential that a quarterback have "quick hands," to get rid of the ball in a hurry. However, he should never turn his wrist. He should use an inward and downward pull of the fingers and hand on the ball. The elbow should lead the way, followed by a smooth, "loose arm" motion, which whips the ball toward the receiver. The speed of the arm and hand action is in proportion to the velocity and distance the ball will travel.

As for the correct arm angle on the pass, the three-quarter to overhand delivery seems the most effective. Roman Gabriel has that, although sometimes he throws directly from behind the ear. I think it depends upon the man himself.

Otto Graham preferred the half-and-half arm motion, which forced the nose of the football to point up as it was released. This action resulted in a softer and an easier pass to catch. Throwing past the ear generally causes the nose of the ball to point down, making it heavy and more difficult to catch.

This motion is not so successful today because of the height of the linemen.

It is advantageous for a passer to be able to adjust his arm angle for a particular type of throw. In the case of a short, quick, bullet pass, the ball would be thrown more overhand past the ear. The passer must lift his arm a little for this type of pass.

On the long pass, he may lower the arm angle and use a little more three-quarter motion to help soften up the ball. We refer to this as a "nose up ball." In throwing the "long bomb," some passers like to exaggerate throwing the elbow out in front of the body, so that the point of the ball will stay up. This long arm action causes the ball to carry farther.

The three-quarter arm motion is often the most natural delivery for most passers. However, the overhand motion enables the passer to throw over the heads and arms of opposing players.

### Release

At the time of release, the shoulders of the passer should be square to the receiver. In releasing the ball, he should draw the fingers and the hand inward and downward. This tends to give the ball the spiral flight so necessary for a properly thrown pass.

When the delivery nears completion, the arm should be extended straight out. The palm of the throwing arm should be facing the ground. The index finger is the control finger, and it should be the last finger to leave the ball. It should point in the direction of the target. The throwing hand comes across the body, and the thumb of the passer is pointed down.

The weight has transferred from the quarterback's rear foot forward onto the front foot. *Above all, he must not throw across his front leg or throw from a flat-footed position.* This is a common error. To assure good "zip" on the ball, the passer must step directly toward the target.

The actual release of the ball generally requires moving forward a step or two from the initial position within the pocket.

### Follow-through

A good follow-through is essential for accuracy and distance. Upon releasing the ball, the throwing hand should come across the body. It should not be hurried. The weight should be on the front foot at the time of the release.

During practice, our quarterback coach, Ted Marchibroda, urges our passers to exaggerate their follow-through movement and to make sure their thumb points toward the ground.

## TYPES OF PASSES

To keep the defense off-balance, a variety of passes and pass patterns should be at the disposal of the offense. Actually, to be effective, the offense doesn't need many pass patterns; just a few basic ones and some counter key passes will do. *It is the manner in which they are executed that is all-important.*

Passes fall into the following three major areas: (1) the pocket pass, (2) the roll-out pass, and (3) the play pattern pass.

### Passing from the Pocket

In setting from the pocket, the passer must make certain that he receives the exchange from the center so that the "fat" of the ball is

A

FIGURE 2-6.   Passing technique. Pushing off the back foot, the passer steps directly at the receiver with his lead foot. Cocking the ball, he executes a smooth arm motion, with the elbow leading the way. For most passers I recommend a three-quarter to overhand delivery, using an inward and downward pull of the fingers and hand on the ball.

B

C

FIGURE 2-6 (continued). Here, Bill Kilmer employs strong wrist action in whipping the ball straight and quickly to his receiver. He executes a complete follow-through; this helps improve his accuracy. Passers must be careful of overstriding: it destroys timing and accuracy.

D

FIGURE 2-7.  *The turn-in pass is thrown to a flanker or spread end who goes downfield 10 yards and then stops. The quarterback (Bill Kilmer here) has to really rifle the ball.*

well seated in the palm of his passing hand. The footwork involves turning and sprinting three steps, then setting. Quickly, it's "1-2-3 and set." This "1-2-3 and set" will place him at a depth of 6 or 7 yards. He should be in a "stand tall" position, ready to step in the direction he will throw the ball.

When passing from the pocket, the passer must remember to stay in the pocket or step up. The linemen cannot block effectively if he leaves the pocket. This is very difficult for young passers to realize and learn and must be stressed during each practice session.

### Turn-out or Turn-in Pass

This pass is so named because the receiver goes in a turn-in or turn-out pattern. It is a medium pass for which the quarterback has to really rifle the ball, usually head high. This can vary, depending upon where the defender is positioned. Sometimes it is better to throw lower. The pass is usually thrown to a flanker or spread end who goes downfield 10 yards, then stops or comes back a couple of steps. (See Figure 2-7.)

Timing is an important factor as far as the turn-in or turn-out pass is concerned.

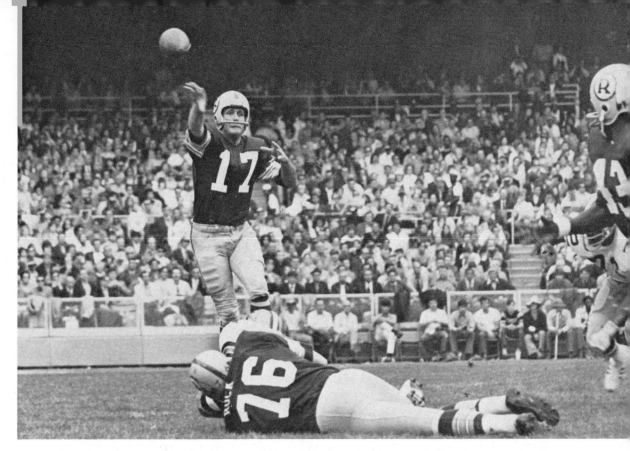

FIGURE 2-8. *Swing pass. The quarterback, Bill Kilmer, gives the flaring halfback a slight lead so he can catch the ball in stride. This pass requires much practice to perfect the necessary timing.*

The moment the receiver turns around the ball should already be on its way. Again, this pass has to be fired very hard and must be accurate.

### Swing or Flare Pass

The swing or flare pass (Figure 2-8) is a relatively short pass with a slight lead that permits the flaring halfback or fullback to run into the path of the ball. The passer should have a slight loft on the ball so that the receiver will be able to take the ball in

stride. It's a much softer pass than the turn-in or turn-out pass. This type of pass is hard to master.

### Long Pass

The long pass is more difficult to complete and is not thrown more than a few times during a game. This is because on almost every play two deep defensive backs will cover any receiver the offense sends. The passer has to really reach back and let it go. The trajectory of the "long bomb" is much higher than that of other passes. The timing of the "lead" to the receiver requires a great deal of practice between the passer and the receiver.

The passer should be cautioned not to throw the ball too hard when executing the long pass. He should develop a rhythm in his delivery. It is very important to get the ball to the receiver quickly as he breaks open so that the receiver doesn't have to break stride. Let him run under the ball. In delivering the ball, the passer must not "cross" the line the receiver is running. If the ball is underthrown out on a line, the receiver can adjust; in fact, he is more difficult to cover because of this.

### Look-in Pass

This is a quick short pass to an end or flanker cutting diagonally across the field. It is called a "look-in" because the tight end takes about two or three steps, looks up, and he has the ball. Some quarterbacks jump before they throw. The reason for the jump is to get above the charging linemen for a better view of the receiver. Although the pro's have pretty much gotten away from the jump pass, some teams use it to some success.

### Screen Pass

The screen pass is a fine weapon. This play often works against a team's putting a strong rush on the passer. We often call it when we need long yardage, and the defense is spread out for a long pass.

Of course, faking by the quarterback and his teammates in the backfield is the key to a successful screen pass. The halfback or the fullback fakes a block moving to one side or the other, but stays in the backfield. In the meantime, the offensive linemen at the defense sift through. Then, they move over in front of the receiver.

We tell our quarterback to take his normal drop-back, as he would in throwing a pass. At this point, he takes a good "hesitation," and then as he drops back farther, he flips a short pass before the onrushing defensemen. It has to be a soft pass, which we like for the receiver to catch on the run.

### The Roll-out Pass

The roll-out, or running, pass is usually a short pass—5 or 6 yards—and can be "thrown" into the flat easily. It is usually a true option run-pass which helps offset a strong pass rush from the inside. Although it doesn't take a great passer to execute this play, the roll-out pass does require a considerable amount of time and practice to perfect.

The quarterback sprints out at controlled speed, while holding the ball in a "ready position." He looks immediately to the area he is running toward, usually the flat.

When using the option on the linebacker, the quarterback keeps his eyes on him constantly. If the defender "pops" across the line of scrimmage, he will unload the ball softly to the receiver in the flat. But if the defender drops out to play pass defense, the quarterback will continue running at top speed.

The running pass has been a valuable weapon for us and we put a lot of emphasis on it. We feel it can make the big play for us—a score. In addition, if we show the running pass, we know the defenders are going to be a little concerned. Therefore, if they know we have the ability to throw it, it helps our running game. The majority of our play action passes are in conjunction with our running game.

The important point for the passer to remember is to try to *set himself* as he releases the ball. *He should avoid throwing the ball when off-balance.* So, have him find a solid footing when he decides to make his throw.

### The Play Pattern Pass

This type of pass involves faking a running play—usually one of your most successful plays—and then setting to throw. The most important point is for the quarterback and the rest of his team to really fake a running play. This pass should look exactly like a run, in which the receiver tries to make the defensive secondary believe he is blocking or just loafing downfield.

Then, the quarterback pulls the ball from the back that he is faking to and either sets in the pocket or continues to roll out. For the most part, play pattern passes include both the short pass and the long ball, which could be a post or a corner pass. The short pass over the middle and the pass out to the sideline are both highly effective. But, again, the quarterback should really fake a running play. He shouldn't give the pass away until he is ready to throw!

### CORRECT MENTAL ATTITUDE

The successful passer realizes that occasionally he is going to be knocked on his back, even after he has thrown the ball. He must be able to concentrate on his target, no matter how many defenders he has around him. He must not let this pressure upset him.

The great passers have the *courage* to hold on to the football until the last split second before throwing it. They are able to stand back in the pocket and take some occasional punishment. Unitas and Starr were

superb at this for years. They knew how to relax and go limp when hit. And if they tried to fight some of those big rushmen, they were going to get hurt.

*Toughness, in my estimation, is one of the biggest factors in becoming a successful passer.* For many years, Unitas was the best quarterback in the league, and one reason is that he was the toughest. While there are others equal to Johnny in passing ability, there aren't as many throwers who are as tough.

A passer must remember not to let interceptions bother him. If he makes a mistake, he must be mentally tough enough to learn from it, to stay loose and be even more determined to succeed the next play. The interception is history, so forget it!

### SPLIT VISION

The passer must develop split vision as much as he possibly can. He has to pick out his receivers and then deliver the ball to them. Most truly great passers are gifted with uncanny perception, along with their judgment and superb delivery.

However, hard work and preparation can help improve the passer's perception. Working every day with the same receivers is a big advantage. Every time he throws a pass, he is prepared for any situation that may arise. If a particular pattern is called, he will know instinctively how to successfully get the ball to a receiver.

Peripheral vision, to a degree, can be developed by preparation—knowing the defense and what he is trying to do. The passer develops a mental picture of where this area will be. This is why he must keep his head turned toward the defense as he drops back to the pocket.

The passer should use as many receivers as possible and try not to limit it to two. Even though the quarterback has an initial receiver, this doesn't mean he shouldn't hit any one of three other men on a particular pass pattern. For example, if the passer finds that the split end is covered on an intended short pass, he might go to the halfback or flanker on some deeper pattern. After seeing the split end is not open, the passer moves his vision back to the left and picks up the tight end or the flanker. If everyone is covered, he will either have to "eat the ball" or make sure he throws it away from the defenders.

Above all, he must never throw the ball into a crowd of defenders. If there is any question in his mind that a defender might intercept the ball, he should not throw it. He might throw it into the ground toward the feet of the receiver, so no one can get it. However, *he must never throw the ball up for grabs.* In some situations, he might decide to dump the ball off to the fullback out in the flat.

In addition to locating his receiver, the passer might have to move around in the pocket. If his primary receiver is covered, he will have to move around, shuffle his feet, and be ready to locate another receiver. The quarterback who is light and nimble on his feet certainly has an advantage in staying out of the hands of the defensive linemen.

## FAKING

Eye and arm faking can prove to be very helpful to the passer. Looking one way and throwing in another direction can be quite deceptive to the defense. By moving his head or eyes just slightly, the quarterback may cause a defender to be pulled out of position, particularly the linebackers. However, I do feel that too much has been made of this in the past.

Another way for the quarterback to deceive the defense is by faking with his passing arm. The passer will pump the ball and thus simulate a throw. As he starts the forward motion of his arm, he just pumps the ball and brings his arm to a stop quickly about halfway through his delivery. This often causes the defender to freeze, allowing the receiver to gain a much-needed extra step.

The bootleg play is another method used to fool the defense. The quarterback will fake a hand-off and then, keeping the ball hidden behind his leg, will slip out into the flat.

## DRILLS

If he expects to play well, the quarterback must also practice well. This certainly applies to throwing a football. A young, aspiring passer can even practice by himself.

1. *Target passing* The old tire drill is still a good one. An old tire hung up in the backyard or one suspended from a crossbar on the goalpost can provide a good target. At first, the passer should stay close enough, then gradually move back. Later, he may practice throwing the ball through the tire while running to his right and then to his left. The passer should go through his steps before passing at the target.

2. *One-knee passing* An effective method used for warming up is to get down on one knee. Simply have two passers play catch, both

down on one knee. The passer brings the ball with both hands to a "ready position," which is about numeral high. Then he raises the ball in a "cocked position," which is around the area of the ear. With the elbow extended out slightly, he snaps the ball with his wrist, throwing only 7 to 8 yards for this warm-up procedure. As he delivers the ball, he should concentrate on having his passing hand finish with the palm down and out.

After he has thrown 10 or 12 passes in this kneeling position, he stands up and passes 10 to 12 yards from a straight standing-still position. He should concentrate on stepping in the direction he is passing. This is most important for balance and control.

3. *High release* The coach can teach a high release by stringing a rope 6 feet high having the passers throw to receivers at normal distances over the rope.

4. *Footwork drill* After practicing 10 or 12 passes from this position, the quarterback can begin practicing his footwork, with the emphasis on dropping straight back and setting himself in the pocket. Here, he practices his footwork at top speed, without throwing the ball. Then, the last step is to practice the footwork and deliver the ball to the receiver at the specific distance for which the play is designated. This calls for a precision type of passing.

# 3

# Pass
# Receiving

*The pass receiver should want
that ball and be able to do something when he catches it.*
**George Allen**

Speed is, in my opinion, the prime requisite of a good pass receiver. An offensive receiver simply has to have the speed to beat those defensive backs because the defensive backs today can run like racehorses.

An outstanding pass receiver, however, has more than just exceptional speed. Besides running a 4.6 or 4.7 forty-yard dash, he has tremendous hands and is capable of making the great catch. He is able to dive for the ball and come up with it. He can catch it over his shoulder. He can turn in the air, twist, and catch the football. Then, after he catches it, he knows how to run with the ball.

If a receiver doesn't have great speed, he will have to work very hard, particularly on his timing and precision work, to be able to perform nearly perfect pass cuts. When the other players have left the field, he is the one who must stay to work on stops, starts, pass cuts, catching the ball, anything to make up for this lack of outstanding speed. Actually, anyone who wants to work hard can become a fine receiver and be able to fit into the pass offense.

Second, a pass receiver must have great faking ability—maneuverability to get open—because even though he may have speed, it won't be enough to get open.

A pass receiver must have a strong desire to catch that football—no matter where it is thrown. It takes real courage for a receiver to stick his head in there and catch the football when he is covered by one or two defenders. There is no substitute for hustle. The more hustle, the more spirit, the more dedication the receiver has, the better he is going to be.

A                                    B

FIGURE 3-2.  Good hands and the speed to get in the open are necessary for a top pass receiver. Here, Bryant Salter goes far down the field to catch a "long bomb," without breaking stride. As he "looks the ball into his hands," his fingers are relaxed and well spread. His arms are also loose and relaxed. Rather than run with his arms extended, he waits until the ball is ready to settle into his hands, then extends his arms and catches it.

FIGURE 3-3.  Tight end Jerry Smith receives a quick pass over the line of scrimmage. A pass receiver should take any pass above the waist with his thumbs in.

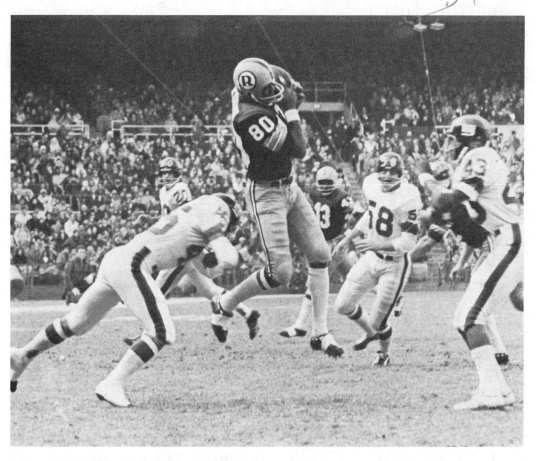

FIGURE 3-4. *The complete receiver must be able to catch the ball in heavy traffic. Although surrounded by the New York defensive secondary, wide receiver Roy Jefferson hangs on to a forward pass thrown by Bill Kilmer. He quickly tucks away the ball.*

## STANCE

We use a three-point stance for our outside receivers. There are two reasons for this. First, we want the outside receiver to feel as though he belongs to the team. Second, we feel he will have more explosion from the line of scrimmage. He must get into the secondary as quickly as he can. If he stands, he is not going to take that first full step.

The upright stance, often used by spread ends, enables the potential receiver to read the defense better, and the receiver can maneuver better in case a linebacker tries to hold him up. On the upright stance, the offensive player should use a jab step and drop his right foot back a little to get extra drive in the first step. With the upright stance, it is very easy to get caught leaning and in motion.

FIGURE 3-5. The pass receiver should "want that ball" and be able to do something when he catches it. Wide receiver Charley Taylor (42) is one of the best at knowing what to do with the football after he gets his hands on it. He has the moves of a running back.

## MENTAL ATTITUDE

In lining up and readying himself to move into his pass pattern, the receiver should concentrate on three things. First, he has to understand, from the films he has been watching, what general type of defense he is playing. Then he has to think, as he looks into the defensive secondary, what they will be doing on this down. Third, he has to consider what he has done before and how the defense reacted to what he did. These are the points he has to think about to help him run an intelligent route.

Whatever route he runs, he will have run it countless times in practice. He has run it so well in practice that he knows that if he runs an intelligent route, it has a good chance of being successful in the game. He thinks to himself that he has done this so much that he has an almost sure completion here. In short, confidence—intelligent confidence—that comes from experience best explains the proper mental attitude we like to see in all our receivers.

We ask our tight ends to take a right- or left-hand stance, whichever is natural. Most of them are right-handed. The tight end should employ a stance that will allow him to take off most quickly. Since nothing usually happens for 5 to 7 yards, we have the ends take a track stance, with the buttocks not so high as those of a sprinter on the track. They place one foot back where they can dig in, so they can really come out of the blocks. The right toe is in line with the instep of the left foot.

FIGURE 3-6. *The three-point stance provides the receiver with more explosion from the initial stance. Here, wide receiver Roy Jefferson executes a comfortable stance with his weight distributed evenly over the three points. This stance also eliminates body lean and sway. This picture shows Jefferson with his head up and his eyes focused directly downfield. He has a comfortable staggered stance with a little weight on his forward hand; this allows for a quick push-off.*

FIGURE 3-7. *The wide receiver can get into the secondary stance more quickly by using a three-point stance. If he stands, he is not going to take that first full step. In many stadiums, it is difficult to hear the quarterback's cadence. Notice Clifton McNeil looking directly into the football. This way he will not move too soon or too late.*

FIGURE 3-8. *The tight end's stance. The right arm, forming a tripod with the feet, should be straight and under the right shoulder. The hips are slightly lower than the shoulders. The right foot is staggered back several inches. The left arm rests above the left knee in a position to explode. The end's head is up, his eyes are open; he looks directly downfield so as not to tip off his intentions. His feet are slightly wider than the width of his shoulders, providing the necessary balance to drive forward or move laterally. If his feet are too close or too wide, the receiver will lack good maneuverability. Alvin Reed demonstrates the proper stance.*

## RELEASES

A receiver must avoid being held up by the defense, since this throws the passer's timing off. Whichever release is used, it must be done with speed. Actually, when the receiver releases slowly there are not many patterns that are effective. He has to release with speed, and then he goes into a glide. This is where he has to drive defenders off with some more speed, and then he will go into his final move.

I don't believe a pass receiver needs a lot of releases. He does need an inside and outside release. Tight ends, for instance, have to be able to step inside as well as out-side. Furthermore, they must learn the correct faking techniques.

We spend a lot of time on releases in our fundamental periods, prior to the passing game. We have the receiver fake a block or "blast"—come off as if he were trying to engage the linebacker and slip him and come on out.

We also use what we call the single head and step fake, in which the end fakes with the head and a step to the outside and then releases inside. Conversely, he can head and step fake to the inside and release outside. Another release would be the double fake, where he fakes to the outside, fakes to the inside, and then comes back to the outside.

Our tight ends also have used with good success a release whereby they actually fake as if they were going to hook the linebacker. The end simply starts out as if he were going to hook the linebacker who is responsible for containment. When the linebacker starts to defend himself, trying not to be hooked, the tight end is able to slip through on the inside.

The *low* release has proven itself quick and effective. The receiver should drop to all fours, scramble along the ground, get up, and then resume his pattern.

The *inside arm* swing is another successful release. As the tight end drives, either to his inside or his outside of the linebacker, he takes his inside arm and makes a great sweeping motion over the top. As the linebackers try to grab hold, the end has a terrific lever that rips their hands off him.

There are other releases that the players just pick up individually, but these are the basic ones.

## HOLDING UP RECEIVERS

Most defenses are continually using stunts or tactics in an effort to hold up the receivers. A

| A | B | C |
|---|---|---|

FIGURE 3-9.   Release with speed. The ability to drive off a defender is essential in getting clear for a forward pass. The threat of having a wide receiver go deep often forces the defense to loosen up their coverage. Here, Charley Taylor, the Redskins' All-Pro, "explodes" from the line of scrimmage.

FIGURE 3-10.   Running an intelligent route. The receiver (here, Charley Taylor) must understand the type of defender and the kind of defense he is playing and how he plans to outmaneuver. He must be able to "read" and understand the total defense. This is an absolute must.

| A | B |
|---|---|

primary objective of the defense is to disguise the direction in which they are going to force the receiver. Of course, if he knows which way they are going to force him, he can normally make an intelligent decision about how to get out.

The defenders who do the best job of holding up the receivers are those who can use their hands effectively. Some players try to hold with their forearms—the forearm lift—and they can deliver good punishment. By the same token, their holding or restricting surface is small, and their range of motion is small, so if the receiver is quick, he can normally elude these people.

Most linebackers have strong wrists and forearms and can extend their arms at least 2 feet in either direction—forward, sideways—and if they have good power, the receiver might find some difficulty.

Normally, the linebackers try to get one hand on the potential receiver's helmet or at least one hand on his shoulder pads. A typical hold would be one hand on his helmet and one hand on his shoulder pad. Others may use two hands on the shoulder pads.

## GETTING OPEN

The most important thing in running a pattern is to drive off the defender. If a receiver cannot drive off the defender, faking isn't going to help. If the receiver does a good job of driving off the defender, faking won't be necessary. However, the defender has to respect a receiver's ability to go deep before he can drive him off.

The threat of beating a man deep, of really exploding off the line of scrimmage, causes most patterns to be open. With more and more speed, there seems to be less and less faking. Faking is still a big part of pass receiving, but with so much speed, the fake is really the drive to the goal line, the threat of beating a man deep.

If the defensive back can just backpedal the way he wants to, he is going to cover almost everything the receiver does. As a result, somehow the receiver has to provoke his movement. He must cause the defender to turn in one direction, losing his balance. With good speed and with explosion off the line, the receiver can provoke him or make him conscious that he is going to go deep on him. The defender will find himself moving backwards faster than he can and then he will get turned in or out. This is exactly what his defense coach does not want to happen. "Don't let them get you turned and throw a touchdown pass!" So, this is where we start, and I think it is most important in our passing attack.

We might start out with a head and shoulder fake, in a particular direction, trying to freeze a man in that direction and then breaking out. This is about the simplest thing he can do. The next simplest move would be a head fake in the direction he is going to end up, coming back with a head fake to the direction in which he is *not* going to go . . . and then coming back in his original direction.

And from there, the pass receiver can go into a variety of maneuvers. He may go into a two-step, which is actually a crossover, a plant in the direction away from where he is going to go, plant, and break in that direction. Or, he could go to a three-step maneuver, the same type of thing.

Our receivers often use a zigzag run, a weave-type run after the defensive back—just watching his feet. Once the defender has been turned in the direction the receiver does not intend to take, he breaks in the direction he intended on going.

Another thing we do is simply run. Let us say we are going to run an "out." We just run at the inside shoulder of the defensive

FIGURE 3-11. *Without breaking stride, wide receiver Roy Jefferson performs a simple look-in pattern against the Kansas City Chiefs. Good receivers have the ability to make their cuts in full stride so the defensive back can't adjust.*

man and continue to run until we force him to turn in that direction and cross his feet. Then we break out.

## RUNNING UNDER CONTROL

We put a great deal of emphasis on running under control, a controlled stride. Coming off the line of scrimmage, we believe, is the most important thing. There has to be an explosion! "You can't come off the line of scrimmage fast enough."

Our young receivers are told: "We want you to go as fast as you can go . . . and still be under control."

The receiver has to be able to make a controlled move when he wants to. After

that, when he comes out of his controlled move, he is coming off his break, and then it is an all-out effort. It becomes a break to the ball, and even though we say all-out, we still like for receivers to have that little extra if they have to go get it—they can pull something from somewhere.

When running under control, the receiver has the ability to cut and angle away from the defender. Saving a burst of speed will help him run away from the man covering him. But when he makes his break, he must really explode! He must use all his speed to get the ball.

## PASS PATTERNS

The Redskins try to employ a precision-type passing attack. We don't depend on trying to

|  C  |  B  |  A  |

FIGURE 3-12. *The strike is a curl-in or curl-out maneuver made after the defender is driven back. Generally, the receiver (here, Alvin Reed) runs at top speed and then settles under control. The ball should be thrown before the receiver makes his turn. After the catch, the receiver should spin on away from the defender.*

FIGURE 3-13. *The curl or strike pattern is one of the three most difficult passes to defense. Flanker Charley Taylor comes down hard, turns in on his curl, and receives a bullet pass. It is essential that the receiver be on balance as he runs the strike.*

A            B

FIGURE 3-14. *One of football's most popular patterns is an 8-yard "slant-in," used by a wide receiver along with his corner patterns. The receiver (here, Clifton McNeil) makes the break quick and sharp. He runs at top speed through the entire maneuver, driving the defender back. Timing is essential in the slant pattern, since the receiver is open for only a fraction of a second.*

fool or out-finesse the defense. Precision passing is what we strive for. Receivers are instructed to go almost to a prescribed depth, then break . . . and our passers know where they will be. The passers can anticipate their break and throw the ball to them. That's the basic thing we try to do.

First, I must say that a pass pattern, no matter how well designed and executed, is no better than the protection given the passer and the accuracy of the pass.

There are actually three basic types of pass patterns:

1. *One-on-one* (*individual*). The receiver isolates the defensive back and tries to outmaneuver him. The most common—and most difficult—pattern to defend against is the outside or sideline break.

2. *Combination pattern.* Here, two or more receivers work together. A decoy clears a zone for the primary receiver. The decoy must make the defender stay with him in a certain zone. He sprints full speed at the defender and drives him back so that the primary receiver can break into the open zone.

3. *Play pass pattern.* This pattern evolves off a backfield action that looks like a run. This action holds the defenders and gives the receiver a slight advantage in getting open. The receiver should try to get into the open as fast as possible.

FIGURE 3-15. *The up or fly pattern. Wide receiver Roy Jefferson (80) gets a step on his defender and outruns him down the sideline. In giving him a good lead, the quarterback should get the ball to him as soon as he breaks open.*

### THE LONG BOMB

On the long over-the-shoulder catch, the passer will throw the receiver a long lead pass over the head. It is important for the receiver to learn to run with his arms in a normal running position. He should never run many yards with his arms extended. He waits until the ball is ready to settle into his hands and then extends his arms and catches the ball. This is one pass where the ball definitely must be "looked into the hands." In pointing his thumbs out, the receiver forms a "basket" with his hands.

By controlling his stride, the receiver is able to slow down a bit if the pass doesn't lead him enough, or he can make that extra effort forward to catch the ball if the passer leads him a little too much. It is very important for the passer to get the ball to him quickly as he breaks open, so that the receiver won't have to break stride. Since a receiver has the speed to cover a lot of ground, the passer tries to let him run under the ball.

*The pass receiver must follow the ball right into his hands.*

## ADJUSTING A PATTERN

Quite often, a receiver has to adjust his pattern into a different area. For example, if he is to run an 8-yard "slant" and a linebacker has come right into the area, he may have to adjust his pattern into a different area, maybe 3 or 4 yards farther. These are things that the quarterback and the receiver have been able to work on during practice. The quarterback will look for the receiver to adjust his pattern, and he knows how the various receivers like to adjust their routes. He knows where to look for them. Of course, if the quarterback thinks there is no possibil-

ity of the adjustment working, he will go to another receiver.

## PRIMARY RECEIVERS

As for the number of primary receivers, we go two ways on this point. First, we give our two outside receivers identical assignments, and they both become primary receivers. Now, the quarterback has a certain defensive man he keys, telling him which man to go to. We do this after the snap of the ball, and it is a very quick thing. Regardless of what de-

FIGURE 3-16. *The goal line pass involves tight competition between the receivers and pass defenders. Here, tight end Jerry Smith, after making a quick release and sharp cut, runs to the corner of the end zone to grab a touchdown pass.*

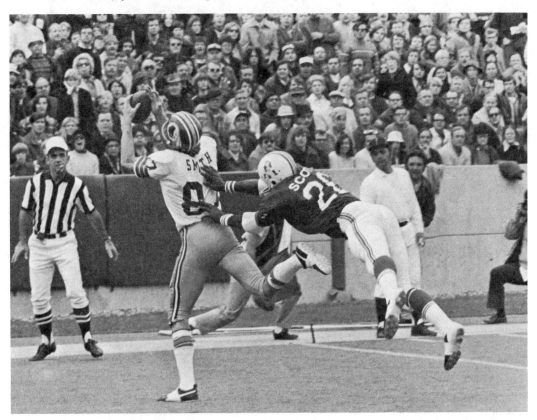

FIGURE 3-17. *Sideline footwork. After catching a sideline pass, flanker Charley Taylor demonstrates some nifty footwork in coming down with both feet in bounds. According to professional rules, if only one foot is planted in bounds immediately after the reception, the pass is considered incomplete.*

fense the opponents have called, or whether they are trying to double up, we have a good pattern on the side, away from the double-up.

In teaching this, we say there is but one primary receiver because after the quarterback makes his decision of who to go to, there is one man.

The other way involves flooding a zone, in which we run either two or three people into a zone, with certain varying routes. We give a linebacker or defensive back the option of who he wants to come up with, actually, a "two on one" situation. When we do this, the quarterback keys the defender we

are trying to put "two on one." Rather than key his receivers, the quarterback keys his defensive man. Now, we just let the defensive man pick out whichever man he wants to cover, and we throw to the other one. So, now, we have two basic primary receivers. We don't do quite as much with that alternate or outside receiver as a lot of teams do.

## THE GOAL LINE PASS

A goal line situation refers to play inside the 8-yard line, where the offense finds the

*FIGURE 3-18. Diving grab. In a tough goal line situation, tight end Jerry Smith fakes his defender out of position to grab a touchdown pass. The tight end often runs his pattern with the threat of force. He can run right at his man and force him to turn. When he turns, the defender is beat!*

depth very restricted. If we are on the 6-yard line, let's say, we only have 16 yards in which to operate. Because the defense plays so very differently in this area, we have to practice a completely separate component of our passing game, rather than combine running with passing.

The defense normally jumps very close to us and very tight. They play man-to-man, and they take an inside position on the receivers—real tough. Here, all we have to do is catch the ball. We don't have to run with it when we get down to the goal line, so the defense must prevent the catch. Of course, by taking the inside position, the defense takes all our inside cuts away, forcing us to throw the outs. This is very difficult to do in this restricted area because their men are playing so close to our receivers.

So, when we get down to the goal line, it becomes a battle, man-on-man, like the one-on-one situation in basketball. Every move our receivers make, the defenders are going to make; this is a very tight, competitive situation. The receiver must try to use any fake or move to get that man out of position . . . just one step . . . and then he should break in there. The quarterback will have the ball waiting for him.

## CATCHING THE BALL

The success or failure of any pass pattern, of course, depends upon the receiver catching the ball. Even the best of patterns is worthless unless the ball is caught.

I don't believe in changing any habits a receiver has if he has had success catching the football. If the player is experiencing some difficulty, then we go back to the basics and try to find where his trouble is.

A            B

*FIGURE 3-19. Look the ball into the hands. The outstanding pass catchers will follow the ball into their hands with their eyes. The head should "pop down" and look right into the fingers. Many passes are dropped because the receivers fail to look the ball in. (Charley Taylor is shown here.)*

### Looking the Ball into the Hands

We like for our receivers to make any catch with both hands . . . and in their hands. They must follow the ball right into their hands. One of the key factors in making a catch is correct movement of the head and the eyes. We spend considerable time on the field emphasizing this skill.

Many receivers do not follow the ball the last 6 inches into their hands with their eyes. Sometimes a receiver will follow the ball to a point about 6 to 8 inches from the body. Then, there comes a place on every catch where he has to move his head in order to keep the eyes on the ball. This is the place where many receivers will not turn their head. The head remains in the position where they were looking back at the passer, and, consequently, they do not follow the last 6 inches into their hands with their eyes. They think they are looking the ball into their hands, but they cannot see the ball the last 6 inches.

We have a little drill where we watch the head *pop down*. If the head snaps right down and looks into the hands, we know receivers are watching the ball. That's one reason why they drop a pass—the head hasn't snapped down right into the fingers.

Another basic point that should be remembered concerning the head is that when a receiver makes his cut, his head should precede his body in the turn. For example, when he makes a sideline cut, he turns into the boundary. Now, the natural tendency is for the receiver to come down, plant, and turn, turning his body as he plants into the boundary. What we want him to do is to come down, plant his feet, and throw his head around. He can turn his head much faster than his body. Naturally, the shoulders and body will follow the head around. This lets the receiver pick up the ball several yards farther than he could if the entire body were turned.

### Running from the Waist Down

We ask our receivers to run "from the waist down." We want the upper body, shoulders, and arms to be involved as little as possible in the running motion. We want it to be a fluid motion. When he runs, the receiver should not overexaggerate and elongate his steps, unless he is in a real footrace with the man going deep. If he can take short or normal steps, his head will be on a more even plane. In other words, the longer steps he takes, the more his head will bob and, as a result, the more difficult it will be for him to keep his eyes on the ball.

### Turning the Hands

One other point we stress is: which way does the receiver turn his hands to make the catch? There is really no hard and fast rule on it, but there is a rule that most receivers use. As the pass receiver is running away from the ball (say he is running a "Corner," a "Flag," or an "Up" pattern), he normally turns his thumbs out, so the hands will form a basket. By the same token, for any ball that he is going to catch, like a "Slant" or "Hook," he normally will want his thumbs

FIGURE 3-20. *The high ball. On the hook or curl patterns, the receiver normally will want his thumbs together, giving him more strength. As a rule, the receiver will take any pass that is above the waist with his thumbs in. This hand position also provides the passer with a good target. The receiver must put the ball away quickly on this type of pass. (Charley Taylor demonstrates hand position here.)*

together. As a rule, any pass that is above the waist will be taken with the thumbs in; any pass below the waist, with the thumbs out.

**A**

**B**

## Changing Shoulders

In catching the ball, our receivers are taught to change from one shoulder to the other. Occasionally when the quarterback is rushed, he puts the ball on a different side than was expected. On this situation, we have the receiver take his eye off the ball and swing from one shoulder back across to the other. This is something he cannot do unless he practices it a lot, and we work on it every day. In several cases last year, it paid off when our receivers made some big catches.

In our system we swing from side to side, depending upon the formation, so our receivers must be adept at catching the ball over either shoulder. Bernie Casey, who played the right side for the 49ers for years, is a good example. When we find a receiver like this, all we do is put him on the other side and give him 90 percent of the work over there and 10 percent from the side he is used to. However, some receivers do have a side they prefer, where they have played the most, but we find they make the adjustment very easily once they get practice at it. Once they get time to work on it, they can play both sides with equal ability.

## Giving with the Hands

The receiver should relax and not fight the ball. Stiffness of the fingers will cause more

*FIGURE 3-21. The low ball. The thumbs of the receiver are out for any pass below his waist. Tight end Mike Hancock forms the basket with his hands as he bends over for the pass. His thumbs are out as his relaxed hands "give" with the throw. He must keep his eyes on the ball all the way. On the low pass, the receiver must flex his knees and bend from the waist.*

dropped passes than anything else. So, he shouldn't grab or stab for the ball. As the catch is made, the hands should "give" with the ball, like an outfielder catching a fly ball. This "give" adds to the smoothness of the catch. Above all, he must remember to catch and have control of the ball before starting to run with it. He concentrates on the ball from the time he sees it leave the passer's hand until he sees it in his hands. He must "look the ball into the hands!" He watches it all the way, even after he has made the catch.

## PUTTING THE BALL AWAY

Once he catches the ball, the receiver must tuck the ball away as soon as possible, so as to prevent a defender from knocking the ball out of his grasp. We give our receivers practice running with the ball. We want them to practice running like a back as soon as they catch the ball.

On all our pass drills, we ask the receiver to tuck the ball away—put it under his arm with a good proper hold on it—and drop his outside shoulder. This is generally the direction the defender will come from, and 98 percent of the time when the receiver catches the ball, a split instant after he has it, the tackler will be there. So we want the receiver to be ready for the blow. He must anticipate it and drop his shoulder to protect the ball so he doesn't fumble. He must put the ball away, quickly and securely. Next, the receiver should be instructed to turn and drive directly upfield as quickly as possible. He can then check the situation and run accordingly.

## DRILLS

Offensive pass receivers are continually involved in a series of wind sprints—short, fast runs; therefore, they must do a lot of running. The pass receiver should practice short, fast sprints of 10 to 15 yards, and should run in a straight line, then cut sharply to the left or right. When he cuts to the left, he must make sure he shoves off from the right foot. When he cuts to the right, he should shove off from the left foot. In other words, he should never cross one leg over the other when he makes his cut.

There is nothing that can take the place of team drill. The ends and backs, all potential receivers, should spend most of their time as a team so that the passer can learn the position of every man on every pattern. In our seven-on-seven period, almost daily, receivers go against the linebackers and deep backs, working on their various patterns. Playing against a top defensive unit like we have helps.

Tight ends, in particular, must learn to run routes with a defender in the way and without interference. Breaks or turns should be marked. They should also be given drill time to work on both one-on-one and two-on-one releases. One or two defenders are placed on the nose of the end with the assignment to try to prevent a release.

1. *Pitch and catch* With a football, two tight ends are stationed about 5 yards apart. Playing catch, they should be instructed to throw high and low, right and left. They should increase the distance apart to 10 or 12 yards.

DIAGRAM 3-1. *Pitch and catch.*

2. *Look the ball into the hands* Lined up in a single line, the ends run pass routes and receive thrown balls from the quarterback. A total of four balls can be used, each with a 2-inch number painted on each quadrant of the ball. Number 1 should be eliminated since it is easy to see. The receiver must call the number of the ball as he receives it, forcing him to look the ball into his hands.

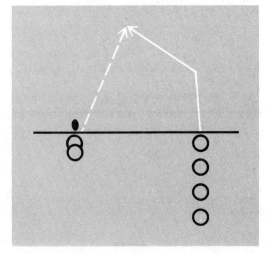

DIAGRAM 3-2. *Look the ball into the hands.*

3. *Bad pass drill* Lining up single file, the receivers run a short pass route and are thrown passes that are difficult to catch, forcing them to make a quick adjustment. A passer or a coach can do the throwing, and the receiver should make every effort to catch the ball.

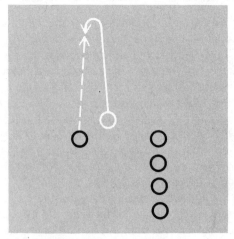

DIAGRAM 3-3. *Bad pass drill.*

4. *Fight for the ball* Two or three receivers are formed in a loose triangle facing a passer at approximately 10 yards. The passer throws the ball up between the receivers, who will try to catch the ball at its highest point and fight recklessly for the ball.

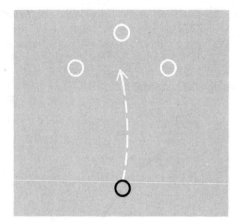

DIAGRAM 3-4. *Fight for the ball.*

5. *Machine gun* Four receivers are placed in a semicircle formation, one with a football. Facing them is a lone end about 6 or 7 yards away, also with a ball. On the signal "Go," the lone end throws his ball to one of the four receivers. At the same time, the end in the formation will throw his ball at the lone end. The moment the lone end fumbles he is "out."

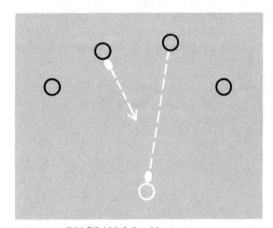

DIAGRAM 3-5. *Machine gun.*

6. *Sideline* A quarterback and center are set up 6 yards from the hash mark into the middle of the field, and the offensive ends are placed on the hash. One at a time, they run on 8- or 9-yard sideline cut and receive the ball just before going out of bounds. A dummy or live defensive back can face the ends.

7. *One-handed drill* To emphasize that pass receivers keep their eyes on the ball while receiving, they should catch with one hand for a short period.

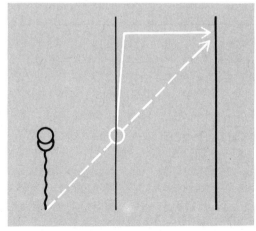

DIAGRAM 3-6. *Sideline drill.*

8. *Catch and run*  A line of receivers runs parallel to the line of scrimmage. The passer throws the ball to the receiver just before he gets even with two standing dummies. The receiver should break immediately between the two dummies and head for the goal line.

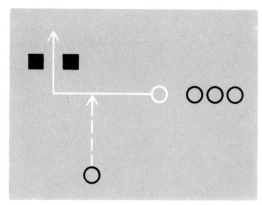

DIAGRAM 3-7.  Catch and run drill.

9. *Two-on-two route drill*  Two receivers who normally run patterns that complement each other execute these routes against a pair of defensive backs. The curl and flat patterns, along with crossing patterns, are some of the common routes used in this drill. Two passers give both receivers the opportunity to catch a ball on the same play.

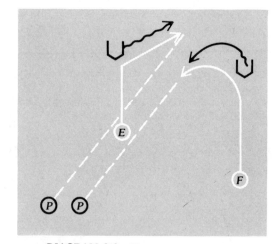

DIAGRAM 3-8.  Two-on-two route drill.

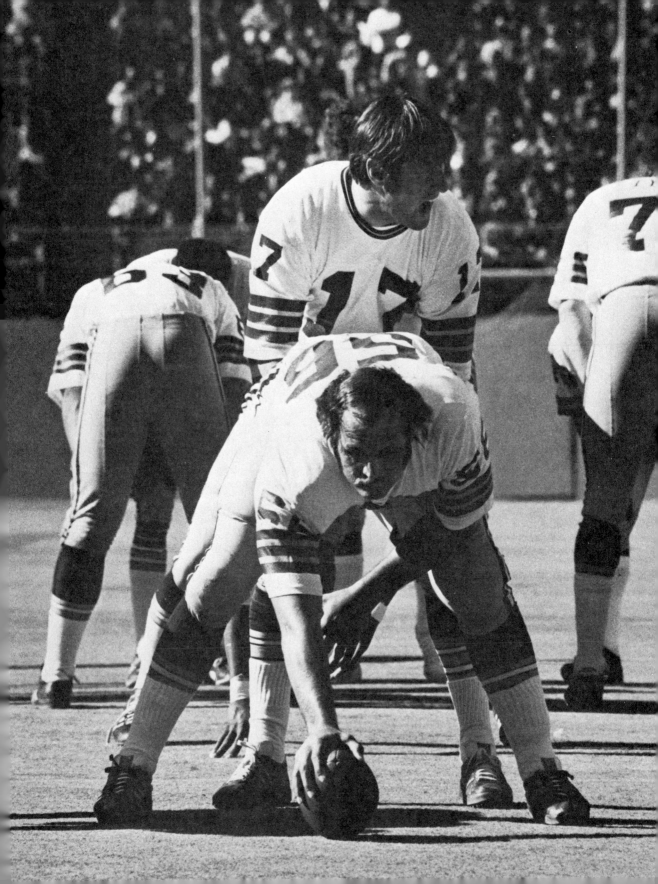

# 4

# Centering

*The center should be just as effective a blocker as the other offensive linemen.*

**George Allen**

The center is a key man on any football team. If he doesn't perform his job of getting the play started by snapping the ball back to the quarterback, the offensive team cannot function.

The center controls the timing of his team, and proper timing is the essence of any offense. If he doesn't execute the exchange properly, the center can cause his team to bog down because of fumbles, miscues, and poorly timed plays. Typically, the center will snap the ball back to his quarterback about 60 to 65 times per game. Therefore, the exchange has to be fast, hard, accurate, and automatic.

Poise and coolness under fire are musts for every center because of the punishment that is sure to come his way. He should be a strong, tough athlete who likes to mix it! He has to enjoy making hard contact with the opposition. If he doesn't explode into a defender with aggressive quickness and power, the defense will surely come to him.

In addition, the center must be able to make the long pass to the punter in punt formation, and to the holder's hands on the placement and field goal attempts. Not enough players consider playing center, but usually there is less competition at this position. Football centers—like catchers in baseball—are always in demand.

In selecting their offensive line, some coaches, unfortunately, fill every other position, then take the leftovers and make them centers. However, we don't believe that "almost anybody" can play offensive center on a football team. The center's position involves considerable responsibility, and by all means should not be filled by the leftovers.

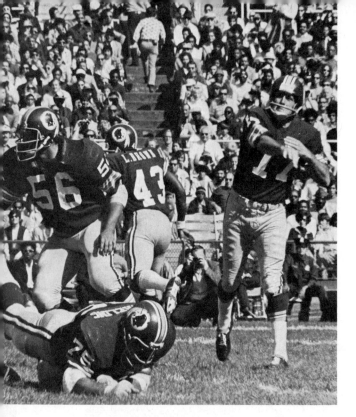

*FIGURE 4-2. Dropping back to protect the quarterback, veteran center Len Hauss (56) is in good position as he looks to help out. An effective pocket has given passer Bill Kilmer the time he needs to get set.*

Above all, the center should be quick. Quickness is more important than size. We call it short speed, speed within a radius of five yards.

A large player at the center position provides greater protection for the quarterback. Moreover, a tall center enables the quarterback to stand higher, giving him a better view of the field and the defense. Another important asset of the center is hustle, providing he has the necessary size, of course. Generally speaking, if the center hustles, his team likewise will hustle. The center sets the pace for the entire offensive line.

To be a pivotal man, a player must have strength to successfully perform his blocking responsibilities. The center should be a punishing blocker who really blasts the middle linebacker when he fires out at him. He has to be able to cut the big tackles, fellows who will be 25 to 35 pounds heavier than he is. His blocks often will determine whether or not the ball carrier will be able to run the shortest line to the goal line—and that's straight ahead!

Therefore, the center has to have the strength to turn the tackles and the quickness to get to the middle linebacker. And, too, when they start playing an odd defense, he has to have the ability to ward off individuals. So, we are asking for a tremendous football player.

## QUALIFICATIONS

The center, like the quarterback, should be a leader. He must be intelligent enough to know the blocking and what is taking place in the backfield. He not only forms the huddle, but he also is the first one up to the line. He has to know the snap count, to get the ball back to the quarterback quickly. Therefore, he must know the situation as far as the last possible movement by the defense. By making the necessary calls and adjustments, he aids the rest of his teammates on the line. In fact, he makes as many adjustments at the line as the quarterback.

## STANCE

The stance of the center is slightly wider than that of the normal offensive lineman, with the feet set as widely apart as the ability to move in any direction will permit without lowering the buttocks. This provides the necessary base to snap the ball back to the quarterback. The important thing is to establish a stance that is comfortable and that can be executed well by the players. By starting with a comfortable stance, the center can effectively carry out his duties of charging and blocking, after executing a successful snapback.

We like our centers to use a staggered stance. By placing the right foot back slightly, the right-handed center finds he has more freedom to make his snapback. The feet are parallel to each other, pointing straight ahead, and are slightly wider than the width of the shoulders. Some coaches advocate a square stance with the feet even and parallel.

The center should be leaning well forward over the ball so that his head is almost up to the front part. The head is up so that his eyes can focus on a point about 5 yards downfield. The shoulders are square, and the back is straight with the hips high enough to allow the quarterback to stand almost erect. His weight should be distributed evenly between the football and the balls of his feet.

He should make sure his knees are pointing straight ahead, rather than kneeing inward. This allows ample space to bring the ball up to the quarterback.

It is up to the quarterback to apply enough pressure to the center's crotch with the back of his hands. This lets the center know exactly where his hands are and provides a target as the center brings the ball up.

FIGURE 4-3. *The center should use a comfortable, even stance, one from which he can move in any direction. While some centers keep the left hand on the knee, others prefer placing both hands on the ball, as George Burman does here. However, everything is done with the right hand. Our centers keep the seams straight up, the way our passers like it.*

## DELIVERY

We recommend that a young center employ the two-hand snapback to the quarterback. The two-hand method is more secure, because the center can bring the ball back a little faster and harder than with the one-hand technique. The one-arm snap does have one advantage in that the center has the free hand and arm that can be used to club away at the man playing on his nose. But, with the two-hand snap, centers have better control. They seem to be a little more efficient in getting the job done.

### Grip

Coming up to the line, the center grabs the ball and positions it the way he wants it. Normally, the laces on the ball are turned end of the ball points at about the level of his knees. He must be careful, however, not to tilt the ball too far forward because the rules state that the ball may not be angled more than 45 degrees from the ground.

Unless he lines up the ball properly and correctly every time, the center cannot be consistent on the exchange. The center should keep his body in the same plane throughout the exchange.

FIGURE 4-4. *Close-up of the grip. The right hand is placed well up on the front half of the ball. The fingers are well spread, and the thumb extends over to the left side of the ball. The left hand is placed on the rear end of the ball rather than on the knee. The left hand is there to balance off the weight. Used as a guide, it comes up as a blocking lever immediately on the snap. The snap is made solely with the right hand.*

## BALL EXCHANGE

The ball exchange from the center to the quarterback must become automatic. Therefore, these two players must practice together countless hours so they have complete confidence in each other.

Although the center has both hands on the ball, it is lifted by the right hand only and should be brought up with all the speed and force possible. The delivery arm hand should swing like a pendulum. The quarterback wants the ball horizontal, so the center has to turn the ball when he snaps it. He does it with one motion—real quick!! It is a natural twist of the wrist. As it comes up, the ball should be turned over so that the side of the ball that was on the ground will contact the hands of the quarterback exactly in the middle of the center's crotch.

The snapback is simply a normal turn, a quarter turn to put the ball between the legs. This is not a difficult maneuver—just a natural way of turning the arm. The quarter turn is faster than the full wrist turn. He just uses the other hand as a guide as he comes up.

Since the laces will still be on the right side, the quarterback receives the ball with the laces across the fingertips of his right hand so that he can pass or hand off immediately without having to juggle or adjust the ball in his hands. It is easier for the quarter-

halfway down on the right side. The right hand is placed well up on the front half of the ball, similar to the position taken for throwing a forward pass. The fingers are well spread, and the thumb extends over to the left side of the ball.

The left hand, which supports most of the center's weight, is placed on the rear end of the ball. The fingers are together with the thumb extended over the top of the ball. His weight is supported by the upper part of the palm at the base of the index finger. He should tilt the ball forward so that the rear

A                                    B

*FIGURE 4-5. Ball exchange. The center (here, Dan Ryczek) keeps his arms stiff on the snap. From a slightly staggered stance, he brings the ball straight up like a swinging pendulum. This action enables the center to get the ball to the quarterback at a quarter turn. As the center drives the ball back and up, his body weight starts forward. As contact with the quarterback's hands is made, the center takes his first step forward. The ball is placed with the laces up into the fingertips of the quarterback.*

back to grasp the ball if the center turns the ball slightly to his left as he brings it up. The ball is then at a 45-degree angle from the line of scrimmage when it reaches the quarterback's hands.

The quarterback places his hands so that the thumbs of each hand are on top, pressing against the crotch of the center. With the throwing hand on top, the fingers of each hand point downward and outward and press against the inside of his thighs. This keeps the quarterback from having one

of his fingers jammed by the ball and will enable his hands to completely surround the fat part of the ball as it comes up to him.

*This is a must:* The center must deliver the ball to the same spot in his crotch every time. Any inconsistency may cause fumbles.

The secret to a good exchange is where the laces wind up. The quarterback wants these laces right under the fingertips of his top hand. Then, he is all set to hand off, pass, or run.

As he delivers the ball, usually the

|  A  |  B  |  C  |

FIGURE 4-6. *The charge. As contact is made with the quarterback's hands, the center (here, Len Hauss) takes his first step forward, followed by the second step, which should be a short, hard-driving step. The feet are well spread so that he has good stability to move into a block. He must drive with explosive power.*

center's buttocks go up, his head goes down, and his back bows. It is very important then that the quarterback's hands ride with the ball and that the center keep his body in the same place throughout the exchange. As the center moves forward, the quarterback must maintain pressure with his hands on the center's buttocks by extending his arms until the ball is exchanged cleanly. Otherwise, a fumble is likely.

## THE CHARGE

The charge of the center depends on the type of block assigned to him. The important thing is to move on the snap. He should start his charge and snap the ball at the same

time. He should not bring the ball up and then start to move. He must move on the snap.

The charge is initiated by driving hard off both feet. The center must make sure that he "fires out" and snaps the ball exactly on the starting count. When the ball is snapped, the center's body is going forward; he has to catch up with it with his feet. If he is going to block to either side, the movement then must be lateral rather than straight.

As contact with the quarterback's hands is made, the center takes his first step forward, usually with his right foot, followed by the second step, which should be a short, hard-driving step. On a pass play, there should be a slight movement ahead, but very slight, though, because the center has to go back for pass protection.

Sometimes, the center will anticipate the signal and center the ball before his linemen have heard the starting count. This has happened many times without being corrected and the other offensive linemen are blamed for not getting their blocks. The defense now will be able to move on the ball and beat the offensive line to the charge. Thus, the offense loses its biggest advantage—knowing the starting count. So, this timing must be watched carefully every day.

Each center and each quarterback are different in their techniques. When fumbles occur on the exchange, the movement of the center should be checked. Quite often, he is guilty of carrying the ball with him on his first step. Or, his snapping action may cause the ball to arrive too low for the quarterback.

The center must be able to cope with the defender who sets himself right up in front of his nose and tries to give the center a rough time. The center can cut him down to his knees by his quickness. He can shoot right out after him and try to drive him back if he is big and strong enough. Of course, if the center is blocking "a Butkus," and if he isn't as big or strong, he is in trouble. But, still, the head and shoulder block and a good forearm might prove effective. Usually, a quick block to try to cut him down at his knees is effective against the big middle backer.

FIGURE 4-7. *Coping with an odd-front defense. The center must be able to cope with the defender who sets himself up right in front of his nose. With the help of an offensive guard, the center can often cut him down with quick and aggressive blocking.*

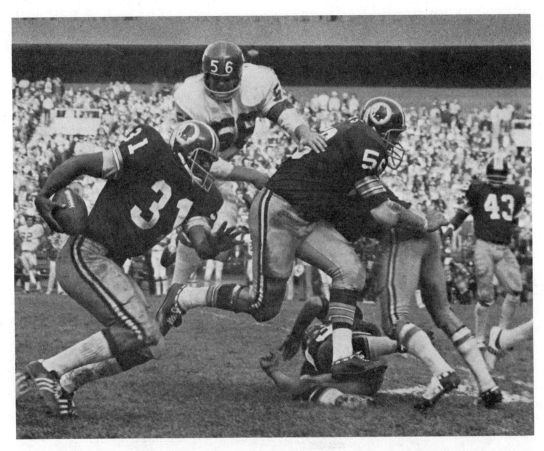

*FIGURE 4-8. Clearing the way. The first quality to look for in a center is quickness . . . the ability to get off the line of scrimmage quickly and move fast for 5 or 6 yards. Here, Len Hauss of the Redskins leads the fullback through the middle. On a running play up the middle, the center often has to take on the middle linebacker straight ahead. He must be quick enough to get to him.*

## BLOCKING

To a large extent, blocking is desire and determination on the part of the player to beat his man and get the job done. If a man is blocked out of the play, normally, the center's work has been successful.

Aggressive blocking is what it takes to perform at the center position. We like to see our center snap the ball, go after his man,

and aggressively block him. He has to "Run him down"!

Blocking the middle linebacker is usually a matter of harassment. It is seldom a crisp block. The center just gets in the middle linebacker's belly and keeps him occupied as long as he can.

Blocking on the draw takes plenty of timing. The center drops his head and drives his shoulder into the linebacker's gut with everything he has. Timing and speed are vital to good blocking for the draw.

With increasing emphasis being placed on the passing game, pass blocking has become an important responsibility for the center. His first job is to pick up the middle linebacker. After that, he is an option blocker, picking up any leakage through the line, helping out the four interior linemen, whoever misses.

Pass protection is probably the most difficult technique for the center, as it is for all offensive linemen. He has to effectively block nose-to-nose so that he will not be defeated. No football team likes the defense to take advantage of a weak center. So, we drill on this by having a defensive man line up against him.

With his knees slightly bent, the center leans forward from the waist, his elbows high and parallel to the ground. The fists are clenched in front of his chest, thumbs in. We

FIGURE 4-9. *Protecting the passer. The center's first job is to pick up the middle linebacker. As an option blocker, he should pick up any leakage through the line. Here, Len Hauss (56) provides strong protection for quarterback Bill Kilmer (17).*

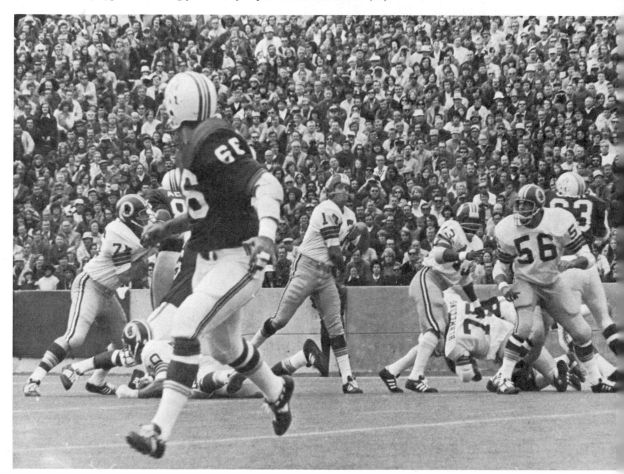

like our centers to drop back about 4 yards, approximately 3 yards in front of the quarterback. At first, it is advisable for the center to look so that he does not end up with his rear in the passer's face. But after awhile, he can sense this position. Good pass protection demands that all penetration be stopped at this point, about 4 yards behind the line of scrimmage.

All in all, the center should be just as effective a blocker as the other linemen. The fact that he shares with the quarterback the important responsibility of ball exchange should not diminish his effectiveness as a blocker. This is the one big advantage over a single wing center.

On a running play going to the right, he will block with his left shoulder. As he snaps the ball with his right hand, he will drive his left shoulder at his opponent, bringing his left hand up to his chest for a broader blocking surface. He should aim his head directly at the man's midsection and slip it by the right side only at the last moment.

The first step with his left foot should be straight forward in a short quick jab. The second step comes just after he makes contact, and then he brings his right foot up under him very quickly at the side of the defensive man. As it hits the ground, he drives off the right foot and lifts him in an attempt to turn the man to the left.

From then on he continues to drive after his opponent with quick, choppy, powerful steps, always working to keep himself between the play and the man he is blocking. If he completes his first block, he should go downfield after another man.

## FORMING THE HUDDLE

The center should take pride in forming a good huddle. One of his responsibilities after each play is to hustle back and establish a point where his teammates will form the huddle for the next play. A point 7 to 7½ yards behind the line of scrimmage is sufficient, where the quarterback can give his signals without the defense interfering or reading what will happen.

A sloppy huddle is the fault of the center, usually a sloppy center. The center should be told to go back to the point and hold up his hand so that the rest of the team can form the huddle and then go straight up to the line for the next play.

We place a great deal of importance on the huddle, the reaction that we have, and the manner in which we come out. Linemen are always looking for a possible tip-off, such as an expression by the quarterback or certain mannerisms by ball carriers or pass receivers. We hope that we are not giving anything away. In fact, during practice, we want our defensive linemen to tell us what they see. After all, what they see, the opponents have got to see.

As he breaks quickly out of the huddle and comes up over the ball, the center should be thinking of his blocking assignment and the technique he will use in carrying out his assignment. The prime concern of the center is the snap count and the importance of delivering the ball at the exact time.

## CENTERING TO THE KICKER

The quickest way to lose a ball game is to have a kick blocked, and usually the fault is traced to a slow or inaccurate pass from the center. I may be wrong, because I don't have statistics to prove this point, but it appears that good centers are becoming scarce. I'm referring to their ability to make the pre-

FIGURE 4-10. *Forming the huddle. After each play, the center must hustle back and es-tablish a point approximately 7 to 7½ yards behind the line of scrimmage.*

cise snap to the holder or kicker. This is why a man who desires to becomes a good center must practice the long spiral pass every opportunity he gets.

When a team lines up in place-kick or punt formation, it becomes the important responsibility of the center to fire the ball back low, quick, and accurately in a perfect spiral.

When the center places his hands on the football, it will be approximately at arm's length directly in line with his nose and the middle of his body. His weight should be distributed evenly on his feet with good balance. In fact, he should spread his legs a bit wider than he would in exchanging the ball.

Centering the ball to the holder on the place-kick isn't really hard. It is more or less a quick lob. The holder, who is only 7 yards behind the center, doesn't want the football coming at him like a bullet. He likes a nice, crisp lob with a steady spiral about 2 or 3 feet above the ground. The ball should come back where the holder wants it. The important point here is that the ball has to come back *at the same speed every time*. Otherwise, the center can destroy the kicker's timing.

On punts, the center does the same thing, but he gets more of his arms into play: his whole body works. In many cases the punter is very far back, but he still wants the

A                                    B

FIGURE 4-11. *Centering to a kicker (Len Hauss and Dan Ryczek). The ball should be at a comfortable arm's length in front of the center. The center has the laces down on the left side. His right hand is under the forward point of the ball. The power in snapping the ball back is supplied by the right hand, with the left hand serving as the guide hand. The spiral is made by rolling the ball off the fingertips of the right hand, while the left hand helps to direct the ball. The center must fire the ball back fast and accurately in a perfect spiral. His target is the kicker's hands. Note the excellent follow-through with both hands. This is one fundamental that is often neglected. Another fault of present-day centers is that they have to pick the ball up before snapping it.*

same kind of pass. The ball must be centered accurately with a firm spiral, and he wants something on the ball. We want speed. This is why the center must put his entire body into this one.

Above all, the center must not watch the ball all the way into the punter's hand. As soon as the ball is passed, he must get himself into blocking position. The ball should be aimed directly at the kicker's hands, in front of the belt buckle.

## CENTERING WITH A DIRECT SNAP

The spiral pass is also used almost entirely by teams that still run from the single-wing or short-punt formations. When I was coaching in college, the first two players I attempted to recruit were a center and a tailback. The reason was that we employed a multiple offense and shifted to the single wing. A good center must know how to snap the ball back to one of the deep backs with accuracy and with the proper speed.

A nice crisp lob is needed, with a good spiral. The center uses both hands on the ball when he passes. The left hand helps with the spin and the speed. Both arms do the job.

The feet of a single-wing center should be spread wider than in a normal stance. Most centers stagger their feet. If the right-handed center will place his right foot slightly back, he will give his passing hand a larger arch to pass through. The knees are flexed for comfort and extra power. The ball should be at a comfortable arm's length in front of the center as he takes his position.

With the laces facing the ground, the right hand should be placed under the forward point of the ball with the fingertips gripping the laces. The fingers of the passing hand should be well spread. Actually, the grip and passing motion are almost the same as those used in throwing a forward pass. The only difference is that now the center is throwing the ball back between his legs.

The left hand is placed lightly along the top of the ball with the fingers almost parallel to the seams of the ball. The left hand is used only as a guide hand since the power in snapping the ball back is supplied by the right hand.

The center should be looking back through his legs and should be able to see at least the lower part of the legs of the man he is centering the ball to. The spiral is made by rolling the ball off the fingertips of the right hand, while the left or guide hand helps to direct the ball to the right point.

On most of the plays in the single wing, the snap should be a soft spiral with a light touch, so minimal follow-through is needed, and the center can quickly bring his head up as he starts to block.

## DRILLS

The center, in his practice drills, must cover all of the situations a center is likely to encounter in a game. Like all offensive linemen, the center must be drilled daily on a wide assortment of blocks. Fire-out, shoulder, reach, reverse, and open-field blocks are those requiring major emphasis.

1. *Stance*  The center candidates, each with a ball, are lined up on a yard line across the field. Together, they go through the various steps in a good stance.

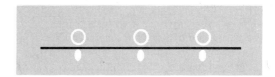

DIAGRAM 4-1.  Stance.

2. *Exchange*  The exchange requires hours and hours of drill until it becomes almost automatic. Daily drill is required if the center is to stay sharp. Even a fraction of a second can make the difference. Every day before regular practice begins, the quarterbacks and centers spend 15 minutes working on the ball exchange. There should be someone on the center's nose in every drill.

DIAGRAM 4-2.  Exchange.

3. *Starting* This usually involves the entire offensive line. The quarterback and a full line should work daily on getting off precisely together and driving out low. The linemen can start into a seven-man charging sled or into shields, bags, or aprons.

4. *One-on-one blocking* When the center snaps the ball, he must make an effective block on a defensive man. A center should never snap the ball without this forward motion. He has to step equally well with either foot. A defender can be placed over the ball on the line of scrimmage. After the exchange to the quarterback, the center tries to drive the defender straight back.

    The pop drill is a very effective one-on-one blocking drill that will teach the blocker to stop the rushman's charge. This drill can be followed with the "pop and recoil," full pass blocking, and heavy bag drills.

*DIAGRAM 4-3. One-on-one.*

5. *Pass blocking and drop-back action* After making the exchange, the center makes a jab step with his back foot and then bounces back about 1 yard. His drop must never bring him closer than 6 yards from the passer. After his 1-yard drop, he should be checked for quickness and position.

6. *Center snap drills* The center snap involving a long spiral pass must be practiced at every opportunity. Some centers find it helpful to practice first each day by standing up and throwing a two-hand spiral from directly overhead for a few minutes before turning around and throwing the ball through their legs using the same motion. The weighted training ball is invaluable for practicing the long snap.

7. *Punt protection, field goal, and extra point blocking* No coach can expect much of a blocking job from his center and still get a great snap. Any block the center makes in protecting the kicker can be labeled a bonus. After his snap, though, the center should come to a hitting position.

8. *Tackling drills* Since the center and all offensive linemen must switch to defense and cover punts, they should have some drilling on the fundamentals of tackling. Since they are limited in time, most coaches confine their preparation to pursuit and open-field tackling drills.

    In drilling open-field tackling, a ball carrier is given a ball and placed in the middle of one of the horizontal lines facing the center. The center's job is to tackle him before he reaches a restraining line. On the command "Ball," the ball carrier tries to reach the other line. This drill allows for open-field tackling but reduces the injury element because of the 3-yard distance.

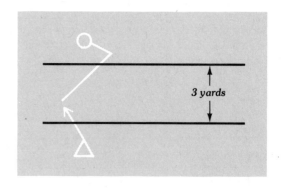

3 yards

*DIAGRAM 4-4. Tackling drill.*

# 5

# Offensive Line

No football offense can succeed without a strong line up front, which can open up the holes and keep the rushmen away from the passer.

Blocking is the first principle in offensive line play. *Fully 90 percent of all offensive action is in blocking. It is the essence of good offensive football.* Therefore, it is the first rudiment a lineman must master, and the line coach cannot stress this fundamental enough.

Successful blocking must be taught in the first three weeks of the season and during spring practice. In order to teach players how to block, drills are necessary to increase endurance and perfect technique. A considerable portion of the practice program should be devoted to the teaching of these fundamentals since blocking is the backbone of all good football teams. Care must be taken to make this part of the practice program as productive and interesting as possible.

Many coaches fail to keep a record of the time devoted to drills and techniques used to teach fundamental blocks. A record of the time spent on each block should be kept on the Time Study Chart on blocking (see Chart 5-1 at the end of the chapter).

In this chapter, emphasis is placed on the following blocks:

1. Shoulder block
2. Reverse shoulder block
3. Trap block
4. Position step block
5. Cross-body block
6. Reverse cross-body block
7. Crab block
8. Double team block
9. Pass block
10. Screen block
11. Downfield block
12. Blocking for kicks

*FIGURE 5-2. The offensive line must be able to open up holes, like the one above giving Larry Brown (43) some good running room.*

All other blocks are secondary or relative to these twelve and originate from different situations that arise on a football field.

The fact that at least 90 percent of all action and energy in offensive football is used in blocking explains why greater supervision should be devoted to the techniques and drills used in teaching the blocking game.

## QUALIFICATIONS

In selecting an offensive lineman, we look for the big, strong man who is quick, agile, and tough and has a great desire to play football.

We like him to have what we call short quickness. That is, we are not looking for 100-yard speed but more like 10, 15, or 20 yards. The ability to move quickly over a short distance is the greatest asset of the lineman. Quick feet and leg power are very important.

Guards and centers are selected for size and agility combined. We will often sacrifice size to obtain that agility and toughness. Of course, the size of the guard should depend on the offense used. If he has to pull out of the line and lead interference, a team must sacrifice size for speed.

The guard has to be one of the toughest men on the field. Along with the center, he is

FIGURE 5-3. *Offensive linemen must be big and strong, but they must also be quick; short quickness is a must! Providing interference for the fullback are guards John Wilbur (60) and Paul Laaveg (73).*

involved in hard contact on every play. On running plays, he must block at the line of scrimmage or pull out and block on outside end sweeps. On pass plays, he has to drop back to protect the quarterback.

A good strong man must be at the center position. He starts every play and is usually in the middle of the action. He must snap the ball to the quarterback with automatic consistency and be a durable blocker.

The tackles are usually the biggest men on the offensive line field. They must be strong and explosive, and have the quickness to block the defensive end. They are usually blocking the biggest man on the defensive line. This assignment determines to a great extent the merit of the offensive tackle.

Regardless of all of their physical at-tributes, offensive linemen have to be sold on playing in the line. Their dedication, or lack of it, will often determine the success of a football team. In short, they must like to hit!

## STANCE

Fundamental to all good blocking movements is a perfect stance. Without a good, balanced stance, it is difficult to start with speed or drive with power after making the initial movements. Most linemen use a balanced three-point stance giving them a solid base to move into their block. From it, they can explode ahead quickly, pull out, or hold against a pass rush.

*FIGURE 5-4. Offensive line spacing has increased the effectiveness of offensive football by spreading the defensive linemen. Using man-for-man blocking, the chief task of the offensive line is to keep the hole open. Shown here are John Wilbur, guard; Len Hauss, center; Ray Schoenke, guard; and Jim Snowden, tackle.*

The Redskins vary the stance, in terms of what is referred to as a balanced stance. We put a little more weight forward, and the stagger is a little greater than for other stances. The stagger should depend on the build of the individual. We like the men to line up with the right foot back, although not farther back than the heel of the opposite foot. The feet are placed about shoulder width apart. Since the position of the lineman's feet may tip off the direction he is going, the guard may suddenly shift his rear foot as the play begins.

The lineman's head is up, the neck is firm, and the eyes are looking straight down the field. His shoulders are parallel to the ground with his feet well up under him. The back is level and parallel to the ground.

The weight is evenly distributed over the hand and the feet. Although the lineman puts weight on the front hand, the forward rock is less pronounced than in the split-T. If a player shows good ability to move forward and sideward, if he can pull, and still has that quick, explosive "pop," we leave him alone.

The right arm on the ground should be in line with the right knee and perpendicular to the ground. When pulling out, this hand isn't as far in front of the shoulder, and very little weight is placed on it. The wrist of the free arm is placed slightly above the knee, with the hand clenched ready for use in blocking.

## STARTING COUNT

Although there are many kinds of starting counts a team can use, the important thing is to keep the count simple. The offensive linemen have a big advantage over the defense in that they know when the ball is going to be snapped. Therefore, they must take full advantage of this factor.

FIGURE 5-5. *Walt Sweeney's balanced three-point stance provides a solid base for moving into the block. The stance should be comfortable and give the lineman good maneuverability. The lineman's head should be up, his weight evenly distributed over the hands and feet.*

FIGURE 5-6. *The charge. The feet of the lineman should be well spread and should be advanced in short, digging, piston-stroke steps. Balance and control are essential. The head should be up, the eyes open. One of the common errors in the charge is to lower the head too soon. Len Hauss is shown here.*

## THE CHARGE

The offensive charge is the quick uncoiling of the line as a unit. Our entire running offense depends on the quickness and power with which our men drive off that line. Since the defensive players are bigger and can use their hands, the offensive line must depend on maximum momentum and surprise in opening up holes for the ball carriers.

Two types of line charges are used in football today: the step charge and the lunge charge. The type of charge or approach a

FIGURE 5-7. *Outstanding blocking ability is a prime requisite of an all-league offensive guard like Gene Upshaw of the Oakland Raiders. Above, Upshaw pulls out of the line to lead the interference for running back Clarence Davis.*

lineman takes will depend on the particular play.

### Step Charge

This charge used against a waiting defensive tackle is executed by driving forward off the front foot while taking a step forward with the back foot. The lineman usually makes contact with the opponent as the rear foot completes its forward movement.

The biggest factor in the initial charge is "two quick steps." He must take short steps to keep both feet under him and give his body the necessary momentum to go for-

ward. So, he must get off his marks fast, as fast as he can, and keep on balance. He must keep his legs driving!

The "step" action only begins the block—to develop a driving force. After the forward momentum gets underway, the specific type of block will determine further movement.

### Lunge Charge

With an opponent playing head-on, the blocker doesn't need any position steps after his lunge. The lunge charge used against hard-charging opponents is executed by driving with considerable force off both feet at the same time. The lineman comes into contact just as or just before full extension of the knees takes place. Once the feet are in their forward position, he takes short powerful steps in a churning driving action. The lunge charge is used primarily with shoulder blocks.

Lunging requires nothing more than straightening of the legs, without movement of the legs. A blocker must never rock back and forth before he makes his lunge. He must explode straight forward without first raising his body. To keep his head up, the blocker's eyes should be kept skyward.

Balance and control are the important factors in the charge. He might "sting" somebody, but if he doesn't have balance after the hit, he'll fall to the ground.

## PULLING OUT

The fundamental technique of pulling and trapping linemen is often neglected by football teams. The Redskins spend considerable time working on this action. This is the sweep-type pull that can pick up the easiest yardage we can get. If we can get a back outside with a lineman in front, we can get away from all those huge people inside, and we can score points out there. We cannot get such easy yardage running up the middle.

There is no deception on the Power Sweep. The two guards simply lead the ball carrier around end. At the snap of the ball, both guards pull out of the line and clear a path for the runner. The blocking back will usually take out the defensive end or corner linebacker.

**B**

**A**

FIGURE 5-8. *Pulling out of the line. In pulling to the right, the guard pivots sharply on the toe of his outside foot (the left), spinning his body in a quarter turn. The first step of approximately 6 to 12 inches is made with the right foot. This places the pivot foot in a coiled position and gives the guard the power to move quickly. The guard should stay low and pump his arm (demonstrated here by Fred Sturt).*

The guards are the keys to the success of the play. They must move out quickly, get out of the way of the runner, and clear the path.

The Redskins employ three basic methods in pulling out of the line: (1) jump pivot; (2) lead step; and (3) cross step. We like the lead step technique (also called the pivot and step) because it enables the pulling lineman to step directly into the hole much faster than does the cross step.

### Jump Pivot

This maneuver is quicker than the crossover in pulling out of the line. In going to his right, the right guard should pivot sharply on the toe of his outside left foot and spin his body in a quarter turn. First, he steps approximately 6 to 12 inches with his lead right foot. This places his pivot foot in a coiled position, providing the power to move quickly. The pulling guard must stay low and pump his arm vigorously.

### Lead Step

In pulling right, the lineman pivots sharply on the toe of his inside, or left, foot, spinning his body in a quarter turn. When he pivots, his outside or right arm thrusts back sharply, turning his shoulders and hips in the desired direction.

The first step of 6 to 12 inches with the right or lead foot will place the pivot foot (or left leg) in a coiled position, giving him the power to move quickly. A longer first step would disturb body balance and prevent a proper rear leg push-off.

In pulling out, it is most essential for the lineman to pivot first on the back foot. He doesn't pick it up at all. He pivots in a 45-degree angle on the ball of his rear foot, and

he should keep the right knee locked in the stance position. The outside guard will pivot on a 45-degree angle any time he pulls for any kind of a sweep. The reason for the 45-degree angle is to make clearance with the offensive back going forward to block a lineman on the line of scrimmage. If the back hasn't cleared yet, the guard may deviate to a higher angle. The locked knee will keep him down, to the point that he can make the first step relatively short, about $1\frac{1}{2}$ feet beyond the pivot foot. He doesn't want a long step of 3 or 4 feet!

### Cross Step

From the basic stance, the lineman pushes off the fingertips of the down hand and pivots on the left or near foot in the direction he is going. Then he crosses over with his right foot. The weight of the player's body should be placed on his pivoting left foot and returned to both feet when the crossover step hits the ground. Some linemen throw their arm vigorously, to help them pivot more quickly.

## BLOCKING

The job of the offensive lineman is to defeat the man in front of him. The more battles he wins in the line, the more battles his team will win in games.

At first, blocking fundamentals are taught against a single dummy. The lineman concentrates on the shoulder block, striving to make quick, hard contact and drive through the dummy. Later, he should work on the traps, cutoff, reverse, and other blocks. We cannot emphasize too much the necessity of daily repetition, along with

**A**                **B**

*FIGURE 5-9. Crossover step. The lineman pivots on the left (or near) foot in the direction he is going. Then he crosses over with his right foot. He places his weight on his pivoting foot, but when the crossover step hits the ground, the weight returns to both feet. When performed correctly, it is a one-motion pivot and drive off the rear foot (Ray Schoenke).*

proper coaching, to teach, polish, and perfect these blocks.

Next comes the one-on-one blocking against a "live" defender. This is necessary to acquire toughness and improve the technique. Later, the linemen progress to team blocking, first on the dummies and later in a scrimmage drill.

### Shoulder Block

The basic block in football is a straight shoulder block. This is the one-on-one. The running attack will succeed or fail depending on how well the linemen execute this block. When I coached the Rams, our offensive line

coach, Ray Prochaska, didn't talk in terms of a right shoulder or a left shoulder block when teaching blocking to the linemen. He had the linemen thinking more of hitting their man with their forehead, then sliding off. The drive block is a favorite among NFL linemen, to drive a defender back. Exploding at the defender, the lineman jab-steps with his left foot, "thuds" his helmet into the stomach, and drives him straight back.

"I tell my men to hit that target in the middle," said Prochaska, "hit the middle with your helmet. This prevents a deviation in his charge. The defender doesn't know what the blocker will do, and the blocker must not give away his intentions as well. As he charges, he will decide what shoulder

FIGURE 5-10.  *Pulling out to block the defensive end, guard Ray Schoenke uses a one-on-one block in leading the way for the fullback. Although he knows which way he hopes to take the man, the offensive guard will run straight at him. At the last moment, he goes into the block he wants, a right shoulder or left shoulder block.*

should be used in the final block. We want him to get as close and tight to his man as he can, and then at the last possible moment, he will slip to the shoulder." Actually, on the up-the-middle plays, the blocking is optional for the offensive linemen. They must drive their opponents whichever way the rushmen first go.

*Approach.* By taking short, choppy steps in the approach, the lineman will have his feet up under him, giving him more blocking power. When he gets close to his opponent, he should muster up all of his strength and explode into his opponent. If the defender is playing on his nose, he should take a short step with his back foot first. This first short backward step will enable him to follow quickly with a step forward.

*Contact.*  The blocker should hit right in the middle of the man with his head, and as he makes the block, he slides his head by him and hits sharply with his shoulder and upper arm. The arm is bent at the elbow, and the fist is on the chest, providing a wide blocking surface.

"The pop of the shoulder, the explosion of the blow is what makes a good block," said Prochaska, "explosiveness in a short distance. You have to have enough drive to stymie the defensive man, and then, it becomes balance and control."

*Follow-through.* After making contact and stopping his charge, the offensive lineman must follow through with short driving steps. After he "pops" the defensive man, he has to keep up after him. The defensive man certainly is not going to stand there. At this point, the lineman has to go for the defensive player with his left shoulder. Good shoulder and head contact is maintained by a well-extended forearm and neck pressure.

The movement of the defender will determine the follow-through foot action.

*Hints on the shoulder block:*

1. *Inside* foot, *outside* shoulder is a good rule for this type of block.
2. Drilling should concentrate on the initial charge.
3. Players should work the bag laterally with the neck and head.
4. A player who is working only on the charge should take the bag straight back, using first one shoulder and then the other.
5. The coach should stress keeping the head up

FIGURE 5-11. *Butt block. Rather than throw his body at a defender, a pulling guard may employ a butt block, a billy goat technique in which he draws a bead on his man's chest, butts him, and keeps going. Here, Ray Schoenke (62) takes on the defensive end of the Dallas Cowboys, Pat Toomay (67).*

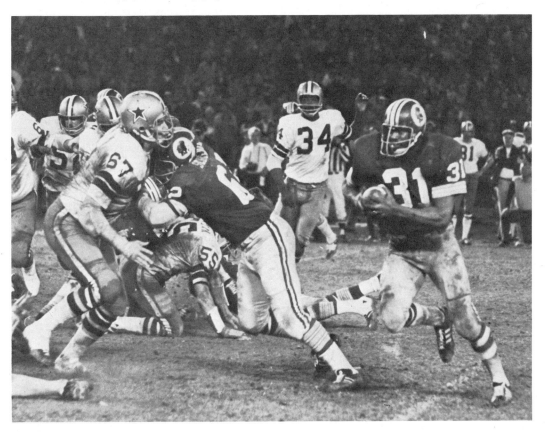

in order to see the target and have the player keep the back straight.

6. The player should aim the head right at the middle of the bag and just as contact is made, slide the head to the side. The shoulders must do the work.
7. The player should work for a good lift with the upper arm, keeping the elbow even with the shoulder to provide more blocking surface.
8. Those players who come up with "strawberries" on their cheeks are usually blocking correctly.

### Reverse Shoulder Block

This block is used on the line of scrimmage against defensive linemen who are reacting to the head of the offensive man on the straight shoulder block. The blocker tries to mislead his opponent by putting the head on the opposite side from where the play is going. It must be said, however, that this is a very difficult block to execute. In teaching this block, the coach should insist on the players' getting their heads across quickly.

The blocker will move out from his stance with a driving step with the foot opposite the shoulder with which he is blocking. The approach is made just as though a shoulder block were about to be thrown, but when the blocker gets close enough to hit the man, he reverses the head and shoulders, contacting the defender in the midsection with his shoulder, neck, and side of the head. The offensive man actually helps the opposing lineman take himself out of the play.

### Trap Block

A trap block is actually a one-on-one straight shoulder block applied from a different position. Everyone along the line must help out on this play, to open up the gates so the trap block can be made. This is because the trapper has to have an opportunity to trap from inside out.

The trap block is used against the opposing lineman who is charging hard deep into the backfield. He is usually two or three spaces from the blocking guard. In order to reach him, the guard has to pull out of the line, behind his own line. In order to pull quickly, he should step with his near foot in a short jab fashion and then step in the direction he wants to go with the far foot.

During the trap block drill, the coach should concentrate on:

1. Proper pulling method.
2. Proper trap block with the guard's head behind the trapped tackle (if the guard is pulling to his right, he should hit the trapped man with his right shoulder).
3. Watching for pointing or pulling out too soon.

### Position Step Block

A position step block is often used by our offensive linemen. Our ends also use this block frequently before going into their pass pattern. The type of block used will depend on what is necessary to prevent a defender from getting into the play. As a result, the blocker wants to momentarily delay the forward movement of the defensive man. In other words, a blocker shouldn't waste himself with a man unless he has to, particularly when the play goes to the other side of the line. After the initial impact is made with the shoulder, he immediately releases his block. Why knock a man down if turning him aside will accomplish the task?

The proper position the lineman has on the defensive man is much more important than the hard contact. If the position step block is applied correctly, the offensive man is actually helping the opposing lineman to take himself out of the play.

## Cross-body Block

Another block the lineman needs is the cross-body block, sometimes called the cut-off block. The body block is used on the line of scrimmage, on linebackers, and downfield on the defensive secondary.

Players should begin the block from what we call "handshake distance." The biggest problem most players have with it is that they want to start throwing the block a "mile away" from their target. After making contact, the blocker will pivot and whip his body across the defender's belt line. Usually, the cross-body is used when a normal pass block fails.

At first, it looks just like a shoulder block, but from there, the blocker slips his shoulder right by and exposes the side of his body. Most players will leave their feet, but when they hit the ground, we like them to roll through the defender. They should work their body around the defender's legs so he cannot get to the ball carrier. They should try to make him come out the back door.

The best way to teach the cross-body block is as follows:

1. Pair off two men. One man holds the bag and one is lined up in front of the bag in a three-point stance.
2. The men rotate after a right-side and left-side block.
3. The blocker starts the raise as if he were going to make a shoulder block.
4. If blocking to the right side, the blocker would:
   a. Shoot the right hand across the bag, about chin level,
   b. Contact the bag with the right hip, and
   c. Drive against the bag, using a crablike motion.
5. Insist the men work on speed, power, and follow-through.
6. This block may be executed from a stationary or running position.

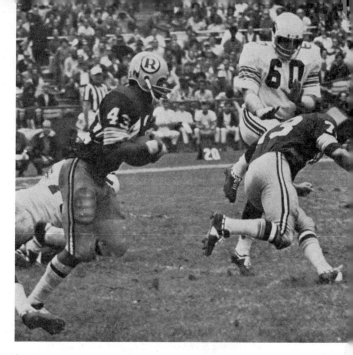

FIGURE 5-12. Open-field blocking. The lineman must have a definite target: the opponent's belt buckle. Many blockers fail to bull their neck. They just keep their head up, neck bulled, and their eyes on the target. Above, guard Paul Laaveg (73) goes after a pursuing linebacker.

7. Errors to watch for in the cross-body block:
   a. Leaving the feet too soon.
   b. Keeping arms too close to body.
   c. Making contact too low.
   d. Hesitating before making contact.

## Reverse Cross-body Block

The blocker begins his motion as if he were going to make a cross-body block. If the blocker is to the right of the bag, he will:

1. Make contact with the right hip.
2. Whip the legs around to the rear of the bag.
3. Keep his body between the bag and the ball carrier, using a crablike motion.
4. Have reversed the position of the feet and head.

In drilling for the reverse cross-body block, the linemen should pair off, with one man holding the bag and one lined up on either side of the bag. The dummy drill will help build confidence before players face live competition.

### Crab Block

The crab block, also known as the single-leg block, is effective against strong opponents who know how to use their hands, particularly the big defensive ends and linebackers in our league. The blocker tries to drive his knee up between the legs of the defensive man. He immediately "crabs" around his opponent, digging with his outside leg but keeping his inside foot stationary. He goes down on all fours and keeps after his man on all fours.

### Double-team Block

The double-team block matches two offensive linemen against the defensive player. We have found it is an effective play to give the attack some needed power. Perhaps the most common situation involves a double-team by the tackle and end on the opposing tackle. In this case, the tackle is the Post man and the end is the Lead man. It's a good weapon to use against a defensive man who is bigger than his own lineman.

The Lead takes a short step with his inside foot and aims for the opponent's hip, just hard enough to break his charge. The Post man swings his shoulders and buttocks around in close contact with those of the Lead, making sure there is no space for the defender to squeeze through. The Post man uses a straight shoulder block, making sure he maintains contact with the opponent. When the team has made contact, they try to keep close together and not let the defender split between them.

In drilling for the two-on-one situation, the players line up facing the coach and are then numbered off by threes. No. 1 faces Nos. 2 and 3 and stays low; on the command to charge he braces against 2 and 3 to provide resistance. Then they practice double-teaming with short driving steps.

The man on defense does not try to break through but he does try to hold the two offensive men so that they will have to put real drive into their charge. It is a good idea to rotate the men after every three charges.

## PASS PROTECTION

The Washington Redskins put a great deal of stress on pass protection. Any football team has to. In the modern game of football, it's pass offense versus pass defense. That's the name of the game in pro football. A team that cannot stop the pass is going to be in trouble, and a team that cannot throw the ball will have difficulty, too.

Pass protection comes from constant drilling. In our league, if a team cannot protect the passer, it is going to be in trouble because all the defensive linemen are good pass rushers. In college and high school ball, a team very seldom has four pass rushers. It may have one man who can rush the passer, but he can be stopped. But in our league, everyone is skilled at this job, so protection is vital. No quarterback can make a living if he doesn't have protection.

We want our linemen to move everything they can in protecting the passer. We want them to keep loose and moving, not to be sitting ducks. The lineman must not let the defensive man latch on to him and grab him. The more movement, the better we like it, just so he keeps his balance.

After making contact with the rusher,

the lineman retreats, sets, and then uncoils again at his opponent. He does this time after time until the quarterback has gotten rid of the ball. "Keep your arms and legs pumping," explained Prochaska, "or else the rusher will grab you and slip by. You have to be able to hit on the run, just keep pecking away at the defensive man to keep him off balance."

## SCREEN BLOCK

The screen pass is an effective move by the offense when the defense is applying undue pressure on the passer. The linemen up front who must do a good job of being "con" men are the key to the success of the offense. After first sustaining the block, they allow their man to think he is about to smear the quarterback, only to learn he's been fooled. However, they shouldn't make it look too easy for the defenders because they will sense something on the "phony" side.

The screen pass can be a deadly offensive weapon if the linemen properly execute their assignments. First, they must brush-block the defensive front four. Then they have to pull out and form a screen along the sideline for the runner.

The screen block is essentially a straight shoulder block. The blocker drives his forearms up toward the head of the opponent, forcing the defensive man to stand up straight. After making contact, he maneuvers his body between the defender and the hole where the ball carrier is to run.

Screen plays require much practice to perfect, but when used properly, they can certainly firm up a sputtering offense.

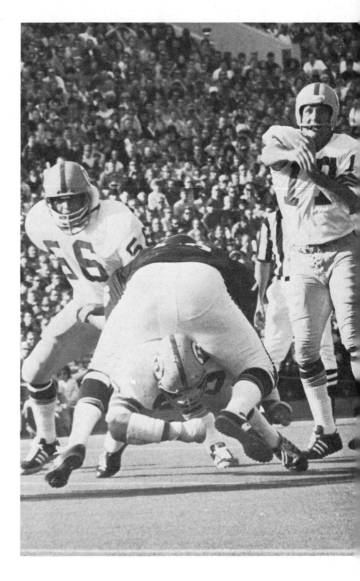

FIGURE 5-13. *Protecting the passer. A fraction of a second is vital to the quarterback. The blocker wants to delay the rushman long enough—usually 3 to 4 seconds—for the passer to get the ball away. Here, the offensive guard goes underneath the defensive lineman. An offensive lineman is in a "4-second business." The only time that makes any difference to him is the first 4 seconds after the center snaps the ball. If he can hold his man out that long, the quarterback can get the ball away. In pass protection, quickness means more than weight or strength.*

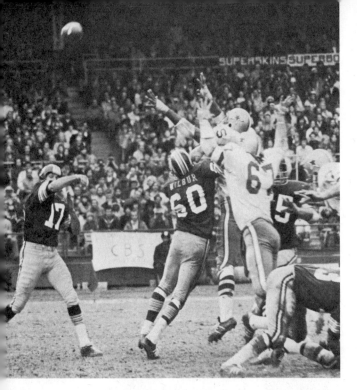

*FIGURE 5-14. Working from the cup, quarterback Bill Kilmer receives strong protection from such blockers as John Wilbur (60), Paul Laaveg (73), and Terry Hermeling (75). This type of protection makes pass defenses suffer.*

## DOWNFIELD BLOCKING

Breakaway plays for touchdowns are the result of good downfield blocking. Therefore, all of the linemen should be adept at throwing an effective block downfield. The downfield block is actually 90 percent desire.

As he approaches the man he wants to block, the lineman gathers himself and then throws his body into the defender, making sure he is close enough to him before he takes off. He will have more blocking surface if he can get his body into the air lengthwise. So, at the moment of contact, he should extend his arms, body, and legs to their fullest.

Downfield blocking is one of the most difficult phases of football to teach. It demands a terrific selling job from the coach. Dummy drills can provide the needed practice for the linemen in downfield blocking. The linemen have assigned dummies to contact and follow a predesigned course.

In drilling pulling linemen, defensive players, either holding dummies or being "live" as the case may be, are lined up in the three defensive positions representing: (1) defensive end, (2) defensive halfback, and (3) defensive linebacker.

## BLOCKING FOR KICKS

Knowing they can give no ground, the offense lines up with their feet widely spaced, set to dig in for the kick try. They should half straighten on the snap, with knees flexed, their heads and fists clenched. All down the line, they have their forearms poised to stop the defender's charge.

## BLOCKING BY THE RECEIVERS

Most of the blocking by our outside receivers involves the downfield body block. An outside receiver either blocks the inside safety or the cornerback on his side. "Quite a few outside receivers in pro ball have a tendency of going down and just pushing, not really doing very much," said Coach Schnellenberger, who coached for me with the Rams. "The best way to get them out of this habit is to get them accustomed to the ground, get them used to rolling on the ground, so that the ground becomes part of the game, and we ask them to do this."

With our tight ends, Jerry Smith has a variety of blocks he has to execute. The "tailor" block is a block we use on our sweep. He splits out 3 or 4 yards, and he has to stand up in the face of the linebacker, hold him on the line of scrimmage for about two counts, and then let him go in the direction he wants to go and shield him on out.

The "M" block is one of the more unique blocks we have. We call it a "Man" block. We ask Smith, our tight end, to come off where we call a "Drive" block, to knock the linebacker straight back, keep his feet, and try to knock him back, and then turn him in any direction that he wants to go because our ball carrier has the option of running the hole that seems more open.

We have a "hook" block for our quick tosses to the strong side. On this, Jerry simply hooks or jumps out and tries to get the strong linebacker or blocks the end. When we throw to the weak side, he has to pass protect as the guards and tackles do.

## DRAW PLAY

The draw is a running play that is made to look like a pass play. The linemen should let their men come in as though they were pass blocking; then they push the rushmen aside, and the ball carrier moves through the hole. The guard must ride his man whichever way he wants to go.

CHART 5-1.  Time study chart on blocking.

|  | Number of minutes for each drill | | | |
|---|---|---|---|---|
|  | 1st Week | 2nd Week | 3rd Week | Total |
| Date |  |  |  |  |
| Shoulder block |  |  |  |  |
| Reverse shoulder block |  |  |  |  |
| Trap block |  |  |  |  |
| Position step block |  |  |  |  |
| Cross-body block |  |  |  |  |
| Reverse cross-body block |  |  |  |  |
| Crab block |  |  |  |  |
| Two-on-one drill |  |  |  |  |
| Pass block |  |  |  |  |
| Screen block |  |  |  |  |
| Downfield block |  |  |  |  |
| Field goal block |  |  |  |  |
| Punt block |  |  |  |  |
| Skeleton backs |  |  |  |  |
| Red dog blocking with backs |  |  |  |  |

Since linemen are bigger and heavier than backs, they usually have poorer agility and movement. Therefore, the coach must use agility drills for the team as well as individual drills to improve each man's capabilities.

We use the board drill a great deal, driving the dummy with short, powerful steps, quicker movement, working on balance. The drills help the player execute the job he has to perform in the game, which is against one man. If he does that, we are going to win!

An offensive lineman has to have good position and body control. Some of the little drills we have might look foolish, getting caught off-balance and whipping up off the ground and jumping around in a grass drill. But all of these drills help the player condition his body so that no matter what situation he is in, the player is in control.

Blocking against a dummy sled is needed every day in training camp and three times weekly during the season.

1. *Stance*  The offensive guards, tackles, and tight ends are placed in a circle or in a line, from which they execute the various steps in a good stance. Facing the coach, they are taught the essentials of proper stance "by the numbers."

2. *Starts*  Since the offensive line must move as a unit, the coach should use drills that involve the entire unit. The lineman must develop the ability to come out of the blocks and keep his body low on the first few steps.

3. *Individual starting drill*  A training aid such as a shoot, a simple rope stretched across poles, can be effective in making offensive linemen fire out at the proper height. Assuming the proper stance, the linemen must time their explosion off the line to the starting signal and drive forward 10 yards. They should be checked on arm action and running form. By using dummies just outside the cage, the linemen can work on all types of running blocks.

4. *Blocking drills*  Drills for offensive linemen should emphasize the basic blocks (fire-out, shoulder, reach reverse, and open-field) plus the pass blocks and tackling drills.

5. *Drills for pulling*  The guards and tackles should form a large circle and assume their normal stance. From the stance position, they are drilled on their basic pivots, starting by

simultaneous pivoting on the left toe and placing the right foot out at a 45-degree angle. The short trap drill involves a gap cross block (wider spacing between the linemen), while on the long pull, the lineman has to get his on-foot deeper than parallel on the first step.

In cross blocking and pulling, the guards and tackles should be drilled for the short curve. A good place for this drill is the goalpost. On cadence, the linemen should pull to the right or left and run a very tight curve as they clear the upright.

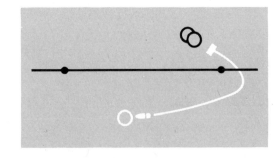

*DIAGRAM 5-1.  Short curve.*

6. *Punt, extra point, and field goal protection drills*  Since guards and tackles use a different punt protection technique, they must be drilled separately from the centers. The

most popular technique is the spread, or nine-man front formation.

While extra point and field goal protection drills are rarely done individually, the coach occasionally will work with one player during the specialty period or after practice. The key coaching point in this type of blocking is for the blocker to anchor his outside foot and never move it.

An effective drill involves placing the blocker between two standing dummies in a hitting position. With one or two rushmen coming through his position, the blocker should make a solid shoulder or shoulders block on them. His anchor foot should be kept in place, though.

7. *Center and guard drills* In the two-on-one setup, the offensive center and one of the guards are opposed by a defensive lineman. The blockers must open the hole by turning the defender. Standing behind the defender, the coach uses hand signals to indicate a two-on-one block or, in the case of the guard fold, a single block by the center while the guard pulls. Pass blocking can be mixed into this drill.

In the two-on-two drill involving an additional defender, the offensive men have an opportunity to practice the various blocks, as shown in Diagram 5-4.

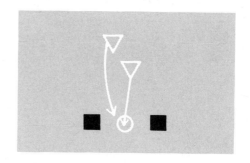

**DIAGRAM 5-2.** *Field goal protection.*

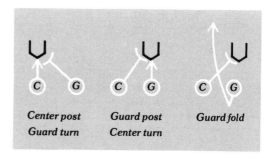

Center post    Guard post    Guard fold
Guard turn     Center turn

**DIAGRAM 5-3.** *Two-on-one blocking.*

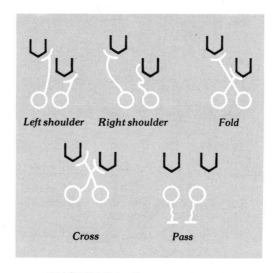

Left shoulder    Right shoulder    Fold

Cross    Pass

**DIAGRAM 5-4.** *Two-on-two blocking.*

8. *Guard and tackle drill* This drill enables linemen at these positions to work on their cross and fold blocking. On the cross block in a short trap situation, the outside blocker fires out first and blocks down, while the inside blocker pulls and blocks out. The puller merely takes a jab step.

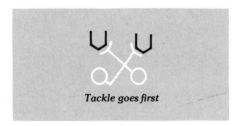

DIAGRAM 5-5. Cross block.

On the fold block, the inside blocker fires across the line first and executes a turn-out block. The outside blocker opens with his inside foot, often blocking on a linebacker.

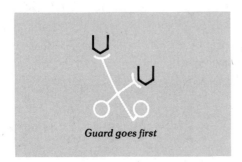

DIAGRAM 5-6. Fold block.

9. *Tackle and end drill* Since the tight end and tackle double-team more than anyone else, they must be given heavy work on two-on-one and two-on-two blocking. The tight end is always the turn man when he works with his tackle. Tight ends should be instructed to step off with their inside foot first and drive straight ahead on their first step. They should learn to turn on their second step.

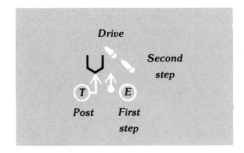

DIAGRAM 5-7. Double-team blocking by the tight end and tackle.

10. *Center and two guards* In working the three-on-three drill, every blocker is signaled to by the coach. The linemen execute the various blocking maneuvers in their offense.

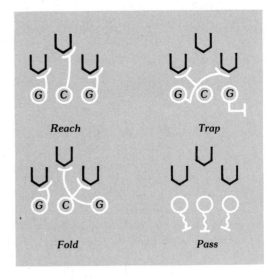

DIAGRAM 5-8. Three-on-three blocking.

# 6

# Offensive Backfield

*The makeup of a great back is heart and determination. He always keeps his feet moving.*

**George Allen**

Speed, determination, and toughness are among the prime qualities of an outstanding offensive back. In addition to having a strong body, the top runners in football have great balance, a sense of timing, and natural instinct. They usually run with their feet close to the ground.

A running back's greatest asset, perhaps, is getting to the line before the holes close and before the linebackers can converge. To do this, an offensive back must develop an explosive start and be able to accelerate quickly. The Redskins' Larry Brown is not the fastest runner in the league, yet he gets his speed in two steps. He probably gets to the line and through the hole more quickly than any other back in football.

The great backs of professional football have the ability to accelerate beyond their normal running speed. Apparently running at top speed, they have an additional burst of speed in reserve.

## QUALIFICATIONS

A back has to have enough speed to be a pass receiver. He is a potential receiver on most pass plays. In college or high school ball, perhaps, most teams can get by with a back who cannot receive a ball because they don't throw the ball that much. But even then, it is going to hurt them.

Whatever the back's assignment may be—carrying the ball, running a good pass pattern, blocking for his teammate—speed plays an important role. If a player cannot run with speed, he will be ineffective as an offensive back.

*Toughness is essential.* To become an outstanding back, a ball carrier has to have

A                                          B

FIGURE 6-2.   In the NFL, a running back must be versatile. In addition to carrying the football, he must block and be able to catch the ball. The Redskins' Larry Brown is a back who can do it all. He is a slashing, aggressive runner who has the mental toughness required of an outstanding offensive back. An excellent deep threat as a pass receiver when coming out of the backfield, Brown is a very effective blocker who isn't afraid to "stick" those linebackers.

courage and toughness because he will have to take a beating.

An important characteristic of an offensive back is maneuverability. He has to make people miss occasionally because if he doesn't, he is not going to stay healthy very long. Running with the ball involves good field vision, the ability to judge distances accurately, the balance to remain on his feet. The back must make quick decisions as to where he will run, while using his interference along the way. A ball carrier must develop the ability to change direction, change his pace, sidestep, pivot, straight-arm, and slip opposing tacklers. As the old saying goes: Lunge, plunge, twist, turn, but keep going!

*Blocking ability* is another quality of an all-round back. An offensive back cannot always carry the ball; he has to be able to block. A determined and sustained effort should be made by every back on every play to block his man, to successfully execute his blocking assignment. The key to all blocks is to get the proper position on the opponent and maintain contact. If every man in the backfield puts forth the same effort that the man with the ball does, few plays will prove unsuccessful.

*The ability to start quickly* is as important for a running back as it is for a charging offensive lineman. There are some backs who are never going to be great because they cannot start quickly. The only time they get going is after they are 10 yards down the field, and they can be stopped before they get going.

To play halfback, an individual must have outstanding speed, good balance, and the ability to move in all directions.

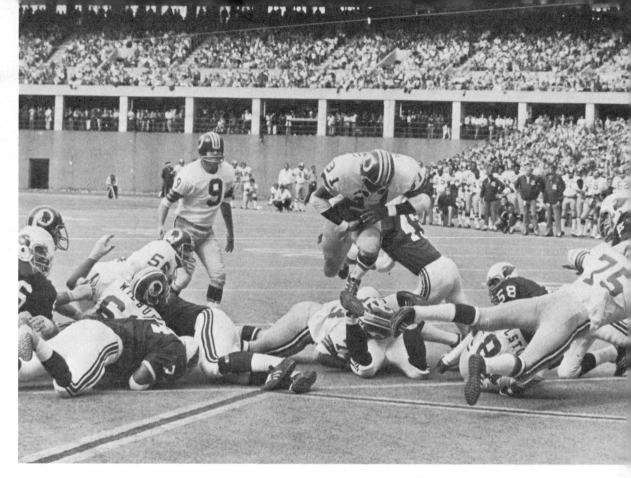

FIGURE 6-3. Running with power. The fullback must hit the line quickly and have the power to bull his way for important yardage. Above, Charley Harraway (31) blasts his way into the end zone for a go-ahead touchdown against the St. Louis Cardinals.

The good fullback must consistently get those 2 yards on third down, even when the defense knows he will be coming. Since he is the power runner in the backfield, he must be big enough to make the tough yardage. He should be a good blocker. He will be called on to explode through the line between the tackles, in addition to blocking for the quarterback and halfbacks. Furthermore, he must have good enough hands to go out on pass routes.

The flanker back does not confine his efforts to merely catching passes. He must also be an able blocker.

The halfback normally lines up approxi-mately 3½ yards deep. He straddles the in-side leg of his offensive tackle. The fullback's position is the same depth but is located directly behind the center and the quar-terback.

## MENTAL AGGRESSIVENESS

To become an outstanding runner, a player must have the desire to play the game, a winning attitude, and confidence. An offen-sive back has to have plenty of desire. Foot-ball is a rough, tough, bruising game and if

FIGURE 6-4. Miami's Larry Csonka will "pick a hole" when he gets the opportunity, but the big 237-pound fullback can pick up tough yardage by running over people. Fast and durable, Csonka is a physical type of runner who has the power and strength to make the big play.

a boy doesn't like body contact and being knocked down, he shouldn't get into it.

An outstanding back has more than speed and size. He has *desire* and *dedication*. Larry Brown is an excellent example. He must want that yard or two so badly that he will smash, twist, or squirm to get it.

Hard running by those in the backfield is often the difference between victory and defeat. A fast-driving back makes the blocking in the line more effective because a block doesn't have to be held very long for a fast runner.

Many games have been lost because a back failed to give his best effort and a first down was missed by inches. A back might ask himself: "Could I have given a little more effort and made those 3 or 4 inches?"

## STANCE

The first fundamental of backfield play is the stance. Regardless of his speed, the back cannot make a good getaway without a proper stance. An offensive back must have one stance for all plays, whether he is going left, right, or straight ahead. Basically, he must assume the same stance, a well-balanced three-point stance, which all ball clubs now use.

"The feet should be approximately shoulder width apart, or slightly wider," said Dick Bass, who played for me with the Rams. "If you are right-handed, you might drop your right foot back just a shade, maybe halfway past the left foot. Your shoulders should be straight, and the neck and head should be up, so that you can see where you are going. Your back is level."

Generally, we like our backs to place a quarter of their weight on their hands. We don't want too much weight forward because our backs have to make more lateral moves than straight-ahead movements. Sometimes this makes it a little awkward if the back is running a dive straight ahead, but in order to move laterally, we have to have it like this. Much of the weight is distributed evenly on the balls of the feet. The inside hand rests comfortably on the ground, while the outside hand should rest on the outside leg.

FIGURE 6-5. Stance. An offensive back (Larry Brown shown above) should assume a comfortable, well-balanced stance and be ready to move in any direction. The head is up, the back straight, and the weight evenly distributed on both feet. He looks straight ahead. This type of stance does not "tip" his intentions.

## TAKEOFF

An explosive takeoff from the three-point stance is essential. A running back must start fast and hard. In perfecting the takeoff, he should work with his quarterback. The back can time his takeoff to the quarterback's call so he explodes on the right count. Being alert is all important! He should find out exactly which way the quarterback calls "hut one, hut two!"

Participating on the track team in the spring has been very beneficial to many outstanding backs in helping them improve their start. In starting, a running back should try to use his arms as much as he can because this helps propel him forward. He should start with short steps and run with his knees high. His feet are wide, with his weight forward. The head and eyes are up looking for the hole to open.

If a team employs a rhythmical count, the back has to anticipate. On the nonrhythmical count, he has to concentrate even more on the sound of the quarterback, and just move as fast as he can.

In taking off, an offensive back can use one of two types of starts: the direct step or a crossover step. On the direct step, he starts with the foot nearest the direction he intends to run. For instance, if he intends to run forward, he will take a short step with his starting foot, driving off full speed on his second step. He should take short, choppy steps until he reaches top speed.

On the crossover step, he will cross one leg over the other in the direction he intends to run; with the same motion, he will pivot on the ball of the other foot. In starting to his right, he will cross the left leg over the right leg, pivoting on the right foot and placing the left foot in the direction he wants to run.

Above all, in starting, an offensive back must never lean or point. To prevent this from happening, he should keep his weight evenly balanced on the balls of the feet.

In short, backfield men must start quickly and be able to run with their bodies under control.

## RECEIVING THE HAND-OFF

In receiving the ball, an offensive back should not be watching the quarterback or the ball. He has his head up. His eyes are looking in the direction he is going and toward the hole he hopes to go through.

FIGURE 6-6. *Following his interference, a running back has to see the entire play. He has to know where the defenders are and where his blockers are. Above, the Redskins' Charley Taylor (42) can go inside or outside, depending on which way his blocker, Terry Hermeling, takes his man.*

The inside arm should be up, providing a large pocket. The outside arm is down, with the elbow close to the body. The inside arm should be parallel with the ground, about chin level. The back should look for the hole, not at the quarterback; the quarterback is responsible for getting the ball to the back.

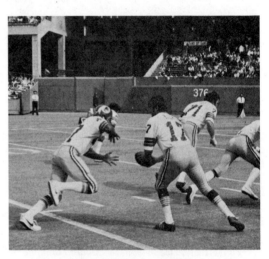

FIGURE 6-8. *Receiving the hand-off. A running back should provide a large pocket, and it is the job of the quarterback to give him the ball. The inside elbow of the back is up as the quarterback (Bill Kilmer) places the ball directly over the left buckle of the ball carrier. After receiving the hand-off, the ball carrier should immediately put it in the pocket. This is important because a ball carrier is often hit upon receiving the hand-off. He should tuck the corner of the ball under his arm.*

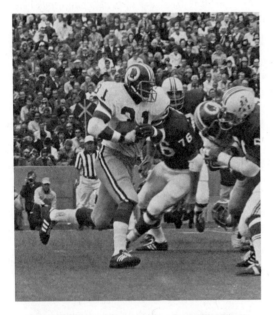

FIGURE 6-7. *Carrying the ball. The ball carrier should tuck the corner of the ball up under his arm and cover the other point with his hand, as Charley Harraway does here. If he has the point covered, it is very difficult to dislodge the ball.*

Once he receives the hand-off, the ball carrier should put it immediately in the pocket, tucking the corner of the ball under his arm and covering the other point with his hand. In this position the ball is difficult to dislodge. The ball should be tucked in immediately and should not be shifted until the back is through the line of scrimmage. Tommy Mason suggested that backs run with the ball away from the pressure (e.g., when running to the right, the ball should be in the right arm with the hand over the point).

In executing a drive (a quick hand-off from a halfback position), the back moves straight ahead three steps, and the quarterback must find him. On the third step, the back's arm automatically comes up and enables the quarterback to set it inside the pocket.

In taking off, the ball carrier should not waste a step. He pushes off his outside leg and steps forward with the inside leg. By doing this, he will get the ball in an open stance, with the outside foot ahead of the inside foot. This provides a good pocket for the quarterback and eliminates the possibility of a runner knocking the ball out of the quarterback's hands.

## FAKING

Since football is a team game, faking is as important to the offense as carrying the ball. The successful execution of every play is dependent on the manner in which those without the ball carry out their fakes. They must convince the defense that they have the ball. A fake should never be considered an optional chore; it is a definite assignment for all members in the backfield.

The player should not exaggerate in faking, but move naturally into the hole as he would if he were the ball carrier. The hands should be held as if taking a hand-off, and the back should look directly toward the hole.

Actually, the best fake a back can give is merely to run hard. He must use the same action for faking as for receiving and carrying the ball. It has been said that if a back isn't tackled on a fake, he isn't doing a good enough job of faking. When he goes through

FIGURE 6-9. *Larry Brown protects the ball with both hands as he bulls his way into the Dallas defense for 4 yards. Anytime a ball carrier is in a crowd, he should hold the ball with both hands. When running, his fingers should cover the nose of the ball. This prevents fumbling. He should keep the ball close to his body.*

with his fake, caution should be taken not to bump the quarterback.

In running in the open field, an offensive back must learn to fake with his head and body. In fact, the head-and-shoulder fake is used to set up the crossover step. This fake is executed by dropping the shoulder and head to one side, drawing the defender out of position. This fake also sets up the side step, which is executed by driving off the lead foot and trying to get as much lateral movement with the trail leg as possible.

The same fake should not be used each time. A player should vary his fakes to keep his opponent guessing. For example, he may run straight at the tackler, fake to the right with his head and body motion, then cut sharply to the left. Or, he may come to a sudden stop before he changes directions.

Faking can be vital in making an offense successful. A good fake will often freeze the linebackers and deep backs, increasing the ball carrier's chances of breaking away.

## BLOCKING

In present-day football, with the wide assortment of defenses, blocking is a key responsibility of every member of the backfield. The blocking chores are not merely left to the linemen up front. What with all the stunting and stack defenses, each back must be ready to contribute to the overall blocking pattern.

Without effective blocking, no offense can succeed. The passer will be forced to throw quickly or not at all. And those who carry the ball will find their holes have been sealed up. So, it becomes a matter of making up one's mind to get the job done. When the play calls for a block, a back has to block!

An offensive back should become proficient in executing the following types of blocks:

### Bob Block

This is the type of block most frequently performed by a back. The fullback uses a "bob" block in handling the end with an inside-out approach. He will use a straight shoulder block and hit him hard at the numbers of his jersey. The halfback, who must be able to block in the secondary, uses a drive shoulder to cross-body style of blocking. The quarter-

back, in leading the sweep, must be able to clean a hole and crack-back on the pursuit with an effective drive-shoulder block.

### Fill Block

With the return to power football and the pulling guards, the "fill" block has become a major block for offensive backs. The term "fill" is what the word implies. The back must fill the gap left by a pulling lineman.

The fullback normally does most of the fill-blocking and does it after faking. Actually, a good faker usually doesn't have to block because he will be tackled.

### Pass Block

In protecting the passer, the back must be able to ward off rushers to his outside and still be aware of the "red-dogger." After firing into the rusher, he recovers back, keeping a wide base and maintaining good hitting position. In handling the hard-charging linemen, he often will fake to the numbers, then get to the defender's legs as quickly as possible.

One of the flanker's most important blocks is a crack-back on the outside linebacker on sweeps. Because of the size of the linebacker, he has to hit 'em low. In blocking the safety, the flanker has to screen him until the back gets up to him. He shuffles along in front of the safety until the ball carrier can cut off him. The flanker leaves his feet and tries to cut the safety down, or he tries to drive through him.

Blocking a defensive end or an end sweep can be a difficult block for an offensive back. Perhaps the key is to move quickly to a point one yard in front of the defender and explode through him. Otherwise, the blocking back will fall short, and the

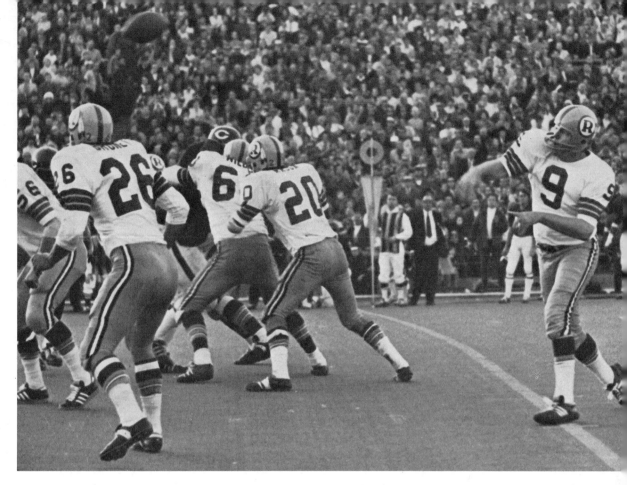

FIGURE 6-10. *Protecting the passer is a prime responsibility of an offensive back. Tommy Mason (20) and Bob Brunet (26), keeping a wide base, combine with the tackles to form a protective pocket around Sonny Jurgensen.*

stronger defensive man will knock him down.

## PASS PATTERNS

An offensive back should spend a great deal of time on running pass patterns. They may look and sound simple, but for pinpoint accuracy by the passer, a pass pattern takes considerable practice.

Among the pass routes used by the Redskins' backs are the Flag or Corner, Flare, Sky, Shoot, Angle, and Circle in.

There are many more. On the Flare, the back drives to the outside with a slight belly. After driving 5 yards, he looks back for the ball and continues on his route. The Flag or Corner involves running a circle, and after coming to a point 8 to 10 yards downfield, he drives to the outside at a 45-degree angle, looking for the ball over the outside shoulder on the break.

On the Sky pattern, the back starts directly toward a point 3 yards outside the strong-side linebacker. Heading upfield, he looks for the ball over his inside shoulder upon crossing the line of scrimmage.

The Shoot route has the back driving at

FIGURE 6-11. *For good balance, a running back should run with his feet apart and use high knee action. Pumping his arms like pistons, he leans forward with the weight on his toes. Above, Larry Brown is under control and always ready to change direction.*

the outside shoulder of the linebacker to a point 2 or 3 yards downfield. Then he breaks parallel to the line at full speed. He looks for the ball over his outside shoulder on the break.

In running an Angle pattern, the offensive back drives to a point 4 yards outside of the linebacker and continues upfield to a point where he can cut back inside the linebacker covering him. When he cuts back, he drives hard to the inside almost parallel to the line of scrimmage, looking for the ball on the break.

The Circle involves a back running a circle, then continuing upfield about 10 yards, where he curls to the inside.

If flat passes have proven successful, a fast man can often free himself deep by first moving to the flat. Then he looks for the ball as the passer fakes a pass to the flat, followed by a burst of speed as he sprints deep to outrun the deep back who has moved up.

There are various ways for an offensive back to delay before going downfield for a pass. He may block momentarily, then break quickly to the outside for a pass.

## RUNNING TECHNIQUE

A great runner has exceptional vision of the field. His judgment of distances is brilliant. His decisiveness enables him to make the right moves and to use his interference to the best advantage. In addition to speed, a ball

FIGURE 6-12. *Speed, determination, and toughness can overcome lack of size, as Mack Herron (42) demonstrates in an explosive run against the Oakland Raiders. Though short in stature, Herron is a constant threat to make the big play for New England.*

carrier must develop the ability to change direction, change his pace, sidestep, pivot, and straight-arm.

On a scrimmage play, the ball carrier has to think about the pattern he's running. Then, when he comes up to the hole and it is closed, he has to think about what his alternative move will be. He usually starts with short quick steps and runs with his knees high. He wants to keep his feet wide, his head and eyes up. His weight is forward. When he is about to be tackled, he lowers his shoulders and drives forward for an extra yard or two.

The ball carrier should put the pressure on the defensive tackler. If he can make a defender declare first and make him lean forward, the running back can give him a left or right step and move around him.

We like our backs to run at a defender until he makes his move, rather than do it 10 yards from the player. Faking alone will not move a defensive man just standing there. He will merely wait until the back has finished faking. Therefore, the ball carrier must run at him until he declares himself.

Once a ball carrier gets past the line of scrimmage, he must use his individual ability to elude tacklers. Along with dipping a shoulder, he might try to change direction at the last minute. He might catch the defender with his head down and get away from him. Quickly reacting to the situation at hand is better than having a set plan.

The head and shoulder fake, side step, crossover step, cutback, limp leg, and zigzag are all open-field fundamentals. Great runners have the uncanny ability to shift gears suddenly and move quickly into high.

The fullback should be effective at swinging away from a filled hole and into daylight. He might find it effective to give the defender a shoulder or a leg, then bust it through him.

The line plunge is a power play in which the runner hits the line with the ball buried in his stomach. His head is down, his knees are high, and he unleashes all the drive he can. Spinning or twisting can gain the runner extra yardage because the tackler has no momentum to knock him off his feet.

A weaving run is made in the open field by swinging the hips and drawing them away from the tackler. The feet of the ball carrier should be well spread when approaching a tackler so that one leg may be thrown forward and outward from him.

### Using Blockers

Knowing how to use his blockers is an important quality of a top running back. A runner should do everything he can to set up the lineman's block. By cutting and veering, he can bring the defender's intercept line across the path of the blocker. The outstanding backs know when to stay with the blockers and when to leave them. Jim Brown was one of the greatest on this technique.

An offensive back must learn how to break off the blocks of his teammates. He not only knows where the blocks are coming from, but he also knows which way his blockers will take their man.

### Balance

A ball carrier should try to keep his feet under him at all times. Leaning too far forward places too much pressure on the legs and results in loss of balance.

For good balance, a ball carrier runs with his feet apart and with a high-kick action. If he runs with his feet just slightly above the ground, he will stumble easily and be vulnerable to even a simple arm tackle.

### Crossover Step

The crossover step is very effective on a waiting opponent. The fundamental to set up the crossover step is the head-and-shoulder fake. Instead of running straight ahead, the runner crosses his right leg over the left just before he makes contact with the tackler.

The ball carrier executes the step by driving a foot as close to the opponent as possible and crossing over with the trail leg. After cutting a 90-degree angle, he fades away from his opponent. As he crosses over, he shoves his right hand against the shoulder or helmet of his opponent.

### Cutting

The cutting maneuver is used to throw the tackler off-balance, which often breaks his tackle. The best time to make a cut is when the defensive man crosses his leg. The runner should try to cut without losing speed. He can cut either in or out and thus force the tackler to change direction. He leads with one leg and then, with a short lateral step, quickly changes direction.

An important rule for all running backs to remember is never cut more than once. After making his cut, the runner should not move too far laterally. As soon as the opportunity exists, he should head up the field.

On outside plays, some backs make the mistake of trying to get outside the entire defense. On sweeps, the ball carrier should turn up field as soon as he is outside the defensive end. As a result, he'll have more room to maneuver and can elude opposing tacklers.

### Change of Pace

This deceptive maneuver is most effective on tacklers coming laterally across the field. The ball carrier appears to be running at top speed; actually, he has some speed in reserve. At the right moment, he releases it to outrun the tackler. Or he may run at full speed, then slow down or stop to make the defender miss.

The change of pace can be practiced by running at an object, an assumed tackler. The ball carrier approaches at three-quarter speed, then crosses away at full speed.

### Straight-arm

This is almost a forgotten weapon. A good straight-arm can be useful for any ball carrier. It is a jabbing motion, in which the runner thrusts the arm nearer the tackler straight out from the shoulder with the elbow locked. Usually, the target is the helmet of the tackler.

The straight-arm is most effective when combined with a good pivot, cross-step, or sidestep dodge. At the moment of contact, all the weight should be taken off the feet to allow the legs and body to swing free.

### Hanging On to the Ball

Running with the ball involves proper carriage, with both points covered, two hands on the ball, and the ball as close in to the body as possible.

### Getting Hit and Landing

No matter how tight a situation, the ball carrier can always manage to turn or twist one way or the other. If he sees a tackler coming and cannot avoid him, the runner might try to hit the defender as he tries to hit him. By just standing there and allowing himself to be hit, he is like a punching bag. When tackled, the ball carrier should be sure he has the ball safely tucked away.

When falling, a ball carrier should always try to hold his elbows in. A fall on the elbows can cause a separated shoulder. Many times when he hits the ground, a ball carrier will get hit after he goes down. Therefore, he should try to roll and curl up in the fetal position.

Some backs will try to explode again after being hit. Occasionally, they can tear the tackle. A defensive tackle, a second after making his hit, will relax momentarily. If the ball carrier can explode once again, he may break the tackle!

## PREVENTION OF INJURIES

Most knee injuries occur when a player fails to see people. Knee injuries come when the cleats are planted into the ground in an odd direction. Many injuries of the knee happen this way. "I have never had to worry about a knee injury from being hit," admitted Mason. "I could always pick my feet up and not get hurt."

The best way to prevent injuries is to "never stop running." Most injuries occur when ball carriers stop running. Many good things can happen if a back will keep his legs going.

Running in hilly areas is excellent in strengthening the legs of running backs, providing the necessary drive in the thighs and hamstring muscles. The steps of the stadium are also very good. They build momentum for that important second effort.

## DRILLS

Football is a game of detail. Fundamental drills are the ingredients that make a great back.

Balance and maneuverability are the prime essentials we strive for in the fundamental drills. I believe that one of the best conditioning drills is running through ropes. Ropes are better than tires because they can be raised to various heights. A player can run the ropes straight ahead or he can use the crossover step. Our ball handling drills start with the quarterback handing off to a back, who first hits straight ahead and then to the side. We like to use a center in these drills to perfect our timing.

The next drill should involve a faking back. After the backs perfect this phase of handling the ball, the quarterback should start handing off to either back.

Our backfield practice begins with starts. We use a center, quarterback, and two halfbacks in this drill. The cadence is called by the quarterback. The ball is snapped and the backs move straight ahead for 10 yards. The quarterback doesn't hand off the ball in this opening warm-up drill. The backs are concerned only with improving the quickness of their start.

There are few drills available to perfect blocking or tackling. A good tough scrimmage will give players the opportunity to show their wares in this department. The best way to teach the shoulder and body technique, though, is by using blocking dummies.

1. *Stance* Offensive backs should spend a few minutes each day on stance. Most teams still feature their backs "down," with a three- or even four-point stance. A very basic drill is to have all the backs line up, one behind the other by positions. After they assume the proper stance, use the starting cadence and have them all start together a few steps. Both forward and lateral starts should be practiced.

2. *Lead blocking* Since running backs are expected to provide interference for each other, they should know how to execute a running shoulder block. A lead block requires exceptional skill, since the blocker is normally not as strong as the defender. Therefore, he must employ speed, momentum, and position to execute an effective block.

This is one of the meanest drills in football. While a held standing dummy can be used, there is really no substitute for doing this one live. Two markers should be placed on the ground about two paces apart. A defensive man is positioned behind but between the markers. Starting his move 3 yards from the defended hole, the lead blocker must blast the defender out of the hole.

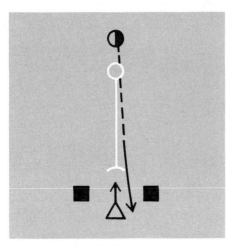

DIAGRAM 6-1. Lead blocking.

3. *End blocking* Offensive backs must be able to block defensive ends or linebackers either in or out. This drill can be done with bags or people. The blocker must *not* show his intention to block either in or out.

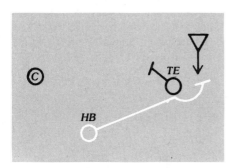

DIAGRAM 6-2. Hook in.

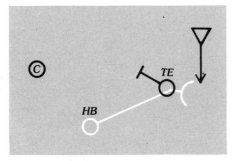

DIAGRAM 6-3. Kick out.

4. *Pass blocking* Two running backs should be set up in formations used in the pass offense. While the quarterback drops back and sets up at 7 yards deep, the two blockers step up and out and block the incoming pass rushmen just outside the wall formed by the standing dummies at the extremities of the cup.

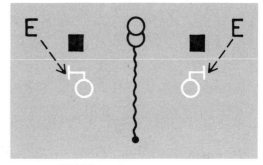

DIAGRAM 6-4. Pass blocking.

5. *Ball handling and hand-offs* Offensive backs need considerable drill on ball handling. Running in a circle, they can throw the ball around, in any direction and to any man.

Another warm-up drill for backs involves the ball carriers running forward and handing off to the receivers.

In another drill, two lines of four players are placed so that they face each other. No. 1 hands off to No. 2, 2 to 3, and so on.

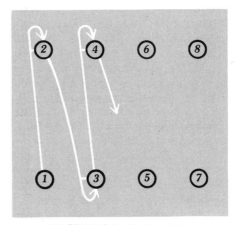

DIAGRAM 6-5. Ball handling.

The pitchout, an important play in today's offensive systems, should be drilled regularly. After receiving the snap from the center, the quarterback quick-tosses to the running back. They should alternate to both sides.

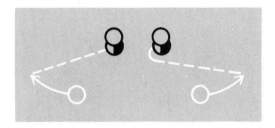

*DIAGRAM 6-6.   Pitchout.*

6. *Faking*   The running backs and the quarterback should be set up in front of a defensive line of scrimmage, with linebackers holding standout bags or shields. Those in the backfield should run through their plays with emphasis on faking.

7. *Ball carrying*   Our ball carriers go through a series of drills that have proven effective for us. We set up about three bags about 15 yards apart and go through a series of four drills that we work on *every* day. First, a back will use a crossover step with a straight-arm. In another drill, he will come up to a bag and "give" the tackler a foot and then take it away. As he gives the tackler his foot, with the other foot he drives away.

In the *double fake* drill, the back comes up to the tackler and gives him the double fake. A single fake is not sufficiently effective. If his opponent doesn't go for the first one, he probably will go for the second. Then, the runner should break away from him.

On the *spin* drill, the back comes up to a tackler and spins away from him, turning his back, if necessary, and spinning away. We also stress lifting the knees high at all times.

In the *gauntlet* drill, each offensive back runs with the ball through two parallel lines of players, each of whom is trying to snatch or pull the ball out of the grasp of the carrier.

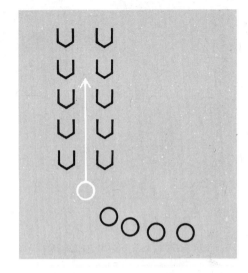

*DIAGRAM 6-7.   Run the gauntlet.*

In the *stiff-arm and sidestepping* drill, a defender is stationed just beyond two standing dummies. The first man in a line of ball carriers runs between the dummies and uses his off arm to jolt the defender on the helmet or shoulder pads as he moves quickly to his right or left.

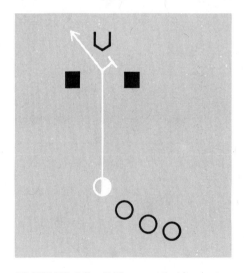

*DIAGRAM 6-8.   Stiff-arm and sidestepping.*

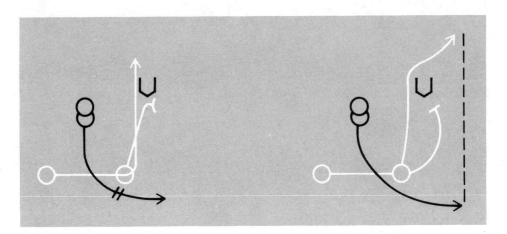

DIAGRAM 6-9. *Sprint-out drill. Left: Kick-out block and running play. Right: Hook-in block and sprint-out.*

8. *Sprint-out drill* This drill provides the necessary work in perfecting the sprint-out play. The lead blocker, particularly, is able to develop his blocking ability. Two plays are employed against two defensive containers: (1) a kick-out block by the near back on a run play inside of him; (2) a hook-in block on a quarterback sprint-out.

# 7

# The Kicking Game

*For the great majority of high school and college teams, the kicking game is the most overlooked phase.*

**George Allen**

No play in football wins or loses as much yardage as the kicking game. This is why the Redskins work every day on kicking, including such fundamentals as protecting, covering, and returning, as well as the actual kick itself.

A strong kicking game is the easiest way to obtain good field position, a major factor in winning football games. The mastery of kicking can determine the position of the team on the field, offensively and defensively.

According to statistics, the kicking game accounts for over 60 percent of the lost yardage and 25 percent of the scoring in the football game, which shows how important kicking is. Frankly, I don't think a team can win a championship without it.

I feel we can win two games each year on our kicking game, and those two might win us a championship. So we work on it every day, all through the training camp and through the season. Next to passing, if a team has a defense and a kicking game, they are going to win a lot of football games because the kicking game can be used as an offense.

Therefore, a coach must find players who have talent in kicking a football. One place where kickers can be found is on the soccer field, where kicking skill receives major emphasis.

The kicking specialist has become a vital part of every football team. Even high school teams have someone who does nothing more than kick the football. Since he never knows when he will be needed, he must be ready at all times. He must be able to come off the bench cold and perform his specialty, often in clutch situations. In the late stages of a close game, his foot probably holds the key to victory or defeat.

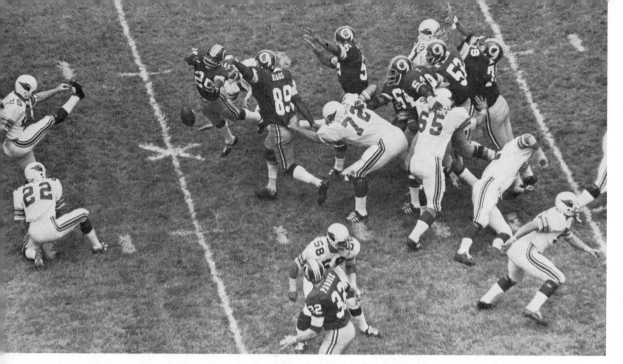

FIGURE 7-2. *A successful place-kick depends not only on the kicker and the holder, but also on the center and blockers working together. Above, Jim Bakken of the St. Louis Cardinals, with his "educated toe," boots one through the uprights.*

During the practice week, the kicking specialist works alone, usually off to one area on the field.

With the adoption of the new pro rules, the "coffin corner" is conversational again. Since on a missed field goal the ball is brought back to the line of scrimmage, an accurate punt can be very effective. Rather than punt for the end zone, it is wiser to try a sideline shot that might go out of bounds inside the 10-yard line.

### PLACE-KICKING

Field goal or extra point kicking demands a team effort. A successful place-kick depends not only on the kicker and the holder, but also on the center and blockers working together. To be an outstanding place-kicker an individual must have good leg power. He should also be well coordinated because kicking requires good timing and coordination.

We break down the place-kick into a four-part machine.

1. The *center* has to get the ball to the holder low and over the spot, without wasting time.
2. The *holder* has to get the ball on the spot, and if he can put the laces in front, it makes for an easier kick. However, if he cannot, he should get the ball on the spot so the kicker can kick through it.
3. Of course, the kicking team has to have *blocking* first to make the four-part machine work.
4. Last but not least, the important *kicker* must kick the ball through the uprights.

Note that in place-kicking a square-toed shoe is more *effective* than the normal round-toed shoe used in punting.

A kicker should try to kick extra points and 40-yard field goals the same way. He should try to kick straight and let the distance take care of itself. The worst thing a place-kicker can do is try to "overpower" the ball. Usually a kicker will try to kick too hard on extra-long field goals (attempts over 50 yards). It's still a natural swing and follow-through whether 30 yards or 50 yards. Every kick should be the same way, with the same rhythm. If he hits it right, the distance will take care of itself. The important thing is to hit it straight.

All the best kickers are talented. When a kicker goes sour, it is usually because he has lost his confidence and concentration. When this occurs, everything is lost—especially timing and rhythm, which are musts.

When Bruce Gossett played for me with the Rams he advised, "Try not to worry about the ones you missed. Just think about the ones you made because it's a 50/50 chance. It either goes in or it doesn't, and you cannot bring it back and kick it over."

### Stance

The place-kicker lines up about three walking strides behind the spot where the holder is going to set the ball. These are just normal steps. Assuming a relaxed position, he stands with his right foot in front of his left foot, squaring his shoulders with the uprights. "I

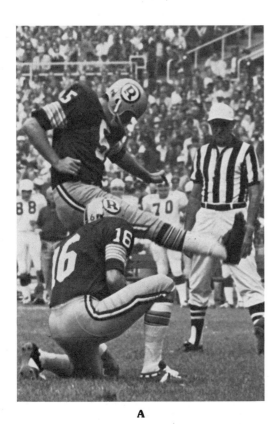

A

B

FIGURE 7-3. *Styles of place-kicking. The orthodox kicker (A) meets the ball straight on, while a soccer-style kicker (B) uses the side of his foot.*

A         B         C

D         E

FIGURE 7-4. *Place-kicking technique.* Holding the Ball. *Prior to the snap, the holder always gives the kicker a good target. He focuses his eyes on the target spot. The index finger of the left hand is placed on the tip of the football. The ball is centered with the laces away from the kicker.* Contact. *With the knee flexed, the kicker finishes with a snap of the lower leg. Immediately after contact, his knee joint is locked, and his toe is pulled up.* The Approach. *Just before the holder receives the ball, the kicker makes his initial step with the kicking foot. The second step is a lunging power step, which comes to a point about 6 inches behind the ball and straight ahead.* Follow-through. *After making the kick, the kicker must continue to keep his head down and follow through. The right foot must be brought straight through on a line with the goalposts.*

keep my weight on my rear foot," explained Gossett. "I like to line my right toe up with the spot on the ground and the middle of the goalposts."

"I keep my eye on the spot, and I can also see the holder's hands. When he throws out his fingers, I know the ball is coming back, and this is a clue for me to start up with my steps to move up to the football."

For extra point tries, the ball is set down about 7 yards from the line of scrimmage. This is the ideal spot.

## Approach

The approach to the ball takes the kicker a step and a half. Just before the holder receives the ball, the place-kicker starts his move. He makes his initial step with the kicking foot. This is a short, momentum-gathering step on the imaginary line he has pictured downfield.

The second step is a lunging power step, which comes to a point about 6 inches behind the ball. This is the step that will give a kicker the power to kick the ball far. As on the kickoff, the last step is the most important step. His eyes are concentrated on the spot where the ball will be placed. He wants to see his toe hit this spot.

## Contact

The kicking right leg should be swung in an arc, with the knee flexed; the kicker finishes with a snap of the lower leg. Immediately after contact, his knee joint is locked, and his toe is pulled up. The heel of the kicking foot contacts the ground first before his toe hits the ball. This helps to lock his ankle and lets him get more power and accuracy into the kick.

On his last step, the kicker's right leg,

from the knee down, is almost parallel with the ground. After bringing it straight behind him, he forces the leg out, and it comes up about the same after he kicks the ball. It's more or less a half circle, from the start of the kick to the finish.

All field goal kickers concentrate on bringing their right foot straight through on a line with the goalposts and then setting the foot back. This way the kicker cannot get a truly bad kick.

In order to kick a field goal, the place-kicker has to have terrific snap and rhythm in his leg. Field goal kickers have exceptional strength in the muscle right above the knee. This is the one that "snaps" every time a field goal is kicked.

On shorter field goals, from 30 yards in, the place-kicker should try to get a lot of height on the ball, so he tries to get under the ball. His heel will first contact the ground and drive the ball upward. On a longer try, the heel will be pretty close to hitting the ground before the toe hits the ball.

On field goal tries inside the 40-yard line, many place-kickers try to hit the ball just a little below the center. Beyond the 40-yard line, they try to hit it in the middle. This results in a slower spin, which makes the ball go farther.

A right-footed kicker may find it more difficult to kick a field goal from the left side of the field, since the angle is tighter and the goalposts appear farther away.

## Follow-through

After making the kick, the kicker must continue to keep his head down and follow through. The type of follow-through depends on the type of kicker. Whereas Lou Groza of the Cleveland Browns had a tremendous follow-through, many kickers do not. They more or less punch at the football.

A                                          B

C                                          D

FIGURE 7-5.   *Holding the ball. The holder's hands, which are reaching for the ball, should form a good target for the center. His eyes are fixed on the ball. If the laces need adjustments, the right hand does the job. The index finger of the left hand is placed on the tip of the ball. The holder must not remove his finger until the kicker has swung his leg completely through. Although we use the left hand in holding the ball, we prefer the right hand. The kicker is able to see the ball better when the right hand is on top of the ball.*

### Holding the Ball

The holder and the center are very important in the execution of a successful field goal. In addition, there are ten other players, the guys who block for the kicker. Their importance is over 50 percent of a successful field goal. The snap has to be perfect; the holder has to get the ball down, and he also has to have the laces turned toward the goalposts. If they are on the side, the ball will go to the side the laces are on.

Many holders like to kneel and place their left knee approximately 1 foot from the kicking tee and to the right side. They may extend their right leg forward, bending it at the knee, to allow the right foot to be flat on the ground. Then they are able to move up, down, or to the side, if the snap is poor.

His hands, which are actually reaching for the ball, form a good target for the center. His eyes are fixed on the ball. After catching the ball, the holder focuses his eyes on the spot where he wants to place it. The tip of the ball toward the center should be placed on the tee. The ball is set in an erect position and held on the proper spot with one finger. The kicker then boots the ball from under the finger.

### SOCCER-STYLE PLACE-KICKING

While my place-kickers have used the conventional style of kicking, there has been a sharp increase in the number of soccer-style kickers, many of whom have been very successful. Coach Ron Marciniak of the University of Dayton is one of the top authorities in the country on the soccer-style kick, and we are indebted to Coach Marciniak and *Athletic Journal* for their permission to use two excellent series of photographs showing kicker Greg Schwarber and holder Jim McVay (Figures 7-6 and 7-7), and the following coaching instruction, which appeared in the September 1974 issue of the Journal.

### Tee Up

After he leaves the huddle, the kicker's first task is to set the tee at 7 yards from the ball. Next, he places his plant or left foot firmly in the direction of the target alongside the tee approximately 3 to 6 inches to the left. Then he should step with his right or kicking foot to size up the proper stride for the impact step. The next distance step to the rear is taken with the left or plant foot.

According to Marciniak, most soccer-style kickers prefer to have the football straight up and down on the tee. Holding the ball with his left index finger, the holder balances it with his right hand, then pulls his hand under his crotch.

### Alignment

The kicker must determine what the line of flight must be in order for the ball to split the uprights and set up his angle of approach. "When a right-footed kicker kicks from the right side," said Marciniak, "he must decrease his alignment angle to the line of the ball. The kicker must compensate his aim for wind conditions and weather, realizing that the wind will affect the flight of the ball. When Greg kicks from the right hash mark, he tries to aim for the outside (right) goalpost because the ball hooks back between the goalposts."

### Stance

The kicker's stance should be comfortable and well-balanced, and his body should lean

*FIGURE 7-6. Soccer-style place-kicking technique (front view). Using a comfortable, well-balanced stance, the kicker (Greg Schwarber) leans forward slightly at the waist. His left foot is forward as he concentrates on the ball. He starts his first step as the holder (Jim McVay) places the ball on the tee. As he prepares to take his first step, the kicker should lean forward. His body weight then shifts to his left leg as he steps first with his right foot.*

N        M        L

F        G        H

FIGURE 7-6 (continued). As the second step is taken, the kicker's right leg is cocked to kick. The point of impact on the ball is made with the middle high instep of the kicker's right foot. His eyes are still on the ball as his foot moves through the ball. A good follow-through provides the necessary acceleration to send the ball soaring for distance and accuracy. (Photos courtesy of Athletic Journal.)

K        J        I

forward slightly at the waist. He should face the ball and stand with his left foot forward of his right foot.

### Concentration

The kicker should concentrate on his center first, then the holder's hands, and finally the spot on the tee. "Concentration should cover kicking through the ball," said Marciniak, "keeping the eyes on the point of impact, and follow-through."

### Approach

The approach for a soccer-style kicker is more difficult than it is for a conventional place-kicker. "A soccer-style kicker must be concerned with angles," explained Marciniak. "He should start his first step as the holder places the ball on the tee. As he prepares to take his first step, he should lean forward, and the weight of his body shifts to his left leg as he steps first with his right foot. As the second step is taken, the kicker's right leg is cocked to kick. In Figure 7-7, Schwarber takes a first step, long second step, and on his third step, he kicks the ball with his right foot. "The three-step kick gives him the momentum and adds body action to his kick," said Marciniak.

### Foot Contact

The point of impact on the ball is made with the middle high instep of the kicker's right foot. His foot meets the lower third of the ball. "We like our kickers to concentrate on the point of impact," said Ron. "He actually sees his foot hit the ball."

From the snap of the ball by the center, to the impact of the kicker's foot, the ball is kicked in 1 second. According to Marciniak, "The maximum time is never more than 1.4 seconds from snap to impact."

### Follow-through

The tremendous acceleration with which the kicker goes into his kick is a vital factor in gaining distance and accuracy. The kicking foot should start its swing about a foot or so behind the ball and extend as far beyond the ball as possible.

"Developing a kicking rhythm is necessary because the style must become mechanical," said Marciniak. "Therefore, he must use the same step and swing each time. Without good follow-through with the kicking leg, the ball will fall short of its target."

### Training the Kicker

The amount of in-season kicking should be left up to the individual, but he should not

FIGURE 7-7 (opposite). *Soccer-style place-kicking technique (rear view). With his left foot forward, the kicker concentrates first on the center, then on the holder's hands, and finally on the tee spot. The kicker (Greg Schwarber) starts his first step with his right foot as the holder places the ball on the tee. The first step with the right foot is followed by a long second step with the left foot. On the final step with his right foot, he strives to kick through the ball. Concentrating on the point of impact, he sees his foot hit the lower third of the ball. To gain distance, he starts his swing about a foot or so behind the ball and extends as far through the ball as possible. Notice that the holder (Jim McVay) gives the center a good target, and after catching the ball, he focuses his eyes on the spot where he wants to place it. (Photos courtesy of* Athletic Journal.)

A        B        C

G        F        E        D

J        I        H

FIGURE 7-8. *The kickoff at RFK Stadium. Mark Moseley (3) prepares to kick the ball deep into the opponents' territory. The important point is for the members of the kickoff team not to move until the kicker is even with them on his approach.*

the summer months and off-season, our place-kickers train with a weighted rubber ball."

## KICKING OFF

Essentially, the kickoff is the same kick that is used for the extra point and field goal. The prime difference is that the kickoff man has a longer approach to kick the ball. He usually takes a 10-yard run at the ball to get a little more power behind him. I believe that most kickers would probably kick the ball just as well by lining up in their regular field goal position and kicking off.

On a kickoff, the kicker has the advantage of using a 2-inch tee to kick the ball off of. "Your foot can hit the ball better," said Bruce Gossett, "and not have as much friction as a ball that's held right on the ground. Also, you can get your weight through better on the kickoff because you're coming at the ball a little faster, and it helps drive your body through the ball."

"On the approach to the ball, I start off real easy over the first 5 yards," said Gossett, "and when I get past the 5-yard mark, I start speeding up. I make my last couple steps a little longer so I can really get my weight behind the ball."

"If you're a right-footed kicker," said Gossett, "after the kick, you want to land on your kicking foot, and if you're a left-footed kicker, land on your left foot. This is the only way you can get all of your weight behind the ball on a kickoff. When you land on your kicking foot, you know you had to go into the ball hard."

If a ball is kicked 5 to 10 yards in the end zone, with a little bit of height, this is an excellent kickoff because the opponents have to decide whether to run it back or not. If they do, we're in good position to force a

tire his leg. "If a kicker is not hitting the ball well on a practice day," said Marciniak, "he should not continue to kick that day."

"Our kickers take from 50 to 60 kicks a day, three days per week," explained Ron. "In addition, they take about 25 kicks on Monday following a Saturday game. During

FIGURE 7-9. *The importance of a good punter is greater today than ever before. With less emphasis on the field goal, more teams will be striving for good field position with a skillfully placed punt. Here, Mike Bragg gets off a long boot against the St. Louis Cardinals.*

fumble or get them inside the 20-yard line. If they don't run it out, they would get the ball on their 20. The best kickoff would be out of the end zone where they can't run it back.

Normally, the kickoff should be high enough to give the kicking team the opportunity to get downfield. However, if the ball is high and on the 7-yard line, it's a poor kick. But, if it is a high kick that is 2 or 3 yards into the end zone, this is an excellent kick.

When the kicking team is behind and must gain possession of the ball, the onside kick is used. However, the ball must cross the opponents' restraining line before the ball is a "free ball."

## After the Kickoff

After kicking the ball, the kicker should try to avoid the man assigned to knock him down, usually the player in front. After looking to see which side the holder is going to, the kicker should go to the other side.

## PUNTING

The value of a good punter cannot be overemphasized. His long, booming kicks can be most instrumental in keeping the other team deep in their own territory.

A powerful boot not only can get a team out of a hole, but can put the opponents on the spot, as with an accurate kick to the coffin corner.

A well-placed kick is sometimes better than a long gain on the ground, or a forward pass, because it puts a team in a hole. And a team has a good chance to score if the defense can keep the opposition down there.

We consider it most important that the punter get elevation on the ball, so we can get down and cover the kick. We are more interested in getting the ball in the air than in having the man kick the ball 40 or 45 yards consistently. We don't care for the individual who is capable of kicking the ball 60 or 65 yards but is inconsistent.

### Stance

In waiting for the pass-back, the punter should assume a comfortably erect stance from 14 to 15 yards behind the center. This distance is far enough back to eliminate the blocked kicks or keep them to a minimum. Most centers get the ball back to the kicker in 0.8 or 0.9 second.

While a three-step kicker may have his left foot forward, other kickers prefer having their kicking foot forward. A balanced stance is essential, in case the snap is to the right or left, high or low. I like a punter to stand with his feet slightly spread, the knees flexed. The weight of the kicker is slightly forward over the forward foot. However, if he crouches too much, this may constrict his kicking action. Many kickers try to step into the snap.

The hands are kept out in front, loose and relaxed, much like a receiver's would be. The thumbs are out and the palms up. Providing a good target helps both the center and the kicker. The center knows the kicker is ready when he gets his hands up and forms a pocket for him.

FIGURE 7-10. *The punter's stance (Mike Bragg). The kicker should stand with his feet slightly spread. His weight is slightly forward over the forward foot. The hands are held out in front, loose and relaxed. The kicker must keep his eyes on the ball at all times in order to avoid a fumble.*

The eyes are constantly on that ball, at all times, as the ball is passed back. Look the ball into the hands. The kicker should receive the ball on his right side. His fingers are extended as if they were going to cradle the ball in—very flexible, not stiff. Rather than force anything, he brings the ball in smoothly. The elbows should give slightly so as to cushion the ball. The hands are relaxed as they give with the ball.

### Holding the Ball

The hands are placed flat along the sides of the ball, with the fingers fairly close together.

The ball should be held parallel to the ground, with the laces turned up. The left hand is nearer the front of the ball, and the right hand is near the back.

The left hand is placed near the front tip of the ball to steady it and is removed during the second step of the kick. Since the ball is cupped in the right hand, all the kicker has to do is turn the front tip slightly to the left, producing a spiral, with the nose of the ball slightly down.

As he drops the ball to the foot, the hand or hands fall away. The hand should not pull away since this might deflect the ball and cause poor contact with the foot. The ball should be held waist high, although this will vary with the type of kick.

## The Steps

Most of the better punters today are three-step kickers. However, results are more important than the particular style a kicker employs. An excellent three-step kicker, for example, may hurt himself by changing to two steps. There are some who find the Rocker step effective.

The punter starts to move forward the moment he receives the ball. The initial step is nothing more than a comfort step straight ahead with the front foot. A long first step might pull the kicker off-balance and disrupt his timing and coordination.

Just prior to planting his last step, the kicker should drop the ball. Then his kicking foot comes up to meet the ball. He should place the ball flat on the foot. If he cannot drop it parallel to the ground, he should have it a little nose down. If the tail end is down, he could have a tendency to hit the back end of the ball before hitting the middle, causing an end-over-end kick. Therefore, the drop is very important.

The forward movement of the punter is similar to a fast walk. There should be no

FIGURE 7-11. Mike Bragg demonstrates holding the ball on the punt. The hands are placed flat along the sides of the ball. The left hand is near the front tip of the ball to steady it and is removed during the second step of the kick. The right arm is underneath the ball to allow for placing of the ball on the foot. The laces are turned up to assure consistency.

hesitation in it once it is initiated. It has to be smooth and precise.

The swing is a pendulum kind of swing. The punter should want his kicking leg straight on contact with the ball. As soon as he gets through, at the bottom of his pendulum swing, he should lock his knee.

## Contact

The contact is, perhaps, the most crucial phase of the kicking action. The ball must be

**A**  **B**  **C**

**D**  **E**  **F**

FIGURE 7-12. *Punting technique. Mike Bragg is a two-and-one-half-step kicker, so his left foot is slightly forward in receiving the ball. The hands are held out in front, loose and relaxed. His first step is a short jab with the left foot; he then fullsteps with his right, followed by the left. Then comes the kick. While taking the two and one-half steps, Bragg adjusts the ball to his hands. Just prior to planting his last step, Bragg drops the ball, placing the ball flat on the foot. He wants to "look the ball all the way on the foot." Over 80 percent of the bad kicks in punting are caused by improper drop of the ball. Notice that the kicking leg is straight when it comes in contact with the ball. The toes are pointed downward and inward. Punting power comes from the right knee snap. At the bottom of his pendulum swing, he wants to get the knee locked. To kick the ball high, contact with the ball should be slightly higher than normal.*

placed out in front of the kicker so that it falls directly onto the instep of the kicking foot. In order to assure proper arching of the foot, he should point the toe of the kicking foot down. He should place the ball right on the arch, maybe a little to the outside.

When contact with the ball is made, the knee of the kicking foot should be bent slightly. As the ball leaves the foot, however, the knee must be locked. The ball should be met by snapping the leg out straight with the ankle locked down. It's the snap in the kick that makes the ball travel. To get the proper snap, the kicker carries the leg forward with the knee bent until just before the ball is struck. Then, he snaps it out straight and locks the joint as the foot meets the ball.

If the kicker places the ball right, the only pressure he will feel will be in the middle of his instep. The ball will feel very good on his foot.

When Pat Studstill played for me with the Rams, he said, "Don't try to kick the ball too hard. When you just depend on brute force, you ruin the smoothness of the kicking action and the long, easy follow-through which is so necessary. Start your kicking swing slowly and continue with increasing speed until it reaches its maximum velocity just as the foot hits the ball."

Concentration plays such a vital role in successful punting. The kicker who takes his eye off the ball will be vulnerable to hooks, slices, and even blocked kicks. A good rule to follow is: "Never look up until your kicking foot comes back to the ground."

As the ball arrives in his hands, the punter fixes his target in his mind, then he trains his eyes strictly on the ball. He watches it as he drops it, as it contacts his foot, and after the ball leaves the foot. Then he watches his foot as it returns to the ground.

"Above all, work on your drop," advised Studstill, "and be sure you are locking that knee and ankle. You will defeat yourself even before you start if you don't do these two things."

"You must kick the ball when it is only 12 to 18 inches from the ground. If the point of the ball dips down, you'll have a bad kick. If the point is up, it will also be a bad kick. You have to drop the ball absolutely flat."

## Follow-through

After making contact, the punter should kick through the ball, allowing his kicking leg to carry through over his head. "You've got to drive your whole body into it," said Pat. "And I think getting the ol' rear end into it is all important . . . just drive in up under it. It's just like making a tackle of a block. You have to get fully into it."

During the kicking action, the punter's back should be bent and his shoulders rounded. When the leg begins to go up, he should straighten his back and throw his shoulders back. The eyes of the kicker should remain on the ball throughout the kicking process.

The punter should come up on the toes of his other foot with his arms outstretched at the sides. After completing his follow-through and bringing his foot back to the ground, the kicker should take a step or two forward to avoid any roll-back action.

It is most important to keep the balance foot on the ground and to stay up at the end of the kick, not fall back. Some kickers like to take a step or two forward after completing the follow-through.

## Time to Get Ball Away

The kicker must always be conscious of the amount of time required to get the ball away. But he must have the poise to remain calm in all punting situations. Most blocked punts are

F        E        D

due to the kicker's taking too much time. We like our kickers to kick the ball in less than 2.2 seconds from the time the ball is snapped from the center.

### Height and Distance

The punt should be kicked as high as possible. At the same time, the punter doesn't want to out-kick his coverage. He has to look at both of these in moderation. A really high short punt isn't a good punt at all, but in the same sense, a long, low punt has a good chance of being returned by the opposition. They will run it right back down our throat. The ideal punt, probably, would be a punt that would stay in the air anywhere from 4 to 4½ seconds and go anywhere from 40 to 45 yards.

The good kicks are spirals. It's just like throwing passes. I'm sure if the quarterback threw the ball end over end, he wouldn't be very effective with it. A bullet spiral will travel a greater distance in the air, and when it hits the ground, the ball will likely roll fast and straight.

The test of a good punter is how well he can kick against a strong wind. Rather than get off a high boot, he must keep the kick fairly low. To do this, he should drop the ball a little lower and turn the front tip slightly down, and not follow through too far.

### Quick Kick

The quick kick can be a useful weapon in high school and college football. The pro game, however, is a game of specialization. Every team in the NFL has a punter who does nothing else but kick. If he came into the game, for example, on a second or third down situation, it would be difficult to conceal his intentions. Furthermore, the pros can score

C         B         A

*FIGURE 7-13. The art of punting. Kicking from near his own end zone, Ray Guy, the brilliant punter of the Oakland Raiders, gets off a booming kick against the New England Patriots. Like other top kickers, Guy is a three-step kicker. In receiving the ball, Ray's left foot is slightly forward. After a short jab or comfort step, he full-steps with his right, followed by the left. Just prior to planting his last step, Guy drops the ball. He wants the ball to fall directly onto the instep of the kicking foot. Observe that he points the toe of his kicking foot down, in order to assure proper arching. He places the ball right on the arch. In picture E, as contact with the ball is made, the knee of Guy's kicking foot is bent slightly. However, as the ball leaves the foot, the knee must be locked.* Punting power comes from the right knee snap.

from long range on any given play, and they don't like to give up the ball until they have to.

There is no defense against the quick kick, and a team can pick up an easy 45 yards. This surprise move is usually on a third down situation with the wind at the back of the kicker. The kicker must not give any tip-off through his stance.

Moving quickly on the snap from his normal backfield stance, he takes an average comfort step back with his kicking foot. He doesn't want to roll back on the heel of his balance foot. The ball arrives in his hands the instant he comes back on his balance foot. This demands split-second timing.

The punter quickly throws his weight forward on his kicking foot; then he takes a full step forward on his balance foot and kicks. The kicking toe must be turned down, with plenty of snap in the leg. The kicker must stay up at the end of his kick. This helps get a bullet spiral with plenty of roll. Since he wants a low kick, about 20 feet in the air, the ball should be dropped a little lower with less follow-through, as if he were kicking against the wind.

### The Coffin Corner

Angling a kick for the corner can be an important weapon, too. If, for example, a punter is on his own 45-yard line, he might draw a bead on the point where the 5-yard line intersects the right sideline. The right-footed kicker usually has a natural pull to the left, so an accurately placed kick might put the ball practically in the corner.

After receiving the snap, the kicker quickly sights his target and steps directly toward it. In order to get away a low one, he should drop the ball closer to the foot, keeping the toe perfectly straight and turned down. The instep should be flat.

Whenever the kicker stands near the middle of the field, he can aim for either corner. The natural pull varies with the individual, and, of course, the wind is a factor, too. Only through practice can he determine the proper allowance to make.

### Problems (Flaws) in Punting

Failure to achieve the desired spiral effect can be attributed to a number of things. First, the punter might not be hitting the ball correctly on his foot and this could go back to the drop. He has to drop it absolutely flat on the instep. Maybe his drop is off just a little. Or, maybe he is not locking his ankle all the way.

Another flaw in punting results from trying to overpower the ball. The kicker usually dubs it when he tries to kick it out of sight. The punter who takes his eye off the ball will likely kick hooks and slices. In trying to see how far he will kick the ball, he will look up too soon.

If a punter is violating the fundamentals, the coach should make him stop immediately and have him start kicking easily in slow motion. This usually will help him regain his form and find the solution to his problem. He will soon realize that it is form, not force, that makes the ball travel.

Some punters have a habit of pointing their left foot to the left as they step through to kick. As a result, they usually move to the left, cross over with the kicking foot, and hook the ball.

# DRILLS

A punter should devote a considerable amount of time to working with a center. The first job is to set the stance, to determine how the feet should be placed at the beginning of a kick. After the kicker has found his correct stance, he should practice making his kicking steps and go through the motions of kicking the football. Chalk marks can be placed on the grass.

The punter must have a center snapping to him for his kicks. He might even have someone make some bad snaps and practice reacting to them. They can be high, low, and to either side.

After he has mastered the fundamentals, he should be placed under as much pressure as possible, preferably during scrimmage. Rushers can be placed on either side of the center out about 7 yards. One rusher from either side is allowed to come on the snap and try to block the kick. The kicker kicks without any blocking. A coach can use a stopwatch and have his kicker practice getting the punt away in less than 2.2 seconds. This is the only way to condition him for game situations.

Kickers should not be overworked. They lose their effectiveness when fatigue sets in, so drills should be limited in time and scope. A kicker must be kept fresh and strong.

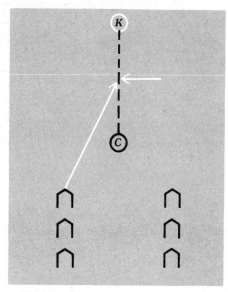

DIAGRAM 7-1. *Punting under pressure.*

# 8

# Defensive Line

*Players on the defensive line are paid to rush the passer, and if they can't rush the passer, they're stealing!*

**George Allen**

*A team of hard-charging, aggressive defensive linemen playing with determination and courage, and in top-notch physical condition, may get hurt a little bit against the run, but it is going to be a difficult team to beat at any place at any time.*

The defensive lineman has to be in good physical condition to rush the passer. It's one of the most difficult phases of all of football. In every play, he is battling that offensive lineman; this takes a lot out of him, and we don't want the lineman to take a couple of steps and stop and watch the pass being completed.

Defensive football is actually "hit and react" football. We like our linemen to concentrate on recognizing the moves of the offense, and then they must react to these moves. The important point is not where the rushman lines up but where he winds up.

An effective pass rush is the objective of all defensive lines. When the offense hits a long one, it usually means the pass rush has broken down, and the defensive lineman is just as much to blame as the pass defender.

The secret to winning in this game, therefore, is getting to the quarterback. That's the main job of the defensive lineman, though he has to defend against the run, too.

Tackling is to defensive line play just as blocking is to offensive line play. If a player cannot tackle, he will prove a weak defensive man regardless of whatever else he can do. Football is a game of "hit or be hit," and a lineman has to be willing to take some hard knocks and dish some out, too. But in order to make the tackle, the player must be able to get into position to tackle. This is where the maneuvers and stunts prove most effective. But unless a player is well schooled in the fundamentals of defensive line play, i.e.,

FIGURE 8-2. *The key to rushing the passer is not how often you dump him, but how much you pressure him. Defensive linemen are the heat men. They must put the heat on the passer and foul up his timing anyway they can. Above, Manny Sistrunk (64) and Verlon Biggs (89) force the Patriots' Jim Plunkett to leave the pocket.*

proper stance, the charge, and the hitting position, all his defensive maneuvers will be worthless.

The inside (or "I") man's greatest asset is his quickness. A quick lineman, particularly one with good lateral movement, is more valuable than a man of great speed. He must have size, strength, agility, and alertness, but most important, he must be quick. *I value quickness more than any other skill a football player can have.* When a coach has a player who can combine size with quickness, that is Utopia!

A huge factor in successful defense is good preparation. On a given Sunday, we want our players to know their opponent's offense like a book.

## QUALIFICATIONS

Quickness is more important to me than height in our outside (or "O") men. We also like a rangy athlete with quickness, although not necessarily blessed with long-range speed. If a lineman has good height, he can get his hands up high and bat some balls down.

Strength is another important quality. We find that all NFL linemen possess good strength, but the great ones have quickness and quick reaction. This is why we work on reactions to situations, reading rules almost every day. The defensive lineman has to continually work on this phase of the game in order to increase a player's reaction to a play.

To be a successful football player, a lineman must have a strong desire for bodily contact, to want to knock somebody down. We like the overly aggressive type who can also take it. In the course of a 14-game schedule, a defensive tackle (we call them "I" men for inside) will take approximately 1,000 or more licks, not counting special teams. In other words, the defensive tackles are getting hit on every play. The defensive ends are the same way, with the exceptions of sweeps away from them when they have to pursue. If these licks are added up over the season, it means that these linemen will have to take quite a bit of hard contact. So, they must be tough to be able to take it physically.

Actually, it takes as many years to develop a topflight defensive lineman as it does a quarterback. Intelligence, determination, concentration, deception, agility, and quickness are as important as size and toughness.

Defensive linemen must be aggressive, alert, and mean. There is always the possibility of blocking a punt, intercepting a pass, or recovering a fumble. A quick-thinking, alert lineman can be an asset to any team.

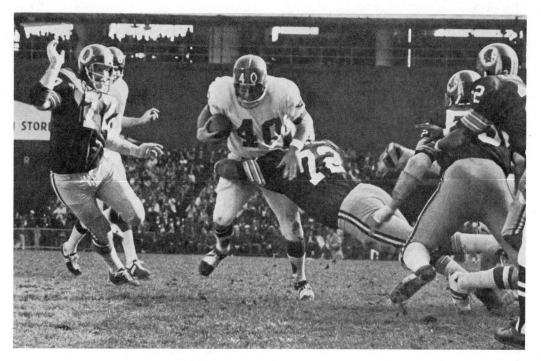

*FIGURE 8-3. An outstanding defensive line can control a game by destroying the opposition from the inside out. The team controlling the line of scrimmage usually wins the game. Here, Diron Talbert (72), the Redskins' aggressive lineman, stops an opposing running back cold with a bone-crushing tackle. His target is the belt buckle.*

A player must have this desire for body contact because it is difficult to instill this strong desire to hit people and get hit. Of course, if the player who is not too aggressive plays with a group of people who are aggressive, this trait can rub off.

## BASIC RESPONSIBILITIES

The responsibilities of those on the defensive line will vary according to the defensive line charges that we employ. Basically, our defensive ends, who are our pass rushers, have run-hole responsibility. The defensive end is responsible for the 6 or 7 hole, which is im-

mediately outside the offensive tackle. On the snap, he has to pick up certain reading rules, and this can change on the run. That's where quickness and reaction play such an important part. He has to charge across the line of scrimmage and, in an instant, change his responsibility or his reactions to the play.

We have our inside people do more things than our outside men because the defense cannot sacrifice their outside pass rush. However, I'm not saying the "O" men don't have reading rules. They have just as many, but they aren't as complicated as those of the "I" men. The inside people, on occasion, will pinch the offense. We send one lineman one way and one another way. We will do stunts inside with them. If it is a

**A**  **B**

FIGURE 8-4. *Quickness has replaced bulk as a defensive lineman's most essential physical asset. With the running quarterback becoming more prevalent, the front line must be able to contain his movement with relentless pursuit. In these pictures, defensive end Verlon Biggs (89) pursues one of the league's best scramblers, Roger Staubach, and finally gets his man.*

basic line charge, about 65 percent of the time their responsibility is to shoulder outside the offensive guard.

Once the linemen charge across the line of scrimmage, they must pick up their reading rules instantly and take off. In short, they do not just come off the ball. A defenseman should have good pursuit. He must be able to chase the ball carrier with quickness.

All defensive linemen must master the following individual fundamentals:

1. *The ability to move.* Every defensive player must move on movement. Instead of watching the ball, he watches the blocker opposite him, and he *moves as he does!* Speed and accuracy of movement are highly important.
2. *The ability to protect himself.* The best way for a defensive lineman to protect himself is to deliver a blow. His prime objective is to strike a blow, neutralize the blocker, get rid of him, pursue the ball carrier, and make the tackle.
3. *The ability to tackle.* The ability to tackle is perhaps the most vital defensive requirement.
4. *The ability to fight pressure.* The defensive lineman should always fight around the blocker's head.

The reading and charging theories of defense are most prominent in football today. A reading defense will hit, then wait to try to read the play. The Dallas Cowboys do a fine job with this style of defense. The defenders flow with the movement of the ball. A charging defense, on the other hand, "bangs" straight ahead across the line of scrimmage as quickly as possible.

Each theory has its advantages and shortcomings. An aggressive, hard-rushing line can be trapped, but it can also place tremendous pressure on a passer. I much prefer the "Jet style" of defensive line play.

For each formation and club, we have different reading rules that might change from week to week. This is in order to give us more effective stopping of a certain play or formation.

The "front four" have the responsibility of closing the middle against running and putting excessive pressure on a quarterback in a pass play. Behind the front four are the three linebackers. The middle linebacker plays 2 yards back from the center. The corner linebackers play head on with the offensive ends and often harass them when they try to go downfield for a pass.

Should a high school or college team employ this defensive alignment? First, they would have to have the personnel. Generally, a coach shouldn't copy another team because quite often, he doesn't have the players to do certain things. Most important, however, his players do not understand the entire defense.

We have great personnel on our front line who can react to a variety of plays. We don't have to use too much trickery, although when we do use trickery, it's quite effective because the opposition doesn't expect it. But our front four are so agile and quick that it isn't necessary for us to sacrifice going against the grain.

## Defensive Ends ("O" Men)

The primary job of the defensive ends is to get at the quarterback, to rush and harass him. They have to be strong enough to hold their ground against running plays and be able to stack up the interference. They must be able to counteract double-team blocking.

On the pass rush, the outside men have options to go inside, outside, or over the quarterback. Basically, the defensive end's initial movement is outside. If he has a man set up who is dropping outside to him, he just has to come back to the inside. That's the only way he is going to have the offen-

sive tackle come back and play it honest. It is to the end's advantage if he can beat the offensive man to the inside. If the offensive tackle is dropping off to the outside and he is giving the defensive end the inside, he should take it.

Defensive ends have to be big, particularly on the four-man line. Along with quickness, they must be counter punchers, reacting to the maneuvers of the offensive tackles. Therefore, they must be able to read the tackle. Some tackles telegraph the way they are going to block, so a defender should observe how the tackle sets up for pass protection and the stance he employs.

Some offensive linemen put a little more weight forward, while others may put a little weight backward. If a lineman really wants to blow out, he may put his right foot back a little farther, or he may get his buttocks a little higher.

## Defensive Tackles ("I" Men)

A defensive tackle should have quickness, the ability to slide around opposing linemen.

These men do not have to be as rangy as the outside men, though. Although they don't need as much mobility, they should be stronger because of the plays hitting directly at them. Quickness, rather than speed, is the quality I prefer. They don't have to worry about containing.

On runs aimed at him, the defensive tackle should be strong enough to hand-fight his guard, then slip through to make the tackle. He often gives the blockers what we call a hand swipe. He hits them in the head with a forearm, then takes the inside. The exceptionally quick tackle can go to his outside as well as the inside, and still be able to get to his objective.

Everyone on the defensive line should know what every man is doing. For instance, if the defensive tackle has an inside spot between the two inside men and if he is going to stunt, his own men should know this.

If he is very quick, a defensive lineman can make a move to the outside and take off back to the inside. The chances are there is going to be a tremendous pileup in the middle area with the stunting action. This will leave a very big hole for the defensive end to react to. He will then have plenty of room to the inside.

If the tackle is rushing to the outside, the defensive end knows the tackle is going to beat him to the outside, and he won't be able to react back. But if he knows the man inside of him is going to the inside, he might tell his own man that he is going to the inside. This is a good opportunity to use the option of going to the inside. However, he has to know when to do it, and what charge to employ that will allow him to do it.

## STANCE

Since a defensive lineman must meet, stop, control, and release an offensive blocker, he should employ a wide stance, staying low and on balance. A strong, balanced stance is important because it enables the lineman to move forward or in slanting directions and deliver a quick powerful blow.

The most common defensive stance used by linemen is the three-point stance. Some coaches prefer to have their guards in a four-point stance. Linemen using the four-point position, however, should not let their knees touch the ground.

A common mistake many coaches make is placing too much emphasis on a rigid type of stance. When it comes to stance, everyone cannot be the same because their physical characteristics are different. My only requirement is that the weight be forward,

with the feet out in a sprinter's stance. The player should line up in a position that does not tip off his intentions. "When he gives cues to the opposition, he is allowing the offensive man to place his hand on his wallet."

I'm only interested in 10 yards—who can get there the quickest, regardless of stance. However, the lineman's feet should be slightly close together, weight forward, and he has his buttocks up. When he does this, he will come out low. By keeping his feet up under him, on the snap, the chances are that he will come straight up, and this is what we don't want to see. We are always working on getting defensive linemen low and stretched out, so that on the snap, they can get across that line of scrimmage. That's where the games are won.

In getting the job done, my recommendation is to allow the best stance for the player and let him come on across. He should not want to copy stances because the arm length, body, and leg length are different. The coach just has to experiment and time the man. We like to time our rushmen a lot in training camp. Have the linemen experiment with different stance; then select one they perform the best with the fastest time.

When Deacon Jones came into the league, he had a problem with his three-point stance. When the blockers would "M-block," fire away right at him, he seemed at a disadvantage. He found that he couldn't get anywhere with someone's head in his gut. So his stance was changed around until he was comfortable and could get out quick. Changing his stance allowed him to hit them first and go past them, before they could hit him.

Actually, the stance on defense is similar to the one used on offense. The chief difference is that the weight is more forward, since the lineman does not have to pull laterally to the line of scrimmage. The feet are

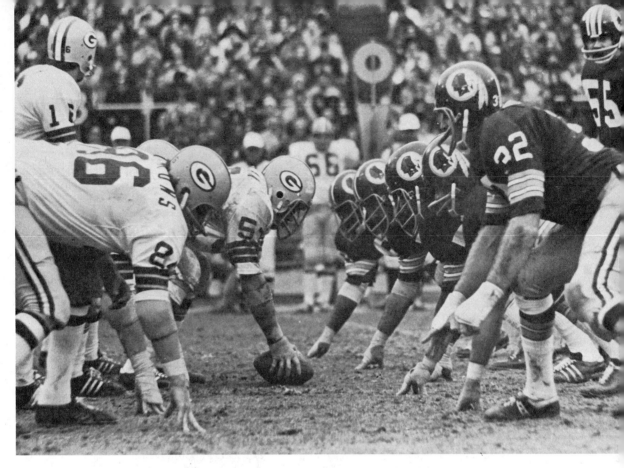

FIGURE 8-5. *A strong, balanced stance enables the defensive lineman to deliver a quick, powerful blow. We prefer a three-point staggered stance, with the weight definitely forward, to allow the rushman to explode off the line.*

placed about shoulder width apart with one foot slightly back in a staggered position, one or two hands on the ground, and the weight forward on the hands. Offensive and defensive stances differ also in that the defensive lineman's body is closer to the ground.

Some defensive ends assume a two-point stance, facing the line of scrimmage with the inside foot forward. However, whenever they are playing tight with a linebacker covering to their outside, they use a three-point stance.

*I value quickness more than any other skill a football player can have.*

## USE OF THE HANDS

All good defensive linemen use their hands to keep the offensive blockers away from their body. *This constitutes the only advantage the rules provide for defensive players.* The hands are used to ward off blockers and to allow the defensive players to get to the point of attack.

## RUSHMEN MANEUVERS

In today's pro football, with the multiple attacks employed by the offense, the charging maneuvers of defensive linemen demand not only quick thinking but also strength and maneuverability. From the skill standpoint, I'm more concerned about the rushman's quickness than any other single characteristic he possesses.

Every defensive lineman has his own favorite maneuvers. We like our young players to experiment and practice all the methods used for defense to see which are the most natural and which they can execute best. In deciding which maneuver to employ, a lineman should first consider the down and tactical situation. He should keep his opponent guessing by mixing his maneuvers. Above all, he should be in position to tackle after he executes the stunts or maneuvers. Quite often, a player might develop his own maneuver. However, new maneuvers should be tested and proven in practice before they are tried in game action.

Certainly, teamwork is necessary to make any defensive line a success. Our linemen have special signals, by which they let each other know what they are going to do. Maybe two will fire in so the other two stay back. Of course, since the situation may change a lot, they have to alter the original plan. But they have played together long enough now so each knows instinctively how the other is going to react to something. And they always cover up for each other.

### Getting Off on the Ball

This must be drilled upon every day both in training camp and during the season. Defensive men should not listen to the signal-calling cadence of the quarterback. They

FIGURE 8-6. A team of hard-charging linemen is always difficult to beat. Here, an aggressive Diron Talbert (72) uses his hands and arms to throw quarterback Dennis Shaw for a huge loss. A defensive lineman must have the strength and agility to punish blockers and quarterbacks with forearm blows and hand slaps. He must intimidate them physically.

The term "use of hands" means the use of hands, forearms, and shoulders to keep an offensive man away from the defender's legs and body long enough to permit him to read, diagnose, react, and get to the point of attack. Many times a defender may not be able to play off a blocker with his hands, but he can play himself off a blocker.

Don't ever forget this! If a rushman fails to make use of his hands, he is never going to reach his potential as a defensive player. Use of the hands is necessary whether a lineman is playing a run or rushing the passer.

B   A

D   C

FIGURE 8-7. *Defensive linemen must be drilled daily on getting off on the ball. Rather than listen to the signal caller's cadence, they must key the ball and move when the ball is snapped. Or, they will key the offensive player and react on his movement. Above, Deacon Jones, one of the greatest pass rushmen in NFL history, demonstrates his pass rush technique.*

must take their initial starting signal from what they see, not what they hear.

There are two ways to perform this vital phase of defensive line play. One method is to key the ball and move when the ball is snapped. The other is to key the offensive player and react on his movement. Actually, some players use a third method in that they combine both keying the ball and reading the offensive man's movement.

Let's say the charge calls for the outside shoulder responsibility of the offensive lineman. We want our defensive man to get there as quickly as possible. We want him to more or less ignore the run and "come off the ball" as fast as he can. If a team drills enough on their reaction to running plays, if it happens to be a run, then they will not likely get hurt.

### Shoulder Charge

The shoulder charge is used in extremely short yardage situations. Some linemen like to charge straight into the blocker and jolt him with both hands on the shoulders. The lineman wants all his weight behind his shoulders to drive his man straight back. When using the shoulder charge, we want the rushman to combine it with the forearm flipper. If he goes just with his shoulder, chances are his arm will be behind him, and the offensive man can get under him. If he comes out very low, using his shoulder and his flipper, he might be able to bring the blocker up as he hits him across the chest. He can bring him up and still stop his movement.

A defensive lineman has to gain control of the line of scrimmage before he is ever going to stop the play. If he comes out with the shoulder alone, we think he will not be as effective. We want him to meet the blocker low with the shoulder and neutralize him. Then he should raise the blocker up and control him with his forearm and other hand. After he whips him, he should release him and make his tackle.

The defensive lineman must always watch his target so he can get a solid blow. After making contact with the blocker, he should locate the ball carrier. He cannot perform this procedure in reverse or the blocker will have the advantage.

### Hand Shiver

The hand shiver is a straight-out shot executed by the defensive lineman using the heel of his hand, and then locking his elbows. The hand shiver is usually used

when he is in pursuit, and a back or guard is coming out to get him. He should extend the palm of his hand out and lock his elbow and give the opponent a real jolt and try to knock him off balance and down. Quite often when players are running, it doesn't take an awful lot to cause them to lose balance.

The forearm shiver is similar to the hand shiver. The difference is that the lineman allows his forearms to make the initial contact with the opponent. He should bend the elbows to a 90-degree angle. The forearm shiver is more popular than the hand shiver because the individual who uses the hand shiver must have exceptional strength for satisfactory execution.

A shiver involves a straight lock with the elbow and getting the shot there. The lineman should come out with the elbow locked, and he should try to stun his opponent right there so he can react to the play.

The forearm shiver is done with both arms and is a protective maneuver to maintain a relative position on the line of scrimmage until the ball is located. One hand is placed on the opponent's shoulder, and the other is on the head. The defensive man should step into his opponent with his back foot, always keeping his feet and legs well back of him. Thrusting his hands forward in an upward movement, he delivers a blow with the base of his palms.

The forearm shiver is often applied in cases where the opponent is trying to use a side body or reach block. It is an effective counter when the center attempts to block the "I" man. The arms are extended and are locked. The locked-arm position helps to keep the blocker away from the defensive lineman's body.

### Forearm Lift

This maneuver is used mostly on close-in blocks, where the blocker reaches the defen-

**FIGURE 8-8.** *The hand shiver is a straight-out shot using the heel of the hand, and then locking the elbows. Above, rushman Ron McDole gives a pass blocker a jolt and tries to knock him off balance.*

sive man much more quickly and with much more power. It is also effective when a rushman attempts to run through a pass protector who is using an upright blocking stance. The rushman uses the forearm nearest the blocker, aiming his arm between the neck and shoulder, under the chest to lift up the blocker.

The defensive lineman comes out of his stance, and he doesn't immediately draw back. He comes right out of the stance and strongly tenses his arm. He tries to make

contact along the shoulders of the blocker or up to the chin or possibly the head. He uses a very quick shot with his forearm and tries to knock his man off balance, and then he reacts to the play. He is thinking about a run, *and he is not thinking about avoiding the man so much as he is beating him right there on the spot to protect his area.*

In using the forearm lift, the lineman meets the power of the block in a lifting maneuver. It is applied in most situations where the opponent is using a shoulder block. This maneuver destroys the force of the offensive block. The arm is driven hard under the chest of the blocker, which forces the offensive man to rise up. The defensive player wants to rid himself of the block so that he can get to the tackle. He must avoid a stalemate because if that occurs the offensive man usually wins.

### Hand Swipe

This maneuver is used by linemen who are quick and agile, against both runs and passes. The rushman executes a fast jab step in one direction as the blocker reacts to meet this fake and comes in the direction of the fake. He uses his hands to swat or swipe him on the head and body compelling him to continue in the direction of his fake. At the same instance, he changes the direction of his feet and goes behind him to the point of attack.

### Submarine

The submarine maneuver is used primarily for extremely short yardage and generally down in tough territory, when the offensive team is close to a touchdown. The lineman takes a very low stance, usually a four-point stance with both arms on the ground. The submarine technique is particularly effective against wedge blocking.

On the snap, the rushman must come out very low and fire right at the offensive man's knees. He should not go any higher than the knees because if he does, he can be driven back. The prime objective is to create a big pileup right there, hoping the runner will run into the heavy congestion. Someone then will likely be able to react to him and prevent him from progressing.

Against certain opponents in specific instances, the lineman will find it effective to fake a high charge, then dive under his opponents. As the opposing player or players charge, they will invariably slide over the back of the rushman. He then raises himself up and is in position to make the tackle. Caution should be taken not to drop to the ground and stay there. The lineman must get his feet under him quickly so he is in position to rise after the initial charge.

### Slanting

Slanting is a maneuver used when the defensive line has picked up a frequency, a certain formation, and they are sure of the situation. The defensive line can be slanted one way or the other, and each man is given a definite hole responsibility. Slanting is employed when the defense expects a run, not a pass, and on the snap, the linemen hit their holes just as hard as they can.

We want the defensive line to get there quickly and disrupt the blocking pattern by the offensive team. Every man must execute his responsibility without hesitation. If he is right, it places him in tremendous pursuit of the play and, usually, he will come up with a loss.

### Going over the Top

This maneuver involves jumping over the two blockers. The lineman either goes over leapfrog fashion with one foot out in front and the other trailing, or he merely dives over headfirst. Of course, this maneuver is not restricted to linemen alone. Our linebackers sometimes use this when dogging to defeat a backfield man who blocks low.

A                    B

C                    D

**FIGURE 8-9.** *The stunt or loop is a quick-change maneuver performed by two defensive linemen in rushing a passer. Here, defensive end Deacon Jones steps to his right—to the inside—and Merlin Olsen, the Rams' defensive tackle, loops behind Jones, to the outside.*

### Defeating the Two-on-One Block

A common defensive mistake is trying to play both blockers. The defender should play either the lead man or the post, but not both. No one is strong enough to defeat two good blockers. Four types of maneuvers used against two offensive blockers are the split, the submarine (in short yardage situations), the limp leg, and the spin-out.

### STUNTING

Stunting by rushmen can be very effective if used intelligently and with moderation. Basically, stunting is exchanging responsibility with someone else. The most important factor in any stunt is to make sure the rushman does not get cut off. If he doesn't replace the man he is supposed to, the defense is vulnerable to a large gain and perhaps a score.

The stunt, or loop, is a quick-change

maneuver that Deacon Jones and Merlin Olsen perform to perfection. Just before the snap, Deacon steps to his right—to the inside—and Olsen loops behind Jones, to the outside. The two rushmen quickly change places, Jones going inside and Olsen, in protecting the now exposed flank, going outside.

By stunting, it is possible to upset the blocking patterns against the run or to spring someone loose to harass or sack the quarterback. Upsetting the running game, causes offensive blockers to begin to hesitate before coming off the line, thereby interfering with their timing and charge. However, stunting is not easy to perfect.

As the offense adjusts to the strengths of our defense, occasional stunts become very effective. This is particularly true if a team is trying to adjust with splits in the line. By doing this, they are weakening some area that we should take advantage of. The best example of defeating splits occurs when the offensive tackle has widened up because the defensive end is beating him outside. The end jumps inside and blows, with the defensive tackle then covering.

The defensive linemen should not stunt just to be stunting. They must have a definite reason or objective. Variations are many and change with various teams, so it is important that they determine the most effective stunts or proper adjustments. Above all, the complete defensive structure must be considered.

## TACKLING

Good technique in tackling is most essential in playing defensive football. Actually, the tackling procedure is similar to blocking, with the added advantage of using the hands and arms. Tackling skill is most dependent on balance, and this is acquired through flexing of the knees, keeping the head up, and distributing the weight evenly on the balls of the feet. In order to maintain a comfortable position, the feet must be spread. To be a deadly tackler, an individual must have an eagerness for contact and he must be proficient with either shoulder.

The type of tackle used by the defender depends on who is carrying the football. If there is a big strong runner coming at him, the tackler probably will hit him low. If the carrier has tremendous footwork, he might want to go high on him. If the offensive player is a real scatback, the tackler has to go high on him, or he might be faked out.

When a team is behind and has to catch up, gang tackling is a must. Even if a team is not behind, it should go for the football. The tackler might find it effective to come on in with one arm; while he is making sure he gets the runner down, he goes for the football. Besides the possibility of a fumble, he will give the runner some good punishment.

### Head-on Tackle

Every tackler must always have a target—this is a must! If a defensive lineman has a ball carrier coming straight on, he should "ram his head right in the midsection at that belt buckle." He will not get faked out if he rams it right in the belt buckle. He must keep his head up, his seat down, and his feet working. The feet should be spread, the back bent, and the arms out from the body. He should move toward the runner and keep his eyes focused on his midsection. The defender must be the aggressor and not wait for the runner. He must go right on into him as soon as he can get the shot. Contact should be made with the shoulder at the break of the hips and stomach. He should dip his shoulder just before contact. The head slips to the side of the ball carrier and remains snug against his ribs. As he makes

FIGURE 8-10. *Defensive linemen must be aggressive, alert, and mean. They must want to knock somebody down. Ron McDole (79) and Verlon Biggs (89) combine with linebacker Harold McLinton to bring down running back Leon Burns of the St. Louis Cardinals.*

contact, he should wrap his arms around the ball carrier and lock his hands behind him with a wristlock, and drive right on through him.

The tackler shouldn't stop there! He must dig his hardest at the moment of contact and continue to drive with short, choppy steps. He must try to carry the ball carrier at least 3 yards and drop him on his back with a driving thrust to the turf.

If the defender is going in belt high, sometimes he can cause a fumble. The ball carrier has the ball under his arms at the waist, and the tackler's helmet might go right at the ball.

When he faces a man head-on, the defender doesn't want the runner to fall for-

ward on him or to break through. So, he must stick that shoulder in his stomach and drive right on through him.

### Side Tackle

The key point in making a side tackle is to take the correct angle of pursuit and be under good body control. The right angle should always be in front of the ball carrier, and the defender should try to anticipate the route he might travel.

We want the head in front of the runner and then the defender should make a hard-driving shoulder tackle. As far as hitting him low or high, again, it depends on the ball carrier. But the important thing is to get the head in front of him because all the runners in our league are very powerful people, and if the tackler's head is behind the ball carrier, chances are he won't make the tackle. The side tackle is the defender's only means of wrapping his hands around the ball carrier. It's just too hard to get his arms around him if his head is behind him. Also, by getting his head in front of him and the goal line, he will be able to get his shoulder into better play and wrap his hands around him. The other way, the runner will probably break his tackle because the defender will never get one hand to the other for a lock.

The tackler should hit the ball carrier at the break of the hips. After contact is made, *the feet should continue to move in a driving motion through the target.* He then drives the runner into the ground.

### High Sideline Tackle

A high shoulder tackle may be used occasionally when the ball carrier has turned the end and is racing down the sidelines. The tackler must have proper balance and good angle on the runner and attempt to drive straight through him. But he must get his head in front of the runner. The tackler must give him a good enough shot, so that the runner will be knocked out of bounds.

In executing this tackle, the proper angle of pursuit is very important. The tackler usually moves in on a 45-degree angle from the line of scrimmage. His eyes should be focused on the runner's neck and shoulder area. He should strive to hit the runner with a strong forearm shoulder lift about shoulder high. The tackler's prime objective is to hit the ball carrier with a powerful lift action in order to send the runner off the ground and sprawling into the sideline.

## RECOVERING FUMBLES

Recovering fumbles is not accidental. The team getting the ball, invariably, is the team that is always after the ball. Recovery is dependent upon *alertness* and *speed.*

The ball is not picked up, but is scooped in. The player actually slides into the loose ball. The dive is low, dragging the hip close to the ground. A pocket is formed by the player's legs and body, and one hand and arm are extended to gather in the ball. The player must remember to scoop it with this extended hand and draw it into the pocket. To protect himself from the impact of other players, he should draw up his knees.

After scooping in the ball, most players find it advantageous to curl up, thus lessening the possibility of injury to the shoulder.

## THE PROPER MENTAL STANCE

The defensive lineman must believe that he can get out there and do the job. He has to want to get out there. I want to see a man raring to go before a game. During the week, I want to see him just itching to get to the game and to enjoy the warm-up and the game, as well as the accomplishments that go with it.

A coach must try to get a unit together who enjoy these different challenges—getting the quarterback, forcing fumbles, "sacking" the passer, and maintaining good pursuit. They must work very hard and be able to sustain the same level of work throughout the game. A football player has to have the stamina to go 60 minutes! *Every play is a big play!*

Most linemen are more effective if they can develop a sense of meanness, to be tough and ornery on the field. However, this mental stance cannot be achieved just by a pre-game pep talk. The conditioning of the mind has to take place throughout the week and on up to game time.

## PLAYING A RUN

The first objective in defensive line play is to get across the line of scrimmage, getting across with the feet as well as with the hands. Each man on the line is charged with an individual responsibility to protect the ground on which he stands or immediately in front of him. However, before he offers help to anyone else on the field, the lineman must first protect his own territory.

After protecting his own territory, the lineman then should go for the ball. A good rule is always to fight resistance. If a blocker is working on his inside, a lineman can be pretty certain the play is inside. Therefore, if he always fights in the direction of resistance, the defensive lineman will be going for the ball.

On the guard pulling to his own side, the "I" men might drive into a tackle on that side with a hand or forearm shiver.

An outside rushman should always assume a play is coming back his way even though the flow is away from him, unless he sees that the quarterback has the ball and is retreating to pass. The "O" men must remember they are the safety valves on all comeback plays.

FIGURE 8-11. *Sacking the quarterback offers a strong challenge to a defensive lineman. In this photograph, Verlon Biggs, the Redskins' huge rushman, is about to throw quarterback Tim Van Galder of the Cardinals to the ground.*

## PURSUIT

*Pursuit is the backbone of all great defensive teams.* I have never seen a great defensive team at any level of competition that didn't have great pursuit. Alert pursuing action of the defensive linemen can keep running and passing gains to a minimum of yardage. Relentless pursuit by eleven men can make up for weaknesses in other areas.

The correct "angle of pursuit" is the key problem. The player who moves along an incorrect pursuit angle will find himself removed from a possible tackle. A correct angle of pursuit will bring the player to or in

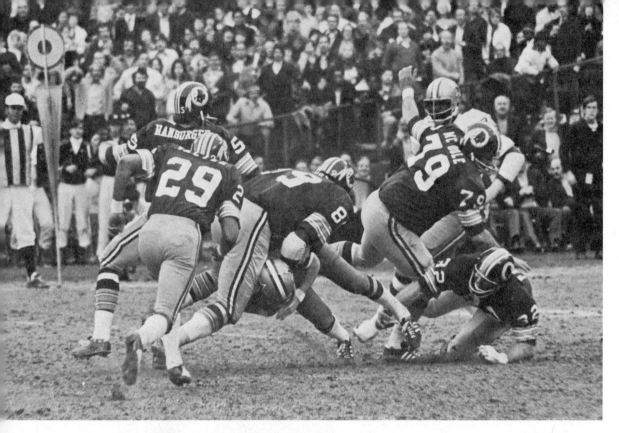

FIGURE 8-12. *Gang tackling and pursuit, a trademark of the Redskins' defense, can be demoralizing to any football team. A host of Washington Redskins, including Verlon Biggs (89), Jack Pardee (32), Ted Vactor (29), Chris Hanburger (55), and Ron McDole (79), combine to stop a ball carrier for the Dallas Cowboys.*

front of the ball carrier, not behind him. The best time to develop the correct angle is during practice while the offense is running plays.

The angle of pursuit depends upon the speed of the offensive players. The defensive lineman must consider his running speed in relation to the runner and the particular path he wants to follow to intercept the ball carrier. He should always stay one step behind the ball carrier while on the pursuit angle.

off to play screens, unless that is his specific assignment. However, if he senses a screen, he should be tough on the receiver and try to knock him down or off balance on his way to the passer. So, he must jam any potential receiver he can reach without going out of his path.

After rushing the passer successfully, outside linemen should look for screens their way. They must play the screen the instant the ball is thrown.

## PLAYING SCREENS

A defensive lineman cannot be an effective pass rusher and be thinking about dropping

## RUSHING THE PASSER

Rushing the passer is the most important part of defensive line play. *A team will do more rushing of the passer than any other single maneuver on defense.* Many coaches and players don't realize this.

The big "front four" have to get after that passer. Having a strong rush line cuts down the necessity of the blitz. Thus, the red dog can be a surprise move rather than an overused move that many teams have to make to get to the quarterback. But we rely on our "front four." They have one job: get the quarterback! Everything else is reaction. If there is a run, they react to a run, but they start off rushing the quarterback. That's my theory on rushing the passer and playing defense.

A pass rusher should concentrate on four points:

1. Line up as close as possible on the ball.
2. Have several possible moves in mind before taking a step.
3. When the center moves his hands, fire through.
4. Come in high, waving the arms to cut off the passer's view.

The down and distance will predetermine every move. On a second and 12 situation, a pass play is most probable. When the defensive lineman decides it is going to be a pass, he determines the type of rush he will employ. Defensive linemen should learn all the "pass giveaways" they can.

There are two basic types of pass blockers:

1. *Riders* The rusher sits back and waits for the defensive man to come to him. While he never hurts him, he still manages to screen him away from the passer.
2. *Fire and recoil* This type will fire out on a defender, then move back and set up for his first charge. Here, the pass rusher should wait for him to fire, then shoot the gap and let him have a limp leg. If he doesn't knock him down with his initial punch, the pass rusher tries to get by him before he recovers and can set up again.

When the offensive man recognizes the move of the defensive player, in most cases he will react a certain way. Usually, he will come right at the hand of the defender and perhaps duck his head. "Once he ducks his head, he has lost sight of you," said Marion Campbell, formerly the Rams' defensive line coach, "and that's to your advantage."

FIGURE 8-13. *A strong pass rush is the "best pass defense" in football. Verlon Biggs, the Redskins' defensive end, stretches high into the air to harass the quarterback. Biggs jumps high with his arms outstretched.*

## PASS RUSH TECHNIQUES

The most important skill that I want my defensive line coach to teach our rushmen is pass rushing techniques. They cannot get too much work on it. We want to start in training camp and go all through the season. We may even want to work on these techniques after practice. If the defensive line coach doesn't emphasize pass rushing techniques in our league, then he is missing the boat, and we are all missing the boat.

In our league, we live or die on our ability to rush the passer. And everybody can improve their pass rushing techniques, no matter how big or slow or strong, fast, or quick they are. This is something that isn't taught too much in high school or college because of the emphasis on the running game.

Pass rushing techniques are essential for any defensive lineman who hopes to stay in the league and make a career out of pro football. *The day of just stopping the run is over.*

1. *Step technique* This charge is used most effectively by defensive linemen. When the outside foot is back, the step charge is a jab step with the inside foot, as contact is made. The lineman should come out using his hands, taking a good hard swipe at the offensive lineman with as little lost motion and time as possible.
2. *Jet technique* The defensive lineman takes off as quickly as he can, low and aggressive, with strong arm and powerful leg drive. On the "jet technique," he drives through the pass protector any way he can. His weight should be forward to meet the block of the offensive guard or tackle. In addition, if he has enough weight forward, he will not be driven back or raised up too high by the pass protector. He must keep his eyes on the passer and not be so reckless that he takes himself out of the play if the passer decides to run or scramble.

3. *Arm raise* The rushman charges forward and, before making contact with the defender, lifts his right arm high into the air and over the head of his man. As he raises his arm, he pushes off his right foot to the outside of the defender. A good job of faking and quick footwork are necessary to ensure success.
4. *Sidestep technique* Linemen who are quick are continually using this technique. The lineman will feint a side step to one side and then quickly sidestep to the other. As the ball is snapped, he moves either foot about 6 inches to the side.

The initial charge must have the force to move the lineman attacked backward and to one side. To accomplish this, he takes his stance in front of the man he expects to sidestep.

In making the fake, the body need not be moved more than is necessary to draw the charge of the offensive lineman. It is similar to a basketball player faking with his head and stepping in one direction and then dribbling off in another direction.

*Playing two blockers.* A lineman should never try to overpower both opponents in front of him. One man at a time is difficult enough to lick. If he wants to play straight through, he must concentrate the force of his charge on one opponent rather than spread it over both. While he attacks one opponent, he must try to elude the other. It is important that the feet move across, causing the other lineman to miss. If he has executed the maneuver properly, he will find himself free and ready for the tackle.
5. *Spin out and spin in* The defensive lineman comes out of his stance and charges into the offensive blocker. He uses a forearm lift, aiming his thrust under the chest to lift up the blocker. After making his initial charge to the outside of the blocker, the rushman makes a quick pivot of his forward (right) foot and spins around in a reverse action to the inside lane of the offensive lineman. This maneuver must be done quickly and should be preceded by a hard straight shoulder charge. The defensive lineman must come out of the reverse spin maneuver down low, on balance, and ready to move in any direction. Although alert and primed for a running play, he will continue his charge and

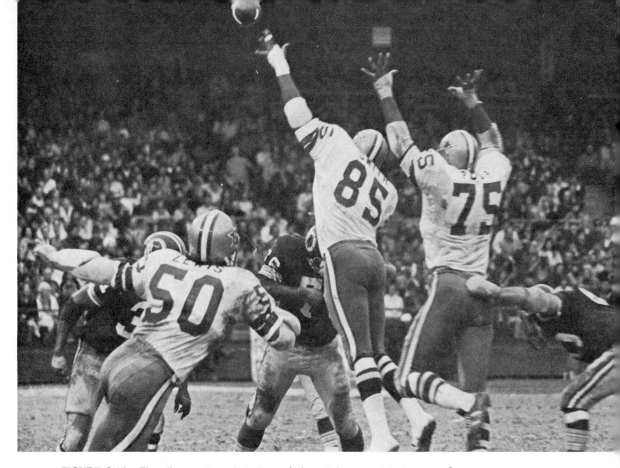

FIGURE 8-14. *The all-out pass rush is the pro's beat defense against the pass. Constant pressure by the Dallas Cowboys' rushmen makes Bill Kilmer throw the ball earlier than he would like. This type of defensive play can result in interceptions and become the difference between winning and losing.*

put pressure on the quarterback if a passing situation shapes up.

6. *Head fake* A head fake is also effective in rushing the passer. The defensive lineman shouldn't drive straight in all the time. When he comes up on the line of scrimmage, he can make a quick head fake to one side and take off on the other side. When he does this, he should reach with his hands and grab his opponent's shoulder and pull him in the direction that he is facing. To do this, he has to have good speed. He can set up these different moves and then come back with something else, something the pass blocker isn't expecting.

7. *Shoulder dip technique* This is the technique used by the defensive ends. Some outside linemen find the shoulder dip highly effective in rushing the passer. However, it has to be used when the offensive tackle has been set up for it.

The defensive end explodes off the ball, dipping his inside shoulder low and hard, allowing the offensive tackle less blocking area for contact. He aims directly at the point where he expects the quarterback to set up for the pass.

8. *Loose leg technique* This technique is more effective for the "I" men. The rushman dangles

the leg at the offensive man and as the blocker makes contact with that leg, he loosens it and allows the leg to accept a portion of a block. Then he proceeds aggressively after the passer.

Most good defensive linemen perform this technique without actually realizing it. Players who use the loose leg technique are extremely quick. They are so quick with their feet and legs that they drive one leg into a man and then take that leg away.

All these pass rush techniques have to be practiced, day after day, all season long. We expect every lineman to know the down, distance, score, and time remaining, as well as the formations.

## PENETRATION

Every move a defensive lineman makes has to be penetration. He cannot make a lateral step one way and go in the other direction because the guard is already set up there, 1 to 1½ yards, and he is waiting while the defensive man is doing all this. The rushman has just so much time to get to that quarterback; therefore, he must make sure that he makes every move with his foot across or in the direction of the quarterback. "If you come across the line of scrimmage," said Campbell, "you will make the offensive man drop back another step. When you come back the other way, he will drop back another step, putting you closer to the quarterback."

The rushman should try to get his man on the run. Also, he has to recognize the depth he sets up. If he is setting up short, he should use one technique. If he is dropping back, he should use another.

Sometimes the defensive tackle will fake to the inside, grab the blocker quickly, and then cut to the outside. However, the inside move is the best for most linemen, and it is the quickest path to the passer.

If two protectors set up to take him, the rusher should go through the outside man. If two protectors set up wide, he should go for the inside one, then change his course and drive over the outside one. This will diminish the chances of the good roll-out quarterback's taking off to the outside.

If the protector likes to throw a body block, the rushman should veer more toward the middle so that he has to throw his block quickly. Then, he will have an easy path to the passer. If an offensive back attempts to block him, he must not fade. He should drive over him and then veer off his outside.

The quarterback run threat should be disregarded against a quarterback who rarely runs with the ball. Instead, the rushman should do everything possible to hurry the passer or prevent the pass from being thrown. Quarterbacks should not be tackled low or around the waist or chest. If he is close enough, the pass rusher should come down with his outstretched arms on top of the quarterback's shoulders and passing arm. If he isn't close enough for that, he should get in the line of the throw and jump as high as possible with his arms outstretched and waving. The quarterback should be forced to throw high over the rushman or around him.

## THE GOAL LINE STAND

In professional football, the most widely used goal line defense is the 6-1, with everyone pinching to the inside. We also remove our linebackers and use a 6-1 jumble by substituting two rushmen for the linebackers. There are many other good goal line defenses, but this is what we prefer at the present time.

All goal line defenses have one thing in common—*penetration*. The defense must penetrate into their opponents' side of the line of scrimmage. Pursuit is not of much value. Penetration is not easy to achieve because most goal line offenses tend to close down; then the defense must apply leverage. The front line must not only drive for penetration but must drive lower than the blockers on the offensive line. This action creates piles, and more running backs are stopped by their own linemen than by any other method.

## EIGHT DUMB WAYS TO GET CLOBBERED ON DEFENSE

Every year in training camp, I go over these eight ways to lose on defense. I want my players aware of these critical errors. While there are a lot of ways to get beaten, these are the critical ones and seem to be the most popular:

1. Don't play the defense in the huddle.
2. GUESS where your coverage is. GUESS what type of pattern your man is going to run.
3. When rushing the passer, STOP when you are blocked. Hope the pass will be complete.

4. STOP PURSUING because you expect someone else to make the tackle.
5. JUMP OFF SIDE, or LINE UP OFF SIDE, and give your opponents an easy 5 yards to keep their drive going.
6. FOUL YOUR OPPONENTS when they are giving you the football. The best ways are holding, pass interference, etc. These are unnecessary penalties.
7. BE GUILTY OF A MENTAL MISTAKE. The best way is by not knowing, or not understanding, your assignment in the defense. The defense breaks down because of mental errors.
8. LOSE YOUR POISE AND START A FIGHT, and get kicked out of the ball game. Not only do we get a 15-yard penalty, but we also lose a regular player. You don't have to take anything from your opponent, but remember that the player who retaliates is always the "one who gets caught."

Every season more and more defensive players are getting themselves and their team in trouble because of the above violations. If a player ever catches himself doing any of these dumb things, he should *stop* in a hurry, because his team could lose a ball game through his stupidity. A player should check himself after each game and see if he is guilty of any of these errors.

## DRILLS

Generally, defensive techniques are first taught in a single dummy situation. We then go to the blocking sled and individual scrimmage drills. Next, we come to the 7-on-7 drills for pass offense and pass defense, running offense and defense. Finally, we work together as a team in 11-on-11 dummy and 11-on-11 scrimmage situations.

Working in 1-on-1, 2-on-1, and 3-on-1 situations, the defensive lineman must destroy the offensive charge and react to the ball. He must beat the man who is trying to turn him and keep him away from his body.

On defense, our drills emphasize exploding, controlling a blocker, reacting to the ball or a man, pursuing, and tackling. In addition to enthusiasm, we emphasize such key points as balance, quickness, and alertness.

Some of the most popular defensive drills follow.

1. *Stance*  With a ball placed on a yard line, the defensive front men are spaced normally off the ball. A second unit is waiting behind them. When a coach or manager puts his hands on the ball, the defensive front men move into their stance. When the ball is pulled, they charge forward a few yards.

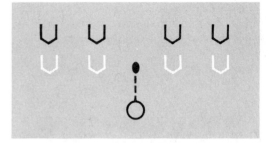

DIAGRAM 8-1.  *Stance drill.*

2. *First step*  A defensive lineman's first step is most important since it is also a hitting step. Contact is usually made on the first step. This first step should be practiced often against a sled, dummy, shiver board, or another player.

    The interior linemen can be divided into single lines of five each. The first man in line should turn around and face the next man in line and get down on all fours. Each man in line will come up, one at a time, and execute his stance and fire forward one step, striking a blow either with his "flipper" or hand shiver.

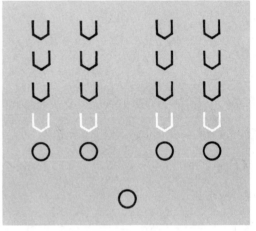

DIAGRAM 8-2.  *First step.*

3. *Reaction*  Since defense involves reaction to the offense's action, the coach should run his defensive linemen through many reaction drills. Most of them can be done by all defensive players.

    Since defensive linemen must be able to "read" blockers, a one-on-one setup can be used at about half speed. The offensive blocker is controlled by the coach, who is positioned behind the defensive lineman. Arm and hand signals can be used by the coach to indicate a reach block, pull, turn-out, down or trap block, or pass block. The defensive man will then react with an appropriate action.

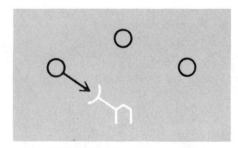

DIAGRAM 8-3.  *Reaction drill.*

The *half circle drill* is one of the favorite Redskin drills used to teach reaction. A defensive lineman can be placed in front of three blockers, who are numbered 1, 2, and 3. On a signal, the defender moves into a hitting position and quickly moves his feet in place. The coach will then call out any number between 1 and 3. The blocker whose number is called moves forward quickly and sticks a shoulder at the defender. The defender steps into the blocker and strikes a shoulder flipper blow and bounces back into position. The coach quickly calls another number, and so on.

Defensive linemen should be taken daily to the big seven-man sled and lined up single file. The first man in line starts out by hitting the first upright with a two-hand shiver and will hit every other upright when rolling.

*Two-on-one* A defensive lineman is placed in front of two blockers. Positioned behind the defender, the coach gives hand signals to the blockers. The defender reacts to defeat each type of situation, such as a single block, down block, pass block, double-team, or trap block. Later, the defensive lineman can engage in three-on-one and four-on-one drills.

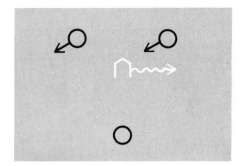

DIAGRAM 8-4. *Two-on-one drill.*

4. *Pass rush drill* This individual drill is a one-on-one situation in which the defensive man executes his pass rush techniques. The rusher must fight through two or even three blockers to get to the passer.

A pile of bell dummies can be used for pass rushers to blast through. Two men, holding air dummies, hit the defensive man in the head or stomach while he is coming through.

5. *Pursuit drill* A defender should be instructed to hit a dummy or stationary blocker and then take the proper pursuit angle to a ball carrier. The ball carrier runs inside and outside either way, cutting back occasionally. This is an excellent drill to teach a defender how to run laterally with his shoulders square to the line of scrimmage.

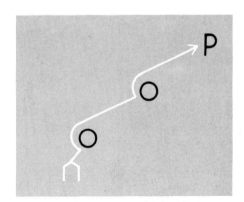

DIAGRAM 8-5. *Pass rush drill.*

6. *Tackling drills* A line of ball carriers face a line of tacklers. The lead ball carrier runs about half speed at a 45-degree angle from the tackler. As the runner approaches him, the tackler lifts the runner up by clasping behind his legs and carries him back 5 yards. The ball carrier is not put on the ground.

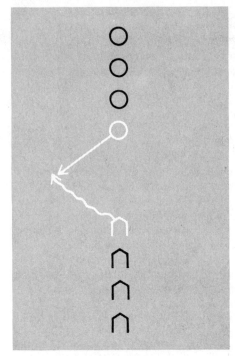

DIAGRAM 8-6. *Dummy position drill.*

Tackling should also be drilled in the open field. Two chalk lines 3 yards apart and about 10 yards long can be used (see Diagram 4-4).

7. *Open-field butt drill* The defensive man delivers a blow into the runner's numbers. Facing a defender about 4 yards apart, a ball carrier starts toward a marker and the defender and then breaks at a 45-degree angle to his left or right. The defender will try to deliver a butt blow with his forehead into the runner's numbers.

8. *Bull in the ring* Five or six players form a circle around the defensive man. The coach yells a number and that man charges into the center to hit the defender. The drill teaches a defensive man to explode on a blocker, to strike out rather than receive, and to retain balance while getting rid of the blockers.

9. *Explosion drill* A fine drill for the tackles and the middle guard is the explosion and pursuit drill. From a four-point stance, the defensive man explodes into the sled with his forearm and shoulder, leaving his legs behind him. After practicing the explosion follow-up (bringing up feet in quick "one-two" succession), the defender will explode and pursue a ball carrier who is stationed behind the sled.

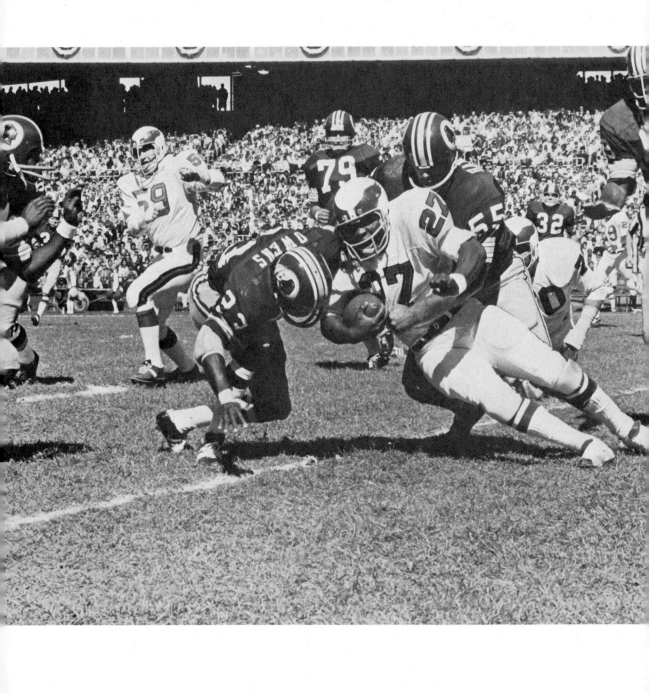

# 9

# Linebacking

Good linebackers have been a major factor in the success of the great defensive teams of the National Football League. In fact, the linebackers are vital in the defensive unit of every football team.

In my opinion, linebacking is one of the most difficult positions to play in football. A lineman must worry about stopping runs, while a defensive back has to think primarily of pass coverage. The linebacker is responsible for stopping both runs and passes. This means he has to be quick, rugged, and a sure tackler. His decisions and reactions to play situations must be made without hesitation, whereas a deep back has time to "read" the receivers.

Generally, I prefer that one of the linebackers act as the defensive general. Therefore, linebackers must possess strong leadership qualities.

While coaches in the past have selected linebackers primarily because of their ability to defend against the running game, I prefer to select our linebackers because of their pass coverage. I'll sacrifice something on the running game to stop the passing game.

## QUALIFICATIONS

The linebacker has to be the best all-round athlete on the defensive team. He has to be fast enough to cover passes and strong enough and big enough to stop runs. I look for a player who is about 6'2" and 225 pounds. I feel this size is just about right for an outside linebacker. Now, if he is not that big, he can still play for us and do a good job. If he is a little larger, like Dave Robinson of the Redskins, that's all right, too. The middle linebacker should weigh about 245, and a height of 6'3" is ideal.

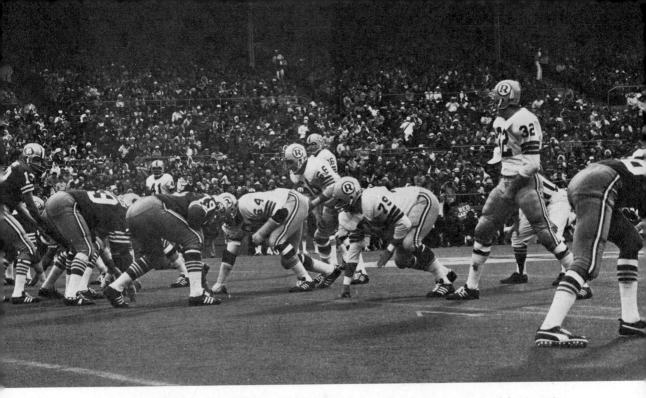

FIGURE 9-2. *The linebackers, for most football teams, are key men in the defensive unit. They have to be fast enough to cover passes and big enough and strong enough to stop runs. Linebackers are tough and aggressive defensive specialists who enjoy the thrill of knocking someone down. Above all, they must have an instinct for the ball—pass or run.*

Anyone who plays in the secondary, whether a linebacker or a deep back, must have quick feet. He must be able to start quickly, whether he is red-dogging or coming out of his coverage or getting into his hook spots. He should have "first-step quickness." He must be quick in moving laterally, forward, or backward with his first few steps. This is why I feel the linebacker should have the footwork of a boxer.

Another qualification of a good linebacker is instinct, the knack of sensing plays. We prefer to call it "instantaneous reaction and recognition." They always seem to know that play is coming and where it is going. Many linebackers seem to have this instinct the minute they walk on the field, but this sensory skill can be developed and does come with experience by watching the same thing over and over. On the other hand, the linebacker should not commit himself too soon.

The middle linebacker has to be agile enough to drop back for passes. He also must have good pursuit from inside out. He has to be sturdy because generally he is facing bigger blockers than the outside linebackers. He is usually fighting off a center, guard, or tackle, sometimes two people. This is why we prefer a bigger man. He must also have the strong hands and arms to shed blockers rapidly and reach the ball as quickly as possible. In addition, he has to have the quickness to rush the passer. This is usually a shortcoming in most middle linebackers.

In short, the linebacker must have a strong desire for physical contact. He must be physically tough enough to be knocked down and get up and knock someone else down.

## STANCE

Before he learns any of the many technical skills of his position, the linebacker must perfect the correct stance. As he waits for the play to develop, the linebacker is low and in a poised position. His feet are staggered, as wide apart as his shoulders, and the inside foot should be forward. The outside foot is kept back to enable him to move without being cut off by some blocker on his side. He is balanced, with his weight on the balls of his feet. His hands and arms are low enough so that he can shoot them forcefully into the

FIGURE 9-4. Diagnosing plays. The linebacker must be able to diagnose plays quickly. He must be decisive, aggressive, and hardnosed. Quickness is more important than long-range speed for a linebacker. Linebackers such as Dave Robinson (89) are large enough and strong enough to shed blockers.

FIGURE 9-3. Stance. The linebacker (here, Harold McLinton) is low and in a poised position. The feet are staggered, shoulder width apart. The knees are flexed and the weight is forward. He should have the footwork of a boxer.

first blocker. They are hanging loosely along the side of his body with the fists clenched, ready to strike a blow at the proper time.

The outside backer generally is playing on a tight end, about half the game. Since his man is only 12 to 18 inches away from him, he can get to him very quickly. Therefore, the linebacker has to be ready for the block immediately.

As the ball is snapped, the linebacker takes a short jab step forward, from 6 to 8 inches, with his inside foot. This action places the feet in a heel-instep or heel-toe position. With the toes pointing straight ahead, the knees should be pointed straight ahead and

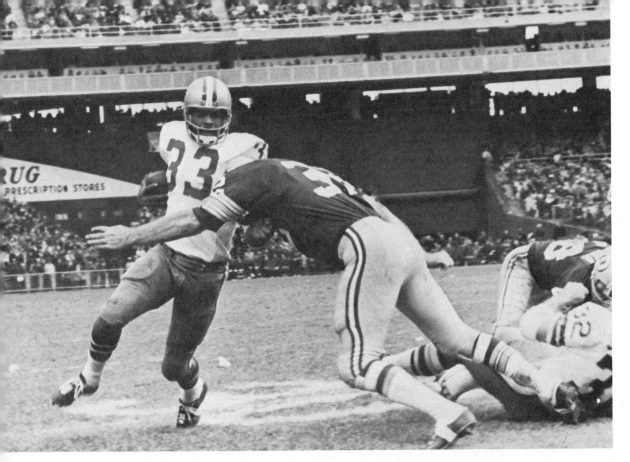

FIGURE 9-5. *The outside linebackers become defensive ends against running plays and defensive halfbacks against the pass. They must have the speed to shut off the end sweep. The ability to move quickly is extremely important, whether they are red-dogging, coming out of their coverage, or getting to their "hook spots." Above, Jack Pardee diagnoses the play instantly and moves up quickly to make the tackle.*

bent slightly. The hips are flexed, with the body crouched slightly in a comfortable position.

## USE OF THE HANDS

No player uses his hands more effectively in pro ball than the outside linebacker. The linebacker must keep opposing blockers away from his body. If he allows a blocker to get into his body, whether he is blocked completely out of the play or not, he is going to get tied up for a second, a second and a half, or longer, on a well-timed play. By that time, the offensive team has the runner through the hole, and it is a matter of chasing him until they catch up with him.

So, we try to work with the shoulder, forearm, or hand shiver to get the blocker away from the linebacker. He might give a little ground but must not be completely taken out of the play. We use the defensive reactor in training camp and try to work on it once a day.

The type of block will determine how the linebacker will try to offset the maneuver. If it is a very low, hard-driving block, sometimes it is easier just to shove the man right on down to the ground. However, if the blocker is coming in waist high, the linebacker may be able to get up under him, raise him up, and make him lose his balance so that he has no more driving power. If the block is high, then the hands alone might take care of it. So, the situation that confronts a linebacker will often dictate how he has to play the block.

## Hand Shiver

The hand shiver is done with the heel of the hand. The linebacker should whack the helmet with the heel of his hand where he gets more power. Naturally, it doesn't always affect a big man, but if he can hit him with a lifting blow and if he is high enough, he can straighten him up and stop his momentum.

## Forearm Shiver

If the blocker is at a spot where he cannot get under him or knock him down, then the linebacker has to use slightly more strength in taking on the block. This is where we use the forearm. The forearm shiver is the most common tactic used in playing off the block. Many linebackers are not strong enough in the arms to stop a blocker with the hands alone.

Our linebackers on the Redskins really are not big people. They are very active with their hands, and they can often be seen using their forearm and the shoulder pad to take on the block. Actually, we work on the hands and wrists every day in camp and try to use the reaction machine at least once a week during the season.

## RESPONSIBILITIES OF LINEBACKERS

A linebacker must remember that he has a job to do on every defensive play regardless of whether the opponents choose to run or pass. If he follows instructions, he should be a factor in almost every play.

### Strong Side

The first responsibility of a strong side linebacker is a running play outside the "O" man. His second responsibility is buzzing to the out-zone, and he must watch the passer as he does it.

On sure passing downs, he should line up deeper and wider for pass defense, unless the defense calls for him to jam a receiver or to red-dog.

### Weak Side

The first responsibility of a weak side linebacker is a running play inside or outside of his "O" man. His second responsibility is buzzing to the out-zone on his side on passes. Keeping his eyes on the passer, he should run backward at an angle.

Receivers must be kept from getting deep downfield, so the linebacker must prevent them from doing so by bouncing, grabbing, or shoving them. The linebacker must never let a screen get outside of him.

### Getting to the Point of Attack

The linebacker usually lines up as close to his "O" man as he can without being "hooked" or "turned in." The distance will vary according to the defense called and the formation used by the opponents.

FIGURE 9-6. *Lateral mobility. The middle linebackers in pro football are always moving laterally with force at an angle into the hole. Middle linebackers patrol the tackle-to-tackle area, tackling anyone who tries to get through. Above, linebacker Myron Pottios moves quickly to his right to stop running back Ed Podolak of the Kansas City Chiefs.*

Taking a medium, controlled stride with his inside foot, he moves to his point of attack, which is right behind the offensive line of scrimmage. He must be low when he reaches this point and he should not rise on his first step.

The more quickly he can get to his point of attack, the more quickly he can start his next movement.

### Meeting Inside Plays

The success of stopping the play will depend on how quickly the linebacker can get to the point of attack and his quickness in play diagnosis. This will come with study and experience.

Keeping low and closing his inside foot quickly, he goes to meet the blocker. He plays through the blocker and keeps his feet moving as he makes contact. On trap plays, he should strike a low, lifting body blow on the trapper. It is important that he see the ball carrier as he plays the blocker.

On inside plays away from his area, when either the fullback or the halfback goes up the middle, the linebacker must hold his ground until he sees the ball. We want him to take a pursuit angle where he will be a

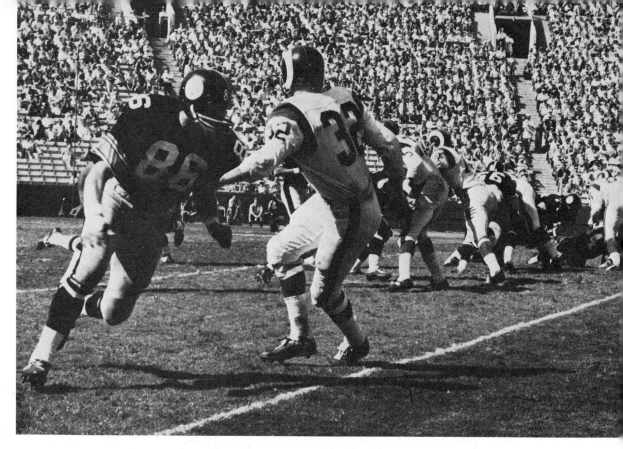

**FIGURE 9-7.** *Looking through the quarterback. In covering a receiver, the linebacker must never turn his back on the quarterback. As he retreats in his pass coverage, Jack Pardee, shown here, is always looking through the quarterback.*

factor in the play. By going too deep behind the offensive line and chasing the play, the linebacker eliminates his chances of making the tackle.

### Meeting Outside Plays

Again, the linebacker must be completely under control at the point of attack. He must not allow himself to be hooked in *at* or *near* the point by one blocker. We tell our linebackers we cannot afford to trade one for one.

The linebacker must not anticipate the outside path of a ball carrier. He should close the inside first. He doesn't want to change his direction until he actually sees the ball and the ball carrier outside him. Then, he should go out laterally and get in position to make the tackle if the runner delays or cuts back.

Once he is certain he sees the ball, he must be sure not to be outside the ball carrier. He should play off blockers and prevent all runners from cutting back inside him. He should try to force the runner and blockers as deep as possible so that his teammates have a chance in the pursuit, but he doesn't want to open the gate between his position and that of his "O" man.

In defending against an outside play, the linebacker must make the tackle if he can,

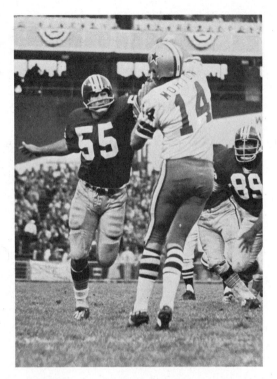

FIGURE 9-8. *Red dog. Reacting on the snap of the ball, the linebacker must take off as if "shot out of a cannon." Here, alert linebacker Chris Hanburger (55) puts strong pressure on quarterback Craig Morton, forcing him to get rid of the ball. The blitz is usually called in a passing situation, and the rest of the defensive unit must try to compensate for the loss of a pass defender.*

When he is sure the flow of the backs is away from him, and there is no back in position to execute a counter play, the linebacker must not chase the play to the opposite flank behind the offensive line. He might "slink" behind his own line, but he must always expect a counter play. He has to make sure the play is not coming back to his side before he "slinks" behind his own line to cut off the runner. As long as there is a near back on his side, whether strong side or weak side, he must be cautious when leaving his spot.

## DEFENSIVE TECHNIQUES

In carrying out his responsibilities, the linebacker employs the following defensive techniques: red dog, drop, buzz, and window dressing.

### Red Dog

The red dog, or blitz, can be a valuable part of any defense. When he goes in too often, the linebacker leaves himself open for a long gainer, but we "dog" just enough to keep them honest. We particularly like to "dog" when opponents don't expect it. With our strong "front four," however, we don't have to blitz very often.

As the quarterback yells out the signals, the linebacker has to be very careful not to tip off the fact that he is going to red-dog. Quarterbacks are sharp people, and they look for it from the way a man lines up. If one hand is quivering, a quarterback might pick this up. If he anticipates a red dog, he will probably change his play and get himself some protection. Or, he will change to a running play which will take advantage of the red dog situation.

If a team has the balance and can get

but he shouldn't go around any blockers to do it. He should always keep his hands in front of him to ward off blockers, and good footwork will help him avoid them.

On wide plays, he must not crash his way over blockers because the play will likely be too far past him by the time he gets himself under control.

On quick tosses, in which the ball is immediately exposed, he must change his normal tactics by taking a direct line out to where he can meet the runner from the outside.

|     |     |     |     |
| :-: | :-: | :-: | :-: |
| **A** | **B** | **C** | **D** |

*FIGURE 9-9.  Drop technique. The linebacker must get back to an outside area or hook area as quickly as possible but never turn his back on the ball. In this series, Pat Fischer uses a crossover with his inside foot as he moves quickly to a zone and to get himself set.*

the good pass rush with their front four, a linebacker does not have to red-dog, thereby placing much less pressure on the deep secondary. No pass defender in football can continually cover speedsters if the quarterback has a long time to throw the ball.

We try to teach our linebackers to try to fool the quarterback. We do not let him know when we are coming and, conversely, we try to have him think we are coming when we are not. So, a linebacker must not tip off the red dog unless the quarterback has completed his audible system. He has the signal caller in a spot when he cannot audible, and the quarterback is stuck with the play that he has called. Maybe, then, he can step into a hole in the line where he can get to him a little more quickly.

## Drop Technique

We use the term "buzz" when our linebackers go to a certain area, whether it be an outside area or hook area. It is extremely important for them to get back there as fast as possible and still see everything that is going on. This technique is particularly effective in playing against the screens and draws.

From pretty much a parallel stance, our linebackers generally use a crossover step. The linebackers' feet are nearly parallel, and as soon as the linebackers have diagnosed a pass, they use a crossover with the inside foot if they want to go out.

Keeping his eye on the passer, the linebacker must get to the area he has to protect as quickly as possible and get himself set.

C                          B                          A

FIGURE 9-10. *Buzz versus pass. In his coverage against the forward pass, the linebacker must never turn his back on the quarterback. He will get many more interceptions if he develops this practice. Above, Mike Bass uses a crossover with his inside foot as he moves quickly to a hook zone. After he reaches his responsibility, he settles in a balanced stance so he can react quickly in any direction.*

Once he approaches this area, he must settle himself in a balanced stance so he can quickly move laterally, forward, or backward instead of just continuing his running.

### Buzz versus Pass

A buzz is actually the coverage of linebackers against the forward pass, getting them out into the hook zones and into the flat zones, getting into those covered spots that the quarterback does not expect them to be in when he is running certain plays.

The buzz, for example, is quite effective against a button-hook type pass. One of the linebackers will call defenses that will be most advantageous to us in getting a linebacker directly in the line of flight of the ball for that hook pass. He can either pick it off

or, if it is complete, he can help punish the receiver so he does not want to catch the ball anymore.

When covering, a linebacker must never turn his back on the quarterback. He will get many more interceptions if he develops this practice. The faster he can get back, the more time he will have to recover and play the ball. So, he should always look through the quarterback as he retreats in his coverage. The deep backs will communicate with him on two calls: "In, In, In," and "Out, Out, Out." The linebacker must also do his share of talking to help them. When he loses sight of the ball, he should stay at home.

The opposing team can be punished much more on defense, so a defender should punish a receiver every pass he catches. He must want to make him cautious the next time he tries to receive a pass.

### Window-dressing

We like our linebackers to do a lot of "window-dressing," in which they jump in and out of the line of scrimmage. We want the offense to look at a defense they are not going to see when the play develops.

## PLAY RECOGNITION

Linebackers must read their keys quickly and effectively. Keys tell them the direction and nature of the play. Never should a linebacker hesitate on defense! Sometimes he will have to act without thinking and without hesitation. If a player hesitates on defense, even for a second, he will be in trouble.

The linebacker must never commit himself until he knows where the ball is. If he does not know where the ball is, he must not move. By playing keys, he usually knows where the ball is. The keys usually go through a triangle from the center on out—the center, quarterback, two guards, and the fullback. He watches which way the guards are going and the way the fullback is leading in.

Other mannerisms that linebackers watch for are the following:

1. Leaning by linemen or backs
2. Staggered position of the quarterback
3. Backs cheating up or back
4. Double-team blocking
5. Splits taken by linemen
6. Adjusting of hands or feet by linemen
7. Quarterback wetting his fingers

FIGURE 9-11. *Pass coverage. Jack Pardee (32), corner linebacker, covers halfback Calvin Hill (35) of the Cowboys on a deep pattern. Executing one of the linebacker's toughest jobs, Jack is in a good position to knock the ball away. In covering a receiver, the defender must never turn his back on the quarterback. As he retreats in his coverage, he is always looking through the quarterback.*

### JAMMING THE RECEIVER

By jamming, the linebacker is trying to hold up a potential pass receiver. By staying with him as he goes along, he can delay his progress down the field. He can either push

him out or let him get by and kind of give him a pull. He can sometimes shove the receiver to the ground. Or, he can "chop him down" the minute the receiver releases.

Our linebackers must be tough because we don't like to see these receivers get out where they can hurt us. Their timing into

A                                    B                                    C

FIGURE 9-12. *Jamming the receiver. When the end is tight, the outside linebacker gener-*
*ally plays him head on and tries to chuck the receiver, jamming or slowing him down.*
*Linebacker Ken Stone shoots for the pads or up under the pads. He tries to get wide receiver*
*Harold Carmichael straightened up so he will lose some of his momentum and speed.*

their pass pattern must somehow be thrown off, whether it means knocking them down, holding them up, or jamming them.

Many times the receiver, in an effort to give himself some space to get a better release, splits out about 2 or 3 yards. Now, he has a two-way go on the linebacker, and it does make it difficult for the linebacker to jam him. It is very hard to hold up a man if he takes a wide release or splits out 3 or 4 yards. In this situation, we like for the linebacker to jam the man vigorously with his hands and, if possible, try to straighten him up.

The running procedure for any runner is a leaning forward motion. He is faster this way. So, if we can straighten the man up, he cannot run quite as fast. The rule says that we can jam him as long as we keep him between us and the ball. Once he gets beside us or behind us, then the hands must be off. The defender cannot do anything more. He cannot trip the man or grab his shirt, or

anything like that. So, it all has to be done as he starts his release. The man must be controlled quickly.

A new NFL rule change has restricted the extent of downfield contact (bump and run) that a defender is permitted to have with eligible receivers on pass plays only. Beyond 3 yards downfield, a defender may hit a receiver only once. An infraction draws a penalty of 5 yards and a first down.

On certain defenses, the No. 1 Sin for a corner linebacker is to let the tight end get an inside release. On many occasions the safety man, who is playing behind the outside linebacker, is positioned a little to the outside of the tight end. If the tight end gets a free inside release, the quarterback merely has to toss the ball 3 or 4 yards to get it to him, and the safety cannot recover quickly enough to knock the ball away before it is caught. So, the corner linebacker has to slow down that tight end on his inside release until our safety adjusts, if it is necessary.

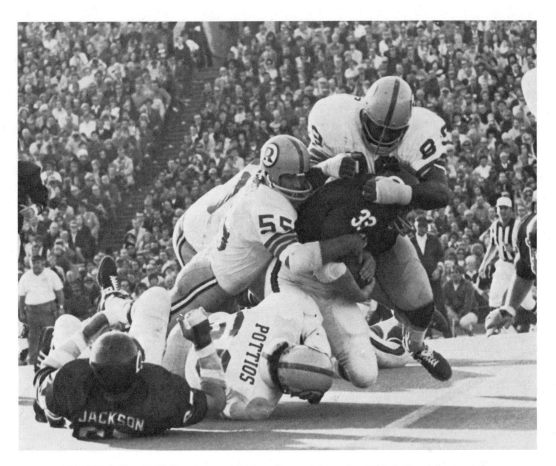

FIGURE 9-13. *We believe in attacking an offense and manhandling it. The defensive team must think aggressively to be savage and ruthless in tackling. They must let the offense know that they are there.* Punish them! *Here, linebackers Chris Hanburger (55) and Myron Pottios (66), along with Verlon Biggs (89), swarm all over running back Gary Kosins (33) of the Chicago Bears.*

## TACKLING

A linebacker has more opportunities to tackle than any other man on the football team. Therefore, he must work on his tackling technique at every opportunity. Actually, 90 percent of being a good tackler is having the determination and desire to really smash into an opposing ball carrier. A good, hard tackle can give a team a real lift. Jolting tackles can also slow down the opposition.

The secret in tackling is: always have a target and keep your eyes open. "I try to hit him in the thighs or the knees," said Maxie Baughan, who played for me with the Rams. "Drive upward hard. Do not go to your knees. On hitches, hooks, curls, and all short passes, hit the receivers hard. You want to jar him loose from the ball."

Smaller linebackers, when tackling big backs, should hit them low. A big, strong linebacker like Dave Robinson can always hit high and overpower the runner.

If a receiver catches a pass in front of

him, the linebacker must tackle him hard enough so that the next time he comes out he will be cautious.

On an inside tackle where a ball carrier is coming through a hole, although the linebacker has some lateral restrictions which confine his movement, he must make a good solid hit either with the shoulder or with his helmet. Above all, he must never take for granted a man is tackled.

### Open-field Tackling

When tackling in the open field, the linebacker *must be sure!* He has to take hold of the runner and bring him down because if he misses, more than likely, it will be a touchdown. Here, the tackle is higher and not quite so aggressive, but it is a sure tackle.

In teaching tackling technique, there are several points that the coaching staff stresses on the Redskins' practice field. In fact, I imagine the players sometimes hear these instructions in their sleep. A tackler must secure a good base since he cannot tackle with his feet together. We emphasize the "good explosion," getting enough "pop" into the tackle to stop the ball carrier's momentum. Regarding the arms, we continually scream: "Lock up, lock up!" When they get the arms around, we urge them to get a good lock on the other arm behind the man and keep their feet apart. If they cannot get the good lock, however, there is the "squeeze tightly!" grabbing hold of some part of the man's shirt or pants.

"Lock up" means for the tackler to squeeze as tightly as possible and pull the man's legs into his chest. If he has hit his man with a good lifting motion, he can take his man right up off the ground. He cannot run very well with his legs locked up against his chest. Now, the tackler must pin him down and drive him into the ground. He must keep after it!

## PLAYING A SCREEN

We want our linebackers to turn that screen in. In other words, just as quickly as they see the screen coming, they must commit themselves to the screen, in terms of getting it turned in. If the linebacker blows through the gap and gets picked off and the screen man gets outside, then all of our interior people, about eight or nine players who probably are chasing this screen, will have to run anywhere from 10 to 20 yards farther before they ever get to the ball carrier.

The screen situation is very similar to the sweep, except that it is delayed. It must be turned in to those people who are coming on pursuit angles.

## DEFENSIVE SIGNALS

Verbal signals are the principal means of calling and controlling defensive formations and movements. Defensive signals are, as far as possible, made up of easily heard and readily distinguishable numbers, letters, words, and expressions.

Signals are composed of two-digit numbers, letters, names, and expressions. They frequently contain three parts: one primarily for the rushmen, one for the linebackers, and one for the deep backs. Although each of these defensive groups is controlled separately by its own part or parts of such signals, quite frequently one signal instructs all three groups.

The defense must be able to *recognize* and *identify instantly* what formations and maneuvers the offense is using. Then, the defensive players must be able to *communicate* with one another easily, accurately, and rapidly what they observe. This ability is of the utmost importance in helping the de-

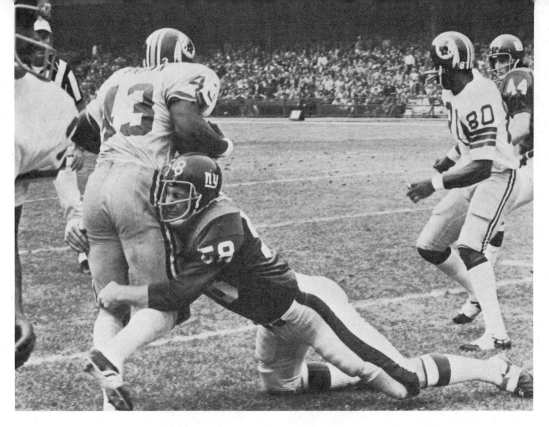

FIGURE 9-14. *A skillful tackler is what a linebacker must become, because of the many key tackles he is called upon to make. He often must defend against a good ball carrier in the open field in a one-on-one situation. Above, linebacker Jim Files of the New York Giants demonstrates tackling technique in bringing down Larry Brown (43) of the Redskins. Observe that Files gets down low and locks his arms around the legs of the ball carrier. However, it is better to keep the knees off the ground to insure leg drive. Below, linebacker Steve Nelson of the Patriots executes a vicious, hard-driving tackle in stopping running back Clarence Davis of the Raiders.*

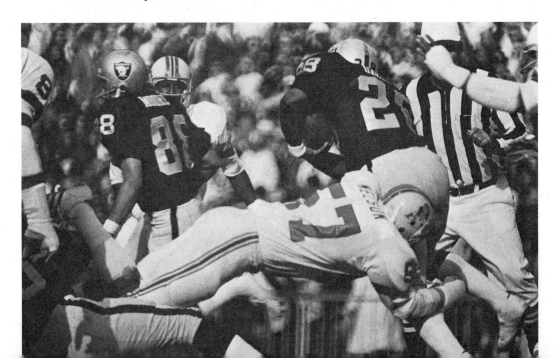

FIGURE 9-15. *An alert linebacker can accomplish feats such as this key interception by Dave Robinson, the Redskins' All-Pro corner linebacker. Dave was able to pick off the aerial by being in the right place by "playing the defense called." Behind the blocking of Chris Hanburger and Brig Owens, he ran the ball down deep in the territory of the New York Giants.*

fense to determine, ahead of the snap, what plays the offense will, or will not, use and in coordinating the efforts of the various defensive players in meeting such plays.

It is also important for the defense to *identify the key offensive players and their positions,* to communicate such information to one another, and to adjust their defensive maneuvers to counter the abilities in order to attain adequate pass coverage and pass rush.

## COMMON FAULTS OF LINEBACKERS

1. Letting an end get inside too freely when he is tight.
2. Looking at the passer and not reacting to a man looking or crossing right behind him. The linebacker must react to the call of the deep back.
3. Not protecting outside on red dogs. The passer has made it to the outside in many instances.
4. Having poor position on a pass when covering a halfback. The linebacker must keep the halfback in front of him at all times and be squared up initially with him.
5. On a quick pitch to a strong back, not being conscious enough of a crack-back block from the flanker.
6. Not being tough enough with the end on goal line and short yardage. The linebacker must control him.
7. Not harassing receiver in his territory.
8. Not converging on the ball.
9. Buzzing before a draw threat is eliminated.
10. Not communicating on the screen or draw.
11. Not jamming "near" ends and controlling their release when possible.
12. Not being in position for tipped or batted balls.
13. Not blocking for interceptions.
14. Failing to alert others of a fumbled ball.
15. Lacking dedicated pursuit (earnest pursuits).
16. Not calling the position of the split ends.
17. Not moving around when possible, giving the quarterback something to think about (window-dressing).
18. Not calling out "pass, pass, pass" on play action passes. The linebacker should call as soon as it is recognized.
19. Not getting depth quickly after a draw is eliminated.
20. Not punishing certain backs when dogging.
21. Overrunning plays away when cut-back threat is a possibility.
22. Tackling too low in open field.
23. Looking into backfield too much and getting chopped down too easily by the slot end.

## DRILLS

Many coaches do not spend enough time in developing the necessary skills needed by linebackers. A few extra minutes of practice each day on these skills can be extremely beneficial.

To be a good linebacker, the player should do everything possible to develop his agility and quickness. Participation in other sports, such as basketball, handball, or tennis, can be very helpful to him in developing his coordination and footwork.

Most of the linebacker's interception opportunities involve moving laterally backward or cutting in toward the ball. Therefore, a linebacker should have someone pass the ball just above his head and run directly at the passer to intercept.

1. *Stance* Because of the variances in defenses, stance drills for linebackers are essential. The style of defense used and the linebacker's position will determine the particular stance. Therefore, the linebackers should be drilled on their stance against a variety of tight and split formations.

2. *First step* This type of drill was covered in chapter 8, "Defensive Line."

3. *Reaction* While some reaction drills were covered in chapter 8, there are a number of drills that are peculiar to linebackers.

4. *Middle linebacker reading drill* In holding down four defensive holes, the middle linebacker and defensive tackles have to work closely together. When the tackles are assigned the two outside holes, the middle linebacker must take the two inside holes, and

vice versa. On all run plays, he has to read the fullback or the No. 3 back on the strong side.

As a result, the middle linebacker and the two tackles should be drilled on their reading assignments. To do this, the offensive holes can be marked with dummies or towels.

5. *Outside linebacker reading drill* (Diagram 9-1) Outside linebackers are either on a tight end or on a split end side. Since most teams flip-flop, one linebacker is always on the tight end and the other is on the split end. Therefore, both linebackers must be proficient at reading reach blocks, turn-out blocks, down blocks, etc. They must be drilled daily on reacting to various keys put on by JV's or B-teamers until reaction becomes instinctive.

6. *Hit-shed drill* Offensive men run straight at the linebacker, who sheds the block with alternating shoulders. This drill can involve several lines operating at once.

7. *React to pitchouts* Reacting to a pitchout or sweep, the linebacker has to learn to play the ball and come up.

8. *Pass rush* (Diagram 9-2) In rushing the passer, linebackers must learn the route they

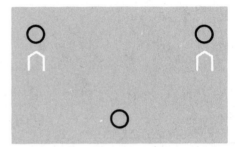

DIAGRAM 9-1. *Outside linebacker reading drill.*

take and how to drive through blockers. Every program should have an area of the field off in a corner with large posts sunk in the ground. Representing offensive line positions, these six posts are approximately a yard apart from tip of shoulder pad to tip of shoulder pad. Thus, the defensive unit can use this area to work on hole assignments, blitz routes, etc.

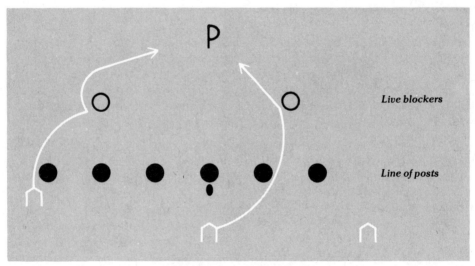

DIAGRAM 9-2. *Pass rush drill.*

9. *Pass drills* Linebackers need considerable drilling in breaking on the ball and catching the ball. While much of their work is covered under semi-group drills, there are a number of effective individual drills against the pass.

10. *Catch drills* From a single file, the linebackers are drilled in running toward the passer. With the passer throwing lead passes, they try to catch the ball at the highest possible point. Then they break off and run at an angle.

11. *Individual zone drill* (Diagram 9-3) This drill teaches the linebackers to get back to their hook area, set up, and react to the ball. On the snap from the center to the quarterback, the linebacker reads the pass, turns, and runs back to his area, looking at the passer over his shoulder. At a prescribed number of steps, he squares up, and the quarterback throws the ball in his vicinity.

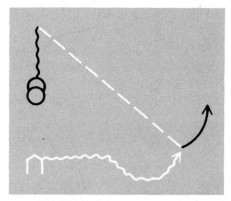

DIAGRAM 9-3. *Individual zone.*

12. *Individual man coverage drill* (Diagram 9-4) On a one-on-one situation, the strong linebackers have to cover a tight end or fullback, using mostly short routes. Keeping the eyes on the receiver and learning how to back-pedal are the key points in this drill. The weak side linebacker is drilled against a back coming out of the backfield.

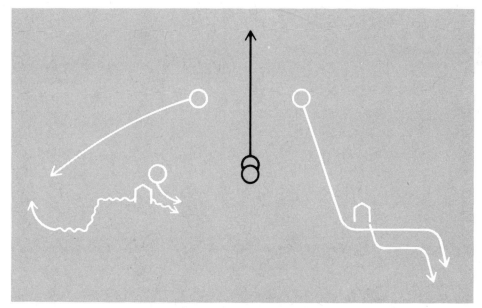

DIAGRAM 9-4. *Individual man coverage.*

13. *Pass-draw-screen drill* This drill teaches the linebacker to play his hook zone and to react to the draw, screen, and roll-out pass. Two blockers in offensive guard positions are alongside the center, with the quarterback and ball carrier behind.

In keying through the guard to the ball, the linebacker must make the proper reaction. When he recognizes a screen, he should yell "screen" and react.

14. *Flyback drill* This drill teaches the linebackers to get back to their hook area, set up, and react to the ball. Three pass receivers are positioned 7 to 10 yards deep and the same distance apart. After setting up 5 yards deep, the quarterback looks and throws to one of his receivers. This drill teaches the linebacker to play the eyes of the quarterback and react at a 180-degree angle to the ball.

15. *Get it* As the passer sets, two linebackers retreat and fight for the ball, while the passer throws between the two men.

16. *Pursuit* Linebackers must be taught the proper pursuit route angles. Using four dummies, this drill involves the linebacker, who pursues to one of four holes and tackles the approaching ball carrier. The coach's command determines the hole. We have an axiom we tell our outside linebackers: "When in doubt, shuffle out."

17. *Tackling* Some of the tackling drills used by linebackers are explained in chapter 8, "Defensive Line."

18. *Eye-opener drill* (Diagram 9-5) Four dummies or shields are placed on the ground 2 yards apart. Ball carriers are lined up on one side of the markers, while the linebackers are lined up on the other side. On the starting signal, the first ball carrier may hit the first hole open or he may fake it and hit another hole. The linebacker shuffles laterally, keeping leverage on the ball. As soon as the runner commits himself, the linebacker stops him with a square tackle.

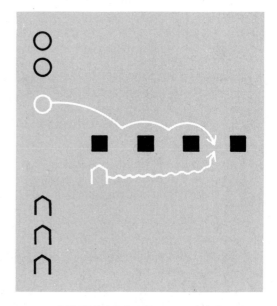

**DIAGRAM 9-5.** *Eye-opener drill.*

19. *Shedding blocker and making tackle* (Diagram 9-6) This drill is essential to linebackers. In this drill, which involves four dummy bags, the linebacker must shed an offensive blocker and then tackle the ball carrier. Markers are placed 7 feet apart, with the linebacker 2 yards from the markers. At the starting signal, the running blocker and linebacker meet in the hole. The linebacker tries to destroy the block, escape, and make the tackle. By widening the gap to 12 or 14 feet, the drill can employ two blockers and two linebackers with one ball carrier.

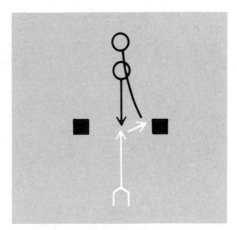

DIAGRAM 9-6. *Shedding blocker and making tackle.*

# 10

# Deep Backs

With today's great emphasis on passing and the pressing need for a stubborn defensive secondary, the deep backs are now being recognized as some of football's most exciting performers. Indeed, this recognition is highly justified when one realizes that pass defense is the most difficult assignment in pro football. Therefore, the defensive backs, those who specialize in pass defense, have the most difficult positions to play. They stand back there and must compete with the fastest, most agile men in the game.

Those who play in the defensive secondary do not become proficient at pass defense overnight. The rookie defensive back has never covered a receiver who possesses the moves and speed of NFL receivers. No matter how fast or how big he is, he must gain the necessary experience to effectively cover these skilled performers.

Star pass defenders are not born. Essentially, they are developed by a step-by-step process of teaching and practice. While some deep backs are gifted with speed and exceptional agility, everyone playing in the defensive secondary can improve by constant drilling.

Every deep back must take pride in his coverage and other defensive skills. He should realize that a good defense will keep any game respectable. There is always hope for a victory when there is confidence in the defense, even when your team is behind in a close game.

Indeed, good defensive backs are hard to come by. Only during the past ten years have coaches played many of their top athletes in the secondary.

The players performing on the corners and the safeties are the last line of defense between the opponent and the end zone. They must know not only their own job but

FIGURE 10-2. To cover, the deep back has to have speed. When the ball is in the air, he should play the ball, not the receiver, and play it aggressively. He should be rough and make an opponent respect him. On the left, Roosevelt Taylor (22) exerts close coverage on wide receiver Leland Glass (46) of the Green Bay Packers. The defensive back should never think he can be beaten on a pass play. The great ones will look defiantly at the quarterback and say to themselves, "Just try to throw it in my area!"

*Whatever you do, don't let those receivers get you turned!*

also the assignments of the other three deep backs, plus those of the three linebackers.

The deep back's best friend is a strong pass rush. Even the best defender cannot hope to cover even an average receiver forever. A deep back must realize that occasionally he is going to get beat. But when he gets beat, can he recover?

## QUALIFICATIONS

The first thing I look for in a deep back is speed. Speed is the name of the game in pro football and a defensive back has to have speed to cover. Second, he must have the ability to react. The ability to react involves quickness. Quickness is more important on pass defense than speed.

There are some deep backs who have speed, but if they don't have quickness, they cannot play in our league. By quickness, I mean the ability to move the hands and feet rapidly in a limited area. There are many good backs who are not exceptionally fast but they are quick. I like our cornerbacks to be able to run a 4.6 forty yards.

Quick hands and feet, good peripheral vision, timing, and body balance are reaction qualities that are necessary for deep backs. On pass defense, the defensive back's reaction ability will determine whether he will succeed or fail. The only way he will improve and develop is through constant drilling.

The deep back has to be tough because those big backs are going to break loose occasionally and run over him, and he will have to bring one down. The defensive back who can "put the leather to someone" will find a place on any football team.

Balance is another important qualification of a defensive back. Whether he is running, jumping, or diving, the player must keep his head and hands in position to see and catch the ball. If a defensive back should slip, he must regain his balance as quickly as possible and continue on to the ball or an area.

The outstanding deep back is an opportunist, taking advantage of every break or miscue by the opposition and making it pay off. When the opportunity presents itself, the "head-up," alert player is ready to make his move, with aggressive action. A deep back must have a strong desire to want to play

FIGURE 10-3. *The defensive back has to be alert but relaxed as he moves up to play the run. The knees are flexed with the weight forward over the balls of the feet. Above, the legs of veteran Cornell Green are flexed so he can react quickly in any direction to the moves of running back Larry Brown (43).*

pass defense. He should want to be the best pass defensive player on the squad.

## STANCE

A proper stance will help the defensive back be physically and mentally alert. A deep back must not become careless in taking his stance. He should work for catlike reflexes. He has to be alert, but relaxed.

The deep back should line up with the outside foot up, so that the heel of the outside foot is even with the toe of the inside foot. The knees and hips are bent slightly. The feet are shoulder width apart. The outside foot is staggered to form a brace for a quick start.

The back is straight, with the buttocks low to allow the weight to be on the balls of the feet. The arms hang loosely down at the side of the body, and the toes and shoulders are squared to the line of scrimmage. The legs are flexed so he can react as quickly as possible in any direction.

The outside or corner defensive backs must take advantage of the sidelines. If the ball is on the hash mark and he is covering a receiver who is positioned near the sideline, the deep back should face *inward* with his inside foot back. In this way, he can view the entire offense and still see his man. In pro ball, however, this is more difficult to do, since the hash marks have been moved in.

## FOOTWORK

No matter how much speed he has, a defensive back still needs drills to develop and improve his footwork. Footwork is a vital skill that every good pass defender must master. Fortunately, it is a fundamental that can be improved considerably through proper teaching.

In covering a receiver, the deep back uses every type of footwork he can possibly come up with. We try to teach our people to backpedal, i.e., to run backwards, while facing the receiver. Defensive backs must be able to shuffle their feet. They have to be able to slide laterally, cross over, and then come out of a crossover. Occasionally, they even have to turn their back on the passer and recover in the manner just described. When covering an out pattern, the proper footwork is particularly important, in order to stay tight with the receiver.

Our deep backs work on running backwards every day. We cannot give them enough of it. In fact, we time our players in running backwards. We clock them for the 15-yard dash, and if a man can run it in 2.5 seconds, that's excellent.

Most defensive backs will run backwards in starting off. When backpedaling, they must lean forward so that their shoulders are over their feet. We never want them to lean backwards because they cannot stop or turn quickly enough.

We believe a "deep" has to be able to carry a man about 10 to 15 yards backpedaling. He must keep the receiver a distance of 3 yards from him until he makes his break. From there, he must turn his legs from one side or the other and run with him. If a deep back cannot backpedal, then he has to come at the snap of the ball. By learning to run and move backwards, the defender will be able to cover a break by the receiver in either direction.

A defensive back must practice his shuffle and glide steps from side to side. He doesn't want to get turned too soon. Many backs make the error of turning on the first fake, rather than wait for a second or third fake and then break.

Naturally, the receiver is trying to get the defensive man to run, to get his feet crossed, so that he can make a break. Conversely, the deep backs covering him are trying to prevent this from happening. Therefore, the deep back must avoid crossing his feet, stumbling, or taking extra steps. Usually, when a back falls or stumbles, it is the result of poor footwork.

Defensive backs must practice running with their knees inward and looking over the inside shoulder. This is similar to an outfielder going after a long drive. The deep back has to develop the ability to sprint when running this way.

## MENTAL ATTITUDE

"They should want to play defense" best describes the attitude and frame of mind we like our players to have. To play to the best of their ability, defensive backs should always be thinking on defense.

B

C

A

D

FIGURE 10-4. *Backpedaling (and breaking right or left). A deep back must develop his footwork to perfection and always be on balance. When backpedaling, it is essential that the defensive back plant the correct foot whenever possible. If he takes an extra step he will lose ground. This is the difference between completion and an incompletion. Here, Ken Houston plants his right foot and pushes off to his left. Notice that he keeps his eyes on the passer. When he plants his right foot, observe the good lean body and the angle, both of which facilitate quickness.*

FIGURE 10-5. *Coming up to stop the sweep can be a difficult play for a deep back. Yet, the cornerback should not be afraid to force those running plays. Above, Pat Fischer (37), the Redskins' tough little defensive back, moves up quickly to stop running back John Riggins of the New York Jets.*

If a football player doesn't know the situation, then he is wasting his time out there. We try to alert our people in the huddle just what the situation is—third and 7 or third and 25. If it is third and 7, we don't want to allow a 7-yard pass. If it's third and 25, 8 yards won't hurt us unless the ball is down close to our own goal line.

So our deep backs have to be thinking about the particular situation. We try to alert the man calling the defensive signals in the huddle. Quite often, we will alert them to make certain he knows the situation.

A good defensive back must have confidence in himself and his teammates. A good pass defender has to feel he can dominate the receiver. He must believe that he cannot be thrown on. We realize he cannot do it every time, but we like for him always to be thinking: "I'm the master of this guy. Just try anything you want, and I'm going to be with you. I'll be breathing right down your neck. And I'm going to take that ball away from you when it comes out here."

Actually, the perfect pass is extremely hard to stop, but that's what we are shooting for—to break up the perfect pass. However, the defense can expect offensive errors and should be mentally alert and ready for them at all times.

Deep backs should not worry about pass completions, but think only of stopping

FIGURE 10-6. An aggressive attitude must be developed on defense. Cornerback Pat Fischer, with help from linebacker Chris Hanburger, treats Donny Anderson (44) rather roughly when the running back of the St. Louis Cardinals tries to break through the tough Washington defense. Notice the fine pursuit by members of the Redskins' front line, Ron Mc-Dole (79) and Verlon Biggs (89).

or intercepting the next one. They must not lose their poise if a pass is completed on them. They should hope the opponents try another so they can intercept it. If they must give ground, they should allow it between the 20-yard lines. Actually, interceptions are mostly a matter of setting the mind to do it.

## APPROACH AND POSITION

The position the deep back maintains on the receiver must always allow him to maintain vision on the passer. The defender must never let the receiver get closer than 3 yards. He must remember that he can get too close as well as get too far.

Of course, the distance the defender plays from his man varies with the respective abilities, plus the down and yardage. Those receivers who don't have great speed and depend upon faking to get open are generally bothered by being played close. A deep back should get in the habit of covering his receiver closely and staying tight on him. He should hound him all over the field. He will find that it is actually easier to cover this way once he gets the practice. If he practices playing him loose, he will play that way in the game.

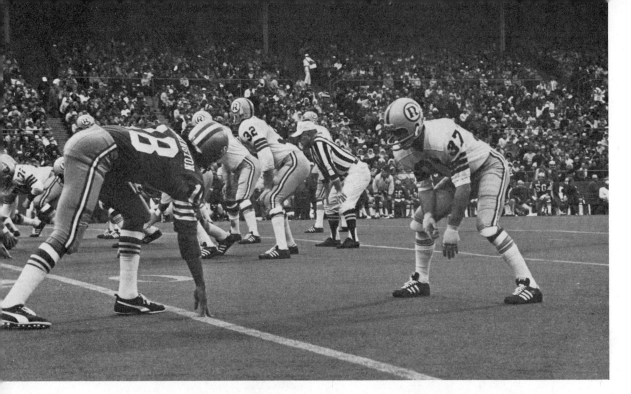

FIGURE 10-7. *Proper position. A deep back should get in the habit of covering his receiver closely and staying tight on him. Above, cornerback Pat Fischer plays a tight press position on wide receiver Gene Washington of the 49ers. The new pro rules have placed tighter restrictions on pass defenses.*

Proper position on the receiver allows the pass defender to do three things:

1. Intercept
2. Break up the pass
3. Tackle the receiver

When a receiver fakes, the defender should merely drop back another step, but he must not decrease his speed or get turned. He should try to keep an outside angle on the receiver. If he does get caught out of position, he must learn to get into a favorable position quickly.

If a receiver is coming at him at full steam, the deep back must give ground rapidly. He doesn't want to be caught waiting for a move. He must learn to judge the receiver's approaching speed.

Once he starts up to stop a play, the defensive back must be aggressive and not hesitant. When the back is going after the ball and has the receiver covered from behind, he should try to keep one arm on each side of the receiver as he goes through his shoulders to the ball. Since almost anything is allowed if he plays the ball, the defender should go through the receiver's shoulders and go for the ball rather than the arms. If he fails to break up the pass, the defender is still in good position to make the tackle. When playing an out, in and out, out and in, curl, stop, and a hitch from the inside, a deep back must remember he can reach across farther by using his inside arm. In addition, he has more force to knock the ball downward.

When a corner deep back is playing a

hitch, he should force the outside receiver inside. He shouldn't go for the inside fake and have him turn outside of him where there is no help.

## ALERTS

To improve their coverage and make possible a cohesive type of defense, the deep backs must do considerable talking with each other. Communication among pass defenders is a must for success. They must repeat everything three times and loudly so that it can be heard. The following are some of the alerts which the Redskins use in communicating with each other:

1. *"Pass, pass, pass"* should be yelled as soon as anyone on defense recognizes that a pass play is on.
2. As soon as anyone on defense recognizes that a screen pass is on, he should yell *"Screen, screen, screen."*
3. Remember *"plaster"* when the quarterback is scrambling.
4. Yell *"powder"* on crack-back blocks on the weak side and on the strong side.

*FIGURE 10-8. Effective communication is vital. Deep backs must communicate loudly with each other in order to alert each other of what is happening. Without talking, it is impossible to be a good defensive team.*

5. *"Ball, ball, ball"* should be yelled when a teammate is going after a long pass and his back is turned. This alerts him that the man he is covering is the intended receiver and that the *ball is in flight.*
6. The linebackers should be directed by yelling *"in, in, in,"* or *"out, out, out,"* when covering curls and hooks. Deep backs must communicate with the linebackers to improve their coverage.
7. The preliminary call for a switch is *far* and *near.* The call on the strong side is *"switch, switch, switch,"* and this must be answered by the strong safety before the switch is on. The call on the weak side is *"take, take, take,"* and again must be repeated by the weak safety.
8. The deep back plays everything as a pass until he is positive it is a run. Then, he should yell *"run, run, run."*

If he is talking, a player is thinking. And I firmly believe that talking takes a great deal of "pressure" off any player. To me, talking is second only to moving the feet as an essential fundamental in good defense.

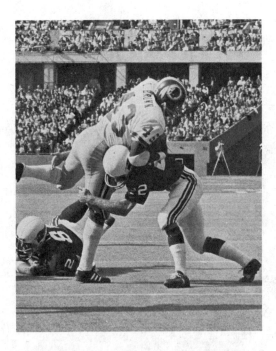

FIGURE 10-9. *Head-on tackle. With the runner coming straight on, defensive back Roger Wehrli (22) of the Cardinals sticks his head into the midsection or the belt buckle. He keeps his head up, his buttocks down, and his feet working. Notice how Roger locks his hands behind the ball carrier with a wristlock and drives right on through the runner. In driving the runner backwards, the important thing is to lift with the legs, not the back.*

## TACKLING

No deep back has ever achieved greatness without combining tackling ability with covering ability. Tackling is the backbone of defense. It is the "blood and guts" of defensive team play.

"You have got to keep your head up!" said Eddie Meador, former Rams' outstanding safety man and one of the surest tacklers in the NFL. "Be on balance and drive through your opponent," said Eddie. "With the big boys, you cannot hit them high. You've got to hit them low!"

While there are various theories on tackling technique, we teach our men to place the helmet in front of the ball carrier. If they miss, the runner is turned back into the playing field where there is some help. Generally, if the tackler places his helmet in back of the runner, if he should miss, the man probably is able to get out to the outside, and a pursuing player either doesn't get there or has a greater distance to go.

When tackling on defense, a defensive back must make sure! Sureness is better than ferociousness. In no other phase of football can one mistake be so costly. There is nothing more discouraging to our rushmen

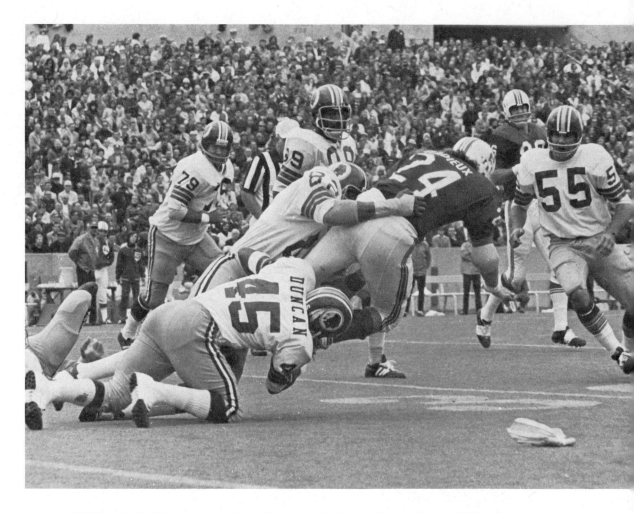

FIGURE 10-10. *High and low. Two Washington Redskins, Speedy Duncan (45) and Jimmie Jones (82), demonstrate the correct execution of high and low tackling. The running back for the New England Patriots has no place to go but down.*

and the entire team than to have a hard-earned point margin wiped out because of a missed tackle.

Courage is no substitute for technique. No matter how much courage a player has, he must be taught the proper fundamentals of tackling. The best way to develop tackling technique is to begin on a dummy, so that a player can gain confidence.

Everyone appreciates a good tackler, and players, fans, and coaches all have the highest respect for the good "hitters."

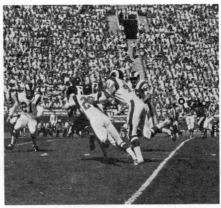
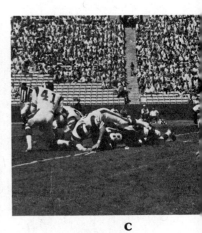

A       B       C

*FIGURE 10-11.   In making a side tackle, the defender must take the correct angle of pursuit. He must have good body control and not allow the runner to cut back inside. In this series, Irv Cross makes a hard-driving shoulder tackle, hitting the runner hip high. His teammates converge on the scene to make a gang tackle.*

## DIAGNOSING RUNNING SITUATIONS

The deep back must determine as soon as possible whether a play is a run or a pass. He should meet running plays as close to the line of scrimmage as possible and make the tackle from the outside in. The deep back must know which side is strong at all times. He watches the flow of the backs.

Prior to the snap, all defensive backs have a key that they try to play. This key will be determined by the type of pattern that will develop, or if it is a run. The key is really their play record.

The deep back should play the area and a man. He must see the men as they come into his area with peripheral vision, watching the passer and playing the ball aggressively from the outside.

First, the defensive back has to cover his man in his area. Then, he can move up to stop a run, but his first priority is to stop the pass. After making a tackle on the line of scrimmage, a deep back can look for a pass behind him on the next play.

Perhaps the only running play the deep backs can really key for is a sweep. They have to pick up interior running plays by the action of the linemen. "I key through the guard and tackle into the halfback," said Meador. "The linemen tell you if it's a running play if they release across the line of scrimmage to block on us. If you see the end is definitely blocking down hard, you can get in there, but again you cannot commit yourself too fast."

If the ball carrier is able to get past the line of scrimmage and into the secondary, somebody has to bring him down. And, of course, before deep backs release their receivers to come up, the play must be a run.

## PASS DEFENSE

With nearly everyone throwing the ball today, the problems of pass defense have assumed new importance. The secret of good pass defense is for the deep back to always have proper position on the receiver. The defensive back must not let the receiver get him turned until his final move. There is an exact position for each defender to assume on each type of pass thrown.

The deep back must backpedal, shuffle, and glide before he ever turns. He must develop this at top speed. To remain sharp and improved, he must practice this every day. I want our pass defense to practice the way we want to play on Sunday. We practice at top speed only.

Great pass defenders exhibit a combination of the following qualities:

1. Aggressiveness
2. Quick reactions
3. Alertness
4. Looking through the receiver into the passer
5. Always hustling when the ball is in the air
6. Determination to get the football

*Confidence is also essential* for good pass defense. When the ball is in the air, the defense must feel it belongs to them. By

FIGURE 10-12. *Bumping the ball carrier out of bounds. With a stiff shoulder and body block, veteran safety man Richie Petitbon (16) prevents hard-running Calvin Hill of the Cowboys from getting into the end zone.*

A       B       C

FIGURE 10-13. *A hard body block. In making a tackle near the sidelines, a defensive back will often drive the ball carrier out of bounds with a hard shoulder and body block. Here, Irv Cross, with assistance from a teammate, demonstrates this technique in stopping a ball carrier.*

having a positive frame of mind, the deep back can help give his teammates confidence.

Many teams use both zone and man-for-man pass coverage in the defensive secondary. The Trojans of Southern California, for example, use at least five zone coverages and two man-for-man coverages.

The most difficult situation for a defensive back to cope with is for a receiver to spread himself out about 16 or 20 yards. Now, a zone pass defense can't be used because the defensive man has gone too wide, and it's strictly a one-on-one situation. Any mistake can mean an easy touchdown.

A football team should have a strong pass defense if it has the following four elements:

1. *Recognition* of the formation and where to line up
2. Knowing the individual *Responsibilities* or the zone responsibility
3. Getting into *Position* on the *Receiver*
4. Moving in to *Intercept* the football

The deep back should not have any doubt that he can cover a receiver, even though his job is more difficult than the receiver's. He must hound him unmercifully until the receiver knows who is the better man and who is the tougher.

### Diagnosing Passing Situations

On passing situations, there are different theories on what the deep back should look for and whom he should keep his eyes on. Some coaches like their defensive backs to keep their eyes glued on the passer, while others have their deep backs look for the receivers to come down. Both require good peripheral vision.

Personally, I think the ideal situation is to be able to see both, so that they can see the ball release and also see their receiver.

Early in the season, we look at a lot of young players. Invariably, their eyes are fixed on the quarterback, and as a result, they are late in getting started, after a man makes his break.

Quite often, when a defensive back is having a problem reacting quickly enough, we will tell him to forget about the ball. We have this rule: "In terms of thinking, you can lose the ball but don't lose the receiver." But, again, the ideal situation is for the defender to be able to look through the receiver to the quarterback so that he knows when the ball is coming, and when there is an interception that we can take it. We are on the football field to play the ball, not to play three downs and walk off. We are there to get the ball on the first down.

If he is having trouble covering a receiver, a pass defender should concentrate on the receiver and nothing else, until he breaks. He should concentrate on his belt buckle, not on his feet or head. Quite often, a defender is beaten and faked because he is attempting to cover too much with his eyes—for example, the quarterback, offensive lineman, and receiver.

After the receiver breaks and *only* after the pass defender gets in stride with him should the defender look back for the ball. His teammate will help him by yelling *ball!* If young defensive backs will try this in practice, they will see how it affects their coverage, particularly for the cornerbacks.

### Tact Position

In running with the receiver, our pass defenders use a tact position, where they can see through the receiver to the quarterback at all times. I like this terminology to describe the exact ideal position for the defender in relation to the receiver. For certain patterns, it is often impossible, but for the major per-

FIGURE 10-14. *One of football's truly great defensive plays was performed by Ken Houston of the Redskins against the Dallas Cowboys the evening of October 8, 1973. On a fourth down and goal situation, with victory hanging on the outcome, the brilliant defensive back stopped Walt Garrison on the 1-yard line after the Cowboys' hard-running back had caught a short pass over the middle.*

centage of situations, we would like to have him assume a proper tact position.

In the tact position the deep back can look through the offensive man into the quarterback. It is the correct position a defender should have on a receiver. If he is in an improper position, he cannot see the ball leave the passer's hand, and he doesn't have a chance to get an interception.

The defensive back cannot allow the receiver to run right on top of him, or he will run right by him before he can recover. So, he has to keep some vertical depth; in addition, he must keep good lateral position on the man. In short, we like our people to employ tight coverage but not to gamble!

The most difficult position to maintain is the vertical position. More defenders are beaten because of this than because of any other factor.

The flight position is the position of the defensive back on the receiver while he is covering and the ball is in the air.

Again, the deep back should read the receiver's belt buckle area. As the receiver breaks off the line of scrimmage, the deep back should glue his eyes on the receiver's belt buckle area. As a result, the deep back is less apt to look at the faking actions of the receiver.

### Playing the Ball

When the ball is in the air, the deep back should play the ball, not the receiver, and play it aggressively. Aggressiveness is one of the most difficult qualities to instill on pass defense. The deep back can be taught to play the ball aggressively first in practice against his own teammates and with helmets. Since many receivers are inclined to be timid, the deep back should be rough and aggressive and make an opponent respect him.

Playing the ball is not something to be taken for granted. It can be taught, however. Proper drilling can teach a man to play the ball while he is covering a receiver. The instant the passer throws the ball, the defensive backs must converge on the receiver. They must not just stand there and look!

In breaking up a pass, the defensive back goes up with two hands because two hands are better than one. He must remember that once the ball is in the air, he and the receiver have equal rights to it. He plays rough and always plays the ball, not the man. Of course, there will be times when he cannot get two hands on the ball, and he will be forced to use one hand. With one hand, however, there is a tendency to tip the ball, so he should make sure he knocks it down toward the ground.

Once the ball is in the air, the defensive backs must converge on the ball. They must knock it down toward the ground, not up in the air. A pass defender should practice developing a "burst of speed" to the ball once it is in the air. Five or six strides with quick recovery at near top speed can be a tremendous advantage. Although the defensive back can gamble a little, he should know *when* to gamble.

When a teammate is covering on long passes and has his back turned, the defensive back should yell: "Ball, ball, ball!" He shouldn't yell too soon, because his teammate will turn to look, and this will slow him down.

There are times when a deep back has his man covered, but because of the type of pass thrown, it will be completed. An effective technique in this situation is to slap at the ball before the receiver can put it away. In most instances he will drop the ball, but the defender is still in position to make the tackle if the receiver holds the ball.

Reaction to a deflected pass is something that must be practiced because it is not a natural type of movement. Deep backs, as

FIGURE 10-15. *When the ball is in the air, the deep back should play the ball, not the receiver. He must remember that once the ball is in the air, he and the receiver have equal rights to it. Here, Pat Fischer moves in front of wide receiver Jack Snow and goes up with both hands for the interception. The defensive back should watch the interception into his hands and then put it away.*

well as linebackers, need this training so they can react correctly when there is a deflected pass, even when they least expect it. Each year, a significant portion of a team's interceptions result from deflected passes. This indicates the value of devoting some practice time to the playing of deflected forward passes.

### Defending against the Short Buttonhook Pass

If the deep back is screened out completely from the ball, he will have to go straight through to the receiver and punish him. If the hook is thrown a little bit high and the receiver has his hands in the air, he can punish a man pretty well by hitting him in the ribs.

If the ball is thrown where the receiver catches it in his stomach, the defender possibly will try to get his arm around and in going for the ball get one hand in. Sometimes he can kick the ball out.

If the ball is caught just before the defensive back gets there, it leaves an unprotected ball. Consequently, there is the possibility of

FIGURE 10-16. *Timing of the ball in flight can pay off in interceptions. Defensive back Mike Bass shows the importance of "playing the ball at its highest point" as he knocks down a long aerial in the end zone. Fortunately for the Redskins, Mike was able to get one hand up for a deflection.*

stripping the man—in other words, coming down hard on him over his limbs, hands, and primarily his arms. It is a hard "pulling down and out" motion, in the hopes that he will flip the ball loose. This may cause either an incompletion or a fumble.

We like our defense men to tackle high on the man who has caught the ball. Some defenders grab the receiver's arms, placing their arms completely around his body, thus preventing a possible lateral. If the defender gets there simultaneously with the ball, he can punish the receiver. However, if he gets there after the ball is caught, he has to make a sure tackle because the defense has reduced their pursuit to two or three men who are in the vicinity of the ball. If the first man does not tackle the receiver or slow him down, the pursuit may not get there.

## Defending against the Long Bomb

The defensive back must always be conscious of the threat of a long pass, in which the receiver goes down, slows, and then sprints downfield. The quarterback tries to hit him on the dead run. On this play, the deep back must maintain vertical depth until the receiver has made his positive break. Then, it is usually a footrace. He cannot always keep the perfect position; in fact, there are some receivers who are difficult to keep up with, stride for stride, in the correct position. However, if the defender can stay stride for stride with his man, at the very last second, he can either get the ball or break up the pass.

The defensive back cannot afford to misjudge deep passes. This is an art and must be practiced. "A good rule to follow is to take one extra step before you commit yourself to go for the ball," said Meador. "Watch the ball all the way and only play the ball."

Above all, a deep back must *never* let anyone get behind him. This is the costliest mistake he can make.

## Intercepting a Pass

The pass interception is one of the greatest and most spectacular plays in football. Intercepting a forward pass is a specialized skill consisting of perfect timing, coordination, relaxed hands, and footwork ability. Unquestionably, it is one of the most difficult skills in football to master. A pass defender running backward is required to cover a lightning-fast receiver running forward. In addition, the receiver has the advantage of knowing where he is going.

A forward pass in the air is a free ball and belongs as legitimately to the defensive team as to the offensive team. Therefore, all defensive men should go after each ball in the air to intercept it, except in special circumstances.

Deep backs should practice making interceptions above the head. If they take it lower and wait, the receiver will usually get it. The defensive back should look the interception into his hands and then put it away. He can be rough as long as he reaches for the ball with two hands. On long passes he should watch the nose of the ball to improve his ability to judge whether to intercept or to break up a pass.

When two defenders cover one receiver, the one who is in position to intercept should yell "my, my," meaning his ball. The other defender stays right there and does not let up, but he is ready for a deflected ball, to block or to help in any way. As a result, the pass defenders will avoid knocking each other off and also will increase their interception chances.

When making an interception in a crowd, the pass defender should be sure to

FIGURE 10-17. *Stripping the man. If the ball is caught just before the defensive back gets there, the defensive back can come down hard on him over his hands and primarily over his arms. It is a hard "pulling down and out" motion, in the hopes that he will flip the ball loose. Here, cornerback Brig Owens (23) makes a high tackle on wide receiver Bob Grim, who has just caught the ball.*

FIGURE 10-18. *Breaking up the pass in the flat. Cornerback Mike Bass (41) makes a great play on a pass attempt to wide receiver Bob Hayes. Defensive backs must be very careful on passes out in the flat since any errors by over-playing can be disastrous, particularly on a wet playing surface.*

twist at the same time his opponent is attempting to get the ball away from him. He will get the ball every time.

## MAN-FOR-MAN COVERAGE

With the forward pass becoming such a potent offensive weapon, more pressure is being placed on the defensive secondary to use man-for-man coverage or work in some combination with the zone coverage. Certainly, the principles employed in the zone coverage cannot be used in man-for-man coverage. Therefore, a set of rules must be developed that can be used in the more difficult man-for-man coverage.

When using man-for-man coverage, the defense has more difficulty getting interceptions. However, pass defenders must use point vision on the receiver and peripheral vision on the quarterback. Some defensive backs make the mistake of focusing so much attention on the receiver that they are never in position for an interception, or they never see the ball in flight until it is too late.

When playing man-for-man coverage, it is better to play too loose than too tight, because it is easier for the quarterback to throw the "home run" pass. Actually, man-for-man coverage is no stronger than its weakest link—a deep back. This is why we devote a great amount of time to perfecting our coverage.

Since it is easier for the receiver to fool the defender than vice versa, a deep back must develop his footwork to perfection and always be on balance. I might say that if he can cover a man in our one-on-one drills, he can certainly cover him in the game. In this type of drill, he needn't be concerned about pass completions, but work for position on the receiver.

During a game, a pass defender never has time to really think out an offensive pattern. Instant reaction is demanded, and this will only occur by constant drilling and is a must with individual coverage. If he finds that a receiver is continually getting too close and is upon him before he can react, more than likely the deep back is watching the action of the backfield. He must never be fooled by play action passes. With man-for-man coverage, he must remember to use point vision on the receiver and peripheral vision on the ball.

When using man-for-man coverage, it is essential that the deep backs talk to one another. Each defender needs all the help he can get, and it is absolutely necessary to work as a four-man unit. They are like the outfield in baseball. *They must develop teamwork!*

## ZONE COVERAGE

The cardinal rule of a zone defense is never let a receiver get behind the defender. This helps stop the long touchdown pass. The drop-back action of zone defenders is more effective against the long pass than other types of coverage.

A zone coverage should be as deep as the deepest and as wide as the widest man in the zone. The defender should always keep his receiver far enough in front so he can see through to the passer. On any zone defense, the defensive back wants to look through the receiver into the passer. He knows there is no need to switch in a zone, and the back never makes his break until the ball is thrown.

The pass defender should carry a receiver approximately 5 yards and do so cautiously. He must watch for a man crossing into his zone. If two men come into one man's zone, the defender is responsible for the deeper man of the two. If he sees two men coming into his zone, he should yell, "Help, help, help!"

Talk, talk, talk is the key to good pass coverage, allowing for the necessary cohesion among the deep backs. Pass defenders should repeat everything three times—loudly—so that it can be heard.

The zone is also simple to learn because the defender has an area to cover rather than an individual, and he plays the ball from the time it leaves the passer's hand. The defender in the zone also has a clear picture up front, which allows him to better distinguish running plays from pass plays, and vice versa. In addition, less speed is required by defenders in the zone because they are covering an area rather than an individual and play him loose.

Deep backs shouldn't worry about short passes being completed in front of them. They may bring first downs, but the long ones will bring the touchdowns. The "home run" pass must be stopped. There is no excuse for this type of pass being completed against a zone defense.

There are a number of disadvantages in the zone defense. First, short zones are usually open for the passer to complete all types of short passes. As a result, an area is left between the linebackers and secondary when the deep backs start retreating immediately because the linebackers cannot drop back quickly enough.

Delayed passes, hook passes, and flood passes are all effective against a zone. All types of screeners, running passes, and drains prove effective against this defense. Unless they are experienced, the deep backs may have problems trying to cover the width of the field.

## THE WEAK SAFETY (JILL)

The weak safety, or "Jill" as we call him, should be the spark plug of the pass defense. He should be the leader in encouraging others to talk. He should call out the down and distance so that the other deep backs can hear him. Since he is a roamer, he has to have some speed to cover the ground.

When Jill is free, he should see the ball leave the passer's hand, enabling him to get more interceptions and increase the distance he can cover. He should also increase his depth, so that he can extend his coverage. By watching the passer's eyes and studying his actions, the weak safety can determine quickly where the ball will be thrown.

His approach and responsibility on wide plays to the weak side are very important. His approach must be made to the outside of the "O" man on his side. The side back will always turn the runner inside to him because his approach is outside. Therefore, Jill must always keep an inside angle on the runner so that he cannot cut back inside of him. He must not overrun the play.

The weak safety must take extra practice on playing the ball so that he will increase his interception distance. He should leave an instant before the ball is thrown and go to the intended receiver.

## THE STRONG SAFETY (SAM)

The strong safety's approach and responsibility on runs to the strong side are most important. "Sam," as we call the strong safety, should always make his approach slightly to the outside of the offensive back when he blocks. He must play everything as a pass first. However, when he recognizes a run, he should "fly up" but be under control to make the tackle.

The side back will turn the play inside to Sam; therefore he must approach from an inside angle on the ball carrier. He shouldn't come up too wide and overrun the play. When a ball carrier doesn't have the necessary speed to sweep wide, he will probably rely on setting up a cut-back.

Sam will key the halfback looking through the offensive tackle and guard. This enables him to quickly make a differential diagnosis between a run and a pass and lets him know whether to expect help from Jill, as he also is keying the same back.

Sometimes the strong safety finds the receiver is continually getting too close and is almost past him before he reacts. When this happens, Sam is probably watching the backfield action. *Never be fooled by play action passes!*

Talking to the linebackers is a good habit for Sam to develop. They can help so much on curls, hooks, etc., if the deep backs will let them know where the receiver is.

When the tight end or slot back blocks and no back releases, Sam is free to read the quarterback and play the ball. However, he should be sure he has communicated with the strong side linebacker before he does this.

The safety man should perfect his footwork for the Drag pass, Cross pass, and the Lookie inside and outside. These are the ones he will face most frequently.

Since Sam usually covers the biggest and strongest receivers, he must hit them low to bring them down. We have learned from experience that the best of the tight ends cannot be wrestled to the ground effectively, because they usually carry their tacklers.

Since the offense sends blockers out after the safety men on virtually *every* running play, they have to be able to fake and bounce away from them, and still stay between the ball carrier and the goal line.

The safety must try to keep them from getting into his body. The tackle will likely come out from the side opposite from where the play is coming off, and he will come fast and hard. Therefore, the safety should come up, stop for a split second, and then make his move away from him.

## GEORGE ALLEN'S TEN COMMANDMENTS OF PASS DEFENSE

1. *Watch the team while in the huddle* and as they break from the huddle.
2. *Call the formation* (Sam's responsibility) and its direction.
3. Line up in the *correct* place with the proper alignment.
4. Call the individual responsibility or the zone responsibility and *know when you have help* and how to use assistance.
5. Indicate, when called upon by the coach, *your play responsibility* whether pass or run.
6. *Recognize and call out* the pattern. Yell "Drag," "China," etc.
7. Get correct *position on the receiver* and maintain that position.
8. Move in for the pass *interception* and play *only* the ball.
9. Yell *"Fire"* for the *interception*.
10. *Block for the interception.* Don't look back for someone to block, but knock down the nearest opponent.

## FILMS

Play recognition can be taught when viewing films by running the play back and forth before its completion. The deep backs can call out "Run" or "Pass," which will help them get more out of the film.

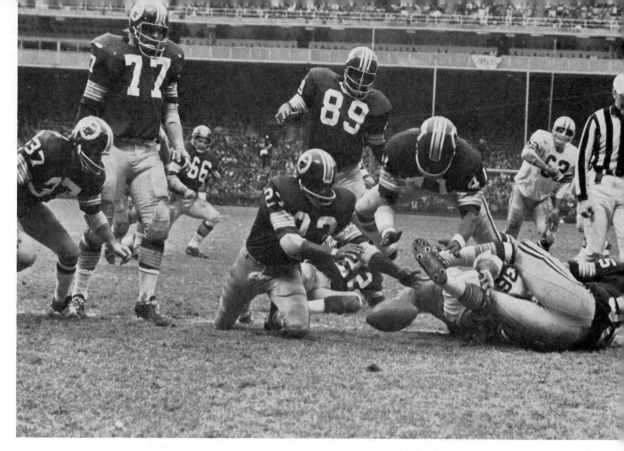

FIGURE 10-19.   *Recovering a fumble. The player must fall on the ball instead of trying to pick it up. Above, cornerback Brig Owens (23) pounces on a loose ball in a game against Green Bay. "A fumbled football draws flies."*

Defensive backs must know the receiver they are covering. They should study him in all the films to know his strengths and weaknesses.

Every time a pass is completed, someone is at fault. So, defensive backs must determine the reasons and study the footwork in the film.

A projector is always available whenever a player wishes to devote extra time to viewing himself and others. Deep backs should analyze film the same as a quarterback. They should check their footwork to see if they made any false steps in covering.

## GRADING

The main purpose of grading is to recognize errors and eliminate them. By grading all phases of the game, careful attention is paid to each movement.

Pass defense men are graded mainly for positioning, as follows:

1. How *close* he allows a receiver to get to him.
2. Playing the receiver *too loose* so that it is impossible to break up the pass.
3. His *position on the receiver* when covering a "Goal," "Drag," "Cross," etc.
4. Whether the receiver got to his *outside.*
5. Whether the receiver got to his *inside.*

## DRILLS

In developing our deep backs, we employ a countless number of drills, most of which stress proper footwork. It is not unusual for our defensive backs to stay after practice and work on their weakness. Defensive backs should try to improve their peripheral vision in practice. All good defenders have this.

One of the most important is the "burst" drill, which is actually an acceleration drill. We try to simulate any break a receiver might make, including coming back for the ball, breaking at a 90-degree angle to the inside or 90 degrees to the outside, and the deeper angle, which we call a goal or post pattern. We try to have the defender counter that break. In other words, he is coming out of a backward run, backpedal, shuffle or slide, or whatever he happens to be using at the time. He has to get into the proper angle of coverage and employ the type of break that he can cover and accelerate. In other words, he must make a complete change of direction and move quickly at full speed again in a new direction.

1. *Stance* The stance of defensive backs is slightly higher than the linebacker's stance. Deep backs must be ready to move quickly without lost motion. The coach can dull his defensive backs by placing them three or four deep in their respective positions and yelling "set." Then they move into their correct stance.

2. *Pass defense* The one-on-one drill is still the best single coverage drill in football (Diagram 10-1). Any type of pass defense, even a zone, still involves man-for-man coverage. If a defensive back does not get enough one-on-one work, he should stay after practice. A deep back must remain sharp, and he needs this every day, especially early in the week. However, his work must be against a receiver.

Defensive backs must drill on interceptions just as the offensive ends work on receiving. Statistics indicate that most interceptions are made while a defender is coming forward into the football. Unless the defender has sufficient training, there is often a clash of hand and ball.

If a deep back finds that he is just missing an interception or arriving a step late, he can improve his interception distance by asking one of the quarterbacks to throw him a few long passes after practice each day. He can leave an instant before the ball is thrown and go to the intended receiver. Five minutes a day will increase his chances for an interception. In

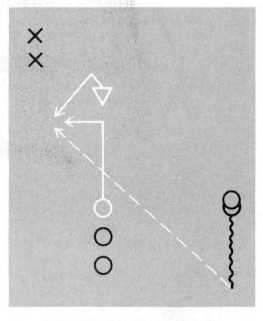

DIAGRAM 10-1. *One-on-one drill.*

practice, the back should return the ball at least 20 yards.

Deep backs and defensive backs should practice running backward every day, in order to improve their footwork and coverage. Defensive backs will be amazed at how fast they can run backward and still cut.

When our backs practice running backward, we increase the distance from 10 yards to 20, 30, and even 40 yards. We even have them race going backward without turning.

The primary purpose of pre-game drills is to warm up all the pass defenders. Deep backs must be loose and supple on the first play of the game. Quite often on the first play of a game, a long pass is completed because the defender was a step slow.

*Fight for the ball* The defensive backs line up in pairs facing the coach. As the coach lays the ball in the air, one player from each line runs forward. Later, the drill can be varied by having the players run backward. In the Cannonball drill, the quarterback throws "bullet" passes to either defender.

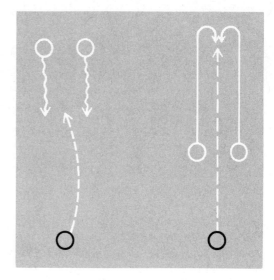

**DIAGRAM 10-2. Fight for the ball.**

*Around the dummy* Facing a passer at about 20 yards, the deep backs are lined up in a single line. A standing dummy is stationed in between at 10 yards. The first man in the line runs forward and circles the dummy and moves backward away from the passer. The passer should throw a variety of passes that will make the defender go get the ball.

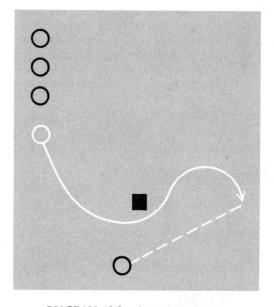

**DIAGRAM 10-3. Around the dummy.**

*Down-the-line*   Positioned on one of the yard lines, the defensive back runs backward as the coach uses the football to point in different directions. Even though the defender is zigzagging, he is running down the chalk line. He uses a crossover step to change directions. After three or four changes of direction, the passer throws the ball. After grabbing the ball, the defender sprints to the outside.

*Interception drill*   The coach throws a line drive interception—high, wide, and low—to a deep back. The purpose of the drill is to give the pass defender practice intercepting the three types of passes, while running forward and catching the ball at various angles. This is one of our favorite game warm-up drills.

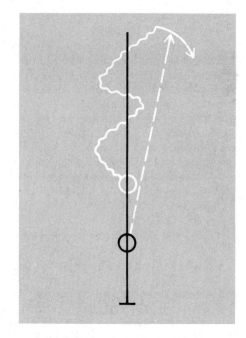

DIAGRAM 10-4.   *Down-the-line.*

*Two-on-one interception drill*   This drill is effective in teaching the deep zone defender to stay in the middle of his zone and cover two men by playing the arm motion of the passer. Two receivers run downfield parallel to the defensive back about 10 to 15 yards apart. The passer throws to one of them.

The defender should stay in the middle of the zone until the ball is in the air.

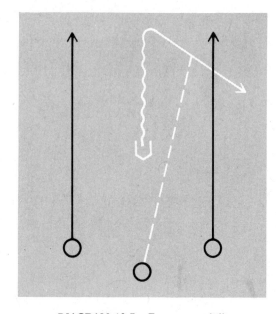

DIAGRAM 10-5.   *Two-on-one drill.*

*Two-in-one zone drill*   Two receivers positioned close together release into the same zone. One cornerback is instructed to cover the deepest receiver in his one-third of the field and then break up on the ball if it is thrown to the short man.

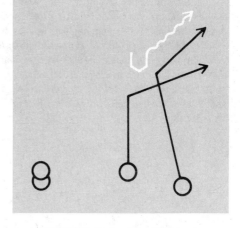

DIAGRAM 10-6.   *Two-in-one zone.*

*Playing the ball*   A receiver is positioned downfield to receive an "out." The defensive back is located about 5 yards behind and 1 yard to the outside. The passer throws the ball slightly to the outside of the receiver, with the defender attempting to intercept or break up the pass.

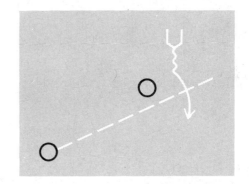

DIAGRAM 10-7.   *Playing the ball.*

3. *Tackling*   Since a number of tackling drills have been presented in previous chapters, the following are drills designed specifically for defensive backs:

   *Sweep tackling drill*   A standing dummy is stationed 12 yards from the sideline. The defenders are positioned in a line just inside the dummy, approximately 8 yards from the dummy. The ball carriers are instructed to run a sweep between the dummy and the sideline. This is an excellent drill to teach deep backs how to use the sideline as part of their leverage on the ball.

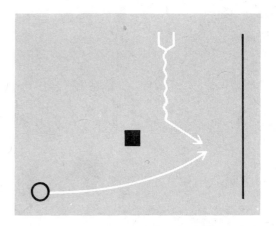

DIAGRAM 10-8.   *Sweep tackling.*

*Sideline tackling*  A line of reserve backs are employed as ball carriers. The coach throws the ball to the first back in line as he moves straight upfield along the sideline. When making the tackle, the defensive back tries to get his head in front. If he fails to get good position, the defender may have to knock or push the ball carrier out of bounds.

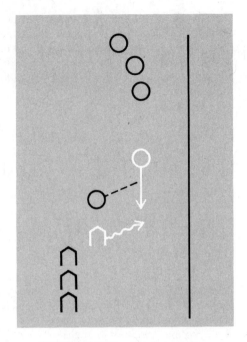

DIAGRAM 10-9.  *Sideline tackling.*

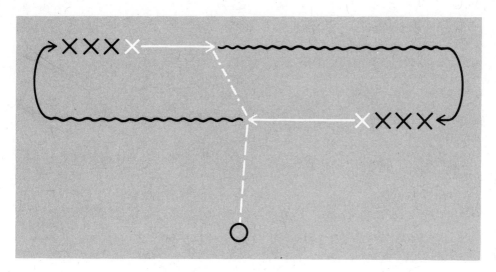

*DIAGRAM 10-10.  Deflected ball drill.*

4. *Deflecting the ball*  This drill gives the deep backs practice in intercepting deflected passes coming from the opposite direction. A hard pass is thrown to the first line of players, who run across the field. They try to deflect the ball to the second line of players, who are 6 to 8 yards deeper.

# Part Two

# Team Play

# 11

# The Offense

*Aggressive, tough blocking combined with explosive, quick-starting ball carriers who run with complete abandon can make any running game go.*

**George Allen**

To counter defenses that have become increasingly sophisticated and complex, the offense has had to develop newer and more potent tactics and strategy. Unquestionably, a stronger conversion to zone defenses has forced the offense to make a number of adjustments and changes.

The running game today is enjoying greater prominence because the hash marks have been moved in, eliminating the short side, and teams are placing less emphasis on the wide-open passing game. Emphasis on zone defenses and more effective pressure on the drop-back passes definitely have had a disrupting effect upon the timing and rhythm of the passing game. More teams are employing a system of multiple and varied defenses which have placed strong pressure on offensive units.

On all levels, quarterbacks with the ability to run have influenced considerably the game of football. Option plays, in particular, have been very effective at countering stacked defenses. The quarterback who can move well enough to get away from the pass rush has become ideal for today's game, even if his passing ability must be sacrificed somewhat. The defensive front line has become so geared to rushing the passer that the quarterback can be a sitting duck if he consistently drops back. In the future, the quarterback's ability to run will become an even greater threat.

Triple-Option offenses have been the most successful and innovative to come along in the last decade. The option maneuver, of course, is the key to the Wishbone attack, with the quarterback either handing off or running himself. If the play is executed properly, the option play can place strong pressure on the defense because the quarterback does not decide whether to run or to pitch the ball to another back until the last split second.

In the Triple-Option Veer the quarterback runs or keeps the ball, or runs and then laterals the ball to a trailing back. Neither the defensive end nor the defensive tackle is blocked—just faked out or run around—thus freeing the offensive end and tackle to block downfield.

Still, there are many coaches who are critical of the trend to the Veer offense in college football. "You can make more big plays that way," said John McKay, coach of the U.S.C. Trojans. "The problem, as I see it, is you can make more blunders, too."

"Every play can end up in some kind of lateral," explained McKay, "and the more you throw the ball around, the more chance you have to make the big play and the more chance you have to make the very poor play."

Actually, the Veer doesn't let a team do much effective passing. Split-second timing is essential to get off the lateral at just the right moment. Since a team has to spend so much time on it, it is difficult to spend sufficient time on the pass offense.

In attacking zone patterns, the majority of passers today have switched from throwing long to their wide receivers and are throwing short to backs darting out of the backfield or to their tight end. These are pass patterns that require little time to set up. The bomb, however, will not be removed from the offensive repertoire. It will always be available against those defenders who least expect it.

Increasingly, gadget plays such as reverses, fake reverses, and counter plays have become effective weapons in neutralizing defensive tactics. A hard-charging defensive lineman fooled by a reverse might let up a split second on the next play, giving the passer the necessary time to hit a wide receiver.

## SETTING UP A SYSTEM

To be successful, an offensive system must have balance and be able to run effectively, inside and outside. A good running attack can open the door for the passing game.

Once the basic alignments and the main formation have been decided, the coaching staff should establish the sweeps, power plays, option, dives, counters, and traps of the running game. It should be kept in mind, though, that it is better to run a few plays well than to run many plays poorly.

The Lombardi system was built around execution, which stressed a minumum of mistakes. There was nothing particularly fancy about it, like a lot of nifty ball handling. Coach Lombardi simply attempted to establish a sound, fundamental game that demanded sharp, crisp blocking and hard-running ball carriers.

Perhaps the key to winning football is to keep the other team off balance. If a team is all pass, its opponents will try to pressure the passer and crowd the receivers, while the linebackers will lie back and wait. Conversely, if a team stays strictly on the ground, the defense will tighten and gang up on the

---

### THINGS TO DO ON OFFENSE

- Move ball over 20-yard line before punting
- Don't give opponent ball outside 40-yard line
- No fumbles
- Three TD's per game
- Five big plays per game

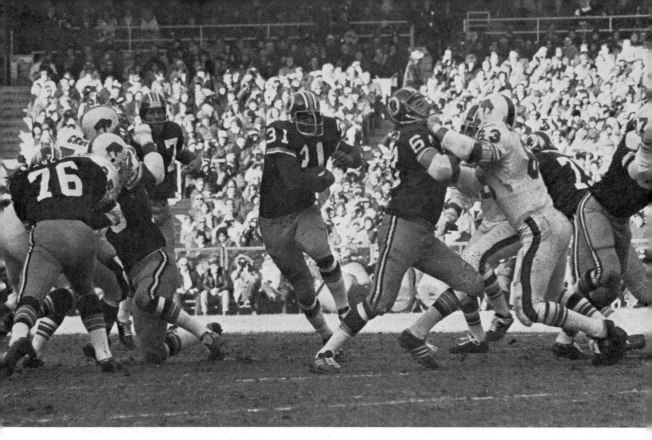

FIGURE 11-2. *An aggressive, quick-starting Redskin offensive line led by Walt Rock (76), John Wilbur (60), and Ray Schoenke (62) opens up a big hole for fullback Charley Harraway. An explosive running game is what makes any team hard-nosed.*

blockers and the ball carrier. The linebackers will be up on the line, supported by a tight secondary.

Therefore, the offense must mix up the plays with backs running outside and inside, play action passes thrown short and long, sprint-outs, pitchouts, the option play, draw plays, and screen plays, all of which will keep the defense guessing. If any offense is to have success, it must have a good end run and off-tackle play. Similarly, every team needs a quick-hitting play with the fullback carrying up the middle.

The Triple-Option play can provide an explosive attack with the quarterback running, throwing, or pitching out. Tactically, the Wishbone is very difficult to defense if it

is executed by competent personnel. However, perfection of the Triple-Option play requires a great deal of time and work.

The Redskins' style of offense is fundamentally simple. We employ an uncomplicated and balanced offense that excels in execution and ball control. We like an offense that doesn't give up the ball, that controls it and keeps it away from opponents. Quarterback Joe Theismann has added another dimension to our offense. He has a strong arm and can run and scramble.

We are constantly striving for a contrived, well-conceived offense, with as few mistakes as possible. Everything we do is based on timing and assignments. This is why we practice a little longer than most

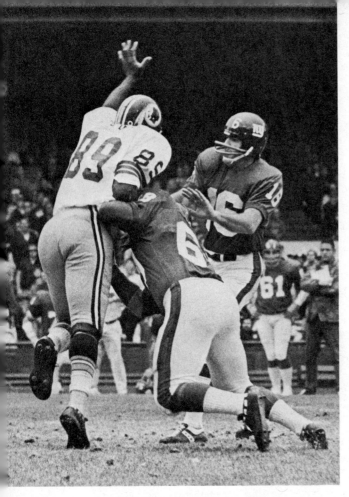

FIGURE 11-3. *Protecting the passer is the key to a successful passing attack. Quarterback Norm Snead of the Giants is given the time to complete a long aerial against the Redskins.*

teams. We don't believe in the gimmicky offense, in tricky maneuvers that might cause us to fumble the ball or lose our timing.

Our passing attack revolves around simplicity and timing, running the patterns the way they are supposed to be run so that the quarterback knows exactly where the receivers are.

While football has become a diverse game, the basic elements are simple. Successful football is still basically sound blocking and tackling. The team that can ex-

ecute individual fundamentals will win, provided that the players work together as a team.

Good blocking, ball carrying, passing, receiving, and quarterbacking, executed by a disciplined, highly motivated team, will result in a winning offense. Although formations have come and gone, the basics are still the same: proper execution, organization, motivation, conditioning, and evaluation. As Vince Lombardi once said: "Formations do not win games. You win with good basic football!"

## THE RUNNING GAME

The great majority of football coaches today base their offenses on a strong running attack, with the emphasis on a good end run and off-tackle play.

A team must be ground oriented. If it is not, it will not be tough enough offensively when, on fourth and one, the players have to grind it out to maintain possession. A strong blocking line is the first requirement for short yardage success. It must eliminate penetration by the opposition. Second, the blockers must have confidence in the man running with the ball. As for the ball carrier, acceleration is his greatest asset. He must be able to turn on the speed in a hurry.

Speed is a priceless strength of any offense. A coach should try to use it to the best advantage. The sweep led by two pulling guards has been one of the most successful plays in football.

Yet, teams are learning how to defense the sweep, for example, by stacking the defense, overshifting, and shooting in the strong safety. For the sweep to be successful, there must not be penetration by the defensive end, strong linebacker, or strong safety. Tosses to the halfback and pitches to the full-

FIGURE 11-4. *The quarterback's ability to run will become an even greater threat in all levels of football. Using option plays, the sprint-out, and the bootleg, the quarterback can place strong pressure on the defense. Here, Roger Staubach of the Dallas Cowboys scrambles for an important first down against the Redskins.*

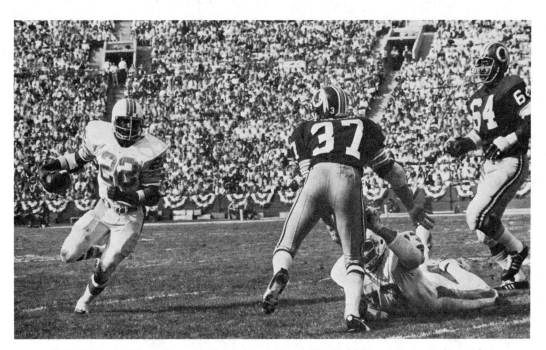

FIGURE 11-5. *Speed is a priceless strength of any offense. Many teams are replacing the sweep with the quick pitchout. Above, running back Mercury Morris of the Miami Dolphins attempts to move around the Redskins' veteran cornerback Pat Fischer.*

FIGURE 11-6. *The basis of a sound running game is effective blocking. Above, offensive guard Dave Herman of the New York Jets demonstrates good position in opening up a hole for running back John Riggins. Observe how he squares his hips and shoulders to the defender in front of him.*

back may be emphasized more in the future. This is because it is possible to get outside with speed and quickness, particularly when the defense is playing tight for the inside running game. While speed and deception are very important, every offense should also feature some power plays in certain situations.

An effective running game can be established only with solid, hard-hitting blocking, up front as well as in the backfield. Aggressive, tough blocking combined with explosive, quick-starting ball carriers who run with complete abandon can make any running game go.

As football becomes increasingly sophisticated and complex, defensive teams are not only using a variety of alignments but are also changing the angle of charge and stunting many ways from each defensive set. To cope with this diverse assortment of charges and patterns, an offensive team must be able to read these movements and adjust the point of attack after the ball is snapped.

Still, many clubs have eliminated fancy maneuvers in an attempt to control the ball. By excelling in execution and ball control, teams can mount long touchdown marches that eat up the clock and keep the ball away from the opposition. By keeping possession of the ball, a team can neutralize the skills of the opponents.

A team should not employ more plays than are needed. Actually, a well-balanced offense can be developed around only twelve plays. For a given opponent, the game plan will involve far fewer plays.

The offense needs to attack only five ways:

- Run outside.
- Run inside.
- Run up the gut.
- Misdirection plays.
- Throw the ball.

### Attacking a Stunting Defense

Since stunting can be confusing to any young offensive team, the following adjustments can be utilized:

- Run outside.
- Widen the line spacing.
- Use quick count plays.
- Use automatics when possible.
- Run power plays.
- Stay basic.

## DEVELOPING A PASSING ATTACK

An effective passing game can prevent a strong defensive buildup against the running attack. To win, therefore, a football team must be able to throw the ball. If the quarterback is not a skillful passer, the defense, by ignoring the possibility of a pass, can tighten up on the line against the running attack.

To employ the passing game effectively, a team must devote a considerable amount of practice time to this method of attack. Normally, a pass-oriented team will devote half of each practice to the passing game. Throughout the season, the coaching staff should continually examine and evaluate the successes and failures of the pass game.

Until recently, the college game has not emphasized the pass as strongly as the pro game has done. A complete passing attack requires considerable time and effort. Seldom does a coach on the high school or even college level have both an exceptional passer and excellent receivers. A good pass offense will be only as good as the players make it. The passers and receivers must be willing to spend much time and effort perfecting the required execution and timing, and blockers must be able to provide the necessary protection.

Yet, there is no more exciting aspect of football today than the passing game. Indeed, the passing game can be a great equalizer against a team that is physically superior.

In developing a strong passing game, the coach should utilize a formation or formations from which both the run and pass can be effective. Teams on the high school and college level should limit the number of pass routes that must be perfected. Whenever possible, multiple receiver or flood patterns should be employed. Complementary patterns should be utilized which can clear the areas of each receiver.

Most teams will designate a primary receiver on any given pass play, although any other receiver should be ready to catch the ball.

The following aspects of the opposing defensive team should be evaluated:

- Pass rush
- Holdup
- Press
- Coverage
  zone
  man-for-man
  combination

The success of the passing game will depend in large measure on those blockers who protect the passer. An effective system of protection must cope with a variety of alignments, stunts, and many types of pass rushes.

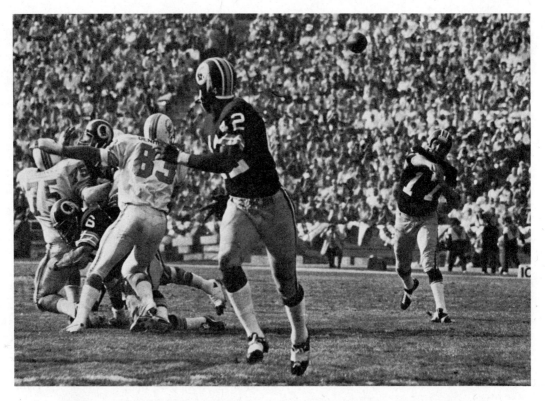

FIGURE 11-7. *Short passes to wide receivers in the flat can be very effective against a defense that concentrates on the bomb or one that is plugging up the middle. Here, Charley Taylor receives a quick throw from quarterback Bill Kilmer. We throw a number of short-outs to receivers.*

Since the opposing defense will spend many hours of preparation to break down the system, the offense must also prepare itself diligently to assure an effective protection system.

An aggressive pass rush can be neutralized by adjusting the pass routes and employing quick passes. The blocking patterns can also be adjusted by using the tight end.

## TYPES OF PASSES

The passing game is divided into six segments: drop-back passes, play action passes, sprint-out passes, option passes, bootleg passes, and screen passes.

### Drop-back Passes

Since it is easier to throw the ball from the set position, the majority of coaches base their pass attack on the drop-back pass. A passer will have better results if he can get firmly set before throwing. However, this action requires more protection.

The quarterback may retreat three, five, seven, or nine steps (see Chart 11-1). As he makes his delivery, he should get the pass away within 3.0 to 3.5 seconds. If he can get

3 seconds, he will be in good shape because his receivers will have had 15 or 20 yards in which to beat their man and break open.

## Play Action Passes

The play action pass evolves from a running play that pins the linebacker down for an instant. With the line carrying out its run blocking assignments, the quarterback fakes a hand-off to one of his backs and passes to a receiver. The key is to make the play look exactly like a run.

Play action develops from sweeps. If the linebackers and deep backs are effective in coming up and stopping sweeps, the offense can beat them by showing the same running action, while a receiver moves behind the defensive backs for a pass.

Many quarterbacks like to roll out to the side, employing either a half roll or full roll action. A play action draw play can be effective off a roll-out pass. With the defense looking for a play action pass, the quarterback then gives the ball to the halfback in the No. 2 hole.

## Sprint-out Passes

The sprint-out can provide the offense with a highly effective passing game. It attempts to

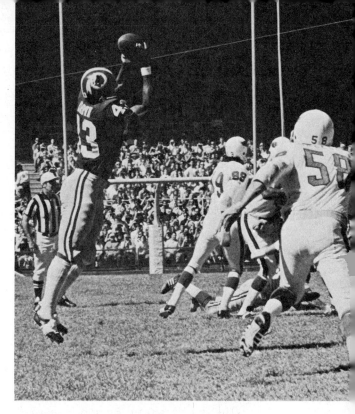

FIGURE 11-8. *One of the biggest developments in football during the past decade has been the emphasis on throwing passes to running backs coming out of the backfield. This has occurred because of the way defenses are playing. Here, halfback Larry Brown moves into the secondary to receive a toss from quarterback Bill Kilmer.*

use one or two blocking backs on the defensive end with the objective of getting the quarterback outside. Once the defense begins to rotate and pursue quickly to the flow of the quarterback, the quarterback will pull up behind the offensive tackle (about 6 to 7 yards in depth) and throw back to the back side.

## Option Passes

Employed usually from the sweep, an option pass can be very effective because the running back can either run or pass.

CHART 11-1. **Drop-back time chart.**

| Drop | Standard Time (seconds) | Times | | | | |
|------|------------|---|---|---|---|---|
| Three steps | 0.9 | | | | | |
| Five steps | 1.30 | | | | | |
| Seven steps | 1.75 | | | | | |
| Nine steps | 1.95 | | | | | |

### Bootleg Passes

The quarterback's action is the opposite of rolling out. After faking a hand-off, he retreats away from the flow, usually protected by a pulling guard.

### Screen Passes

Screen plays can help make an excellent passing attack because they can discourage a good pass rush. To draw in the four rushers, the quarterback in the pocket must appear to be passing deep. The keys to a successful screen play are the guards and blocking back, who must be good actors. They must look like they are pass blocking.

The lead guard has to have the correct timing. He must release on time. When he goes, everybody goes.

The double screen is another effective pass play, in which the quarterback looks to one side, then looks to the other side.

In conclusion, the screen pass is a play you have to stay with. The 49ers employ the screen very well because they keep using it. The thing I like about the screen is that it is a game breaker. It is a more reliable play to get you 40 or 50 yards at one crack than any other play in football.

### PASSING PATTERNS

With increased emphasis on the passing game, colleges and high schools now employ as many as ten or twelve different pass patterns, in addition to their many variations (Diagram 11-1). To fully exploit all types of defensive secondaries, a short release man and a deep receiver are involved in all the patterns. The short release man can exploit the red-dogging linebackers of the defense.

They also leave vital short pass zones open, such as the flat, hook, and curl zones.

Most college patterns are built on the flood basis, primarily because most college teams are still predominately and primarily zone teams. The high schools employ pretty much the same tactics. By forcing the deep man to cover deep, they have the underneath man practically open.

Many teams have been successful in building a set of patterns for man-to-man and another set for the zone. They run a crossing pattern and a pick pattern against a man-to-man defense. Against a zone operation, they will employ a flood kind of pattern.

### Favorite Patterns

Many coaches feel the curl is the best pattern a college team can run. The sideline also ranks high as an effective route for a receiver. The sideline and up, a deep pattern calling for tremendous speed, and the flag are also popular. Perhaps, the most successful pattern in the sprint-out pass is the halfback flare. The comeback route can also be consistently effective with both drop-back and sprint-out techniques.

Combination routes can be worked successfully with the tight end. One man might be sent deep while the tight end is brought shallow across under him.

Individual patterns run by most college and high school teams are listed below.

*sideline.* an "out" pattern of 12 yards.

*curl* (or *hook*). the receiver comes down hard, turns in on his curl, and receives a bullet pass.

*sideline and up.* faking the quick "out" and breaking back up.

*post.* receiver breaks down for approximately 12 yards, fakes to the outside, and breaks to the goalpost.

*flag.* drives to inside of defensive man as if run-

ning "deep slant" or "curl," then drives off inside foot to corner.

*slant* (*in or out*).   cutting off the outside foot, the
receiver makes his break quick and sharp, in a
slanting angle.

*hitch*.   a quick pass to an outside receiver.

*flare*.   a swing out by a back into the flat.

*circle*.   breaking right off tackle and swinging back
up into the linebacking area.

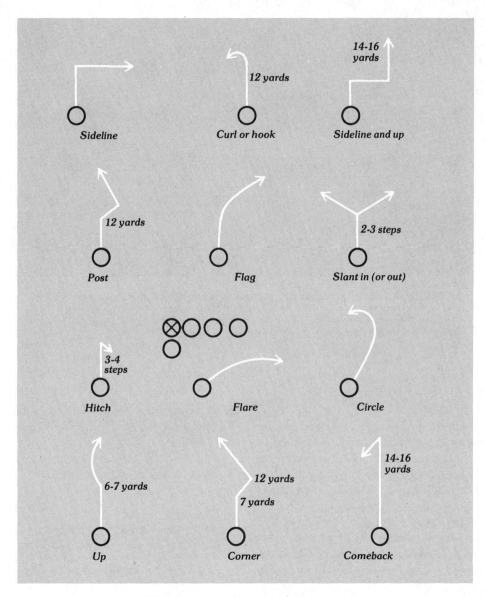

DIAGRAM 11-1.   *Individual routes for receivers.*

FIGURE 11-9. *An accurate passing game can puncture a zone defense by exploiting the cracks, or seams, where one zone adjoins another. Here, wide receiver Charley Taylor finds a hole in the defensive secondary of the Dallas Cowboys, as defender Mel Renfro arrives too late to break up the pass play.*

### ATTACKING A ZONE DEFENSE

When throwing against zone defenders, the quarterback has to have some extra time to throw. Normally, zone defensive backs do not pick up the receivers right away. They stand in the middle of their seven zones (usually four up and three deep or three up and four deep) and wait. Therefore, the quarterback must wait, too, until his receivers can get to the edges, or seams, of the zones.

These are the holes between the zones. The offense should send the flanker wide to one side, while the split end goes wide to the other. These maneuvers will widen the holes and provide the seams for the receivers. Passing deep against some zones can be a big mistake.

In attacking the four short zones, the 10- to 15-yard defensive zones are broken down into distinct areas:

- A flat on both sides
- A hook on both sides (Y, tight end)
- A curl on both sides (X and Z, wide receivers)

The Slot formation has been very popular because it floods the zone by placing more receivers than one man can handle into an area. This flood pattern has been used very successfully by Miami's Paul Warfield (X) and Howard Twilley (Z). Twilley's fly route takes the defender deep and Warfield runs an out-and-up route.

What makes a zone defense tough is an aggressive, hard-charging front four. As a result, screens and draw plays work particularly well against zones.

As the pass pattern develops, the quarterback reads the defense being used. His receivers have optional routes against combination double coverages or zone defenses. The passer has to "read" the option that follows a predetermined plan and hit his receiver in the cracks or seams of the zone defense.

Recognition of the defense is not easy to teach and learn because the receivers must spot the plan on their first step across the line, at the same time the defense is trying to disguise it. The keys are the defenders on the side of the receiver, the safety man and defensive cornerback, plus, at times, the linebacker on the respective side.

## TRAINING THE QUARTERBACK

The coaching staff should spend as much time as possible with each of their quarterbacks, both on and off the field. They must assist the quarterback in acquiring a thorough understanding of the game plan and help him learn how to study the opposing defense as well as his own personnel. In choosing his plays intelligently, the quarterback must have a thorough knowledge of both offensive and defensive football.

The quarterback must learn how to take advantage of defensive tactics, like audiblizing at the line of scrimmage to counter different alignments. This calls for a complete knowledge of the blocking assignments of every

man on every play, against every type of defense. Therefore, the signal caller must be able to recognize quickly the various defensive formations that confront his team. He must know the characteristic fakes and patterns of his ends and backs and anticipate the break before the receiver makes it.

Along with his coach, the quarterback should go over every phase of the scouting report. The opponents' defensive weaknesses against rushing plays should be discussed. He should know the opponents' weakest as well as strongest defensive performers.

Most teams have two or three quarterback meetings each week. The Tuesday meeting should cover the defenses expected from the upcoming opponent. The use of game films is most helpful in enabling the quarterback to evaluate what is happening on defense. Later in the week a coach should review the sideline signal system with the quarterback.

## CALLING THE PLAYS

Sensible play selection is essential to team success. While many coaches still prefer having their quarterback call the plays, an increasing number are employing a simple system of signaling plays from the sideline. Using hand and finger signals, the coach is able to communicate both running and pass plays to his quarterback on the field. Certainly, the coach is better qualified to call plays for his quarterback. Besides his superior experience, he handles the play calling during practice and is responsible for the analysis of the game films. In addition, he is in telephone communication with assistant coaches in the press box. Yet, shuttling players in and out of the game tends to take something away from the quarterback's position as a leader.

If his team has an effective passing game, the quarterback should not hesitate to pass on first down. The surprise element is a major factor in making a pass play successful on first down.

"First down is the most important down," said Coach Ted Marchibroda, who formerly coached our quarterbacks. "You are in charge because you can either run or pass. What you want is at least 4 yards so you can dictate to the defense again on second down. If it is second and 8, they are dictating to you. But if it is second and 3 or 4, you can either throw the ball or run it—and the pressure is on the defense. So, on the first down, call the best plays you have."

"Always know exactly where you are and what the situation is on first down," said Marchibroda. "Call the plays you have worked on the most, the plays that are working the best, the bread-and-butter pass or run. These are the positive plays."

"When you call positive plays on first downs," said Ted, "you get more third and short situations. Third and 1 is better than third and 4, and the better your call on first down, the better your chance for third and 1. With positive calls on the first play, you also get more fourth and short situations."

Using the right personnel on big plays is very important in play calling. The quarterback (or coach) should know who the best blockers and runners are. He also should know where the defense is weak, or relatively weak. He should go to the best receivers. It is vital that he know who is in the lineup at all times—his lineup and the other team's—so that on every big play he can match his strength against their weakness.

## NUMBERING SYSTEM

The play selected in the huddle is a combination of the series and the hole in the line. While the numbering system varies with the team, for plays in the 40's, the right halfback will be carrying the ball; in the 30's, the fullback; and in the 20's, the left halfback is the ball carrier. A play in the 30 series through the 7 hole would be 37. (See Diagram 11-2.)

As a rule, the outside legs of the guards are the 2 and 3 holes; the outside legs of the tackles are the 4 and 5 holes, and so on. Interior linemen are normally spaced 2 to 3 feet from each other, while the tails of running backs are generally $4\frac{1}{2}$ yards from the line of scrimmage.

While they are not numbered, pass plays are identified by the intended receiver and the route he is to run.

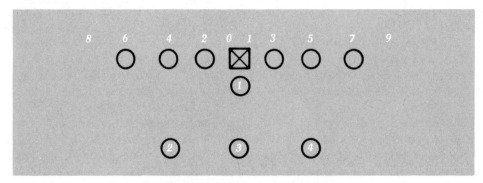

DIAGRAM 11-2. The numbering system.

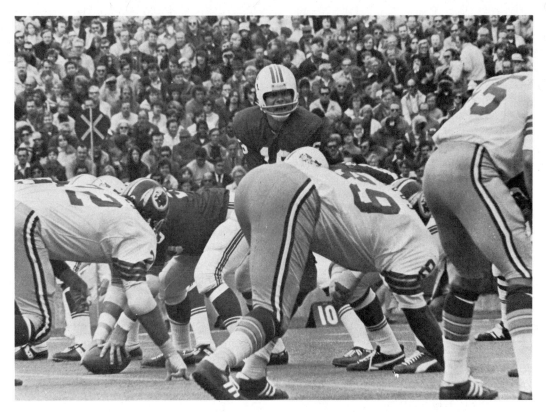

FIGURE 11-10. *The quarterback should examine the defenses at the line of scrimmage. If he sees that the intended hole is jammed with defensive men, he should be able to call a simple automatic. Jim Plunkett of the New England Patriots is shown looking the defense over.*

### X, Y, and Z

The receivers are numbered as follows: X, the split end; Y, the tight end; and Z, the flanker. While the split end is positioned on the line of scrimmage, the flanker back is not.

### SIGNAL SYSTEM

After calling the formation, the quarterback indicates to the ball carrier whether the tight end is left or right, the hole number, and then he gives the snap count. For example, if he calls an end run, he would say: "Red right [formation], 29 [left halfback through right end] on 3 [snap]. Break!"

### AUTOMATICS

A system of automatics or audibles can produce excellent results, with a minimum of practice time. Yet, automatics are seldom used on the high school level.

Actually, calling a change-up on the line

of scrimmage is not difficult. In the huddle, the quarterback will say, "34 on 3." The "34" is the play number and the "3" the snap number. On the line, if the play stands, he will call "Set!" two meaningless numbers, and then "Hut! Hut! Hut!" On the third "Hut!" the center snaps the ball.

However, if the quarterback decides to convert to another play from 34 on 3, he will call "Set! Three!" and then the new play number. The repetition of the snap number "3" means that a change-up is coming, but an opponent will not be able to tell whether the play number is real or not because he does not know what snap number was set in the huddle.

Or, the quarterback can use the color system of calling an audible. Each week a different color is "live." If the signal caller calls out the color and a new play, he has audibled to that play. Half the time, the color is just a dummy call. After an audible, the play is automatically run on "Hut two!"

To avoid confusion, automatics should be kept to a minimum. Some favorite pass plays used as automatics are the following:

- Flat out pass to either side
- Fast goal to either Z or X
- Look-in to Y (tight end)
- Running game audibles

## BLOCKING SYSTEM

Blocking should receive major attention by the coaching staff throughout the season. With the sophisticated and changing defenses of football today, we like to teach simple blocking patterns instead of line calls. One-word assignments are much more easily memorized and understood by the linemen. As a result, any blocking system should refer to one-word rules.

### Line Calls

Line calls by the center enable the offensive line to adjust to the defense's shifts. Essentially, line calls tell the line to block "even" or "odd." *Even* refers to an ordinary block: *odd* designates angle blocking, i.e., scissors by the center and guard, or cross-blocking by the guard and tackle.

### Rule Blocking

Before rule blocking was used, linemen blocked according to the defense they faced on any given play. In short, the defense dictated the man a lineman was to block. In rule blocking, the center, for example, drive blocks the man over him. If none is there, he will release and fan back. If a guard has to cut off the man over him, and none is there, he will release and seal the first inside linebacker.

Unquestionably, rule blocking has simplified the blocking assignments for the linemen. Linemen no longer have to learn a different assignment for each defense. Therefore, the defense is no longer able to call the shots.

On running plays that are built on the theory of running to daylight, a blocking lineman will take a defender where he wants to go. If he wants to go inside, he will drive him inside, while the running back runs outside.

To understand his defensive opponent, a lineman must know how he makes his initial charge, how he reacts and keys, and the maneuvers he may employ.

### Offensive Line Splits

Line splits have been responsible for eliminating the odd-man defensive lines with the big middle guard on the center's head.

Shifting the guard an extra foot has widened the gap between the defensive tackle and the middle guard over center. With the offensive tackles moved out another gap, the defensive tackles have had to stay inside and play on the head of the offensive guards. The defensive ends have also been forced to come inside to play the role of defensive tackles. As a result, the corner linebackers have had to protect them outside.

## ORGANIZING AND WRITING OFFENSES

After he determines the blocking technique system for his team, the coach must develop a method of writing up and presenting his offensive plays. These write-ups will include coaching points and drawings of plays.

Coaching staffs spend hours each week applying their blocking rules to the defenses they expect to face on the weekend. As important as blocking rules are, a coach should not overlook the task of keeping the fundamentals of blocking sharp and crisp.

For quicker teaching and learning, the various assignments and rules should be placed on a "weekly assignment sheet."

### Offensive Worksheets

Mimeographed sheets of different defenses are very effective in enabling the coaching staff to check quickly on the players' blocking assignments against different alignments.

### Categorizing Offensive Plays

For ease in learning and communication, the various phases of offense should be categorized into different systems. They are

**FIGURE 11-11.** *A great block by veteran offensive guard Ray Schoenke has opened up a gaping hole for fullback Charley Harraway to move through the left side of the Houston Oilers' defense.*

given different priorities and placed in a logical sequence.

The following blocking systems in the passing game are categorized:

- Drop-back
- Sprint
- Quick pass
- Roll
- Draw
- Screen
- Goal line

### Selecting an Offensive System

The football coach should try to fit his system to his team's talents and personality, as well as his own. Ideally, the personnel should dictate the offense. During the pre-season training program, the coaching staff must find the basic offense the team is most ca-

FIGURE 11-12. *The cut-back play provides the blocking required for necessary yardage situations. Led by pulling tackle Walt Rock (76) and fullback Charley Harraway (31), running back Larry Brown turns the corner against the Dallas Cowboys. Strong pressure is placed on defensive end Larry Cole of the Cowboys.*

pable of running. Ideally, though, spring practice is the time to set up the offense. The type of quarterback will often determine the style of offense.

No matter what offensive system is employed, plays should be selected in series that relate to one another. A series is a group of related plays that come off a certain backfield action. For success in execution, each series demands players with particular skills and attributes.

Unfortunately, some coaches attempt to recruit players whose college experience conforms to their predetermined system. They would be wise to fit their system to their personnel instead of deciding first on a system and then trying to find the personnel. Essentially, the plays should be within the team's physical ability to execute consistently well.

Generally, if his players tend to be big

and slow, the coach should concentrate on straight-ahead, hard-hitting plays, while a more wide-open attack can be employed if the players are small and fast.

## Two-minute Offense

The two-minute offense is a contingency plan for the final 2 minutes of the first half and final 2 minutes of the game. Few high school teams employ it because they lack the highly developed skills and time for practice possessed by professional players.

Through the years, top NFL quarterbacks like Johnny Unitas, Bart Starr, and Roger Staubach have expertly moved their teams on long scoring drives. In the 1972 NFC play-off game with the San Francisco 49ers, Staubach directed his Dallas team to two touchdowns in the closing 2 minutes to win 30–28.

From his own 45-yard line, Staubach connected on two consecutive 8-yard passes to Walt Garrison, who ran both out of bounds to stop the clock. After a 19-yard aerial to Billy Parks, and a Cowboy time-out, Staubach hit Parks again on the goal line for a touchdown.

On an attempted onside kick, Mel Renfro recovered for the Cowboys. On the first play, Staubach scrambled up the middle for 21 yards. Then, Roger passed to Parks on the left sideline for 19 yards, stopping the clock with 56 seconds remaining. The winning score came on the following play when Staubach found Ron Sellers in the end zone. Indeed, it was a superb demonstration of the two-minute offense.

### High School

Many high school teams have been successful with the Pro-set and Pro-slot formations, with some modifications. The Split Wing T formation has been bolstered by the use of split ends and flanker backs.

The Power T has been one of the most prominent offensive sets used by high schools in Ohio, relying heavily on power off-tackle and power sweep plays. Since a Power series needs more players at the point of attack, tighter formations are usually necessary. Two-on-one blocks are very common at the attack area.

The Power I series of double-team blocking involving numerous pulling linemen and leading backs has become a popular offense in both high school and college football.

The I formation, with the single split end with the slot, or a wide flanker and split end, has been used successfully, also. While the I offense is simple and effective, it does require

**CHART 11-2.** Popular offensive attacks.

| Formation/System | Pertinent Assets |
|---|---|
| Regular I | Quick sweeps, inside power |
| Slot I | Quick sweeps, weak-side attack |
| Pro I | Passing wide, inside power |
| Power I | Short yardage, goal line |
| Triple Option | Dictates to the defense |
| Pro-set | Drop-back passing, versatile running |
| Pro-slot | Flood passing |
| Wing T | Deception |
| Full House | Power running |
| Slot T | Strong-side passing, weak-side running |
| Double Slot T | Four quick receivers, flexibility with motion |

specific talent, which colleges can recruit but the high schools cannot. The I calls for a quarterback who has outstanding running and passing ability.

Since few teams on the high school and college levels are blessed with the strong-armed drop-back passer, the sprint-out pass should be considered. A fair passer with some running ability can make the sprint-out a potent weapon of the offense. The sprint-out pass is particularly effective when used from the I formation.

### College

The offensive system used most prominently on the college level in the early 1970's has been the I formation, and its variations. Such powers as Notre Dame, U.S.C., Oklahoma, Alabama, Nebraska, Michigan, Ohio State, and others featured the formation in an effort to attack the odd-front, Monster-type defense that has been so effective in college football.

From the I backfield alignment, the offense can attack the entire front with the best ball carrier running behind the best blocking back. Utilizing the quarterback run-out option, the off-tackle play, the sprint-out or roll-out pass—coupled with a roving wing-back—gives the I a multitude of advantages.

In the past several seasons there has been a marked increase in the use of the Triple Option system of attack, involving Wishbone and Veer formations. The "Triple" produced outstanding results at Texas and Houston and has attracted numerous followers, many of whom had been successful advocates of the I formation.

For two decades, the Pro-set has been a popular formation on the college scene. With countless passing possibilities and a variety of running potential, the formation continues at all levels of football.

Following World War II, there was quite a transformation from Single Wing football to T football. During the process, the Wing T formation became very popular, because it had some appeal to coaches of both schools of thought. The Wing T has maintained a considerable following and provides a very deceptive and consistent means of attack.

San Diego took a Single Wing type of football and made it I formation football. Their offense requires a tailback with great speed. Indiana has used the I offense exceptionally well, utilizing the quarterback run-out option, the off-tackle play, and sprint and roll. Their offense is geared to the outside. They run very few plays (about six running plays), but strive for flawless execution with these. The fullback's running play consists of a direct hand-off, and he "runs to daylight."

Michigan State also works from the I formation, featuring pitch sweeps and options. They also run a lot from the Slot formation, featuring the lead dive and the sprint-out. A favorite play of the Spartans is a Power draw. Their best counter is a fake option, slot counter. Teams pursue so quickly on defense today that the offense has to have counters to try to slow them down.

As an example of their highly diversified attack, M.S.U. runs six types of passes: (1) fake option, (2) belly action, (3) bootleg action, (4) sprint-out option, (5) pitch sweep, and (6) drop-back.

In varying degrees of popularity, the Full House, the Slot T, Double Slot T, and others are very much a part of college football.

## OFFENSIVE SYSTEMS

The following formations have met with much success.

### The I Formation

The I formation (Diagram 11-3) generates a powerful inside running attack, since the fullback is in position to lead the tailback on running plays. The fullback can also hit inside quickly. When the I formation was introduced, the idea of putting the tailback 7 yards back, rather than 4 or 5, was repulsive to many coaches. But the additional depth of 2 or 3 yards has given the ball carrier an opportunity to run to daylight. Designed originally to provide the quick outside thrusts, this formation affords excellent opportunities for sweeps, as illustrated in Diagram 11-4.

As with most successful systems, the ability to run off-tackle (to either side) made

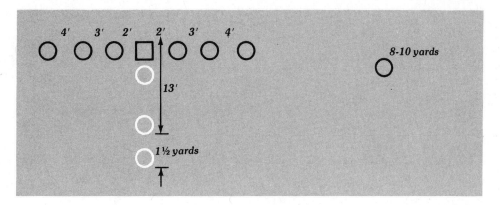

*DIAGRAM 11-3. I formation.*

this one of the "bread and butter" plays of the formation (Diagram 11-5).

Knowledge of the defensive symbols illustrated in the accompanying box is necessary to read the following diagrams.

| SYMBOLS OF DEFENSIVE PERSONNEL | |
|---|---|
| △ | Rushmen or defensive men (in three-point stance) |
| ☐ | Linebackers |
| S | Deep backs inside (safeties) |
| C | Cornerbacks |

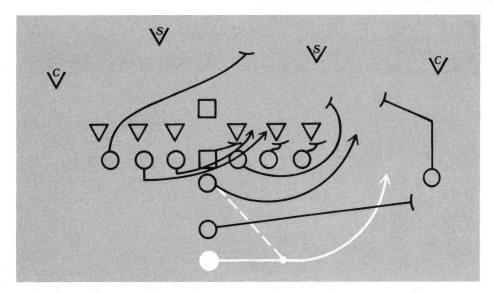

*DIAGRAM 11-4. I formation sweep versus 6-1.*

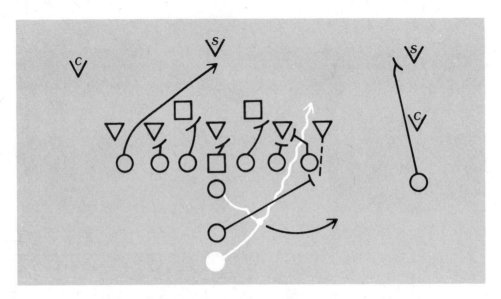

*DIAGRAM 11-5. I formation off-tackle versus Oklahoma.*

The Draw play that evolved proved particularly effective, because the passing attack is based primarily on play action to the strong side. See Diagram 11-6.

### The Slot I Formation

The Slot I formation (Diagram 11-7) features fine strong-side passing and good weak-side

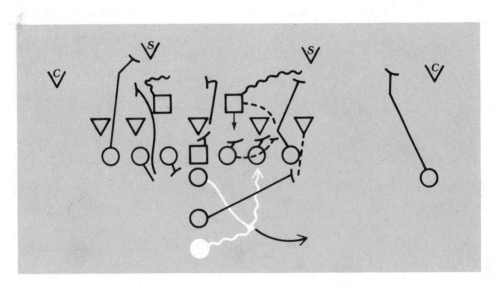

*DIAGRAM 11-6. I formation draw versus Oklahoma.*

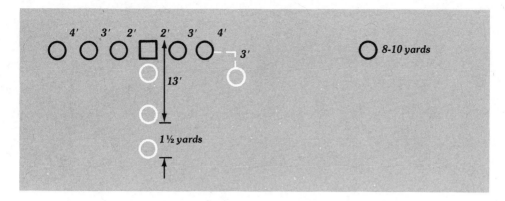

DIAGRAM 11-7.  *Slot I formation.*

running. The I slot adds greatly to the regular I in the number of variations available. The tight end drops back to become a wingback. The flanker back moves up to become a split end. It gives great deceptions on reverse plays, since the wingback can get the ball quickly after the quarterback has faked to the fullback or tailback.

With the threat of a wingback counter inside, the formation discourages defensive

pursuit, a problem which has plagued the regular I since its inception.

By having a wingback on the strong side instead of a tight end, the off-tackle play is curtailed somewhat. However, the formation has fine strong-side passing potential, with numerous combinations, involving the wingback and split end.

A typical strong-side pass is shown in Diagram 11-8. The quarterback's first key is

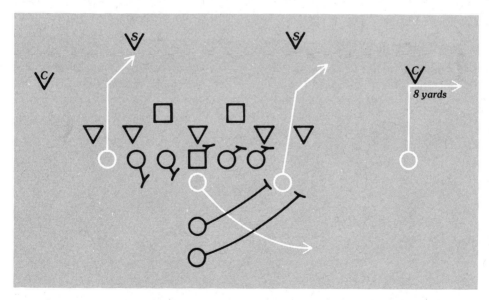

DIAGRAM 11-8.  *Slot I sprint-out pass versus Oklahoma.*

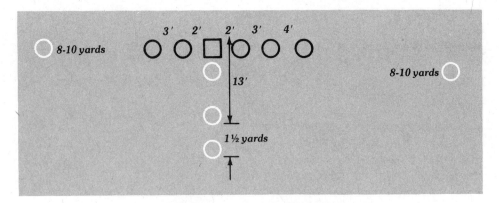

*DIAGRAM 11-9. Pro I formation.*

the reaction of the cornerback. In the event he retreats, the quarterback throws immediately to the split end. If the cornerback holds, the quarterback switches his attention to the wingback. On a zone rotation, the quarterback throws to the wingback in the "Seam." If the wingback is covered, the quarterback runs a sweep.

### The Pro I Formation

The Pro I (Diagram 11-9) is a balanced formation that provides considerably more passing potential than the regular I, yet retains a great portion of the running threat.

Defensing the problems presented by two wide receivers, containing the quick sweeps, and stopping the inside power game is quite a task. As used at U.S.C., this system of offense has produced consistent success.

### The Power I Formation

The Power I (Diagram 11-10) features good deception that is effective in tough yardage territory and provides strong inside running. It has been used by most teams as an "addition" to their normal formation. In short yardage, goal line, or ball control situations,

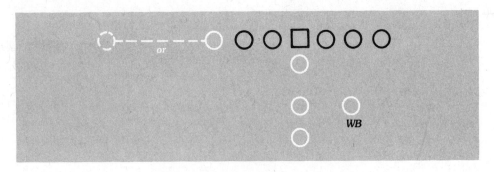

*DIAGRAM 11-10. Power I formation.*

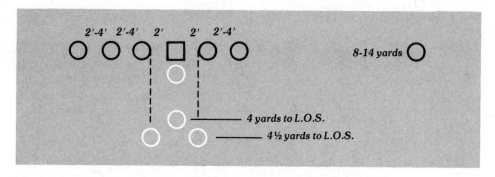

2'-4'  2'-4'  2'   2'  2'-4'

8-14 yards

4 yards to L.O.S.

4½ yards to L.O.S.

*DIAGRAM 11-11.  Wishbone T formation.*

this is an ideal formation. It has great power and deception, since both the fullback and wingback can lead to block on inside running plays.

### The Triple-Option Offense

Employing multiple backfield alignments, the Triple Option is a powerful running formation with excellent deception. The complete offense is based upon the unique concept of one basic play. In executing this play, the quarterback is permitted to select any one of the three points of attack while the play is in progress. As the play develops, the reaction of the defense enables the quarterback to determine where the offense will attack.

The Triple idea does not dictate a specific alignment or formation. However, the Wishbone I formation, pioneered at the University of Texas by Darrell Royal, and the Houston Veer, developed by Bill Yeoman, have become big favorites. Both offenses feature the running quarterback.

The basic play from the Wishbone has the fullback hitting the offensive guard-tackle gap, expecting to receive a hand-off from the quarterback (Diagram 11-11). Meanwhile, the quarterback "meshes" with the fullback

and determines if this gap will be the point of attack. The quarterback's decision is dependent upon the reaction of the first defender inside the defensive end.

If the defender does not respect the threat of the fullback (comes across the line of scrimmage), the quarterback simply allows the fullback to keep the ball and the guard-tackle gap becomes the point of attack.

Now, if the defender inside the defensive end does respect the threat of the fullback and closes down, the quarterback keeps the ball, thus eliminating the offensive guard-tackle gap as a possible point of attack.

As the quarterback withdraws the ball from the grasp of the fullback, he continues running toward the defensive end. At this point, he will focus his attention on the defensive end and make a second decision.

If the defensive end moves in to tackle the quarterback, the quarterback tosses the ball back to the trailing halfback, who establishes a 5-yard "pitch-relationship" with the quarterback. If the defensive end crosses the line of scrimmage or drifts out to protect against the possible pitch, the quarterback keeps the ball and turns upfield. The basic play from the Wishbone is shown in Diagram 11-12.

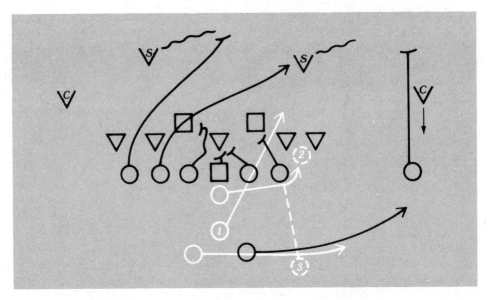

DIAGRAM 11-12.  *Triple Option (Wishbone T versus Oklahoma).*

As stated previously, the Triple offense is not confined to a specific backfield alignment. Coach Yeoman of the University of Houston, one of the early proponents of this offensive approach, applied the Triple from a wide-open formation (Diagram 11-13). A growing number of college coaches are now employing the Houston Veer because they want a Triple Option offense from which there is a constant passing threat.

To confuse the defense still further, the other plays used in this intriguing attack—the

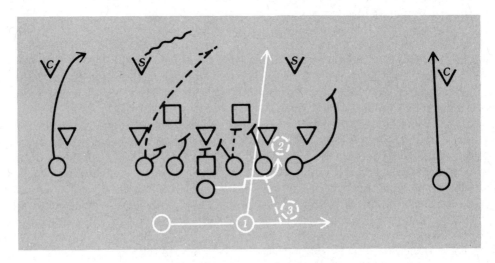

DIAGRAM 11-13   *Triple-Option Veer versus Oklahoma.*

FIGURE 11-13. Pro-set. Although it lacks power inside, the Pro-set can provide a wide-open attack. This is my favorite formation in pro football. By employing two wide receivers (not shown) out to both sides, the formation forces the defense to spread. With only two running backs in the formation, it lacks a back leading inside plays.

counter, the counter option, and various play action passes—all begin like the basic play.

The Triple makes slanting and other stunting maneuvers dangerous and forces defenses into predictable interior alignments.

The theory behind the Triple is extremely simple. It is predicated on the assumption that anything the defense does can be wrong. However, successful execution requires considerable practice by the quarter-back in reading the intentions of the defense; also, perfecting the quarterback-fullback "mesh" on the basic play is a demanding technique.

### The Pro-set Formation

The Pro-set (Diagram 11-14) is the best balanced offense in pro football for running and

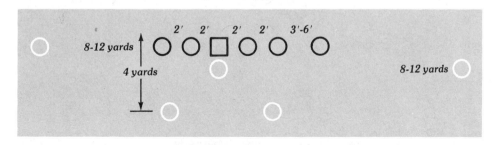

DIAGRAM 11-14. Pro-set formation.

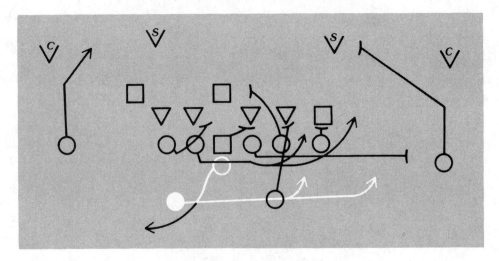

DIAGRAM 11-15. *Pro-set Power sweep versus Pro defense.*

passing. You can do everything from this set to put pressure on the defense. The backfield is split or divided with wide receivers out to both sides to take advantage of the dropback passing game featured by this formation.

Basically, the Pro-set offense has the tight end split somewhat in order not to be pinched in when he wants to release the forward pass. Also, from the split position, the tight end can isolate the man defending against him so he can get a one-on-one block.

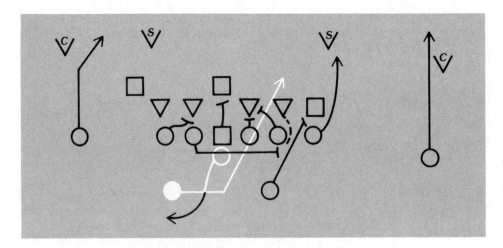

DIAGRAM 11-16. *Pro-set off-tackle play versus Pro defense.*

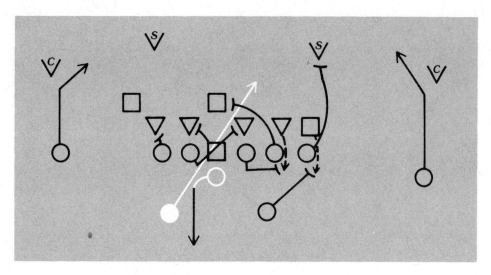

*DIAGRAM 11-17. Pro-set, quick toss versus Pro defense.*

With the two wide receivers out to both sides, the Pro-set offense can run such plays as the Power sweep (Diagram 11-15), the isolation play, off-tackle play (Diagram 11-16), the quick trap (Diagram 11-17), and the quick toss to either side (Diagram 11-18). The quick toss can break a game open with quickness and surprise. A back with speed can get outside with stunning quickness. The pros' "bread and butter" play against the Pro defense is the Power sweep.

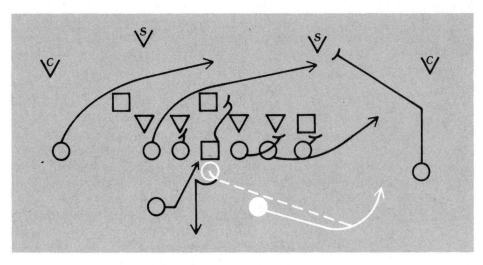

*DIAGRAM 11-18. Pro-set quick toss versus Pro defense.*

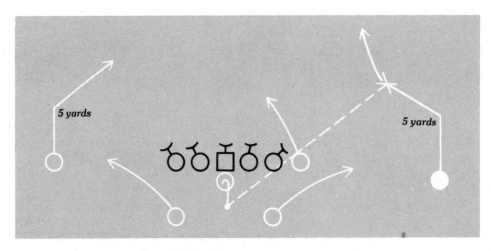

DIAGRAM 11-19. Look-in pass.

On the Power sweep, the flanker blocks in on the safety and the onside guard blocks out on the contain man. The offside guard and the runner will cut off the isolation block of the tight end, a "Daylight Play."

Diagrams 11-19 through 11-24 illustrate six of the most popular pass plays from the Pro-set formation.

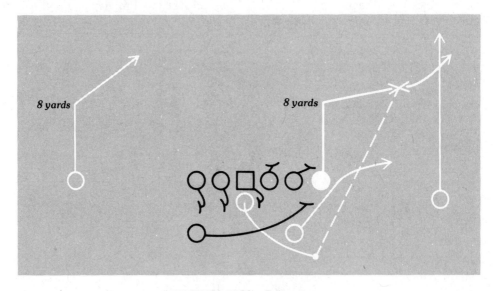

DIAGRAM 11-20. Roll-out pass.

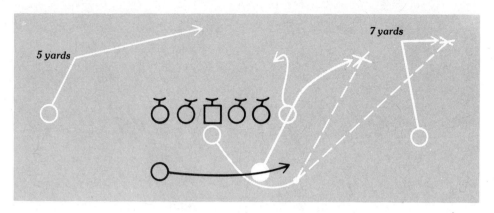

DIAGRAM 11-21.   Goal-line pass.

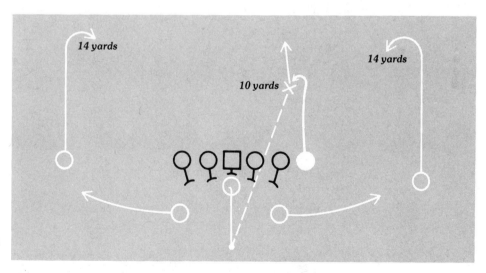

DIAGRAM 11-22.   Hook pass.

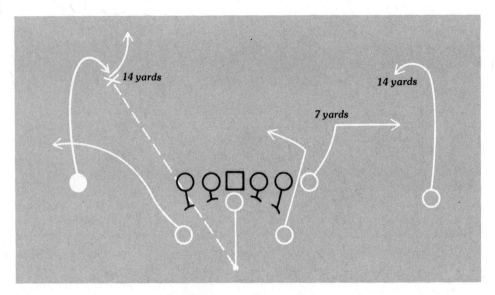

DIAGRAM 11-23.  Curl pass.

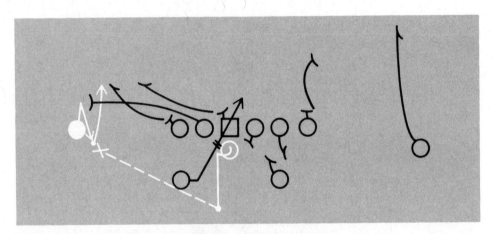

DIAGRAM 11-24.  Screen pass.

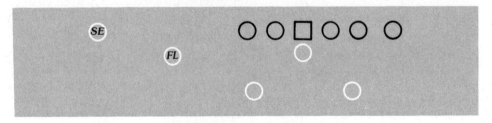

DIAGRAM 11-25.  Pro-slot formation.

## Pro-slot Formation

A variation of the Pro-set is the Pro-slot formation (Diagram 11-25), which provides strong-side passing combinations and weak-side running. It allows for quick-hitting plays up the gut. The split end is spread, and the flanker is in the wide slot position.

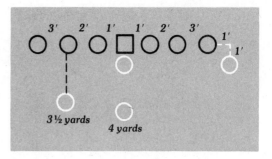

DIAGRAM 11-26. *Wing T formation.*

## The Wing T Formation

Essentially, the Wing T (Diagram 11-26), is a four-back attack, which provides a threat of three quick, deep receivers. A strong running formation, the Wing T allows for good deception and misdirection and forces the defense to place an additional man on the line of scrimmage. Placement of the wingback creates an additional gap that widens the defensive front and usually dictates an eight-man type of front.

Designed for consistency and ball control, the Wing T allows for an excellent misdirection attack, which can slow down the aggressive, fast-flow type teams. Diagrams 11-27 and 11-28 illustrate the deception incorporated in this offense.

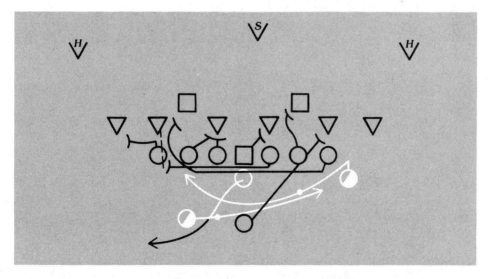

DIAGRAM 11-27. *Wing T counter versus 6-2.*

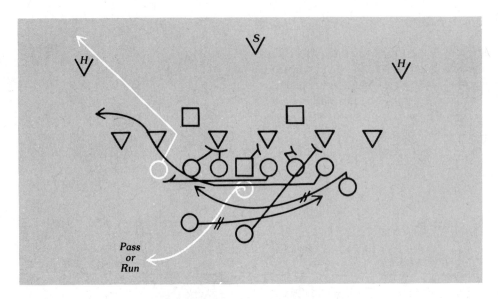

DIAGRAM 11-28. Wing T counter pass option versus 6-2.

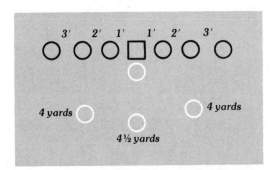

DIAGRAM 11-29. Full House formation.

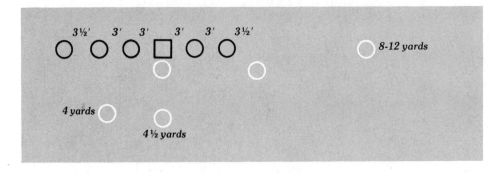

DIAGRAM 11-30. Slot T formation.

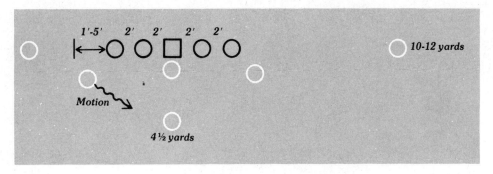

*DIAGRAM 11-31. Double Slot T formation.*

Diagrams 11-29 through 11-31 show other popular formations likely to be seen on the college gridirons. The Full House is a strong running formation with deception. The Slot T provides a good weak-side running attack with good strong-side passing combinations.

Prior to the snap, the Double T is an excellent passing formation.

# 12

# The Defense

*Defense, in my opinion, is the name of the game.*

**George Allen**

A strong, aggressive defense is the only sure road to victory. To win consistently, a football team must not only prevent the opposition from scoring but it must get the ball. By attacking the offense, the defense can get possession of the ball.

The importance of defense must be given major emphasis in any football program. I believe a good defensive team has a chance to win every game because it will not allow many touchdowns. To win with defense, to come up with the big plays on defense is the total defensive attitude that must be developed.

No single type of defense in football can stop every running and passing play. This is particularly true with today's multiple offenses. Therefore, to cope with the multiple offense theory, defensive football has become increasingly sophisticated and complex. The defense has found it necessary to adopt a basic multiple approach of their own, including several alignments and adjustments. Against a team that executes the Triple Option well, I do not believe the opposing defense can stay in one defensive alignment. From each defensive set, they must change the angle of charge and stunt various ways.

The success of the Wishbone T has forced some defensive teams to place more than seven players on or near the line of scrimmage. A Triple Option quarterback is involved in considerable reading and keying, which requires split-second decisions. As a result, a change of assignments by the defensive end and the outside linebacker through stunting and switching can disrupt the quarterback's ability to read.

The multiple theory involves changing defensive fronts before the ball is snapped and after the ball is snapped. These moves are basic and the rules are simple enough that high school teams as well as college elevens

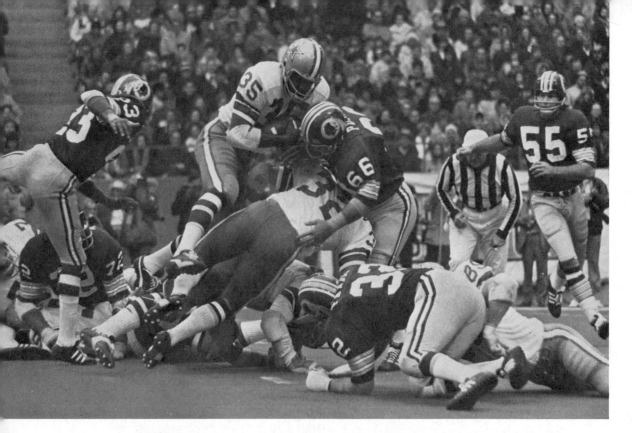

FIGURE 12-2. *A group of smart, quick, tough, aggressive determined football players can make any defense work. The basic alignment is secondary to the individual qualities of the players.*

may apply the multiple theory to their defensive football system.

Actually, the basic alignment employed by the defense is secondary to the individual qualities of the players. A group of smart, quick, tough, aggressive, determined football players can make any defense work.

The zone defense has continued to be prominent along with the multiple defenses—overshifts, undershifts, and stacks in the line. Many teams are combining zone and man-to-man coverage. By using various alignments and by disguising their rush maneuvers and coverage, the defensive team can give the offense a difficult time.

My philosophy about football defense can be summed up in one word: ATTACK!

*A team that cannot play defense cannot win.*

We believe in attacking an offense and man-handling it. Constant drive must be exerted by the defense, never letting the offense get the upper hand. The defense has to take over the game and make the offense play their game. It must never give them the strong suit to work with.

We like our defensive players to have the attitude there is nobody better than we are. They can handle anybody. "I don't care who they are, we will take them on!" is the mental attitude we like them to have.

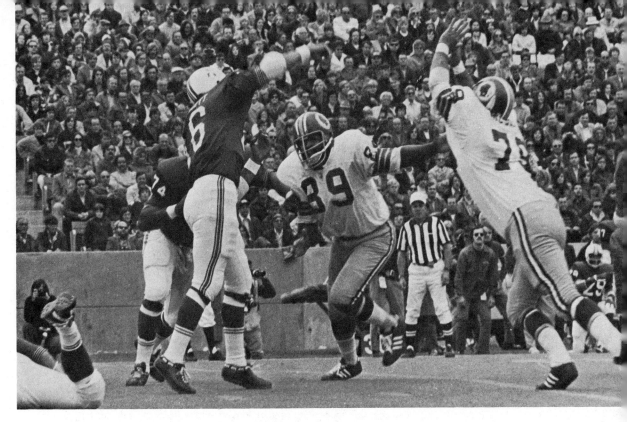

**FIGURE 12-3.** *An effective pass rush is the objective of all defensive lines. When the offense hits a long one, it usually means the pass rush has broken down. Here, Jim Plunkett has time to get away his throw.*

---

```
┌─────────────────────────────────────┐
│   THINGS TO DO ON DEFENSE           │
│                                      │
│ • Hold opponent within 15-yard line │
│ • Hold opponent to less than 3 yards │
│ • Forced three fumbles               │
│ • Five big plays                     │
│ • Three sacks                        │
│ • No run over 25 yards               │
│ • No long touchdown passes           │
│ • Intercept two passes               │
│ • Stop all third and 3, third and 4 plays │
│ • Allow 17 points or less per game   │
└─────────────────────────────────────┘
```

We want our defensive team to think aggressively, to be savage and ruthless when tackling. We want them to attack by stunting, looping, and, on occasion, by blitzing. The defense must always be thinking positive—to get that ball!

Members of the defensive platoon must go out on the field and not kill, but hurt their opponent. They must let the opponents know that they are there. Punish them!

The defense has four major goals:

• Prevent the score
• Get the ball
• Gain vertical field advantage
• Score!

Remember, the defense can score five ways, while the offense has only three ways.

*The team wins or loses on defense.*

FIGURE 12-4. *A strong desire for bodily contact. Players on the defensive unit are aggressive, alert, and mean. They must want to knock somebody down. We want them to attack the offense and manhandle it. Above, Diron Talbert (72) gets his man!*

**DEFENSE CAN SCORE**
1. Blocked punt
2. Fumble
3. Pass interception
4. Safety
5. Punt return

**OFFENSE CAN SCORE**
1. Pass
2. Run
3. Field goal

## A SUCCESSFUL DEFENSE

A sound defense is built with a foundation of ends and tackles, whom we call rushmen. The linebackers are added, and the cornerbacks and safeties provide the secondary lines of defense.

The line, however, is where the foundation must begin. A weak pass rush will mean an unbearable pressure on the defensive backs. Since the linebackers will have to help them, the defense against the running game will be weakened.

An ineffective front four against the run will force the linebackers to stay in close and play mop-up all the time. As a result, the deep backs can expect little help on pass coverage.

But stick a couple of big, tough, hard-charging studs on that front four, and the game situation—offense versus defense—takes on a different look. The quarterback will be pressured into passing, uninhibited linebackers can call their shots, and coverage by the defensive backs will be far more effective.

## CHARACTERISTICS OF GOOD DEFENSE

Successful defense is characterized by the following elements:

*An Aggressive Defense.* An aggressive attitude must be developed on defense. A few fiery, aggressive players can inspire an entire defensive team. If the coach can get two or three players yelling, before long he will have his entire squad chanting and hitting.

*Think Tackling.* Each player on the defense must believe that he is going to make a tackle on *every* play.

*Good Pursuit.* Described as the barometer of desire, pursuit is one of the distinguishing characteristics of a good defensive team. After recovering from the initial charge and the block placed on him, the player moves toward the direction of the play. Good pursuit can keep a 50-yarder down to 15 and hold a touchdown to a field goal.

The defense, however, must guard against reverses or counter plays. Proper pursuit angles and relationships to the ball must be stressed at all times.

*Gang Tackling.* The surest way to stop a ball carrier is by gang tackling; a relentless

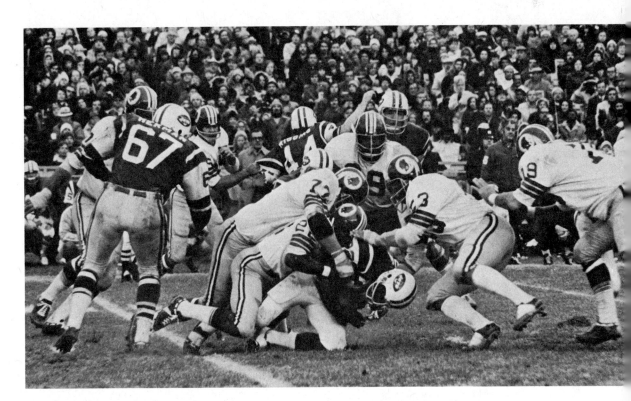

FIGURE 12-5. *Gang tackling. Nothing is more demoralizing to the offense than gang tackling by the defense.*

FIGURE 12-6. *Stopping the run. By attacking the line of scrimmage, the front line can force blocking errors. Staying off the line, the linebackers read the blockers and then pursue toward the ball.*

surge of all members of the defensive unit should stop only when they hear the whistle.

*Good Field Position.* Having good field position is of great importance in determining the outcome of a football game. The team that can consistently gain a favorable field position will have a strong advantage. The point of exchange refers to the spot on the field where the offense surrenders the ball to the opponent.

*The defensive team should try to determine what the opponent will do and try to call the defense accordingly.*

Favorable field position on exchanges results from the following:

- A solid defense
- A consistent offense
- A strong kicking game
- Avoiding turnover errors

FORMULA FOR A GOOD DEFENSE

- **Aggressive down linemen**
- **Alert linebackers who can read offense**
- **Strong pass rush**
- **Deep backs who can play the ball and tackle**

## RESPONSIBILITIES

### Defensive Line

Attacking the offense should be the prime objective of the linemen up front. Rushmen, as I prefer to call them, must dominate the line of scrimmage. They have the vital responsibility of taking on the blockers, defeating them, and making the play. Or, they will pursue the play or rush the passer.

Much of the time, the defensive line will try to penetrate the offensive line to force them into errors and mistakes. On every play, each lineman should anticipate making a tackle.

A variety of defensive alignments and charges must be employed. As a result, the offense will not be able to concentrate on one defense or charge. On each play, a defensive call will determine which alignment and charge will be used. Then, everyone on the defense must be prepared to execute properly.

In defending against the Triple Option, for example, the end and outside linebacker must know their contain and force responsibilities. A "me-you" relationship of containing and forcing the ball through stunting and switching can confuse the quarterback's ability to read.

The front line must learn the dozen or more ways they will be blocked and how they will defeat those blocks. Essentially, they have the following responsibilities:

- Charging
- Neutralizing the charge of their opponent
- Avoiding being blocked
- Locating the ball
- Moving to the ball

*The defense should have a sound knowledge of what to expect on game day.*

FIGURE 12-7. *Outside linebackers such as Chris Hanburger (55) who can defend against both the run and the pass are hard to find.*

Since the rules prevent the offensive interior linemen from moving farther than 1 yard downfield on pass plays, the moment an ineligible receiver moves farther than a yard downfield, the defense can safely assume that the play is a run.

### Linebackers

The linebacker positions are the most demanding in football. Linebackers must be able to stop the runs at the line of scrimmage, in addition to covering short zones and sometimes deep ones. They are responsible for plugging up holes in the line or covering a pass receiver. After jamming the tight end, they often have to sprint backward 15 yards to protect their zone. They must be

FIGURE 12-8. *A sound defense should be effective against both the run and the pass. To confuse offensive blockers, the defense should continually alter its alignment. Above, the out-side linebackers have momentarily changed the four-man front to a six-man front, but they are prepared to handle pass coverage responsibilities.*

prepared to stop both draw and screen plays.

The prime responsibilities of linebackers are the following:

- Reading
- Attacking
- Retreating
- Tackling
- Using the hands
- Using the feet

The keys of the three linebackers are as follows: Sam, the strong-side linebacker, keying the natural progression of blockers from the tight end in; Mac, the middle line-backer, watching a triangle of guards, center,

and fullback; and Willie, the weak-side backer, watching the guards who pull and keying the weak back.

### Deep Backs

The two cornerbacks and two safeties are key players who can prevent touchdowns. To a great extent, their effectiveness is dependent on the ability of the front four to rush the passer. The linebackers must assist them, though, by staying tight with receivers through the "seams," the weakened areas between zones. Then, the deep backs must play a tight man-to-man or zone coverage.

Deep backs have the following coverages:

- Man-to-man, weak safety free
- Man-to-man, weak safety committed weak
- Man-to-man, weak safety committed strong
- Man-to-man, double teaming flanker or split end
- Zone to strong side
- Zone to weak side
- Weak safety blitz
- Okie prevent zone

In addition to pass coverage, the cornerbacks and safeties have run support responsibilities. In supporting the front four and middle linebacker, they often have to rush up to contain a running play or force it to the inside.

The safeties on each side make the calls for run support. Typical terms are *crash* (the cornerback contains); *stone* (the safety contains); and *bomber* (containment by the linebacker).

A key defense, such as the 4-3 key, is based on automatic reactions by the deep backs. The two defensive halfbacks (cornerbacks) and safety men will key their actions to what the weak-side back does, that is, the back away from the flanker. If he pass blocks, for example, the weak-side safety will go deep and play the ball.

## DEFENSIVE TECHNIQUES

In attacking the offense, the defensive linemen employ a variety of defensive charges and techniques. These maneuvers and actions prevent the opponents from being able to zero in on one defense or charge. Of course, proper execution is of great importance.

*quick.* from the alignment call, the tackles move quickly into the backfield. They should be ready to read the blocker as they move.

*inside.* the tackles drive hard through the offensive tackles. The angle of penetration is much greater than for the quick technique.

*slant.* used by both guards and tackles, the slant move is made from a head-up position on the offensive blocker.

*go.* the go is the same as the slant, except that the defensive lineman penetrates to the left.

*middle.* used by the guard, the lineman takes a controlled jab step to the center. He must stop the charge of the offensive center or guard and get to the ball.

*wide.* similar to a middle, the guard takes a jab to the outside.

*read.* used by both guards and tackles, the primary key will determine their reactions and movement. The defender must stop the charge of the blocker and rid him by striking a blow and using his hands.

## STUNTS

Movements by the defense other than their basic charges are termed *stunts*. Some stunts are a combination of a slant or loop charge by a lineman or end and a read-key by the linebacker. With the linemen slanting to the left, the left linebacker might shoot the gap between the guard and tackle.

If the offense should effectively pick up these stunts, the defense should continually alter its alignment, thus confusing their blocking assignments.

Down linemen can move over or line up in the gaps, where they can shoot the gap or charge to their right or left. The linebackers can play directly behind them in a stack alignment.

Jumping around by the defensive team just prior to the snap can further confuse both the signal caller and the offensive linemen, who will be forced to readjust their blocking assignments.

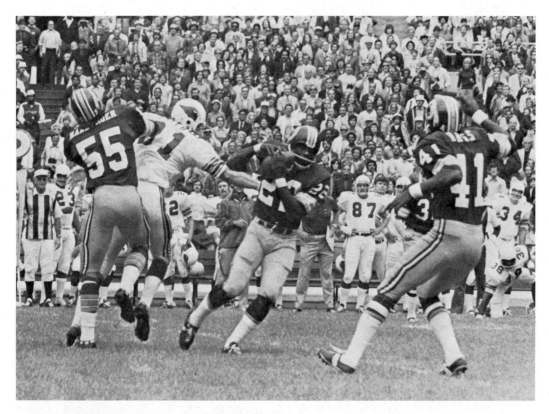

FIGURE 12-9. *Pass defense demands an effective coordination between the rush and the coverage. Pressure on the passer by the front rushmen has made it possible for the Redskins' defensive secondary to come up with the football.*

The *blitz* involves sending one, two, or three linebackers across the line with the four front men. It has two purposes:

1. Get the quarterback.
2. Force the offense to keep additional personnel back to protect him instead of going out as receivers.

When a linebacker blitzes, it is important that he get to the quarterback. Otherwise, he places considerable pressure on the secondary. If the quarterback reads the blitz, he can audible and send a receiver into the vacated middle.

*Pinch* is a stunt involving the down defensive linemen, while the cross charge of two adjacent down defensive linemen is termed a *limbo*.

## PASS DEFENSE

*The key to successful pass defense is simple—rush the passer!* The front line must rush the passer so that he will not have a long time to set up and throw. A longer time than five to six counts makes it difficult for the defensive secondary to hold the pattern and cover the receivers.

Pass defense, therefore, demands a

coordination between the rush and the coverage. The linemen must pressure the passer so the job of the deep backs is not so difficult.

Three methods that are often used to stop a passing attack are (1) an all-out rush by blitzing or pressuring the passer; (2) delay and knock off the intended receiver (bump-and-run); and (3) maximum coverage with a minimum rush.

All teams now use the zone defense in some form, varying it with man-for-man coverage or combinations of both. Since many high school and college coaches feel they are not able to compete with their opponents on a man-to-man basis, they commit themselves to the zone defense. Even though a team may play a strictly zone defense, however, it should understand man-to-man techniques.

In a third down and long-yardage situation, some professional teams will bring in a fifth defensive back and take out a linebacker. They double-cover the wide receivers, and the substitute defensive back covers the tight end, like the Redskins' famous Nickel defense.

The red dog, or blitz, is probably used more on the high school level than on the college level. The blitz is not used to a great

FIGURE 12-10.  *The front line must rush the passer so that he will not have sufficient time to set up and throw. In this game situation, an erratic throw enabled the Redskins' cornerback to pick off an interception.*

A            B

*FIGURE 12-11. Get that ball and score! By attacking the offense, the defense has an opportunity to score. Here, rushman Bill Brundige's sacking quarterback Joe Namath of the Jets has enabled teammate Verlon Biggs to pick up the loose football and run it in for 6 points.*

extent in college football because most of the teams do not use a drop-back pass. It is difficult for a linebacker to zero in on a quarterback if he does not know what side he is going to.

The college teams will blitz more on a half-line basis than on a full-line because of the great running ability of some quarterbacks.

### Man-for-Man

Each eligible receiver is assigned to a deep back or linebacker in the defensive secondary. In the man-for-man defense, a secondary man will line up relatively close to the line of scrimmage. When the ball is snapped, he moves with the receiver, keeping him slightly to the inside. When the ball is thrown, the defender leaves his man and moves to the ball.

Occasionally, two defenders may find it

necessary to switch men after the ball is snapped.

To prevent the receivers from having so much room to maneuver, fake and make their break, corner men occasionally play the bump-and-run technique. They will line up about $1\frac{1}{2}$ yards from the receiver. As the ball is snapped, the defender steps into the receiver, bumps him, and holds him up. Then he has to stay with him the rest of the way downfield.

In the NFL, downfield contact and the bump-and-run technique have been restricted by a new rule change which states that beyond 3 yards downfield, a defender may hit a receiver only once.

### Zone

The principle of the zone is that people cover an area, rather than a prescribed man. Indeed, zones are being widely used on all levels of football today.

On a zone pattern, all defenders in the secondary will keep relative distances between themselves until the ball is thrown. Then they immediately move to the ball.

A zone defense can be particularly effective if the front line can get to the quarterback or exert enough pressure to make him unload the ball before the zones get too big.

The weakness of a zone defense is that an accurate passer can exploit the gaps or holes in the defense. If a receiver can find these cracks, or seams, a skilled passer can hit him as he makes his break. The wider the offense spreads itself, the more pronounced these gaps in the defense become.

Defensive teams are becoming more proficient at disguising their zone coverage. For years, quarterbacks have been told to read the actions of the defensive strong safety. If he moves toward the tight end, the defense will be man-to-man. If he backs up, or veers over to the side, the defense is playing zone coverage.

To counteract this, a tight safety might fake a move toward the tight end, and then drift into a zone. Alternatively, he might switch assignments with another defender, or combination coverage might be used.

While the zone defense reduces the effectiveness of the long pass, it also can leave huge holes for running plays. As a result, the concern of defensive coaches is how to stop both the long pass and the run.

In combining zones and run support, the deep backs have a responsibility for "rolling up," while the linebackers drop off in the other direction. This maneuver results in four short zones and three deep ones.

Run support can be established by giving containment responsibilities to the linebacker or cornerback. In the event of a pass play, however, they will stay in the short

zone. As a result, the player can contain the run, in addition to playing a zone.

### Three-Deep and Four-Deep Secondary Coverage

Essentially, the three-deep secondary is easier to play than the four-deep alignment. Also, since the pass is not as potent on the high school level, a four-deep secondary is not always necessary. By going with a three-deep defense, one man can help up front where the running game is a greater weapon.

*Three-Deep Secondary.* The assignments of the three men remain the same. The two halfbacks must cover the deep outside zones, while the safety covers the deep middle. The defensive halfbacks will maintain their positions 8 to 10 yards deep and move to the outside. The safety will give ground as he moves back with the flow of the play.

*Four-Deep Secondary.* The entire unit must move together, maintaining relative position with one another. When the ball moves to their left, they will rotate in that direction. As the passer drops back to throw, the secondary men also drop back. On a running play, the defensive backs will move up quickly.

The two safeties always react as a team. As the cornerback moves up, the safety to the side of the play has deep outside responsibility, while the safety away from the play covers the deep middle zone.

### Monster Defensive Secondary

Since most long gainer plays are directed to the wide side of the field, the Monster defense features an extra man playing on the wide side of the field on all occasions. When the play moves away from the Monster man, he will move back to become the middle safety.

The flexibility of the Monster defense can reduce significantly the pressure on the linebackers and secondary. This is why many teams have used this alignment in recent years.

## TRAINING THE DEFENSE

To be an effective unit, the defense has to know everything the opposing offense does. Therefore, the coaches and players must spend a considerable amount of practice and meeting time trying to anticipate what the offense is going to do. They receive a play-book almost as large as the one given to the offense. To combat the blocks by the offense, those on the defense must learn a variety of maneuver techniques, stunts, and blitzes. They have keys to be learned—that is, movements by the offense that will tell them where the ball is going, what blocking to expect, and how to defeat it.

Teaching emphasis on defense should be based on the ability to run and to pursue. The coaching staff must emphasize all-out pursuit, being in on every tackle on every play. The players must be taught to accelerate to the ball. Defenses that allow players to read on the move can result in more aggressive play.

### Basic Skills

The following fundamental skills should be incorporated into the practice plan and practiced enthusiastically at least 15 to 20 minutes daily:

FRONT LINEMEN

- Tackling
- Reaction, one-on-one
- Go and slant techniques
- Pass rush
- Area blocking
- Keying

LINEBACKERS

- Tackling
- Block protection
- Pass drop
- Rush techniques
- Keying

DEEP BACKS

- Pass drop
- Tackling
- Playing the ball
- Man coverage
- Zone coverage
- Disguise
- Block protection
- Five under
- Keying

In teaching assignments, the coach should remember: the simpler, the better. In their communication to players, coaches should try to use one-word terms. Players should be allowed to concentrate on such fundamentals as reaction, movement, pursuit, and tackling.

A football team can prepare itself effectively without a great amount of total scrimmage, which often results in injuries and physical punishment. Essential skills such as full-speed reactions and pursuit can be developed without unnecessary scrimmage. Actually, a team's physical preparedness is often related to the players' mental preparedness.

High school and college coaches have told me that they feel the poorest-taught fundamental on their levels is the pass rush. On the pro level, we live and die on our ability to rush the passer. Consequently, we practice and study this crucial aspect of defense with religious dedication.

As closely as possible, practices must resemble actual gamelike situations. Unless these game circumstances can be created, it will be difficult to prepare players for game competition. Players should be able to react and pursue at full speed, even though they are not allowed to tackle.

Having a good scout or preparation team can be a very important element in preparing a defensive team for an opponent. The preparation team must be able to show the defense what offense can be expected. It should be able to execute an opponent's favorite rushing and passing plays.

## Defensive Game Plan

Just as the offensive team receives a game plan, the defensive unit should receive a similar tactical plan in line with the offensive strategy expected from the opponents.

Each week the head coach will prepare the following defensive write-ups on the upcoming opponent:

- The team's own defenses
- Scouting report
- Offensive sets and plays of opponents

A field chart will contain the actual defensive game plan based on the opponent's down and distance tendencies.

A sample defensive game plan is provided in chapter 15, "Training Program."

## Charting Tendencies

A tendency chart can be prepared by breaking down past game films and feeding the information into a computer. The chart will list the opponent's plays from a dozen or more formations. For example, from the

Brown left formation, first down and 10, they may use the 30 series, employing the sweep and off-tackle plays in the same direction.

The players should take notes in their playbooks on their opponent's tendencies while the information is projected on a screen from an overhead projector. The chart should include the score, time left, and location of the ball.

*Defensive Charts.* The opponent's defenses should be listed, including the number of times each defense was used against the various downs and yardage situations. The offensive formation and the location of the ball are correlated with the down and yardage situations.

## THE DEFENSIVE SIGNAL CALLER

The importance of an effective signal caller on defense cannot be stressed too much. He is the key to success for the defensive unit. Even though the defensive calls may be made from the bench, he must understand the game plans thoroughly so he can make any needed adjustments on the field. He should have a complete knowledge of both offensive and defensive tactics. Therefore, the coaching staff should spend as much time with him as they do with the offensive quarterback.

Good leadership qualities, of course, should be a must for the player calling the signals. Poise under fire and the ability to maintain composure are some of the intangibles of an outstanding defensive quarterback.

The signal caller on defense must be able to recognize distribution of strength. He should have the skill of a field general in matching his defensive strength with that of the offense.

In making his call in the huddle, he should advise his teammates of (1) down and distance, (2) the defense, and (3) possible plays or formations to expect.

## DEFENSIVE SIGNALS

The calls made in the defensive huddle give directions to each of the three dimensions of defense. If the defensive quarterback calls out: Pro Ed Right Cover 3, he has signaled the following:

- a Pro front, standard 4-3 defense
- Ed, a stunt by the tackle and end
- Cover 3 instructs the deep backs to play coverage number 3, man-to-man, weak safety free

The defensive huddle should be set up as soon as the play ends. On the professional level, the outside linebackers call out the down and distance, while the middle linebacker and weak safety look for their signals from the defensive coach on the sideline.

FIGURE 12-12. *The coach should be prepared to make the necessary adjustments in his team's defensive strategy. Here, Coach Allen helps his two corner linebackers, Chris Hanburger and Jack Pardee, diagnose an unexpected offensive alignment.*

When sending in signals from the bench, many coaches use a system of fists and open hands, such as one arm for defense and the other for coverages.

As an example, the right fist might mean defenses 1–4, while the right open hand could be defenses 5–8. A left fist might imply coverage 1–4, and a left open hand means coverages 5–8.

By practicing this routine from the opening day of practice, the middle linebacker and weak safety will not likely get their signals crossed in a game.

## DEFENSIVE GRADING SYSTEM

An effective grading system will enable the coaching staff to evaluate exactly how well those on the defensive unit perform. It can provide the motivation so necessary for improvement and better performances.

The system can give the defensive players points for their successes and their errors. One point can be awarded for getting a part of a tackle, while an unassisted tackle receives two points. Mental errors can be categorized as follows:

$M_1$. technique
$M_2$. pass rush
$M_3$. pass coverage
$M_4$. causing a penalty
$D$. dog play

The most difficult positions to grade, with the sole exception of the quarterback, are those in the defensive secondary. The reason is that so many variables might have determined whether a pass was complete or incomplete or whether the defender had his man covered. One also needs to know whether he failed to cover his man when he

FIGURE 12-13. *The defensive huddle should be set up as soon as the play ends. The calls provide information for all dimensions of defense, the front four, the linebackers, and the deep backs.*

was away from the point of attack. The secret of pass defense is for the defensive back to always have proper position on the receiver. There is an exact position for each defender on each type of pass thrown. The defense must be taught the correct position on the receiver for the curl, slant, out, etc.

We have used the grading chart to evaluate the entire team for the last ten years. It is a very fair way of grading, in that the defensive men are graded only when they are at the point of attack. However, they can pick up additional grade points if they perform their responsibilities and pursue and hustle, even though they may be on the off side. Since every man cannot be graded the same, this chart is broken down into three separate areas: Rushmen (defensive linemen), BU's (linebackers), and Deeks (defensive backs).

CHART 12-1. Defensive grading sheet.

| DEFENSIVE GRADING SHEET | | | | | |
|---|---|---|---|---|---|
| Name | Total | First | Second | Third | Fourth |
| | | | | | |

# DEFENSIVE GRADING REPORT

REDSKINS vs. COWBOYS    Date: _____    Coach:   George Allen

| Name | All Players S | P | T | MT | A | SQ | HP | EE | NE | OR | BB | AX | BLK | RF | Rushmen CT | CE | RA | BU's R | PR | INT | Deeks R | PR | INT | PP | PE | Final Grade |
|---|---|---|---|---|---|---|---|---|---|---|---|---|---|---|---|---|---|---|---|---|---|---|---|---|---|---|
| Talbert | -1 | -2 | 7 | 1 | 4 | 3 | 4 | 2 | X | X | 1 | X | 1 | 1 | -2 | -3 | -1 | | | | | | | 64 | 55 | 86% |
| Houston | X | X | 6 | 1 | 3 | X | X | 2 | X | 2 | X | 2 | 1 | X | | | | | | | +5 / -3 | +6 / -1 | 1 | 44 | 39 | 88% |
| Hanburger | -1 | X | 8 | 1 | 5 | X | 1 | 1 | X | 1 | 1 | 1 | 1 | | | | | | | | +4 / -1 | +5 / -1 | 1 | 61 | 54 | 88% |

## GRADING SYMBOLS

S   Spot (initial location)
P   Point (destination of charge)
T   Tackles
MT   Missed tackles
A   Assists
SQ   Sack quarterback (tackle passer)
HP   Hurry passer
EE   Extra effort
NE   No effort
OR   Obstructing the receiver
BB   Batted balls
AX   Axing
BLK   Block
RF   Recover fumble

*DEEKS*
R   Reaction (run or pass)
PR   Position on receiver
INT   Interception
PP   Possible points
PE   Points earned

*BU's*
R   Reaction (run or pass)
PR   Position on receiver
INT   Interception

*RUSHMEN*
CT   Timing of charge
CE   Elevation of charge
RA   Recovery angle

## POINT STRUCTURE

| | | | |
|---|---|---|---|
| S | 1 | *Rushmen* | |
| P | 1 | CT | 1 |
| T | +3 | CE | 1 |
| MT | -3 | RA | 1 |
| A | 1 | | |
| SQ | 6 | *Linebackers* | |
| HP | 3 | R | 1 |
| EE | +3 | PR | 1 |
| NE | -3 | INT | +6 (TD pass allowed -6) |
| OR | 1 | | |
| BB | 1 | *Deeks* | |
| AX | 1 | R | 1 |
| BLK | 1 | PR | 1 |
| RF | 6 | INT | +6 (TD pass allowed -6) |

*The secret of good performance at critical moments is found in drill.*

This grading chart is an off-season project. It is too time-consuming to keep up during the season, unless the head coach has enough assistant coaches to be able to assign one of them to work on it several days a week. It serves as a guide for estimating improvement as well as for grading, because the coach is grading strength as well as weaknesses. The best way is for one coach to grade the entire defensive team; in that way they are all being evaluated the same way. Every coach on the staff will come up with a different grade if asked to check the film. It is a big project for one man and at times it is advantageous to have the defensive line coach grade the rushmen and to have the defensive back coach grade the backers and secondary. Still another way is for the line coach to grade everyone with respect to runs and the secondary coach to grade all eleven men with respect to passes.

## Grading Points

The team defensive grading form has a sample of player grading for each defensive areas. The manner of grading and the points awarded (or penalties given out) are described below.

To show how individual grading works out, let us take the case of Ken Houston, a defensive back (Deek). Note that when there is a box with an X inserted, this shows that no grade was given in that area.

All possible points are now added up, the total here being 44, and the figure is placed in the PP column. Now all minus numbers are subtracted from the possible points and this remainder will give the coach the player's points earned. This figure is placed in the PE column. Now the percent-

age grade can be arrived at by dividing the possible points earned (the grade here being 88 percent).

If a deep back or linebacker allows a touchdown pass, it counts minus 6 (−6) points. If he intercepts, it counts plus 6 (+6) points. If a long pass is completed for a touchdown, everyone is penalized 1 point and the particular defensive back is penalized 6 points. The coach cannot blame just one player. If the line had rushed better, perhaps the quarterback would not have had the time to get the pass off.

## Analysis and Grading

Written tests are often used by coaches in early two-a-day practice sessions, to enable the coaching staff to make sure the players understand all of their defensive assignments. The test may require a short written answer or a diagram of the correct defensive course of a given illustration.

## TERMINOLOGY

To help eliminate defensive mistakes, defensive personnel should have an efficient method of communicating with one another. In addition, the gaps at the line of scrimmage should be numbered from the center out; for example, the guard gaps on either side of the center comprise the four areas.

While space will not permit a complete terminology sheet, the various defensive alignments should be defined.

*odd defense.* a man on the center; these defenses are usually in the 50's.

*even defense.* defensive men lined up on the offensive guards, with no man on the center (40's or 60's).

*combination.* a defense that utilizes both the odd and the even principles (Oakie-Eagle).

*gap defense.* one or more down defensive linemen located in the gaps.

*seven-man front.* the defensive linemen and linebackers number seven, with four men in the secondary.

*eight-man front.* defensive linemen and linebackers number eight, with three men playing in the secondary.

*four deep.* four defensive backs employed in various types of pass coverage.

*three deep.* three defensive backs used.

*pass-run ratio.* the normal ratio of pass rushers to pass defenders, usually 4–7 or 5–6.

*man.* one back or linebacker assigned to cover a receiver by himself.

*free safety man.* pass coverage in which three defensive backs cover three receivers man-for-man and are supported by a safety in zone coverage.

*rotate.* from a three-deep or four-deep secondary alignment, the outside halfback comes up to cover the outside flat and the inside safety covers the deep outside.

*invert.* from a four-deep alignment, the inside safety covers the outside flat area and the halfback backs up to cover the deep outside area.

*prevent.* an alignment used to prevent the long pass when time is running out.

*press.* a defensive halfback or linebacker employed in a tight position on a wide receiver in either a zone or man-to-man coverage.

*eagle position.* a defensive linebacker positioned over the offensive tight end.

*goal line defenses.* alignments used when facing a goal line situation, inside the 5-yard line.

*short-yardage defense.* alignments used on third and fourth downs with 1 or 2 yards needed for a first down.

## FORMATION RECOGNITION

Every man on the defensive unit should have a thorough knowledge of different offensive formations and the particular strengths of these alignments. In Chapter 11, they are given a thorough discussion.

Some of the most common formations employed by the offense are illustrated in Diagrams 12-1 through 12-11.

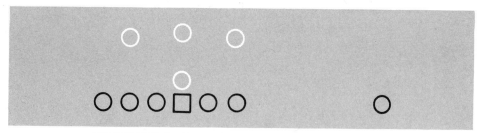

**DIAGRAM 12-1.** *T formation (three backs in tight backfield).*

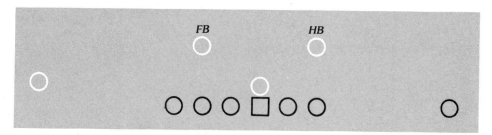

**DIAGRAM 12-2.** *Red formation ( flanker on opposite side of halfback).*

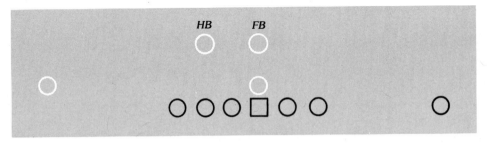

DIAGRAM 12-3. Brown formation (flanker on same side as halfback).

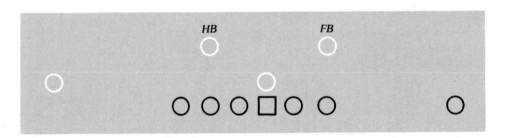

DIAGRAM 12-4. Green formation (fullback in halfback position).

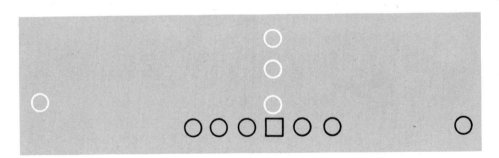

DIAGRAM 12-5. Blue formation (two backs in straight line I behind quarterback).

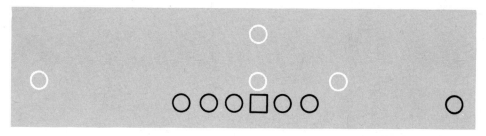

*DIAGRAM 12-6. Double wing formation (two receivers on each side of center).*

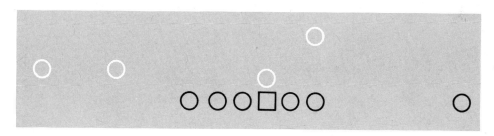

*DIAGRAM 12-7. Triple formation (three receivers on one side).*

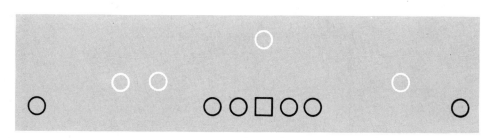

*DIAGRAM 12-8. Spread formation (quarterback is deep; backs are on each side).*

*DIAGRAM 12-9.   Tan formation (combination of brown and blue).*

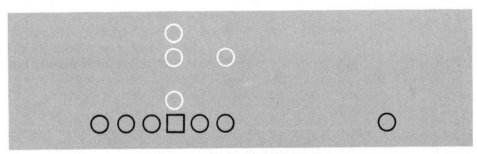

*DIAGRAM 12-10.   Pink formation (combination of red and blue).*

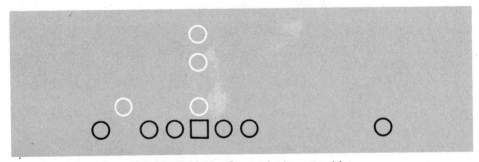

*DIAGRAM 12-11.   Strong slot formation (slot is inside tight end).*

## DEFENSIVE ALIGNMENTS

From the early days of football, defensive formations or alignments have undergone a succession of changes. Many teams will use as many as three fronts or formations, from each of which they can call six or eight different defenses.

Coaches today are positioning their players where their abilities will be most effective. Basically, the 4–3 (or Pro-4 defense) is the soundest defense against both the run and the pass. The three linebackers are in good position to move against the run quickly and still be able to move back into their pass defense areas.

Generally, however, it appears that defenses are moving out of the traditional 4–3 defense. As early as the 1960's, a number of teams abandoned the four-man front and started stacking their players, also hiding them in "overs" and "unders." They felt they lacked the type of personnel the standard 4–3 demands.

The great success of the Triple Option attack from the Wishbone T offense has been largely responsible for forcing the defense to place more than seven players on or near the line of scrimmage. One of the most popular of the eight-man front alignments has been a Split-6 type of 4-4 defense, with a three-deep secondary. In the 4-4 defense, a "me-you" relationship must be assigned to the outside linebackers and defensive ends on every play. Changing assignments through stunting and switching can hurt the quarterback's ability to read the contain and force players.

The stack has proven to be a very effective defense. Blockers must react in a hurry as linebackers wheel and deal out of their stacked, hidden positions. The stack does not have to originate from an odd-front defense. Using a pure 4-3, the Green Bay Packers under Coach Lombardi employed stacking principles when he assigned his defensive tackles the job of pinching inside, keeping the blockers off his middle linebacker.

To use a stack, a team should have the right type of defensive linemen. They must be quick and be able to penetrate the gap and tackle people.

Ideally, a coach should have a defense that works effectively against both the run and the pass. While there is no perfect defense, defenses like the 5-2-4 or the 4-3-4 work better against the pass. The 6-2 and the 6-1 generally are effective against the run.

From any alignment, the defensive team must have plays that will stop the offense if the defensive quarterback has diagnosed the point of attack. For example, the 5-2-4 defense, in which the ends and tackles shoot to the inside, should stop all inside plays. Or, the ends and tackles may slant to the right or left. If a strong pass rush is needed, one of the linebackers might blitz.

Strong against the running game, the 5-4 is one of the most effective defensive alignments for attacking the Triple Option.

Because of the alignment of the defensive end, the Split-4 defense can be very effective against the sprint-out pass. The Pro-4 is less effective in containing the quarterback's route.

To confuse offensive blockers, the defense should continually alter its alignment. From the 5-2 front, the nose guard and the right down linemen, for example, can move half a man to their left, lining up the gaps between the offensive linemen. The linebackers will play directly behind them. A stack alignment of this type can place considerable pressure on the offensive linemen by confusing their blocking assignments.

In the Pro Zip defense, the strong-side linebacker, Sam, moves closer to the flanker to assist the cornerback. Since this maneuver may create a weakness against the run, Mac should compensate by moving farther out.

In shifting over to the strong side, the odd-man line moves its strength to the side the offense is expected to attack. A massive tackle moves head on in front of the center.

In the under shift to the weak side, the strong defensive tackle is in front of the center, while Mac is in front of the strong guard.

In attacking the throwback on a sprint-out or roll-out pass, some teams will rotate their defensive secondary immediately on ball flow. The linebackers, however, must not flow quickly on the first movements of the quarterback, unless both offensive backs are sent to the sprint-out side.

The defensive end, of course, must attempt to stop the quarterback's route and force him to pull up and throw the football. Once he reads a sprint-out coming his way, he should assume a low position immediately, keeping his outside foot back and away from the blocker. He should meet the blocker quickly.

### Eight- and Nine-Man Defensive Fronts

With only three defensive secondary men, the strength of an eight-man front is on the running game. Considerable pressure is placed on the run and the quarterback. These defenses include the Split 4-4, 5-3 defense, Monster 5-3, 4-3 Monster, 4-4 Tandem, Wide-Tackle 6, Gap-8, and 7-1 Diamond.

A four-deep secondary is utilized by a nine-man front defense. The cornerbacks are able to rotate forward, or the inside safeties can invert to help protect against the run. Some of the nine-man front defenses are the Oklahoma 5-4, 4-3-4, 6-1 defense, 5-4 Slant, Eagle-5, 6-5 Goal Line, and 7-4 defense.

### High School

High schools teams can get the best results through simplicity, by avoiding highly involved combinations on slants, pinches, red dogs, loops, and other stunts. Assignments must be kept as simple as possible so that players have a complete understanding and can concentrate on coverage and interceptions.

Indecision must be eliminated from football! A player is more likely to react quickly if he has less thinking to do. Stunting, particularly, is a difficult phase to chart in advance. Keys and rotations require an enormous amount of time.

Against the Split T, the Notre Dame defense is an excellent high school defense because its primary objective is to stop the run. Generally, high school teams have more kids who can run than can throw.

High school teams have employed the professional 4-3 formation scaled to their personnel and requirements. The chief concern, though, is to make the 4-3 stronger against the running game. A secondary defender can be brought inside, changing the 4-3 to a Split-6. A regular practice is to use 4-3 as a combination with many other defenses.

The Monster 50 defense is still popular in some areas of the country, although the trend is moving away from it to the Notre Dame defense. The 50 defense is an unbalanced defense used against strong sets, unbalanced line, or teams with unusually strong running tendencies. This defense involves a gap charge and may utilize a zone or man-for-man coverage.

The Split-6 type of defense has achieved much prominence with high school teams over the past five years. The alignment used most places the linebackers inside of, or stacked behind, the rushmen, who are aligned in front of the offensive guards.

The Oklahoma defense is still one of the most popular types of defense employed on the high school and college levels. Perhaps it is even more popular today because people can play four deep, which makes it effective against the forward pass. The Okie requires quick linebackers who can react.

Since most high school teams do not have exceptionally large players, they must use a more diversified type of end play. While the play of the linebackers and the deep secondary is basically the same, the end and tackle play is changed in order to: (1) split the option, (2) stop the off-tackle play, and (3) stop the "sprint and roll."

The most difficult play to defense is the option. Therefore, the defense must get enough flexibility in their end play to be able to switch up and change their play at the corner.

### College

The basic defenses commonly employed today on the college level are the Oklahoma 5-2, Monster 50, Pro defense, Notre Dame 4-4, and Split-6. In this era of multiple offenses, many college defenses have adopted in one form or another a theory of multiplicity within a simple framework of defense.

Any defense can be given a basic multiple approach, either by stacking men in a gap or shifting and sliding them to one side or the other. Basically, the linemen and linebackers are trying to do the same thing, but they are being moved around a little. Play after play, most coaches rarely set the same defense.

College and high school linemen are using various pro techniques and maneuvers. Some linemen will vary the depth that the man will play off the ball, either playing tight on the ball and attacking or playing off the ball and reading.

Team stunts can be essential to a successful college defense. Stunts such as looping and slanting enable the defense to get an effective pass rush. Commonly used against larger players, the stunts are very simple and can be implemented without changing from the regular defensive alignment. The slant, popular in the Arkansas

kind of defense, involves running at an angle, while looping is stepping laterally.

If a team has big, strong defensive tackles, the Notre Dame defense can give good versatility. These two big tackles, from a pinched position, must come hard through the outside shoulder of the offensive guards. The ends play a crashing game, and a standard three-deep secondary may be used.

Various college coaches have been able to adapt the pro defenses effectively to their requirements, particularly to make the defense multiple enough to attack the run and the pass.

Because of its flexibility and consistency, the Arkansas Monster 50 defense compares favorably with many other popular defenses. Because of this, it is regarded as an excellent field position defense.

The Oklahoma 5-2 defense, for years one of football's favorite defensive alignments, is still popular today because of its effectiveness against the forward pass. The 5-4 version of the Oklahoma defense is stronger against the running game.

### DEFENSIVE SYSTEMS

Knowledge of the accompanying defensive symbols is necessary to read the diagrams that accompany descriptions of the various defensive systems.

---

**SYMBOLS OF DEFENSIVE PERSONNEL**

△     Rushmen or defensive men (in three-point stance)

☐     Linebackers

/S\     Deep backs inside (safeties)

/C\     Cornerbacks

---

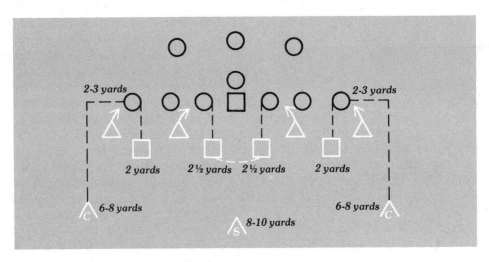

DIAGRAM 12-12. Notre Dame 4-4 defense.

## Notre Dame Defense

The Notre Dame 4-4 defense (Diagram 12-12) gives good versatility, but unless a team has big strong defensive tackles playing on the outside shoulder of the offensive guards, their "pinched in" position is not as effective as playing a man straight up where he can move outside more effectively.

In a pinched-in position, the defensive tackles are often not big and strong enough to withstand the block of the tackle coming down, and they end up in a caved-in position. Therefore, when using the Notre Dame defense, a smaller man can play straight up so he can react to either man more effectively.

The front four men, the tackles and the ends, come hard all the time. The two outside linebackers play on the inside shoulder of the tight end. The outside linebacker to a split end side can line up in varied positions. The two inside linebackers play inside the legs of the defensive tackles, while the secondary will be in a three-deep alignment.

While the Notre Dame defense is in better position to trail the guard pulling across the center and to kill the short trap, pursuit to the outside is not as good as with other defenses.

## Pro 4-3 Defense

In the Pro 4-3 (Diagram 12-13 and Figure 12-14), the tackles must possess quickness and durability, in addition to size and toughness. The ends should have good height and lateral movement. The linebackers should be sound thinkers with the ability to read the play. The cornerbacks and halfbacks should have height and good lateral and backward movement.

In employing the Pro 4-3, a four-point standard should be used:

1. Protection against the wide running game.
2. Protection from tackle to tackle against traps, quickies, and power plays.
3. Providing a defensive man in all possible passing areas.
4. Applying constant pressure on the quarterback on passing situations.

FIGURE 12-14. *The basic 4-3 defense is a 6-1 as the players line up, but it is a 4-3 in action. This is because the outside linebackers do not go in unless they are blitzing. They play on the line of scrimmage and drop off when the pass shows.*

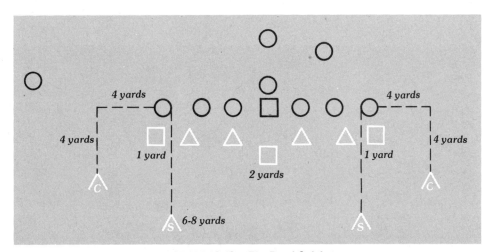

DIAGRAM 12-13. *The Pro 4-3 defense.*

As many as five different stunts are used with this defense. On all plays, the front four "blow" across the line one yard and pursue the football. On these stunts, the defense should try to get different movement from the linemen and linebackers. The Pro defense features a four-deep coverage, allowing their men to rotate to either side.

The 4-3 defense has been successful in attacking the Triple Option, similar to the tactics employed by the 5-4 defense.

The 4-3, also called a Pro-4 defense, can stop the swing option by utilizing secondary support to the front defenders.

### Arkansas Monster

The Monster defense (Diagram 12-14) receives its name from the adjustment of one defensive man to the strength of the offensive alignment or to the wide side of the field. A team will line up in an unbalanced front but will slant and loop back to a balanced front. The Monster man gives his team six men on the wide side of the field with only five to the opposite side.

The basic Monster 50 defense consists of two main parts, the forcing unit and the

containing unit. Five main variations may be employed:

1. The odd-front Monster
2. The Wide-Tackle 6
3. The 6-1-4
4. The 27-Front
5. The Monster Stack and 4-4 Stack

### Split-6

With the Split-6 (Diagram 12-15), the rushmen, the four interior men, can charge through the four interior gaps in the offensive line, thereby creating a Gap-8 defense with hard penetration. Or, they can play it straight and make it difficult for the blockers to get to the linebackers with a Gap-8 blocking scheme. The Split-6's may be divided into either the 4-4 or the true 6.

### Oklahoma Defense

The Oklahoma version of the 5-2 defense (Diagram 12-16) is a very strong defense against the running game. It does have some coverage limitations, due to the inside posi-

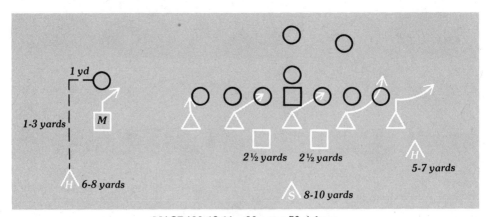

DIAGRAM 12-14.  Monster 50 defense.

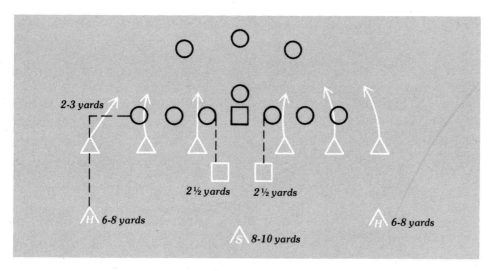

*DIAGRAM 12-15. Split-6 defense.*

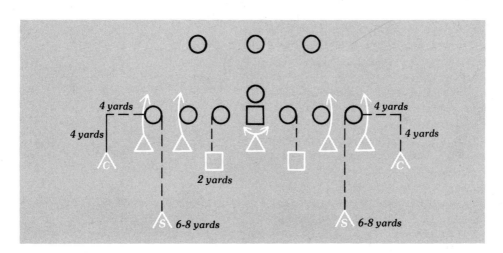

*DIAGRAM 12-16. Oklahoma 5-2 defense.*

tion of the linebackers. The Oklahoma 5-2 defense is being used more and more by professional teams. Effective at attacking the Triple Option, the defense provides an extra linebacker in position to offer a variety of blitzes. It is a pursuing and containing type of defense. Many teams like to slant and angle from the Oklahoma. Considerable flexibility exists for stunting up the middle, as well as on the corner.

## 4-4 Defense

With the success of the Wishbone T and its explosive Triple Option attack, many defensive teams are placing more than seven players on or near the line of scrimmage. Perhaps the most popular of the eight-man front alignments has been the 4-4 defense (Diagram 12-17) with a three-deep diamond secondary. In defending the Triple Option, numerous teams are using a Split-6 type of 4-4 defense, as shown in Diagram 12-15.

Either the outside linebacker or the defensive end has the responsibility of containing the quarterback and the pitch man. They should call either "me" or "you" in regard to which one has containment of the pitch man.

The use of a rotation of the three-deep zone coverage into the play action can be another aid to the defense of the Triple Option. The on-side defensive halfback can be rotated up to the line of scrimmage to provide a double contain of the pitch man.

The Split-4 is an effective defense in stopping offensive plays up the middle. The defensive tackles can either align or slant down over the offensive guards.

## The Pro 4-5

A basic defense, the 4-5-2 (Diagram 12-18) provides a four-man front, with five linebackers, and two safeties. The four-man pass rush can be remedied by stunting with linebackers and safeties. This defense is vulnerable to an offensive alignment that can release two receivers quickly to one side.

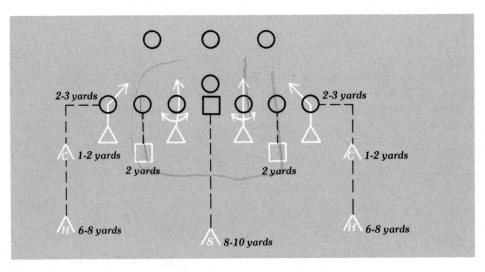

DIAGRAM 12-17. The 4-4 defense.

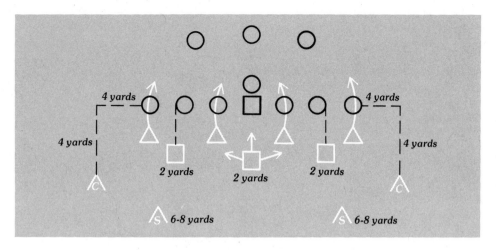

DIAGRAM 12-18. Pro 4-5 defense (good against the pass).

Group leaders in each segment will give a signal indicating the alignment and the stunt to be used. Besides the calls by the two group leaders in the line and linebacking segments, one of the backs will make a verbal call that will indicate the alignment and play of the three defensive backs, such as "Rover," "Green," and "Blue."

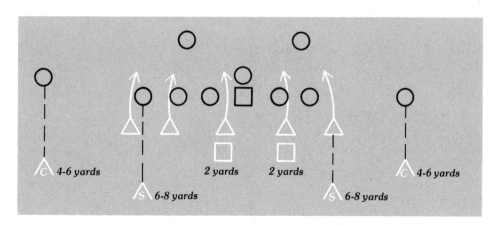

DIAGRAM 12-19. Stack defense (toward the offensive strength).

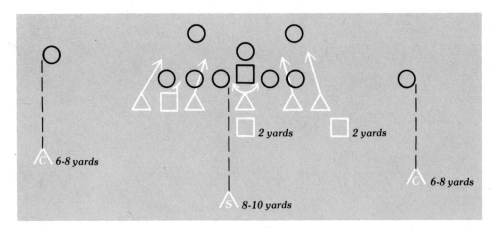

DIAGRAM 12-20.  The 5-3-3 defense.

## 5-3-3 Defense

The 5-3-3 (Diagram 12-20) offers many different combinations of alignments for both the line and the linebackers. With three linebackers, a wide variety of stunts can be run.

As many as five men can rush against the pass. An eight-man front can make running very difficult. In passing situations, there is three-deep coverage and the linebackers are responsible for the flat area and short coverage such as the halfback out.

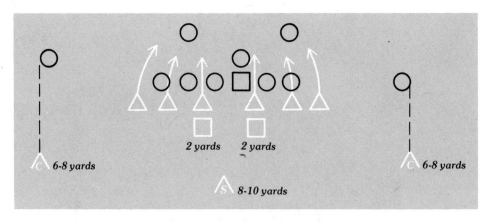

DIAGRAM 12-21.  The Gap defense.

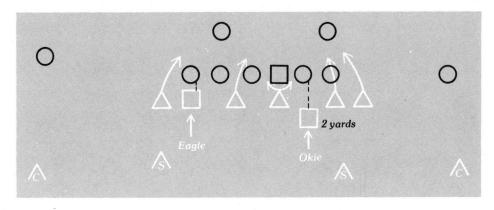

DIAGRAM 12-22. Combo (Oakie-Eagle).

In obvious passing situations, the 5-3 defense has caused considerable pressure on opposing quarterbacks. The Miami Dolphins have employed Bob Matheson (53) as a quasi-lineman and linebacker. He had the option to either drop back in the Dolphin's airtight zone defense, or rush the passer on an all-out blitz.

The pro's have been going to the 3-4-4 Okie defense, with the three down linemen defense. The Dolphins call it "53," while other coaches call it the prevent defense.

## Goal Line Defense

The best deep goal line defense is what everybody on the college level calls the 6-5 (Diagram 12-23 and Figure 12-15). Behind the six men on the line are two linebackers and the outside backers. This alignment provides the power and strength necessary to stop a plunge or surprise forward pass. On the snap, the six down linemen must charge off the ball, shooting the gap to penetrate as quickly as possible.

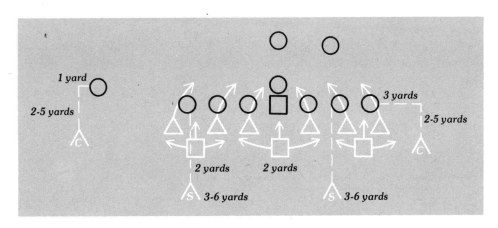

DIAGRAM 12-23. The 6-5 Goal Line defense.

FIGURE 12-15. *Attacking at the goal line. The ball carrier must be stopped immediately. The defensive guards may execute a pinch maneuver by driving their inside shoulders into the center. The linebackers must attack quickly and forcibly to the ball.*

In attacking at the goal line, penetration by the defenders is necessary. The ball carrier must be stopped immediately. Once flow of the play has developed, the linebackers must attack quickly and forcibly to the ball.

Other effective goal line defenses include the 7-4, the Gap-8, and their variations.

If there are inches to go, the defensive guards can execute a pinch maneuver by driving their inside shoulders into the center. Slanting by the two guards is another effective method.

On goal line situations, many teams will employ off-tackle power plays. The defense can slant the entire line outside or use a gap charge in the tackle-end seam by the defensive end. Or the defensive tackle may use a gap technique inside while the end loops out. In a similar stunt, the defensive tackle will slant outside while the halfback stunts the guard-tackle seam.

Man-for-man coverage is commonly used whenever the goal line defense is called, or as soon as the opposition reaches the 15-yard line.

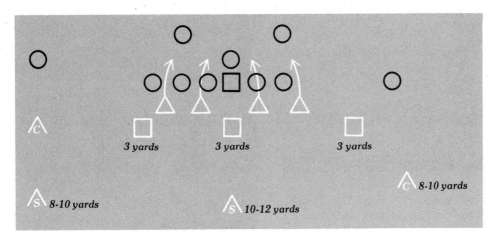

*DIAGRAM 12-24. Prevent (4-4-3) defense.*

## SPECIAL COVERAGES

### Prevent Defenses

The purpose of the prevent defenses (Diagrams 12-24 and 12-25) is to ensure that the offense will not be able to break a play for long yardage. Three of the most popular prevent defenses are 4-4-3, 3-5-3, and 4-5-2. To get maximum speed and mobility, secondary men are often substituted for down linemen and linebackers. In both the 3-5-3 and the 4-5-2, the deep defenders play pure zone while the linemen rush and force the play. The 3-5-3 is an easy alignment to get into from the 5-2.

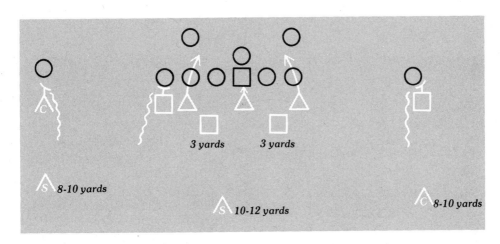

*DIAGRAM 12-25. Prevent (3-5-3) defense.*

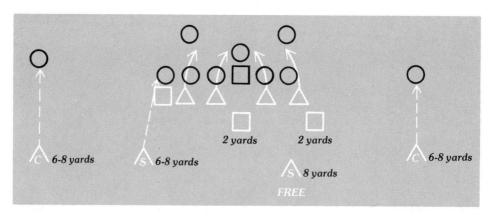

*DIAGRAM 12-26. Free safety man.*

## Free Safety Man

In this pass coverage, three defensive backs are responsible for three receivers man-for-man and are backed up by a free safety in zone coverage (Diagram 12-26).

## Press Defense

The press defense (Diagram 12-27) employs a defensive cornerback or linebacker in a tight position about 1 to 3 yards on a wide receiver. The coverage can be zone or man-to-man.

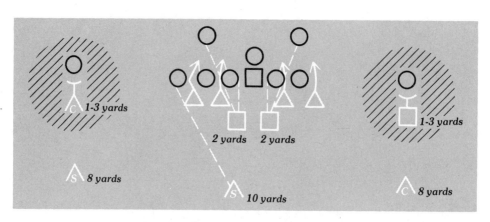

*DIAGRAM 12-27. 4-4-3 Double coverage (press).*

# 13

# Special Teams

Special teams are important, because the kicking game is vital to winning. If a team does not have a good punter and kicker, it is in trouble. I saw the need back in Los Angeles when I was the first professional coach to hire a full-time special teams coach.

Unfortunately, for the great majority of high school and college teams, the kicking game is often overlooked. Yet, one out of every five plays in a football game is a kick of some type. Good teams with excellent offenses and defenses often blow a game on a punt return, a blocked field goal, or a weak punt.

Special teams are the kickoff and kickoff return teams, the punt and punt return teams, and the field goal and extra point teams. While they have been described as the third team in football, special team players are actually first team players who believe they are doing their best on every play.

"I am as happy for a guy who makes a tackle inside the 20-yard line on a kickoff as I am for the guy who makes an interception on defense, or a long run on offense," said Chris Hanburger. "I honestly believe that is one of the reasons the Redskins have had so much success."

"Special teams will tell you one thing," Vince Lombardi once said, "Who wants to hit and who doesn't. You find out right away."

Indeed, those on special teams soon learn that they have got to hit or be hit. Playing with abandon, they have a genuine desire for body contact. Emphasis is not so much on size and strength as it is on motor skills. In addition to motor skills, position ability, and desire, these men must be tough and play without fear.

FIGURE 13-2. Kicks are involved in everything special teams do. Too many good teams with excellent defenses and offenses blow a game on a blocked field goal, a weak punt, or poor coverage on a punt return.

FIGURE 13-3. The Redskins work on the kicking game every day. As assistant coach Kirk Mee times his kick, Mike Bragg gets off a punt during pre-game practice.

We have tried to make special teams attractive. Some of our past teams were given catchy names such as Guillory's Gorillas in honor of our special team captain Tony Guillory. We also try to instill pride in the players on special teams.

A special teams coach is something that should have been thought of years ago. Occasionally, we will spend a full day working on the special teams, making sure that each man knows his assignment perfectly. For special teams to be successful, every man must strive for absolute perfection.

FIGURE 13-4. *Special team players like Bob Brunet are fast, aggressive, courageous, and ambitious. A man who likes to hit and keep hustling should make a top special team player.*

FIGURE 13-5. *Much emphasis today is placed on overall game preparation for the special teams. Assistant coach Paul Lanham, who is responsible for the Redskins' special teams, devotes almost as much time to group meetings and field practice as do those who handle the regular offensive and defensive squads.*

*Dedicated, inspired athletes playing with pride on special teams can contribute greatly to winning a championship.*

FIGURE 13-6. *Proper alignment of kickoff team. Mike Moseley prepares to kick off from the 35-yard line, as the rest of the Redskins use a bowed line. The kickoff for high school and college games, though, is still from the 40-yard line. Those on the kickoff team are assigned lanes of coverage. Lanes 1 and 2 are the most critical, since the majority of kickoffs are returned up the middle.*

The kicking game offers some very important offensive possibilities. A well-executed punt or a carefully planned return, for example, can give a team strong ground-gaining capabilities. Therefore, we allot sufficient time during practice for a variety of team kicking drills and procedures. The best way to get a kicker used to the intense pressure is to create pressure conditions in practice.

The recent changes in the kicking rules for pro football place even greater importance on this phase of the game. At this writing, the new rules include the following:

1. Goalposts have been moved back to the "end line."
2. During a kick from scrimmage, no player of the kicker's team (other than the two outside men) may go beyond the line of scrimmage until the ball has been legally kicked.
3. All field goals attempted and missed from the scrimmage line beyond the 20-yard line result in the defensive team's taking possession of the ball at the scrimmage line.
4. The kickoff is from the 35-yard line.

While the preceding rules apply to the professional level, much of the discussion on the kicking game is based on current college and high school rules. In chapter 14, pages

351–352, the authors have attempted to provide a comparative study of these and other rules relative to the various levels of play.

Many teams use the double row coverage instead of a single line. The threat of a long run is less when a second line backs up the first. If blocked, a player will have the opportunity to get up and back up the front line. The possibility of the return man going all the way is considerably less if every man gives all-out coverage.

Many teams use six players as lane men who are responsible for sprinting downfield in assigned lanes. Three players must penetrate the blocking pattern and move immediately for the ball carrier.

In the past, large and durable players were assigned to cover kicks; however, more and more backs are being assigned to this unit. Open-field tackling skill and the ability to avoid blockers are more important than size and strength.

Positions on the kickoff team are numbered L1, L2, L3, R1, R2, etc., according to the side of the kicker they are on.

Since a kickoff is a dash from the 40-yard line to the opponents' 20, a coach should make an effort to get all the speed he can into his kickoff team. When the kicker moves by them, the other members of the kicking team begin their run. Actually, it is a sprint for everyone. Still, a kickoff team will need some size, particularly in the middle to meet the wedge.

Since many kickoffs are returned up the middle, the most critical are lanes 1 and 2. They are covered by the all-out sprinters and wedgebusters. Those responsible for the in-

*Coverage men should know where the ball is. They should stay in their assigned lanes regardless of what happens.*

---

> ## SPECIAL TEAM PLAYERS
> - **Kicker**
> - **Holder**
> - **Snapper**
> - **Punter**
> - **Blocker**
> - **Wedgebuster**
> - **Returner**
> - **Tackler**

*A kicker only wears one hat—hero or goat. He either makes that winning 40-yarder with 30 seconds to go or he muffs it.*

side lanes will encounter the wedge, and, should one of them fail his responsibility, a gap in the coverage will open up.

## KICKOFFS

While booming the ball through the end zone can be an effective approach to a kickoff, very few kickers can do it consistently. Good coverage on the kickoff, therefore, is extremely important because it determines the field position of the return team. (See Diagram 13-1.)

Containing the ball and the man carrying it is the chief responsibility of the kickoff team. Members of the kickoff team are assigned lanes of coverage, which are designed to effectively contain the returner. Some teams use a bowed line when kicking off, while others employ a relatively straight line of ten players a few yards behind the 40-yard line.

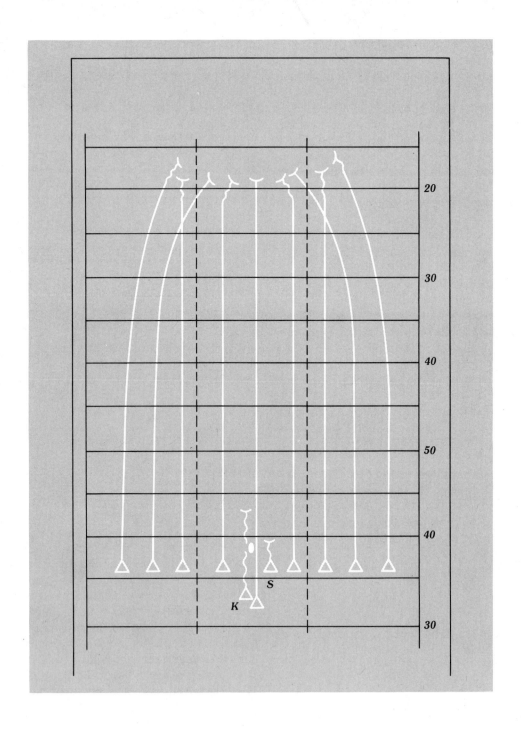

DIAGRAM 13-1.  *Kickoff coverage.*

FIGURE 13-7. *The wedgebuster, also known as the hot man, has the responsibility of as-saulting the four men in front of the kickoff returner. Above, the Redskins have formed a strong wedge in front of Speedy Duncan, their elusive return man.*

Skirting the wedge and getting to the re-turn man is the responsibility of players in lanes 4 and 5 on each side. The kicker, acting as the final safety, stays back near the 50-yard line with another safety man.

Two fast backs who are positioned as the third men in from each sideline have a key responsibility of forcing the action. They must make the opponents show their play. The two outside players have to be strong enough to protect the sidelines and force the play to the inside.

The wedgebuster, known as the hot man, has the responsibility of assaulting the four men in front of kickoff returners. After determining the strength of the blocking, he will hurtle his body into the four blockers with speed and abandon. His prime objec-tive is to scatter the wedge and open up an alley for his teammates to run through.

On a sideline call, the receiving team aims for a lane between the No. 4 and No. 5 men of the onrushing team. The kickoff men are numbered from the middle, or kicker, five on each side, to the sidelines. The No. 5 man has the responsibility of hugging the sidelines and turning in all ball carriers. Nor-mally, the receiving team tries to block him out and the No. 4 man in. However, if the No. 4 man hangs back, the sideline return could go through the No. 4 and 3 men.

On the up-the-middle return, the receiving team employs cross blocks. The blockers on both sides crisscross in their charge upfield, with the idea of knocking everyone to the outside and creating a funnel up the middle.

## ONSIDE KICK

For even the most skilled kicker, the onside kick (Diagrams 13-2 and 13-3) can be a difficult task. The ball has to be kicked two lanes over in front of the man in the second lane. The perfect distance, of course, is just beyond the legal distance of 10 yards.

To get a sideways spin that will put the ball on the left side just over the 10-yard zone, the ball is kicked on the top right corner. Five men on the kicker's left, sprinting at full speed, try to recover the ball as soon as it passes the 10-yard required area. The five players on the right side move to the left to back up and protect against a possible return.

As shown in Diagram 13-3, the ends are sometimes deployed 4 yards back.

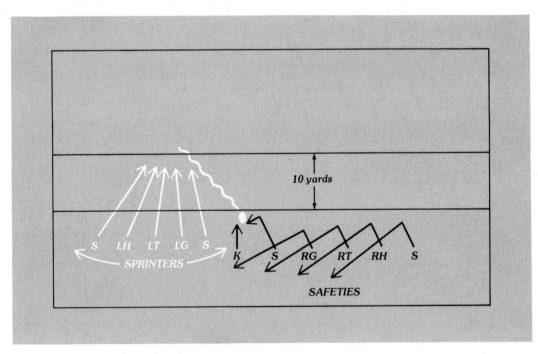

DIAGRAM 13-2. Onside kick alignment (kicking team).

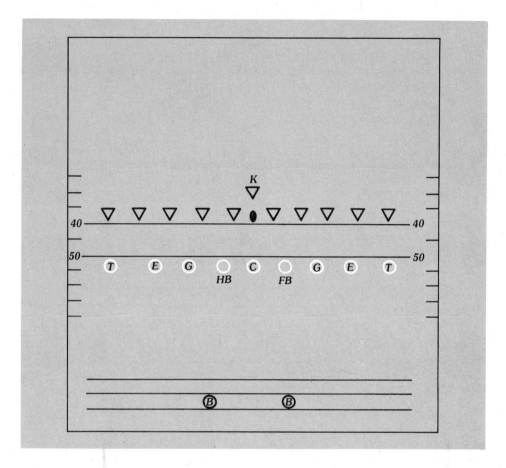

DIAGRAM 13-3.  Onside kick alignment (receiving team).

## KICKOFF RETURNS

Returning a kickoff is one of football's most exciting plays. Yet, it is also one of the most overlooked phases of the game. Since a miscue can cost valuable field position if there is a bobble, the receiver must catch the ball at all costs. Kickoff returns are important not only tactically but also psychologically: they can demoralize an opponent.

Rather than set up complicated plays on the kickoff, most teams structure their return to achieve maximum security. They employ a few plays they can use, and one day during the week, Thursday or Friday, is designated as kick day, when they polish these plays. Getting the ball back to at least the 30-yard line is their primary goal.

There are only three basic kickoff return plays: run to the right sidelines, run to the

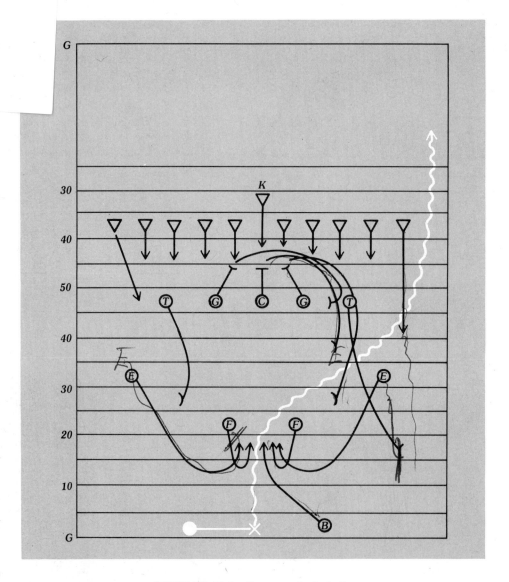

DIAGRAM 13-4. *Returning the kickoff.*

left, or go up the middle. The play is called before the kickoff. Many teams use a wedge return to force everyone outside of the wedge by sheer numbers. The ball carrier tries to stay in behind the wedge as long as he can, and any time he sees daylight, he may break off to the outside. He shouldn't get out of the wedge too soon, though, nor should he stay in it until he falls over his blockers. Whichever return is called, the runner must remember that the straight line still is the shortest distance to the goal line.

Many high school teams have been successful at using a wedge to attack the middle.

The wedge, four men tightly packed, operates from a position directly behind the front trio. The wings, usually ends or quick linemen, are located on either side of the front rank. Since they are responsible for picking off the wide men in open territory, they have to be good open-field blockers.

Finally, the two kick returners are positioned on the goal line. One man fields the ball, while the other makes the call, whether to down it or run it. If the kickoff is a high one and the coverage good, the second man will instruct his teammate to stay in the end zone and down the ball. Low kicks and short kicks should be returned. The four players who make up the wedge will set up about 10 yards ahead of the point where the ball is

*FIGURE 13-8. In returning the kickoff, the ball carrier should catch the ball and get to the wedge as quickly as possible. Here, Bob Brunet displays the running speed required of a good kick-return man.*

The popularity of the wedge can be attributed, in part, to the fact that the average high school player cannot kick the ball an excessive distance. As a result, a ball carrier who receives the ball on the 15-yard line usually lacks the running room to allow for complicated blocking patterns to develop.

Generally, the kickoff return team is broken up into four phalanxes. In the front rank of three linemen, one man is assigned to the kicker if he is capable of making a tackle. The other two players are responsible for the men on either side of the kicker, known as the wedgebusters.

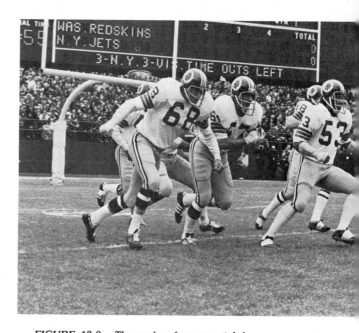

*FIGURE 13-9. The wedge, four men tightly packed, should be composed of linemen or heavy backs who are good blockers. The ball carrier stays within the protection of the wedge until he sees an opening.*

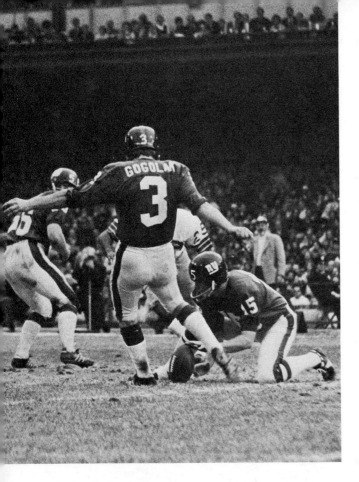

FIGURE 13-10. Soccer-style kickers like Pete Gogolak of the Giants hit the ball with their instep instead of their toe, providing a greater surface with which to hit the ball. While soccer-style short cleats are effective on a dry field, they are no good on a muddy day because the planted foot will often slip.

tection of the wedge. Then, he should attempt to break through it into the open field.

Every kick- and punt-return man has his own style. "I try to get a visual picture of how they are bearing down," explained Herb Adderley. "Sometimes I try to draw them in at the wedge in the middle. Then, if I can get the end man too close, so he commits himself too soon, I figure with my speed I might be able to turn the corner before he can recover."

To assist the return man, the wall men should have a definite side to peel back. "Wedge right" or "wedge left" will indicate the peel area. They should have a variety of blocks to employ. Quite often, they will double-team the two outside men to the side of the wall.

## PLACE-KICKING

Perhaps the biggest breakthrough in the kicking game has been in the area of field goal kicking. Professional and college teams now seek young soccer players who might have the right leg for field goals. Still, the side-footed soccer kickers have not taken over the game.

"I think the soccer style permits you to kick farther," says Pete Gogolak (Figure 13-10). "For accuracy, straight ahead is just as good. Our way we can put much more power into the kick. You can put your body into it. But the straight-on kicker seems to punch the ball with his foot."

In addition to a skillful kicker, the essentials for a successful placement are good solid blocking, a good center hike, and the holder of the ball (Figure 13-11). It requires weeks of practice at training camp and hundreds of kicks in practice during the season.

caught. At the command of "Go," the wedge attack is launched forward against the kicking team. The four men of the wedge are told to "Run over the opposition!" In using the wedge effectively, all members must remain on their feet. Essentially, all blocks are from inside out of the running shoulder type. Until he sees a break in the defense's line, the ball carrier should remain within the pro-

## BLOCKING ON PLACEMENTS

For maximum kicker protection, two of the biggest linemen should be positioned in the line to block (Diagram 13-5). Quite often, two linebackers will be employed as halfbacks with blocking responsibilities.

The offensive line blocking is shoulder to shoulder. The blocking linemen should make themselves as big as they can, thereby stretching the corner as wide as possible (Figure 13-12).

To prevent any gaps, the line must tighten as the blocking is applied to the inside. The defender who runs around this wall of blockers will seldom interfere with the kick. The average time for a successful placement in pro ball is approximately 1.3 seconds. Based on studies of the angle of the defensive charge, the optimum distance is 7 yards back of the line.

A blocking lineman should be instructed never to move his outside foot. He must be responsible for anyone trying to penetrate between him and the player next to him.

FIGURE 13-11. *A skilled holder on placements is almost as important as the kicker himself. Since laces can foul up the placekicker, the holder has to spin the ball and bring it down within a second.*

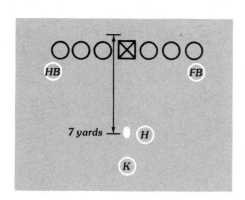

DIAGRAM 13-5. *Point after touchdown and field goal formation.*

## BLOCKING PLACE-KICKS

A blocked kick (Figure 13-14) can be a tremendous psychological advantage for the defense that can spark a team to victory. The best side to rush from is the right side, which is the open side. The ball is not shielded by the holder's body. Many teams will overload on one side and a quick defensive back will fly in from the outside and try to block the kick.

Yet, many blocked kicks come from the inside, from the "alley." This alley opens up when a defensive lineman shoulder blocks or pulls his man out of the way. By doing so, he creates a gap for a teammate to rush through.

FIGURE 13-12. *Blocking linemen who have the physical equipment to make the widest possible corner should be utilized for point after touchdown and field goal placements. Stepping with their inside foot, they must seal off the inside gap. The corner halfback or fullback should face out at a 45-degree angle and protect to the outside without moving the inside foot.*

FIGURE 13-13. *A place-kicker must have 1.2 to 1.5 seconds to get his kick away without fear of getting it blocked. Here, Curt Knight connects on a long field goal attempt against the St. Louis Cardinals.*

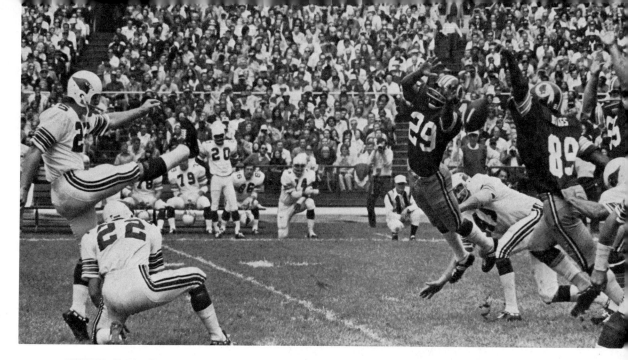

FIGURE 13-14. *Blocking the kick. While teammates tie up blockers, one fast defender soars in from the outside to try to block the kick. While the outside rushman, Ted Vactor, could not get his hands on the ball, the Redskins were able to partially block the field goal attempt by Jim Bakken of the Cardinals.*

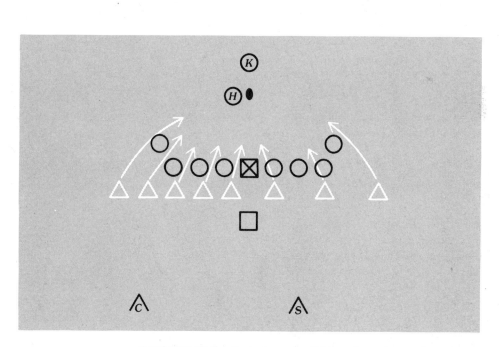

DIAGRAM 13-6. *Rush team for field goal and point after touchdown kicking.*

FIGURE 13-15. A booming punt. When a team cannot make a first down, or a touchdown, it can pick up half the distance of the field with a long, high punt. Mike Bragg of the Redskins demonstrates how a punter should kick through the ball, allowing his kicking leg to carry through over his head.

## PUNTS

A good punter can prove a tremendous asset to any football team (Figure 13-15). His long, booming kicks can be most instrumental in keeping the other team deep in their own territory.

Today's punters try to keep the ball high to discourage runbacks. "The higher I kick the ball, the longer it stays in the air and the more time it gives our guys to get downfield," explained Ray Guy, whose "hang time" on punts averages out to somewhere between 4.8 and 5 seconds.

Indeed, height can be just as important as the distance of a kick. If a 40-yard punt is returned 15 yards, the kicking team nets only 25 yards. Therefore, the net yardage after the kick and the return is the true assessment of punting. The return yardage on the high and long punters like Guy, Jerrel Wilson, and other top NFL kickers is less than 5 yards. As Vince Lombardi used to say, "The quicker the ball gets to the receiver, the quicker it gets back."

Punters who kick for accuracy and not necessarily distance can also do their team considerable good. An accurate coffin corner boot that goes out of bounds on the 2-yard line can put the opposition in very poor field position.

During punting practice, one of our coaches will time two items with his stopwatch: (1) the time it takes between the center's snap and the sound of the kick, and (2) the amount of time the punted ball stays in the air. We feel either one can be more important than the actual distance of the punt.

We figure you have to get the punt off in approximately 2 seconds. We are always clocking our punting team, from the time the ball leaves the center's hands to the time it leaves the punter's foot. The distances we have kicked from and the desired times are as follows:

15 yards—2.2 seconds
13 yards—2.1 seconds
10–11 yards—1.9 seconds

With the kicker 4 or 5 yards deeper, a greater burden is placed on the center. While the spread formation provides superior downfield coverage, for a high school team, whatever advantage is gained is not worth the risk of a blocked kick or a poor hike from the center.

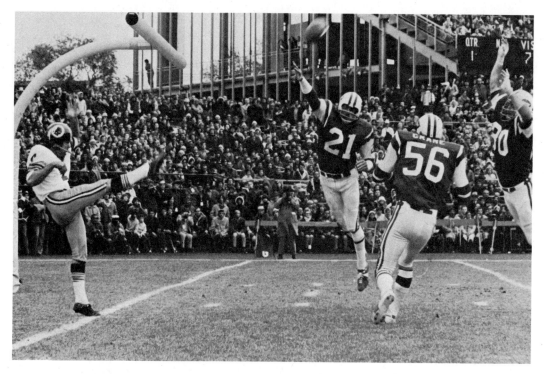

FIGURE 13-16. *A quicker kicking delivery will mean fewer blocked kicks. If a punter can hang the ball in the air 4.6 to 5.0 seconds, his job will be secure. Mike Bragg is shown here.*

## PROTECTING THE KICKER

Strong protection is of tremendous importance to the man kicking. Even when a kick is not blocked, his effectiveness is greatly hindered if he is hurried. Blocking must be strong up the middle. After the snap, the center, guards, and tackles pass block for two counts and then release downfield. Protection must be particularly heavy on the side of the kickers.

### Punt Formation

The regular punt formation is of two general types:

1. *Tight balanced line.* The ends are split about 5 yards. The two backs protect the kicking side of the kicker, and one back protects the off-side. The first responsibility of the interior lineman is to protect their inside seams toward the center. The outside foot and leg must remain stationary to prevent any leaking at the seams. Most punters, when using the regular formation, will line up 10 to 12 yards from the center. Many high school teams still use the closed punt formation with a tight balanced line in preference to the spread type used by professional and collegiate teams.

2. *Spread protection* (Diagram 13-7). This type of protection tends to spread the defending team, diminishing the threat of a blocked kick. However, a team shouldn't employ this technique unless the center is able to snap the ball at least 13 yards with good accuracy.

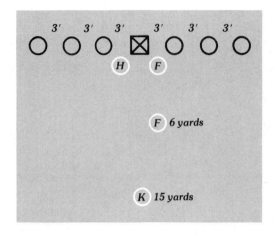

DIAGRAM 13-7. *Spread punt formation.*

## PUNT COVERAGE

Good punt coverage (Diagram 13-8) is based on the ability of the punter not to outkick his coverage. We spend considerable time in practice working on punt coverage. The fact that our opponents' return percentage has been poor is proof that our attention to punt coverage pays off.

Many coaches teach the recoil technique. Standard splits are established at the line, and the linemen recoil and drive off their inside foot. After recoil, they release outside and move into the proper coverage lane. The backs fire out to form a consistent wall of blockers.

### Field Goal and Extra Point Protection

The team protection used in the field goal and extra point kick is identical. The kicking team will line up in a tight line from end to end. The responsibilities of the linemen are to protect inside. The offensive backs will line up tight behind and slightly outside of each end. Although they are primarily concerned with inside protection, they have a basic responsibility to bump any rushman going to their outside. The holder lines up 7 to 8 yards behind the center.

The center's long pass must come back quickly as well as accurately. He should not hold the ball too far out in front, since a lack of power can result.

In the 1972 play-off game in San Francisco, a bad snap cost us the ball game. The ball was also poorly handled by our punter, and the 49ers fell on it in the end zone and got a touchdown. The following year, we added 3 minutes to our practice sessions—to eliminate bad snaps.

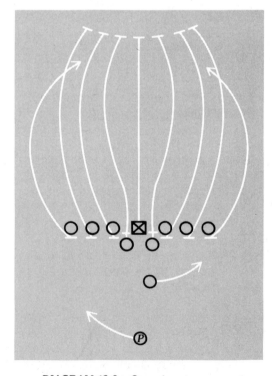

DIAGRAM 13-8. *Spread punt coverage.*

## PUNT PLAYS

To cut down the pass rush and have more effective coverage, a team should have a few run and pass plays in their arsenal. An end run to the left side or a reverse employed with deception can be very effective. The screen pass right is another effective play from the punt formation. After taking his normal steps, the kicker straightens up and throws the ball out to the fullback in the right flat. In the huddle, the quarterback should call the name of the back and a specific pass route.

## POOCHER PUNT

The poocher punt, which demands a skilled punter, can be an effective weapon in placing the opponents deep inside their own 10-yard line. Those on the coverage unit try to down the ball before it rolls into the end zone. The kicker should kick the ball so that it lands dead with a minimum of roll.

### Tight Punt

When punting inside the 3-yard line, a team will tighten the line. While the tight punt formation provides better inside protection, it restricts the coverage. After releasing, those on the coverage must spread or fan out in effectively assuming their coverage lanes.

Once in a while, a coach will make a decision to take a safety when his team is forced into a tight situation, described above. In this case, he should instruct his kicker and team to take a safety. I can recall Miami Coach Don Shula making this decision in a playoff game against the Cincinnati Bengals. It worked to the advantage of the Dolphins, too.

### Quick Kick

For teams lacking a strong offensive threat, the quick kick can gain considerable yardage. Indeed, a well-executed quick kick can be a big morale booster for a team.

The element of surprise is an important advantage of a quick kick. Often, the ball will take a long roll, since no one is usually back to field the punt. In his haste to retrieve the ball, the return man could very well fumble the ball away.

Ideally, the fullback should handle the quick-kicking duties. Although a team can quick kick on any down, it can also be effective on fourth-down situations. When they see the offense line up in a regular offensive formation, the defense will often hurry in to protect against a run or pass. A quick kick over their heads can set them back a considerable distance.

Perhaps the most effective method of quick kicking is the rocker step technique, which eliminates the kicker's backward movement and allows him to kick quickly. Although the change is difficult to detect, the fullback and halfback line up one yard deeper than usual. On the snap of the ball, the kicker (the fullback) will take a rocker step backward with his left (nonkicking) foot. Then with the ball in his possession, he steps forward with his left and kicks with his right foot.

Another method can be used, but it is less effective. The fullback, about one count prior to the hike, backs up quickly three steps and kicks the ball.

## RUSHING THE KICKER

Rushing the kicker is of great importance to the defense. Indeed, a blocked and recovered punt can be a great morale builder for any football team.

## The Punt

Perhaps the most effective method for penetrating the blocking pattern is overloading the defending halfbacks at one end or the other. The tackle and end will often work together on the kicker's offside. The prime objective is for one of them to draw the back out of position, while the other rushes up the alley. Also, two linebackers might be sent in on one side with the hope that one will be overlooked.

Another technique is to drive directly up the alley either by overloading or by moving the center out of the way. In the roll-out procedure, one man will grab and pull the center out of position. This opens a hole for another defender to break through up the middle.

On the snap of the ball, the outside rushers, usually halfbacks, will jump inside of the offensive ends and rush aggressively to the kicking area. We instruct our rushers to aim for a point 2 yards or so in front of the anticipated impact of the punter's foot and

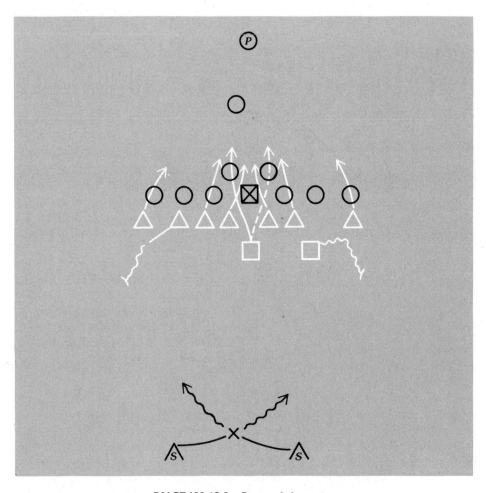

DIAGRAM 13-9.  Punt rush formation.

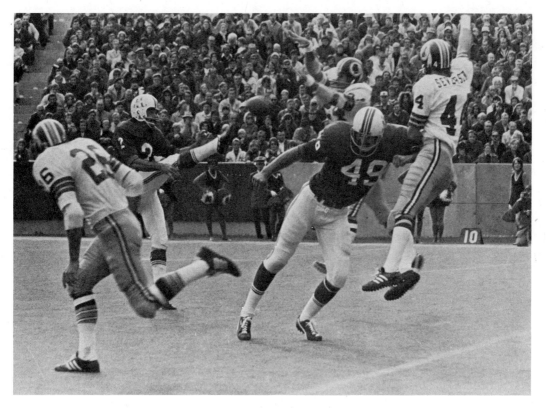

**FIGURE 13-17.** *A blocked and recovered punt can be a great morale builder for any football team.*

the ball (Figure 13-17). We go up, not dive. They are told repeatedly, "Don't leave your feet!"

### The Place-kick

The eight-man rushing line is generally used in attempting to block the field goal or extra point. As in blocking the punt, overloading and pulling stunts are used.

While a blocked kick can give a team a great boost and good field position, players should realize that roughing the kicker can give the opposition the ball back and an automatic first down. We also caution them not to be off-side.

### FIELDING THE PUNT

The punt can be a dangerous offensive weapon if the receivers do not handle the ball correctly. Actually, a punt can be a most difficult ball to handle, whether it be end-over-end, spiral, floating, or wobbling.

In catching a punt, two rules are of prime importance. First, the receiver must never be off balance, and second, he should always watch the ball. He follows the ball all

A          B

FIGURE 13-18. *In fielding the punt, the receiver (Ken Stone) must be in a balanced position and keep his eyes on the ball from the moment it leaves the kicker's foot until it is safely in his hands. He should put the ball away as quickly as possible.*

the way from the moment it leaves the kicker's foot.

Most professional teams use twin safety men. The man who is not receiving will advise the catcher about the tacklers pounding downfield. If they are too close, he'll yell, "Fair catch!" Otherwise, he'll tell him, "Plenty of room!" By providing this information, the receiver can concentrate strictly on the ball.

Generally, we tell our backs to "Fair Catch" a high punt and return a low, long one. A fair catch forfeits the receiver's right to advance the ball. He extends and waves one hand only above the head, and after catching the ball, drops one knee to the ground. He must catch the ball; otherwise the ball becomes free.

When the receiver catches the football,

he should hesitate for a split second. There are two reasons for this action. First, the receiver can get a quick look at his pursuers; it also gives his blockers time to get back to him. Then he can break down the middle, hoping to draw in the tacklers.

The duty of the other safety man is to block the first tackler downfield so the receiver can break down the middle. When the ball carrier sees the second tackler, he'll cut right or left toward the sidelines, according to the play. This maneuver will provide his blockers enough time to get back and pick him up.

We like the receiver to catch the ball with a combination of hands and chest. He will find it effective to lift up to the balls of his feet for the catch. We feel he can get a quicker takeoff by doing this. But the most important point is keeping his eye on the ball until it's safely in his hands.

Once in a while, a receiver will gamble and try to catch a punt on the run, but this is risky business. It is also dangerous to field a ball bouncing along the turf, but sometimes he has to take the chance.

A returner should be instructed not to field a punt inside his 10-yard line. If he is near the 10, he should stand there but never back up from it to field a kick.

## RETURNING PUNTS

When he sends his special team or players in, the coach should indicate whether he wants a right or a left return. Seldom does a return man move up the middle. For many teams, the familiar wall return has been used consistently. (See Diagram 13-10.)

Two methods are most often used:

- Criss-cross of the two deep backs

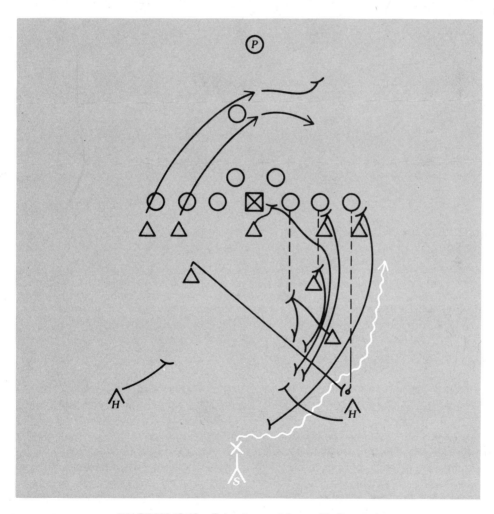

*DIAGRAM 13-10. Returning punt from odd alignment.*

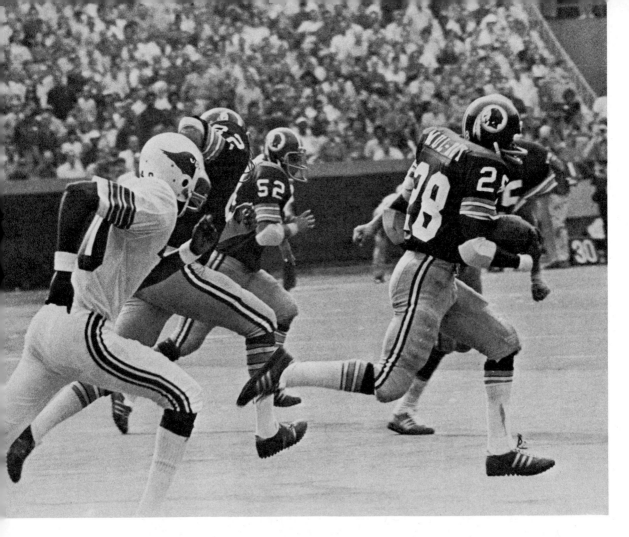

FIGURE 13-19. *A long run can have a demoralizing effect on the kicking team, as well as giving the receiving team a strategic advantage. Here, Herb Mul-Key, the former Redskins' kick return performer, breaks loose on a long 97-yard touchdown run against the St. Louis Cardinals.*

• Free back serving as a personal blocker for the ball carrier

Most teams use two plays on a punt runback, right or left. The call is given for the punt by the defensive captain in the huddle. The simple left or right call becomes a necessity created by the peculiar blocking problems created by punting. The blockers on the receiving team must first break through the line to force the punt, then circle around and rush back down the sidelines to provide interference for the punt receiver.

On the wall return to the right, the defensive right end will determine the depth at which the ball will begin, depending on the distance of the punt. About 10 yards from the receiver and approximately the same distance from the sideline, he will turn in and wait for a tackler to come to him. At 5-yard intervals, the rest of the line will peel back and form the remainder of the wall.

The defensive end away from the wall, after rushing the punter, should loop around to become the last man on the wall. We often have three men delay or block the offensive end to the side on which the wall will be run.

As the fielder receives the punt and the wall forms, he will cut wide either to his left or right. Generally, a return man will return outside to give his blockers time to set up their wall.

Every football team should devote at least 5 minutes a day to practicing the wall punt returns. Some teams prefer working on kickoff returns three times a week. Ideal days for practicing kickoff and punt returns are Monday and Friday, since they are normally light workout days. Rather than finish a practice with windsprints, many teams will end a session with several punt and kickoff returns.

# Part Three

# ORGANIZATION, TRAINING, AND CONDITIONING

# 14

# Organization of the Football Program

A Football Season: a period of time
that becomes one big game. Any game
can become a season, any minute can
produce a game-winning play, and any
play can make a winning season.

**George Allen**

First-rate organization—along with superior personnel—is the surest way to achieve team success. Many coaches do not know what the word organization means. Careful attention to the details of organization is a must for any football team. Since the beginning of the National Football League in 1920, the most successful coaches have been men who excelled in organization, like my former boss, George Halas, Don Shula, Hank Stram, and Paul Brown.

The story of the NFL has shown that no team of individual stars has ever won a championship. The team has to be a 40-man unit! I have found from past experience in college and professional football that the only way we can win is to play together as a team.

Perhaps the most important thing on a football team is the exact timing that comes from playing together week after week. Injuries, whether in the line or backfield, can wreck this timing and precision.

Our practice program is set up to accomplish basic objectives. We do not go out just to have a 1½- or 2-hour practice. We go out on the field to accomplish something, and we will give as much time as is necessary to accomplish a goal. The time element does not bother us too much. If it's 5 minutes, it is 5 minutes. If it is 20 minutes or an hour and it takes that much to do it, that's what we will do. We have found that if we just go out to practice and warm up, we gain nothing. The players, as well as the coaches, understand this. We probably have longer practices than most teams.

Everybody must work together. You can
have the Pro Bowl squad, but if everybody's not working together you won't
win.

327

FIGURE 14-2. *Football is a game of detail, a highly complicated game that requires intelligent planning and direction. Tactical moves must be made quickly and decisively, both on the sidelines and in the locker room at half time.*

Organization involves more than the scheduling of available practice time so that every minute is used to the best advantage. It includes game plans and evaluations, staff assignments, and the utilization of scouting reports. Certainly, a carefully planned schedule is necessary if the practice program is to be successfully adapted to the needs of the squad, such as previous games, player grading, and film studies of future opponents.

*Organization is the foundation of all successful football coaching.* This is just as true

*Football is a game of detail.*

in the handling of high school and college teams as it is in coaching play-for-pay professional squads. Organization is the basis of the whole game.

Winning football depends not only on how well organized and coordinated the coaching staff is, but also on the efficiency of scouting, player assignments, and practice sessions. Checklists, forms, charts, schedules, scouting reports, and drill diagrams should be available and ready for use. The practice schedule should be developed so that *every minute pays off,* and the coaching staff must make the best possible use of time all year long.

# OFFICE OF THE FOOTBALL COACH

**STAFF ASSIGNMENTS**

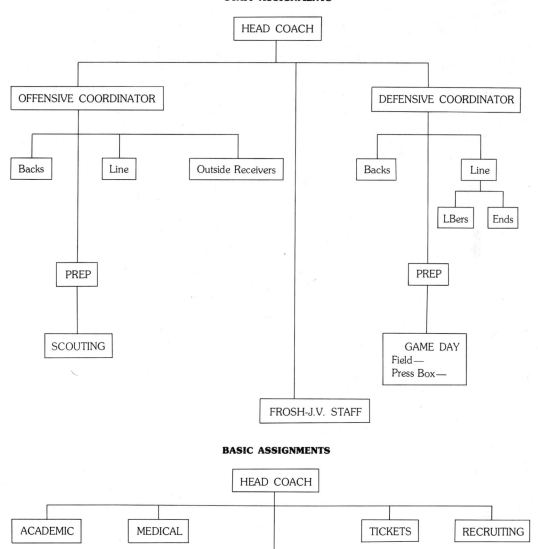

**BASIC ASSIGNMENTS**

*FIGURE 14-3. Organizational plan for high school and college football programs.*

Since coaching football is a year-round job, a yearly organizational plan must be prepared and followed as closely as possible. An outlined plan of organization to be administered by the head coach should be prepared for the entire year. He must realize that no detail or technique is too small to be ignored.

Building a football program on the high school or college level is a cooperative effort and includes the school administration, faculty, community, and the news media. If the coaching staff does not have the support and cooperation of the school and community, it is not possible to produce a high-caliber football program.

Winning is the science of being totally prepared. Preparation can be defined in three words: *leave nothing undone.* No detail can be too small. No task is too small—or too large.

The difference between success and failure is so minute it cannot be perceived by most of us. Nowadays, there is practically no difference between one team and another in the NFL. And usually the winner is going to be the team that is in better physical condition and better prepared.

## TEAM MANAGEMENT

The organization of a football program involves many aspects that the coach should be concerned with year-round. Indeed, the job of a head football coach can be a 12-month assignment, especially at college and professional levels.

The management of a football team includes the following areas:

1. Conditioning and training
   a. Off-season
   b. Pre-season
   c. During season
2. Team selection
3. Game preparation
4. Facilities and equipment
5. Maintenance of the playing field
6. Public relations
7. Player recruitment
8. The budget and its uses
9. Making the schedule
10. Planning for trips
11. Selecting officials
12. Scouting needs

Many of football's most successful coaches divide their day into a half-dozen categories, such as general, staff, medical, alumni, public relations, recruiting, offense, defense, and the kicking game. Employing a checklist, they will cross off each item after it is done.

## ORGANIZATIONAL CALENDAR FOR COLLEGE PROGRAMS

### June

1. Check players' final grades.
2. Write out and run off 6-week weight and running exercises.
3. Check the film trading agreements.
4. Follow up on summer clinic reservations.
5. Reevaluate entire spring football program.
6. Make out summer assignments for staff members.

### July

1. Attend football clinics (2 weeks).
2. Send for college films.
3. Review fall teaching schedule and organize office hours.
4. Evaluate pass defense.
5. Check with grounds keepers about new turf and plans for game and practice field.

FIGURE 14-4. *The coaching profession takes long hours, and we may well have the longest hours in the business. Shown here is the 1974 Redskins coaching staff. Front row (left to right): LaVern Torgeson, defensive line; Ted Marchibroda, offensive coordinator; George Allen, head coach; Charlie Waller, offensive backs; Joe Walton, offense. Back row: Ralph Hawkins, defensive secondary; Dick Bielski, offensive receivers; Bill Austin, offensive line; Bill Hickman, special assignments; Paul Lanham, special teams; Jim Hilyer, weight training; and Kirk Mee, general assignments.*

## August

1. Finish running off defensive alignments and stunts.
2. Reevaluate and finish viewing various college films.
3. Prepare checklist for basic attack and practice schedules.
4. Work on players' notebooks and finalize basic offensive attack.
5. Meet with student trainers and football managers.
6. Request transportation for scouting.
7. Check on pre-season football scrimmage date.
8. Organize detailed practice schedules.
9. Conduct pre-season staff meetings.

*To play as a team, everyone must feel part of it and care for everyone else.*

## September

1. During first week, evaluate, rate, and discuss football personnel.
2. Formalize game plans for the first game.
3. Obtain films of opponent's games.
4. Keep master scouting plan up to date.
5. Work on the kicking game.

## PRINTED MATERIALS

### The Player's Notebook

Before summer practice begins, notebooks should be put together by the coaching staff. These notebooks contain the results of countless hours of film analysis, grading, and systematic review. Then, as the season moves along, new material is added to the looseleaf-style notebook (8½-×-11-inch paper), including scouting reports, game plans, adjustments in offense and defense, and notes and diagrams recorded during team meetings.

On the professional level, we like our players to write down many of the plays and diagrams themselves. We lecture and they write. Writing the material down facilitates learning. The offense receives one playbook, and the defense gets another book. Both books run more than 1,000 pages, and we expect our players to read and study them.

Every player is responsible for updating his notebook and recording new information, plays, or maneuvers. We make it a practice to check the notebooks periodically.

The notebook covers the chief rules, field regulations, dressing room requirements, injury prevention, diet, daily fitness, and calisthenics. Playbook material includes.

1. Formations
2. Hole-numbering
3. Pass and backfield patterns
4. Play diagrams
5. Signal calling and checking
6. Defensive manual

### Program Checklists

Checklists or outlines should be used in all phases of the football program. In addition to specific skills, drills, and techniques, the checklist can save valuable time in preparing

daily and weekly practice schedules. Individual defensive and offensive line position lists are particularly valuable. As each assignment is accomplished it should be checked off.

### Pre-season Team Brochure

Each year on about August 1, a brochure can be sent each football candidate. This brochure is designed to acquaint everyone with the plans for the season. Some of the major things the brochure covers are:

1. Pre-exam schedule (physical exam, equipment, etc.)
2. Game and practice schedule
3. Training program, including proper diet, etc.

### Post-season Brochure

A brochure made up by the staff can be distributed to all football candidates, and includes the following:

1. Statistics from the season just completed
2. Returnees for the upcoming football season
3. The upcoming schedule
4. Tips on growth and development
5. A three-part conditioning program

### Season Report

The coaching staff must enjoy a friendly relationship with the administration and the faculty.

The administration should be provided with a complete report on the previous football season. The report should include:

1. Participation
2. Record
3. Success of the program
4. Failure of the program
5. Grades and attendance
6. Equipment and facilities

7. Physical condition
8. Needs
9. Comments
10. Outlook

## Defensive and Offensive Ready Sheets

After a careful study of the scouting reports and movie breakdowns, defensive ready sheets are written and diagrammed. A detailed written and illustrated defensive ready sheet is important for each defensive position.

The offensive sheets consist of a rushing sheet and a passing sheet. The coach in the press box uses his offensive ready sheet in calling down plays from the press box.

## Other Printed Materials

- Offensive plays ready list (8-×-10-inch cards in plastic envelope)
- Diagrams of running plays (8-×-10-inch cards; 20—24)
- Diagrams of pass plays (10 × 14 inches)
- Defensive charts (8-×-10-inch white cardboard)(opponent's defenses)
- Frequency chart of offensive plays
- Offensive pass blocking against the various defenses

## RULES AND CLUB POLICY

At the start of the summer training season, members of the Washington Redskins are given a printed copy of the General Rules and Club Policies, which are applicable for the entire season. The copy reads: "You are expected to conduct yourselves as gentlemen at all times and in a manner that will reflect credit upon you, your teammates, the Washington Redskins, and the National Football League." The rules continue:

1. Keep yourself neat and clean at all times.
2. Team members will eat all meals at the prescribed time. It is mandatory that you attend the *Breakfast* period each morning.
3. It is *your* responsibility to be on time for all practices, meetings, and other appointments. Do not rely on someone else. Excuses will *not* be accepted.
4. Drinking of hard liquor will not be tolerated.
5. Curfew for all players is 10:45 P.M., unless told otherwise by the head coach. Lights out is at 11:00 P.M. in training camp and this means that each man must be in his own room and bed.
6. No loud radio, television, phonographs, or musical instruments will be allowed in the dormitory area.
7. Every player must weigh *in* and *out* every day. A fine of $100 per pound will be assessed for overweight players.
8. Every player will wear prescribed uniform and there will be no exceptions. A protective face guard will be worn by all personnel unless permission has been secured from the head coach. While on the field of play, or practice, the helmet will be worn or carried at all times.
9. All players must have their ankles taped before every practice and game.
10. The club reserves the rights to impose and require observance by the players of *reasonable* standards of personal conduct. Players must conform to, and abide by, the rules and restrictions established by the Club to protect and safeguard the game of professional football.

If a team has the proper mental attitude to begin with, training rules take care of themselves. I like to think we have fair training rules, but at the same time, I think they are as strict as necessary. We have a bed check at 11 o'clock every night during training camp, as well as every night we are on the road. I have had to fine only two ball players for missing curfew. I don't like to fine a player, but if I have to, generally, the fine is not a token one.

FIGURE 14-5. *An efficient and devoted secretary can be a tremendous asset to any football coach and program. Shirley Krystek, my personal secretary both in Los Angeles and in Washington, handles a multitude of secretarial assignments and assists in the presentation of technical materials. An extremely dedicated young lady, she has been of inestimable value to me and my football programs.*

## THE BUDGET

Each year, the head coach of high school and college football programs prepares a budget, or a statement of the anticipated expenditures and receipts for the coming season. A budget is an estimate of costs in regard to the purchase, care, and repair of equipment and uniforms, home game expense, travel, scheduling of games, medical expense, care and maintenance of the field, awards, and all other expenses involved in maintaining a team.

Home games involve the expense of officials, policing, and advertising, which must be planned so as to conform to the budget as closely as possible.

The budget is largely based on past expenditures and receipts, but changing conditions, from year to year, may require careful planning and control.

## PURCHASING

Although exact procedures for obtaining approval for expenditures may differ from school to school, the head coach usually fills out a requisition form (including catalog number, price, size, etc.) and submits it to the director of athletics for approval. After the requisition has been approved by the business office, a purchase order is issued.

### Dining Hall

Our grocery bill at training camp comes to around $40,000, including $14,000 for meat alone and as high as $600 per meal.

A pro team will drink 1,440 gallons of fruit juice after practices. Other expenditures are:

$3,000 in fruit
300 gallons of ice cream
600 pounds of cheese
500 loaves of bread
350 dozen rolls

### Film

Over 65,000 feet of film are used by a pro team filming exhibitions and regular season games. The total cost of all films amounts to over $75,000 for three prints of each contest.

## MEDICAL ASPECTS

Mandatory medical examinations and medical history should be taken at the beginning

FIGURE 14-6. The medical staff plays a vital role in the success of a football team. Injuries must be treated quickly and effectively. Here, Dr. Pat Palumbo, the Redskins' team physician, assisted by Bubba Tyer, assistant trainer, diagnoses a head injury sustained by quarterback Bill Kilmer.

field and all player protective equipment meet high standards.

### Selecting Talent

Classifying the talents and shortcomings of the players is one of the most important phases of organization.

Qualities to be considered include relative speed, tackling ability, range, passing talent, and blocking ability. Along with the physical qualities a *burning desire to win* is a quality every coach is seeking in a player. Players with this will to win and competitive attitude are the players who will be at their best in the fourth quarter when a few plays will decide the outcome.

The shrewd and wise coach is able to make adjustments with his personnel to compensate for a deficiency in quality or numbers.

of each season. Physical conditioning should be proper, gradual, and complete.

A physician should be present at all games and practice sessions (Figure 14-6). The team trainer, whether he is a coach or noncoach, should be adequately prepared and qualified. Insurance plans should be made available to squad members.

There should be strict enforcement of game rules. Above all, the technique of "spearing" or "goring" must be eliminated from the game of football.

Since statistics show that the majority of player injuries occur during the first 10 days of practice, extra precaution should be taken in an effort to keep injuries to a minimum. The players can help considerably by being in top condition when they report, but the coaching staff must make sure the practice

FIGURE 14-7. All football staffs should have offensive and defensive personnel boards. Above, Tim Temerario, director of player personnel for the Redskins, records some new information on a player.

FIGURE 14-8. *Looking for new talent. The Redskins were the first team to conduct large-scale free agent camps throughout the United States. Starting in March, camps are held in nearly a dozen major cities. Here, Coach Allen puts the clock on one of the young prospects.*

## TRAINING ROOM

The training room is for taping, first aid, and the treatment of injuries. It is a place of business and is not to be used as a lounge. Absolutely no horseplay is tolerated in the Redskins' training facilities.

We are constantly striving to keep these facilities "big league." Players are told: "Don't throw old tape, soiled white goods, equipment, or any other articles on the floor." We have provided disposal containers for refuse. So, we want our players to use them and keep this area orderly and sanitary.

It is the responsibility of each player to report injuries to the trainers immediately. On the morning following the game, it is their responsibility to report for treatment to get all the "bumps and bruises" taken care of.

Treatments are given before and after practice and immediately after the evening meeting. "Never miss a treatment period!" the players are told. "You must be able to go full speed to help yourself and the Redskins." By observing training rules, an athlete will be a better football player.

## EQUIPMENT

Proper equipment should always be worn when playing such a highly competitive game as football. Moreover, the very best equipment available should be worn by a player when engaging in contact. Failure to do so will not only contribute to poor blocking and tackling but will increase the possibility of injury.

Football, with all its body contact, demands that properly fitted shoulder pads and helmets be worn, together with snug-fitting pants that keep the tight guards and hip pads properly positioned. Backfield men and receivers, as a rule, wear only shoulder pads and helmets, modified hip, thigh, and knee pads, plus the usual tape on their ankles. Such protective equipment is necessary not only to prevent injury but to provide added protection in case an injury has already been sustained.

The use of synthetics has made equipment lighter and stronger. Protective pads fit the contours of the player's body to provide greater protection.

We urge our players to take care of their equipment and not to throw it around. We do not like to see our men dress sloppily for practice, just because it is practice. Instead, they should have pride in their appearance every time they go on the field with their team.

Indeed, it costs a lot of money to outfit a football player. Locker room costs, such as training devices, medical supplies, tape, and just the maintenance of equipment, can be a sizeable sum for a squad of 40 players, averaging well over $20,000 annually.

## Uniforms

Equipment and clothing have become more carefully styled, flexible, and, of course,

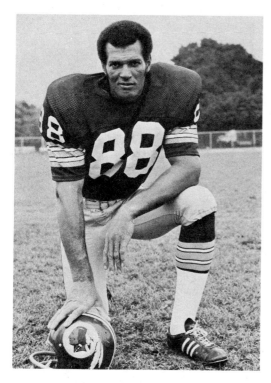

*FIGURE 14-9. Uniforms are more style-conscious today. Nylon is lighter and more flexible and gives a player complete mobility. Stretch nylon fits more snugly and keeps the protective equipment in place like a rubber band. Alvin Reed poses here.*

more expensive. Even the necklines of jerseys are often specially sewn, stocking specially cut, sleeve lengths specially measured.

Numbers have been enlarged, and names have been added to the back of the jerseys. Today, the tendency is toward impressing numbers under heat, and impressing of vinyl, rubber-type numbers right into the jersey. The vinyl numbers are lighter in weight and stretch with the jersey.

## Shoes

A very important piece of equipment is the shoe. The shoes must be comfortable, and they must support the joints of the foot and ankle. The shoe cleats should always be checked before every game and practice to make sure they are the proper type for the condition of the field.

Many styles have flooded the market, ranging from the traditional seven-cleat shoe to the multicleated soccer shoe. Shoes today are changed like underwear, with careful regard to both the type of playing surface and the weather report.

Many shoes being used are lightweight, thin-soled, and badly supported. Many foot injuries result from wearing improperly constructed shoes.

## Protective Pads

The shoulder pad has become the most personalized piece of equipment, designed for size, for position, often for the individual. The knee pad is now made of better foam and contoured more exactly to the joint. The thigh pad, once placed in the middle of the leg, has been shifted to the outside, where there is more and harder contact. Hip pads have become less cumbersome and lighter.

**FIGURE 14-10.** *Maintenance of equipment demands the close supervision of an equipment manager, such as Tommy McVean of the Redskins, who is shown here adjusting the face guard on a new helmet.*

### Safety Pads

For years I have been searching for ways to improve our 11-on-11 practice period to make it resemble game conditions without actually scrimmaging. I want my defensive players active and mobile yet fully protected during the drills. I want my offensive players to be able to get their timing down against a defense that reacts normally.

The problem always has been the protective gear worn by the defenders, which has been either too heavy, too bulky, or both. True, it gives protection, but it limits the defensive player's normal speed and reaction.

In these new, lightweight pads, I believe we have the answer to this problem. The three pads are called: safety hand, safety power elbow, and safety power arm. All three are light and extremely easy to put on or take off, and they do not limit the defender's play in any way. I think these safety pads are a giant step forward in football teaching aids. With them, an 11-on-11 drill will be as close to a real game as it is possible to get. They have aided our players tremendously, both offensively and defensively.

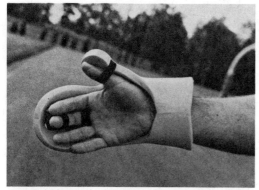

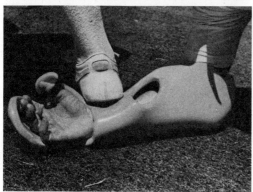

### Helmet

The greatest safety concern has been with the head and the helmet. Restyled, better-fitting helmets have been responsible for cutting down facial injuries; for example, better padding is now used on the rims. Helmets that fit too loosely can be lifted from behind and cause a broken nose.

## FACILITIES

Proper facilities should go along with a good football program. If the team is to play in big league fashion, the coaching staff should provide facilities that are as near top caliber as financial assests and ingenuity will allow. Office facilities should include a sound filming system and other administrative aids.

Football is such a complicated game that three or four different practice areas must be run at the same time. All in all, the practice site should be large enough to accommodate five large areas where the following groups drill:

1. Defensive backs
2. Offensive backs
3. Defensive linemen
4. Offensive linemen
5. Quarterbacks and receivers

The development and construction of a training room for the treatment of injuries and a weight training room will provide the physical conditioning necessary for championship play. Equipment and locker room facilities should meet good standards of operation.

*FIGURE 14-11. These lightweight pads are extremely easy to put on or take off during practice. They do not limit the defensive men in any way. These innovations of mine (with a patent pending) are called (top to bottom) safety hand, safety power elbow, and safety power arm.*

### Redskin Park

Creating Redskin Park was a major coaching accomplishment. I wanted Redskin Park because I think it is important to have a place the players can call home. When a player comes out here, he is preparing himself to win. There is no extraneous activity. Having students and people right off the street milling around is not conducive to winning football. Whenever the players come into this area, they can concentrate on football and winning. It helps morale.

We have not only a grass field but an Astro-Turf surface as well. When we are scheduled to play on Astro-Turf, we should practice on it. Our practice fields are all properly lined and marked in 5-yard segments and with hash marks. These markings are necessary to create down and distance, particularly for the passing and kicking phases of the game.

We now have a punting machine, so we will not wear out our kickers. This machine actually kicks spirals, so that now we can practice catching punts. When we are going to face a left-footed punter, the machine will spiral the ball the other way. The ball fades away.

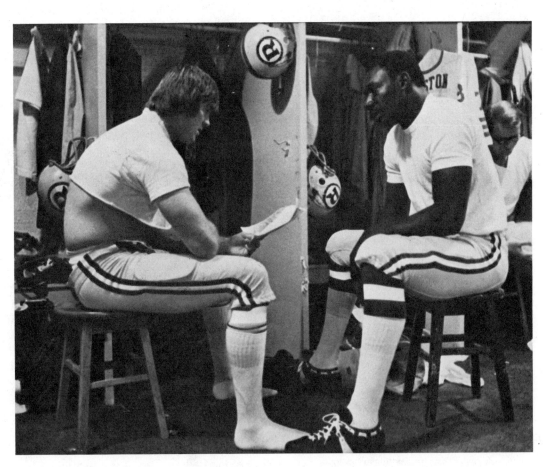

FIGURE 14-12. *Clubhouse comfort. While the dressing room facilities of schools and colleges need not match the NFL in quality, each player should have a stool or bench in front of his cubicle or locker.*

FIGURE 14-13. *Redskin Park is the Utopia in football training facilities, which I feel every professional team will have in the future. Located in Herndon, Virginia, about 25 miles from the nation's capital, the magnificent football complex was developed at a cost of $750,000. The two practice fields offer both grass and Astro-Turf, and each field is properly lined and marked in 5-yard segments and with hash marks. The huge building includes the administrative offices, clubhouse, training room, weight room, and handball and basketball courts.*

Basic equipment on our practice field includes:

- Seven-man sled
- Two-man crowthers
- One-man crowther
- One-man sled
- Big dummies
- Hand shields
- Large shields
- Chutes
- Netting
- Reactor
- Hand shiver board
- D-O dummy sled
- Punting machine

## Turf Drainage

Melvin Robey, superintendent of Purdue's athletic facilities, and Dr. W. H. Daniel, turf specialist in agronomy at Purdue, are co-inventors of a new system in turf drainage. Several major athletic installations such as Ross-Ade Stadium at Purdue University are successfully using this system,* which allows

* Prescription Athletic Turf, Inc., Lansing, Michigan.

FIGURE 14-14. The new D.O. dummy sled has six units on 36 feet. The power posts are on one end, and the dual pads are on the second side. Both sides can be used for offense and defense. (Manufactured by Marty Gilman, Inc., Gilman, Conn. 06336.)

FIGURE 14-15. The latest gadget in the Redskins' training arsenal is an automatic punting machine made by Garver Industries. Here, assistant coach Paul Lanham prepares to "punt" the ball high and long to the Redskins' punt return men. It is easy to get the robot kicker to zoom the ball up to 100 yards or better.

man to manage the root zone in turf. Suction pumps tied to collector pipes and slitted drains draw the water through a sandy sub-surface, leaving the playing field firm—even after 2½ inches of rain, according to Alex Agase, head football coach at Purdue.

## SCOUTING

The more information a football team has about the opponent the greater chance there is for victory. This is why teams of all levels place considerable emphasis on the scouting phase of their organization.

Even at the high school level, the head coach should organize an effective scouting staff. Sources of personnel are members of the coaching staff, former players, and friends of the coaches.

When scouting a team, the individual scout must:

1. Take away the most important material he can obtain.
2. Exploit the weaknesses of the team scouted.
3. Above all, never guess.

### Weekly Scouting Report

A scout must give a written report to the coaching staff. Normally, he will also give an oral report to the squad and answer any questions the players may have.

The scout, if not the coach, is concerned with transportation, film exchange, scouting materials, scouting techniques, and scouting schedules.

A good scout should have on hand the necessary forms and be ready to jot down as much pertinent information as he can. He shouldn't trust his observations to memory.

In taking the play-by-play, the scout should use a format that contains space for four diagrams on each page.

While a defensive play-by-play is not required, a summary of defenses should be reported relative to normal long- and short-yardage situations.

A written scouting report should include:

- Title sheet
- Personnel (offensive and defensive)
- Formations (basic)
- Favorite runs versus our defense
- Favorite passes versus our defense
- Basic defenses (goal line and short yardage)
- Punting game
- Kickoff game

### Key-sort Card Scouting

This card contains all of the most important offensive information on one side and all of the defensive information on the other side (Figure 14-16). The card enables the coaching staff to gain the most important sta-tistical tendencies of the opponent.

## FILM GRADING

The most accurate method of evaluating football players, as well as coaching methods and techniques, is by grading the game films. The film is run over and over until the coaches have graded and written down their players' scores.

We will run a play over and over, maybe a dozen or more times, examining each man and trying to determine how each man might have reacted better.

Some positions are more difficult to play than others, and the passing grade varies ac-cording to the situation and the degree of dif-ficulty. For example, on pass plays, the inte-rior linemen should make 85 percent of their

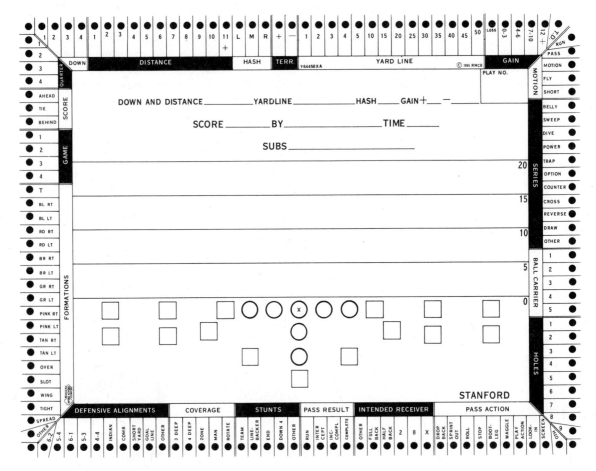

*FIGURE 14-16. The scouting card contains the most important offensive information on one side and all defensive data on the other.*

blocks, while a passing mark for a split end on running plays might be 55 percent.

As I have explained in chapter 10, deep backs are graded on a plus-and-minus point system. On a good day, a defensive back will break even. If he has a plus score, he played an outstanding game.

During the off-season, each player's performance is examined closely. Too many bad marks can cost a player his job.

Plays are examined just as carefully as players. The resulting statistics can tell us which plays are consistent ground gainers and which are unreliable. The strengths of various defensive alignments get the same careful study.

## COMPUTERS

The most widely recognized use of electronic computers in football has been for scouting. Yet the most far-reaching application has involved play analysis, team tendencies, and the game plan. The IBM 360's and Univac 108's have been very important to those football programs with the finances to afford them. Teams in the National Football League, of course, have used them extensively.

Increasingly, computers will play a major role in providing detailed scouting reports on opposing teams and in assessing the strengths and weaknesses of its own personnel, plays, and overall game plan.

Yet, a computer is no better than the information put in it. A computer will provide play analysis by down and distance, field position, and formation.

Detailed scouting reports on thousands of college players are fed into a centrally located computer, which processes them and relays the information to each member club of the NFL. The computers do in a few minutes what it used to take a full staff of scouts and coaches weeks to accomplish.

FIGURE 14-17. *Films are a great training aid. In addition to game films, every practice session is filmed, and the films are developed within 15 minutes in a special darkroom next to the team's dressing quarters. Nate Fine, our chief photographer, is one of the best. While college and professional programs are able to utilize 16 mm equipment, high schools can save money by using an 8 mm camera.*

They rate size, speed, weight, attitude, stance and agility, reaction, desire, ability to learn, aggressiveness, scholastic aptitude, history of injuries, etc. In short, the computer can tell the coaching staff what to look for in a football player.

## STUDY TIPS

Off-season preparation for high school and college football also involves checking on grades, hitting the books, and making certain that prospects are eligible for participation in football in the fall. Most low and failing grades are due to one or more of the following reasons:

1. Failure to study
2. Careless, sloppy, incomplete, or late homework assignments
3. Goofing off, inattention in class
4. Failure to grasp or understand class material

The coach should develop the practice of talking over study problems with his players and guidance counselors to determine if study hangups can be overcome.

The following are some suggested tips for study:

1. Keep accurate notes and review before each class or exam.
2. When studying, try to forget about outside problems.
3. In reading textbooks, underline important ideas or sentences.
4. Find out when you study best, i.e., morning, afternoon, or evening.
5. Attend classes regularly.
6. Keep up with each class to avoid cramming.
7. Find a comfortable place to study, free from distractions, and on occasion isolate yourself from others.
8. Be familiar with location of library resource materials. Take advantage of an orientation tour of the library.

## TRAVEL POLICIES

When traveling to out-of-town games, members of the football squad should keep in mind that they not only represent themselves but their school and community as well. Therefore, their standard of dress and appearance should be taken very seriously.

Among the policies adopted by many school teams when traveling are:

1. Report ahead of scheduled time. The bus will not wait.
2. No gambling, whatsoever!
3. Do not take candy or food with you.
4. Be neat, well-dressed.
5. Coaches will sit with their players on the bus.
6. Arrange in advance the meals at restaurants.
7. Members of the squad must eat and stay together.
8. Each player must take care of his own gear.
9. Be quiet on the bus going to the game.
10. Players must return with the team, unless excused by head coach.

While on the road, Redskins players are required to wear a coat and tie at all times, unless they are instructed otherwise by the staff. They are required to take care of all their incidental hotel charges upon checking out of each individual hotel. The club will take care of their room charge only.

## GAMBLING

Gambling is a very serious problem in all sports. Our players are explicitly told to avoid any association with gamblers. In addition, they must be very careful of strangers who attempt to strike up a conversation. Under no circumstances are they to discuss the physical condition of members of our team, or any other subject that might give aid to gamblers.

I cannot completely express how important this is. We urge our players to always be on the alert regarding this problem. If they are approached by anyone, at any time, whom they feel is suspicious, they should report it to me or the management personnel.

## THE MANAGER

The importance of an efficient, dependable student manager cannot be overemphasized, particularly on the high school level when the head coach may be limited to one assistant coach. A well-trained manager who is responsible, prompt, and a good organizer can be a major asset to the football program. Space will not permit me to list the countless details and responsibilities which the coaching staff can delegate to their managers. I might say, though, that they should be treated with respect by the players as well as the staff.

Most programs on the college level have several assistant managers who are underclassmen, and one man will work up to become the varsity manager during his senior year.

## PROMOTING THE FOOTBALL PROGRAM

### Fund Raising

The success of the football program in most high schools and colleges rests in large measure on gate receipts and money-raising projects. The quality, as well as the quantity, of equipment, facilities, and program supplies is determined by how much revenue comes in. The work of booster groups, in particular, has been a huge source of income for high

school and college football programs. The coaching staff can work closely with the booster club in raising money to purchase football equipment and to help pay for insurance.

Fund-raising dinners have been big revenue producers for the football program. Candy sales and promotion of exhibition basketball games have also proven successful. An annual faculty-student basketball game proves a winner time after time. Many athletic booster clubs have annual membership drives which provide the club with the bulk of its revenue. Usually there is a $1.00 individual membership fee, and a minimum fee of $5.00 for commercial membership.

Weekly booster meetings during the football season prove highly popular to club members. The head coach or one of his assistants would be present to narrate the films.

### Public Relations

The news media provide the principal link between the football coach and the public. Therefore, it is in the best interest of the coach and his program to cooperate to the fullest extent when dealing with the press and with radio and television.

Team support, particularly of gate receipts, is directly related to the coverage of the team by the news media. Keeping the public informed and interested is the surest way to bring them out to the stadium.

In dealing with the press and radio-TV people, the football coach should:

1. Be honest, cooperative and fair.
2. Refrain from playing favorites with reporters.
3. Provide fair treatment to all media.
4. Request the availability of a sports information man who can coordinate the distribution of all news.

FIGURE 14-18. *Before and after each game, the head coach has a responsibility to be available to the writers and radio-TV people. Coach Allen is shown here meeting the press after a big game in Washington.*

5. Never use the news media as a propaganda or psychological tool.
6. Admit newsmen to the dressing room just as soon as possible after the game (Figure 14-18).
7. Never expect a reporter to be a cheerleader.
8. Invite reporters to attend practice sessions and meet with them after practice.
9. Reserve the press box and camera locations for the working press.

### "Selling" the Football Program

Football organization, whether on the college or high school level, involves "selling" the values of football to the athlete, his parents, the faculty, the administration, the student body, and the community. The idea that "football is a very worthwhile endeavor" must be promoted to the fullest.

A football coach has to be a salesman. He must sell not only himself but the sport as well. Therefore, he should welcome the opportunity to speak to almost any group on his program.

The following techniques should be considered by the football coach in promoting his program:

1. Send out weekly news releases containing information on the progress of the team.
2. Information brochures should be distributed to the news media and to opposing schools.
3. Inform the parents about what their sons are doing. Write to the prospects and parents. Arrange home visits.
4. Organize a booster organization. They can play a significant role in the success of the football program.
5. Have the Quarterback Club meet at lunch every Monday during the season. They can hear a report from the coach and replay the football game. Invite members of the team to a post-season special luncheon.
6. *Encourage a strong contribution from the cheerleaders.* They have their own effective gimmicks for promoting team spirit and getting the team up for the game. Besides leading the cheers, the song girls spend considerable time painting pep signs and organizing the pep rallies.
7. Hold an annual awards banquet, highlighted by a presentation of a "hardnose" award to the most deserving player. In addition, awards can be given to seniors for the following honors: most improved, most spirited, most coachable, best offensive back, best defensive back, and best defensive lineman.
8. Have clinics conducted by college mentors. Clinics can be a key factor in improving the style of play.
9. Encourage the players to watch college and professional contests, either in person or via TV.

### Publicity

We remind our players that they are engaged in professional football and that our success is dependent on not only how many

*FIGURE 14-19. The success of a professional football team is dependent not only on how many games it wins but also on how many fans attend the games. The gate receipts of college and even high school football games make a major contribution to the financial support of the entire athletic program.*

games we win, but also on how many fans attend our game. Therefore, publicity and promotion play an important and very large part in our program. When not actually engaged in a team function, their first responsibility will be to the publicity department. They are expected to perform these duties with the same enthusiasm as those which are directed by the coaches.

Our relationship with the press, radio and television people, and others of the publicity field is extremely important and at our training camp and in our clubhouse these people are our guests and should be treated accordingly.

## COMMUNITY SERVICES

Throughout my coaching career, I have had the desire, and a responsibility, to provide services to the community, particularly to those groups or individuals who needed assistance most. While my time is limited during the football season, I have gained considerable personal satisfaction during the off-season from my participation in numerous projects and worthwhile causes.

A head coach of a professional football team is in a unique position to help other people. This community involvement is very challenging and highly gratifying. I know the majority of coaches at all levels of play have given a considerable amount of their time to serving the community in some way.

With a sense of pride and pleasure, I would like to list some of my contributions:

- General chairman of the Washington area Summer Jobs for Needy Youth program. Over 16,000 jobs were secured for the summer of 1974.
- Establishment of three scholarships to: Gallaudet College for the deaf and dumb. Morningside College, Iowa (my first coaching job); helped establish a scholarship dinner for the forgotten American Indian, perhaps my favorite charity, a project co-sponsored with the Washington Touchdown Club.
- First president of the Red Cloud Athletic Foundation, formed in 1965.
- Visiting children's and veterans' hospitals in the Washington area.
- National honorary chairman of Kidney Foundation fund drive, 1973.
- Honorary chairman of the D.C. Special Olympics for retarded children, 1972.
- Assisting the recruiting drive for Boy Scouts of America.
- Conducting instructional clinics for young athletes.
- Involvement with the President's Council on Physical Fitness and Sports.
- Assisting such organizations as the Big Brothers, March of Dimes, Lion's Eye Bank

and Research Foundation, Christian Service Corps, the D.C. Association for Retarded Citizens, Goodwill Industries, National Conference of Christians and Jews, and Justice for Children.

***The message of good sportsmanship exemplified by the Washington Redskins is especially important to our young people, many of whom are upholding team members as models to pattern their own lives and careers.***

**Walter E. Washington**
**Mayor, Washington, D.C.**

## *BUILDING A FARM SYSTEM*

Winning high school teams typically are blessed with a successful feeder or farm system. To be successful, the high school program must have an organized feeder system. This applies to "Pop Warner" or a midget league, and touch or flag football programs at the lower levels.

Ideally, the entire football system of the city or community should be under the direction and leadership of the head football coach at the high school. This enables everyone to teach the same method. The junior high school players are oriented at an early age to the varsity system. The sophomore team plays a full schedule, and those juniors and seniors who do not make the varsity play a full schedule against the smaller high schools.

A typical feeder program begins with touch football in the fifth and sixth grades. Tackle teams start with each seventh grade room and each eighth grade section. Pop Warner and other little league tackle football programs have accelerated rapidly across the nation.

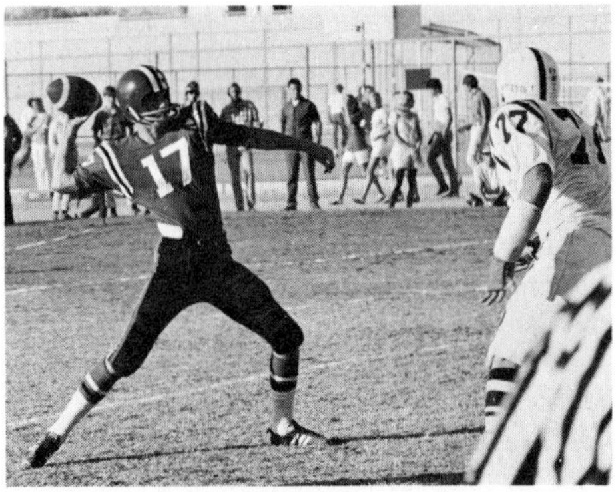

*FIGURE 14-20.* ***Building a feeder system is important to almost all winning high school programs, whether it is "Pop Warner" or a midget league program at the lower levels. George Allen, Jr., above, profited from a sound youth league program and later led his Palos Verdes (California) Sea Kings to a 7 win, 2 loss season, the second best record in school history.***

## *RECRUITING*

A high school coach is often asked by his players to offer guidance in choosing a college. Therefore, he should have a proper understanding of the recruiting process. I feel a coach has a responsibility to his athletes to take time to educate them as to the ways of recruiters. The players should understand that a recruiter is a coach who is trying to sell his university to the athlete and his parents.

The coach should not attempt to influence a boy as to his choice of college but only give advice. He could discuss with the boy which size of school and caliber of competition might offer him the best opportunity for success. Rather than choose a college for its athletic reputation, the student should understand the importance of choosing a school for the degree his education will lead to.

## NEW RULES CHANGES

From 1934 until April 25, 1974, the rules were fairly standard in the National Football League. True, free substitution had come in the 1940's but basically it was the same game and the same strategy.

For two years, the NFL owners and coaches had been debating rule changes. Then, the league acted, approving a wide range of changes designed generally to make the game more wide open and to help the offense. Whether or not they have accomplished their purpose is anybody's guess. I remarked at the time that "If they'd met another day, they probably would have brought back the flying wedge."

### Sudden Death

Under the new rule, in effect for preseason and regular season contests, a professional game can still end in a tie if neither scores after 15 minutes of overtime. Up until that point, however, it is still sudden death and ends when either team scores by a touchdown, field goal, or safety. The previous rule is still in effect for all post-season games: the first team to score is the winner and the game cannot end in a tie.

There is no sudden death on the high school and college levels of play.

### Kicking Game

The goal posts were moved from the goal line to the end line, thus opening up the end zone to a pass attack. Indeed, the move has affected the point after, in that the conversion rate is no more a 99.9 percent situation.

The kickoff in the NFL is now from the 35-yard line instead of from the 40-yard line. This move has opened up the kickoff return and given the return men an edge they need and cut down on kicks into the end zone.

The kickoff for high school and college games is still from the 40-yard line. In high school play, if the kickoff goes out of bounds, the ball is not re-kicked. From the 40-yard line on down, the ball comes back to the 40. However, if the ball goes out before the 40, the ball is played from that spot.

On the college level when a kickoff goes out of bounds untouched, the receiving team may either take possession where it went out of bounds or require the kicking team to accept a 5-yard penalty and kick again.

### Missed Field Goals

In situations involving missed field goals, the ball reverts back to the line of scrimmage or the 20-yard line, whichever is farther from the goal line.

On the high school and college levels, the ball comes back to the 20-yard line. Any ball kicked into the end zone cannot be advanced; the ball is dead.

### Crossing the Line of Scrimmage

Members of a professional team kicking from scrimmage (punt or field goal) cannot cross the line of scrimmage until the ball is kicked. The new pro rule does permit two eligible receivers, one on each side of the line, to go downfield before the ball is kicked. Other members of the kicking team must remain at the line until the ball is kicked. The penalty for violating this rule is 5 yards from the line of scrimmage.

Offensive linemen on the high school and college levels are not restricted from crossing the line of scrimmage before the ball is kicked.

## Passing Game

Roll blocking and cutting of wide receivers is now illegal in pro games. An eligible receiver, other than anyone lined up as a tight end, cannot be blocked below the waist. Penalty: 5 yards and first down.

On the college and high school levels, the receiver can be hit and knocked off his feet at the line of scrimmage but not held.

The professionals have restricted the extent of downfield contact (bump-and-run) a defender is permitted to have with eligible receivers (on pass plays only). Beyond 3 yards downfield, a defender may hit a receiver only once. Penalty: 5 yards and first down. There is nothing like this in the college game, however.

The new pro bump-and-run rule says that a defender may hit a potential pass receiver only once and may not ax him—cut him down with a rolling block on the scrimmage line. This rule was intended to bring back the deep passing game.

## Penalty Change

The penalty for offensive holding, illegal use of hands, and tripping has been reduced from 15 yards to 10 yards, when the infraction occurs in the area of the line of scrimmage and 3 yards beyond.

The penalty is still 15 yards in high school and college contests.

## Blocking Change

Wide receivers blocking back toward the ball (crackback block) within 3 yards of the line of scrimmage cannot block below the waist. The "initial contact" must be above the waist. Penalty: 15 yards. The high school and college programs have the same rule.

Blocks below the waist were causing too many injuries. According to the new rule, the principal force of the initial contact must be on the jersey of the defensive man.

While the wide receiver cannot block below the waist, the wing back can if he is less than 4 yards out.

## Pass Receiving

On the professional and college levels, a pass interference penalty is at the spot of the foul, first down. For high school games, the penalty is 15 yards from the line of scrimmage, with an automatic first down. If the interference is committed in the end zone, the ball is placed on the 1-yard line, first down.

On pass receptions at the sideline boundaries, the pro's have to have both feet in bounds after a catch. High school and college receivers, however, need only place one foot or any part of the body in bounds after receiving a pass before stepping out of bounds. In the 1974 Rose Bowl game, Lynn Swan's right hip came down inside, making his reception legal.

Another rule difference concerns the quarterback as an eligible pass receiver. While a pro quarterback is ineligible to receive a pass, the high school and college quarterback becomes an eligible receiver after he hands off to a running back.

## FUTURE CAREERS

Professional football has been a springboard to success for many former players of the Washington Redskins and other teams in the

FIGURE 14-21. *A half-century of dedication and effort has established the National Football League as the major sports attraction in America. The great pioneer owners of the past, like George Halas, George Preston Marshall, and Wellington Mara, have been replaced by the modern executives of today, men like Art Modell, Lamar Hunt, Tex Schramm, Carroll Rosenbloom, and Edward Bennett Williams. Above, Williams, owner of the Redskins and a brilliant attorney, is presented with a game ball by Coach Allen, after a Redskins victory.*

National Football League. Many NFL players have advanced quickly to important positions in industry, commerce, and the business world. A player in the pro leagues can not only earn a sizeable income during a five-month season, but he can employ himself in the off-season apprenticing in the field he has chosen for his long-range career. In addition to an attractive pension, he can retire from football with a substantial savings account.

## LEAGUE GROWTH

Professional football has come a long way since the first game was played on September 17, 1920, in Canton, Ohio, when the actual birth of the National Football League took place. In the splendid publication *The First Fifty Years,** Bob Oates, Jr., wrote,

\* Produced by NFL Properties, Inc.; distributed by Simon & Schuster, Inc.

"The earliest professional football was played by teams in small midwestern towns, often supported by companies as a promotional venture. Players were offered salaried jobs and allowed to practice and play football and other sports on company time."

In 1926, the National Football League comprised twenty-two teams from coast to coast, but when the Great Depression struck in the early thirties, the League dwindled to only ten teams. In 1933, the League was broken down into two five-team divisions, which remained intact until the 1960's. The only alteration occurred in 1950, when three teams—Cleveland, San Francisco, and Baltimore—came into the NFL from the All-American Conference, which existed from 1946 to 1949. By the end of the 1950's, professional football had matured, and in the words of Oates, "the NFL was on the verge of a booming success."

Through the foresight, hard work, and organizational skills of league executives and club owners, combined with crowd-pleasing play and masterful coaching on the field, the league has grown to unprecedented proportions. In the 1960's, the twelve-team league literally exploded into a twenty-six-team setup. A decade of spectacular growth occurred, highlighted by the nationwide appeal of televised football.

Expansion franchises were nurtured in Dallas, Minnesota, Atlanta, and New Orleans and a rival league, the American Football League, organized in 1960, merged with the NFL in 1966.

Regular season paid attendance set a record in 1973 when 16,730,933 fans attended 182 NFL games. Overall attendance including pre-season and post-season games increased to 15,500,586 for an average of 57,838. With new franchises in Tampa and Seattle, the NFL, under Commissioner Pete Rozelle, has expanded to twenty-eight teams and is regarded by many as the major sports attraction in the U.S.A.

# 15

# Training Program

No system will be effective if the
players are not well grounded in fundamentals through a training program.

**George Allen**

The backbone of any football operation is a well-organized program of practice and training. I have always felt that tough practices will lead to winning football. We try to utilize every minute possible in preparing for our opponents and our practice sessions.

To play with confidence, a team must feel that everything possible has been done to prepare fully for the coming game. Practice sessions can mean the difference between a strong and poor performance. Indeed, your team will play the way it practices.

The caliber of a coach is not what he knows but what he can teach his players. Teaching is most effective when it is done during practice, when there is time for both repetition and close supervision. The best-drilled team usually makes the fewest mistakes and manages to win the close games. After mastering the fundamentals, the players must be integrated into a smooth-working team.

The Redskins have two types of football practice schedules. Early in the summer, we concentrate on teaching techniques, while our game plan schedule during the season is designed for a specific opponent.

A successful training program includes the following components: conditioning, play execution, timing, defensive recognition and coverage, development of new talent, team spirit, and morale, team depth, and prevention and treatment of injuries.

While rigid, demanding training sessions can produce feelings of fatigue, a football team will be more successful in avoiding the fourth-quarter injuries that often are the result of poor conditioning and fitness.

OF THE
NATIONAL FOOTBALL LEAGUE

PRO-FOOTBALL, INC.
13832 REDSKIN DRIVE
P. O. BOX 17247-DULLES
WASHINGTON, D. C. 20041
(703) 471-9100

Dear Squad Member:

I firmly believe that everyone on our squad should report to
camp with the feeling that this year has to be the Redskins year.
The coaching staff would like you to report in the very best shape
ever. We want you to be prepared to be willing to sacrifice and
pay whatever price is necessary to make you play to the best of
your ability. In doing so, you will help make the Redskins the
team you and I would like it to be.

To get our season off to a rousing start, we must have a
training camp that will be tough and hard hitting. If you report
over your assigned weight at training camp, you will let me know
exactly what you think of our Redskin football program. By being
in tip top condition both physically and mentally, we will be able
to move quickly into the technical aspects of the game.

So let's be ready to go! Come to camp with desire and dedication that this is the year we will go all the way. NO obstacle
must stop us from reaching our No. 1 goal.

Best personal regards,

George H. Allen
Head Coach and General Manager

FIGURE 15-2.    Summer letter to team members.

## SUMMER MONTHS

During the summer months, the coaching staff must keep in touch with their players. They should provide them with the necessary direction in their individual or small-group conditioning work. In effectively motivating the players, many high school and college coaches will send them as many as three or four letters during the summer months.

In addition to important reminders, the letters will pertain to the following topics:

- Reporting weight and general information
- What to expect in the fall
- Workout schedule, offensive and defensive terminology sheets
- Workout schedule; offensive and defensive assignments

*A player who practices well will play well.*

## PRE-SEASON TRAINING

Opening day normally is a day for physical exams. Each player is given a complete exam of the upper and lower body, including the complete muscular and bone system of each man. All of these things are checked to be certain if each player is in good enough shape to play this game. They have to pass a very stringent physical examination. Various aptitude tests are taken by the rookies that give us an idea of their potential. We also believe in a complete eye examination.

When our players report, we want them to be able to run a mile. Some teams will have their players run four laps, with one minute's rest in between. Players who report to camp overweight should receive special treatment.

From the opening day of training camp to the last, every practice session and class meeting should be planned carefully to prepare the team for the season.

The opening weeks of practice involve two workouts a day, one in the morning and one in the afternoon. Most coaches like to have a squad meeting before each session. Every other evening there is usually another meeting, in which the team is broken down by position into smaller groups. The coach in charge of the position conducts the meeting.

Two-a-day workouts are held until the week before the opening game. While some physicians maintain that the majority of injuries occur during double practice sessions, a football team needs the twice-daily workouts to accomplish all the conditioning work. Once the season begins, a team lacks the time to spend on conditioning.

Most high school and college coaches prefer 1½ and 2-hour practice sessions. Once the season gets underway, they will hold practice 2 days for two hours a couple of days a week and possibly for one-half hour less on the other days. The final workout on the day before the game is usually never more than 30 to 45 minutes, in addition to a squad meeting.

### The Practice Plan

The following general segments make up the daily practice plan:

1. Meetings
2. Calisthenics
3. Specialty period
4. Group drills
5. Individual drills
6. Team development period
7. Kicking

*FIGURE 15-3. Training camp. A football team needs the twice-daily workouts to accomplish all the conditioning work. Superb physical conditioning is essential in championship football.*

*Physical conditioning and training are the heart of a successful football program.*

A pre-season calendar should present in chart form every practice session and indicate the introduction of plays, defenses, and kicking game plans. This calendar should be on display in one of the meeting rooms.

Many coaches will prepare a chart of fall objectives and points to emphasize during the season. The objectives are categorized by offense, defense, and the kicking game.

Posted schedules should give the details on the uniform of the day. Full gear means: helmet, pads, jerseys, pants, and cleats. Sweats and sneakers mean a less strenuous routine.

### Season Notebooks

When the players arrive back on campus, we give them an offensive and defensive season notebook to keep during the entire season. They are instructed to index the small spiral notebook and then we review the entire offense and defense systems. Each player is

| **MORNING** *(Concentration on offensive football)* | | **AFTERNOON** *(Concentration on defensive football)* | |
|---|---|---|---|
| *8:00–8:45* | Tape and dress | *3:30–4:15* | Tape and dress |
| *8:45–9:00* | Specialty period | *4:15–4:30* | Classroom meeting |
| *9:00–9:05* | Stretching exercises | *4:30–4:40* | Specialty period |
| *9:05–9:20* | Calisthenics, cadence, and agility drills | *4:40–4:50* | Calisthenics, cadence, and agility drills |
| *9:20–9:25* | Bertha (offensive fire-out) | *4:50–4:55* | Bertha (defensive pursuit) |
| *9:25–9:30* | Perfect tackle technique | *4:55–5:05* | Perfect tackle technique |
| *9:30–9:50* | Individual offense | *5:05–5:25* | Individual defense (fundamentals such as key, movement, blow, pressure, and pursue) |
| | A. Fundamentals of the play-of-the-day | | |
| | B. Review past fundamentals | *5:25–5:35* | Group defense |
| | C. Coordinate line and backs | *5:35–5:55* | Half-line |
| *9:50–10:20* | Half-line (offense vs. defense) | *5:55–6:10* | Unit defense |
| *10:20–10:40* | Pass offense (individual and team) | *6:10–6:20* | Punt returns |
| *10:40–10:50* | Team offense (¾ speed, no tackling) | *6:20–6:30* | Conditioning period |
| *10:50–11:00* | Conditioning period | *6:30* | To the showers |
| *11:00* | To the showers | | |

responsible for keeping up his notebook and recording coaching points, plays, and defensive maneuvers. The notebooks will be checked periodically by the coaching staff.

### Agility Drills

Linemen and backfield personnel work in separate groups, under the close direction of the coaching staff. A typical routine may include:

- Running in place
- Running left and right
- Sprinting forward and backward
- Quick turns left and right
- Forward and backward rolls
- Carioca left and right
- Crab or bear walk
- Hitting the ground and up on feet

Linemen perform many of their agility drills on a seven-man sled, such as:

- Hit and react
- Fire out on sled, retreat, and assume hitting position (left and right)
- Hit sled, spin, and assume hitting position

Backfield drills include:

- Running through tires with a football
- Running through rope ladders
- Obstacle course

### Offensive Drills

Drills should be developed to teach and improve every technique or skill required in a team's offensive system. Backfield drills involve:

- Stance
- Ball handling
- Play paths and hitting holes
- Quick starts in all directions
- Fumble prevention
- Blocking (fill and power blocking, downfield)
- Trapping
- Pass protection

Linemen drills include:

- Stance
- Quick starts (with quarterback cadence) and firing out
- One-on-one techniques
- Pulling left and right
- Trap and screen blocking
- Lead and wedge blocking
- Cross blocking
- Double-team blocking
- Pass protection blocking
- Downfield blocking
- Hit and drive (sled work)

Pass receivers work on individual skills such as:

- Releases from line of scrimmage
- Faking
- Pass routes
- Pass receiving

## Offensive Group Drills

Group drills enable a segment of the offense to work alone against several members of the defense.

*Middle drill* The center, quarterback, two guards and fullback are employed against an even or odd line with one or two linebackers. Two dummies are placed at the offensive tackle positions.

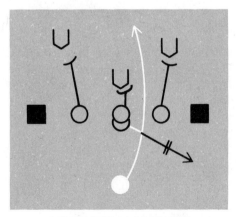

DIAGRAM 15-1.  *Middle drill.*

*Off-tackle drill* Seven members of the offensive unit run off-tackle plays against two defensive linemen. Kickout blocks should be mixed in between the fullback and the guard or tackle.

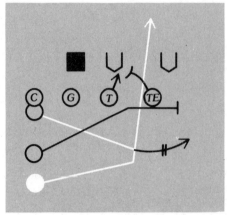

DIAGRAM 15-2.  *Off-tackle drill.*

*Sweep and option drill* Sweeps and options are run against the defender in front of the tight end and a cornerback and strong safety backing up.

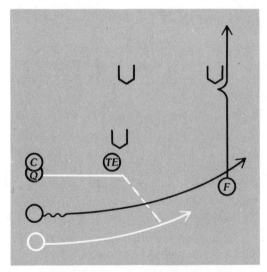

DIAGRAM 15-3.  *Sweep and option drill.*

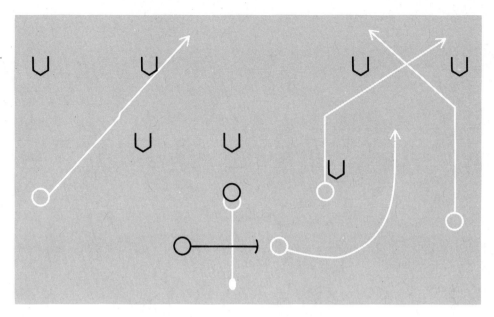

DIAGRAM 15-4. *Skeleton pass drill.*

*Skeleton pass drill*   With emphasis on the passing game, the backs and ends should receive considerable drill time against a full perimeter of defense.

*Interior linemen drill*   With the backs and ends working on the skeleton pass drills, the remaining five interior linemen should be involved in a group drill of their own. Pass blocking and interior run plays receive the major emphasis. Two offensive lines can alternate against five defensive rushmen. A spare quarterback can be used to take the ball from center and set up, but he does not throw. A stopwatch can be used to make this drill highly competitive.

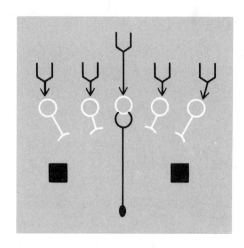

DIAGRAM 15-5. *Interior linemen drill.*

FIGURE 15-4.  *Big Mona pass blocking drill. Veteran offensive guard Walt Sweeney keeps his feet moving and stays in front of the bag. Drills of this type are needed to improve each man's capabilities.*

*Half-line drills*  The offense is divided into two groups: (1) strong side, consisting of the tight end, strong tackle, strong guard, and center (a full backfield will scrimmage against half a defense), and (2) weak side, involving a center, a backfield, a weak guard and tackle, and a split end.

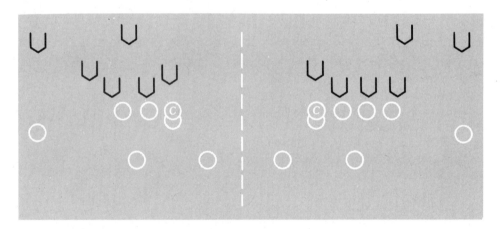

DIAGRAM 15-6.  *Half-line drills.*

## Offensive Unit Drills

Lining up on the 20-yard line, full backfield units run all their plays up and down the field. In addition to working on individual skills, the purpose of these drills is to teach proper running paths and coordinate the timing of all the backs. All plays should be run at full speed.

Likewise, the offensive linemen are divided into either full-line or half-line units. These periods are used to teach the blocking assignments for each offensive play against various defenses. Members of the coaching staff look for errors in stance, line spacing, and techniques of blocking. We like to start out with the linemen holding dummies and then progress to game situations.

By dividing the offensive linemen into right- and left-side units, on-side blocking can be taught to both sides of the line at the same time. The same procedure can be used to teach downfield blocking. After our half-line unit drills, we put both sides of the line together to coordinate their timing and movements.

## Offensive Team Drills

The entire offensive unit can work together on such team drills as the hash mark drill, up and down the field, stationary drill, and scrimmage.

While the offensive unit should get work moving from one hash mark to the next, the stationary drill involving two huddles enables the coaching staff to check the line of scrimmage. One team is huddling while the other team is running a play.

## Defensive Drills

Drills should be performed daily to teach and improve defensive techniques and skills.

*Linemen.* The following drills are done on a seven-man sled or one-on-one line situations:

- Defensive stance
- Reacting to snap of ball and firing out
- Delivering a blow and gaining control
- Shedding a blocker

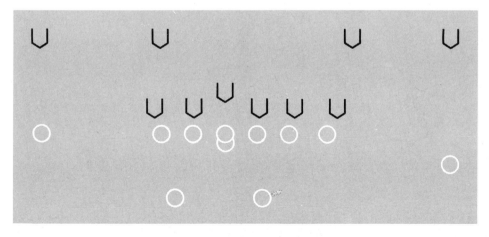

DIAGRAM 15-7. Stationary drill.

- Tackling
- Pursuit of ball carrier
- Reacting to running plays, such as draws and traps
- Reacting to pass plays

*Linebackers.* Drills for linebackers should be run that will develop the following skills:

- Stance
- Reacting to keys
- Pursuit to ball
- Tackling
- Shedding a blocker
- Blitzing
- Reacting to running plays
- Reacting to pass plays

*Deep Backs.* The following skills should

be practiced by those in the defensive secondary:

- Stance
- Reacting to keys
- Pursuit to ball

### Defensive Semi-Group Drills

Semi-group drills enable a segment of the defense to work alone against several members of the offense.

*Trap and power drill* The purpose of this drill is to teach two defensive linemen to play the trap, with the emphasis on reaction. In this full-speed drill, the defensive linemen are able to work against the various blocking patterns.

DIAGRAM 15-8. Trap and power drill.

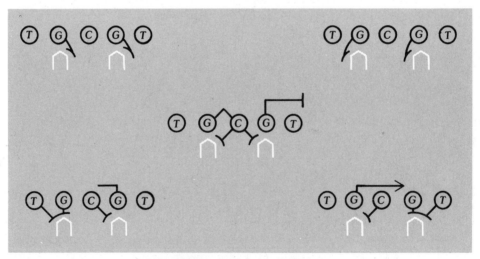

DIAGRAM 15-9. Five-on-two drill.

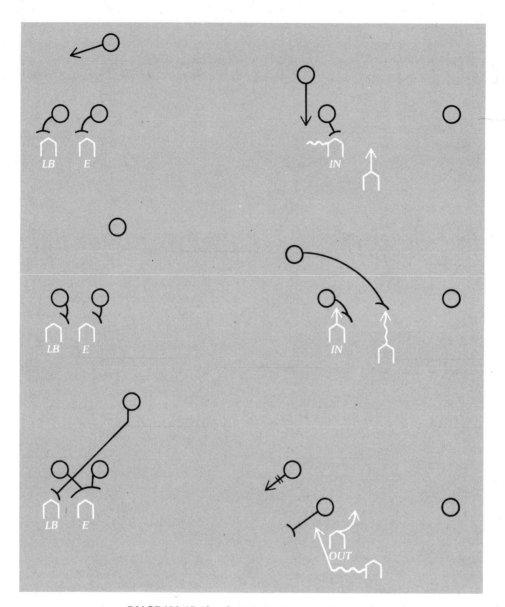

DIAGRAM 15-10.   *Outside linebacker and end drill.*

*Five-on-two drill*   This is similar to the previous drill but now you line up five offensive blockers against two defensive linemen in an even defense. Using a huddle every play, the defenders can work against all the blocking patterns that affect the middle.

*Outside linebacker and end drill*   Often called the triangle drill, this is an excellent drill in giving the end and strong linebacker practice at closing the off-tackle hold, certainly a "must" in any brand of ball. The offensive linemen are instructed to execute reach, turn-out, cross, and double-team blocks. On the split end side, though, the weak linebacker and end must continually use inside and outside techniques.

*Pass rush drill* This semi-group drill enables the defense to work on pass rush, draw, and screen defensive maneuvers and features pass show with pass, draw, and screen blocking.

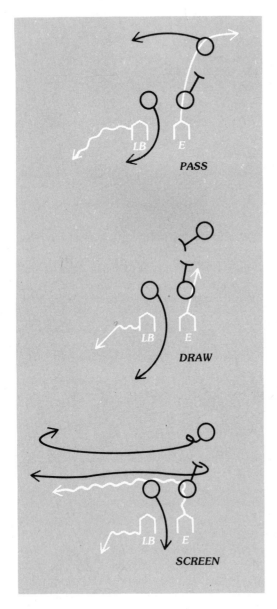

DIAGRAM 15-11. *Pass rush drill.*

*Sam and Mike pass drill* This drill provides good training for the strong and middle linebackers or a linebacker and safety against a combination coverage. It shows the linebackers at which point they should play man-for-man or a combination zone. In Diagram 15-12A, Sam and Mike must play an inside-outside zone on the No. 2 and 3 backs. In Diagram 15-12B, Sam plays the No. 3 man while Mike blitzes, or vice versa.

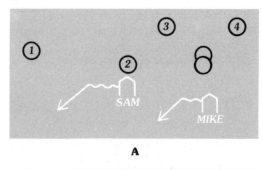

A

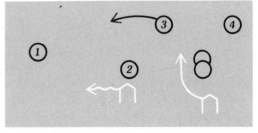

B

DIAGRAM 15-12. *Sam and Mike pass drill.*

*Double-cover drill* Two defenders are employed against a wide receiver, with short and deep coverage. The defender can get right on the receiver's nose and attempt to "dog" him tight for 10 yards. Or, he can fake getting on him and then back up and zone him. When the short man loses him, the deep man picks him up.

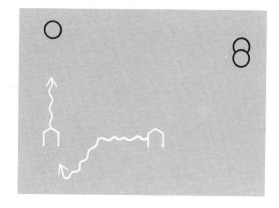

DIAGRAM 15-13. *Double-cover drill.*

### Group Drills

*Half-line scrimmage* Similar to the offensive drills described earlier, the emphasis is now on defense. The offense is instructed to run their strong-side offense mixing running and passing plays. The strong-side offense is on one side with the weak-side offense on the other side.

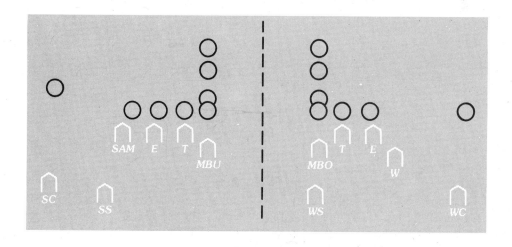

DIAGRAM 15-14. *Half-line scrimmage.*

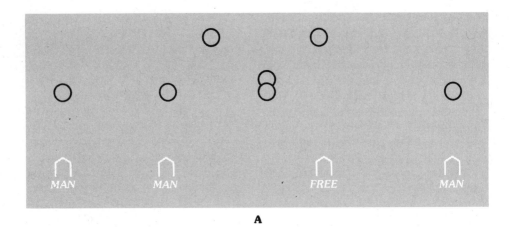

A

B

*DIAGRAM 15-15.   Four-deep recognition drill.*

*Four-deep recognition drill* This drill provides an excellent opportunity for the three or four deep defenders to look at different formations and make their calls. The offensive people, consisting of a full backfield, two ends, and a center, need only line up in this drill. After each huddle, the four defenders make their calls and line up.

*Four-deep versus patterns drill* Using the same setup as the preceding drill, we now have the offensive people run their routes, such as crossing patterns, hooks and curls, post, etc. Early in the season, the players should merely walk through the routes and coverages.

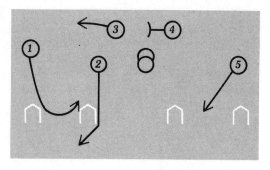

DIAGRAM 15-16. *Four-deep versus patterns drill.*

*Lapping drill* This is a zone drill involving the four deep backs against a passer. The rotation should be called, such as a three-deep, and the passer throws the ball between the defenders. A marked field should be used so that the defenders can "lap" with the sideline.

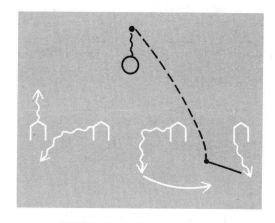

DIAGRAM 15-17. *Lapping drill.*

*Defensive team drills* The entire eleven-man defensive unit will work against seven offensive linemen, the quarterback, and various backs. Team drills can emphasize pursuit, interceptions, full-speed work, and types of situations such as the goal line.

FIGURE 15-5. *Footwork is nearly everything in football, whether on offense or defense. This is why one of my favorite training camp drills is running through the ropes. The ropes help improve eye and foot coordination and strengthen ankles, knees, and legs.*

## FALL TRAINING PROGRAM

### Practice Sessions

Our practice sessions are always busy. The players move from drill to drill, area to area. They are always moving (Figures 15-5 and 15-6). We believe a team plays like they practice, and if the players are allowed to practice sloppily, they are going to play a sloppy game.

The coaching staff can tell halfway through the week pretty much what kind of frame of mind the players will have on Sunday and what has to be done to get them going. Sometimes we have to shock them, while on other occasions we will handle them softly.

The head coach is responsible for determining the tempo of the practice, the schedule plan, and the time designations on the field. While practices can be tough and the repetition killing, this is where the rigid discipline so necessary in football success can be instilled in the team. Football's most successful coaches have been tough and demanding disciplinarians, particularly during practice. "Run that play again! Run it until you do it right!" Over and over, the same moves are drilled into the players. But repetition and drill, no matter how boring and routine, can pay off with a victory on game day!

We like to see our players fight aggressively, even tenaciously, for starting positions. Linemen should dig in and attack the sled with everything they have got (Figure 15-7). Defensive backs engaged in a coverage drill should try to outdo one another. Meanwhile, the coaching staff is yelling words of encouragement: "Stay with him! Give it a good pop!" The practice field is a scene of hustle and spirit, with a lot of hand slapping and some growling as well.

FIGURE 15-6. *Drills are most essential in developing the various skills of the defensive lineman. Here, players on the defensive line go through a brisk workout with the shiver machine.*

FIGURE 15-7. *Defensive back Bryant Salter works hard against a dummy sled in perfecting his tackling technique.*

The coach who allows his practice to get out of hand, to get loose, will find that his players will continue to practice that way. It becomes a matter of habit. Every practice is a game, so to speak.

We like our players to be punctual, even early, for all practices, games, and departures. We urge them to use the time after practice to improve themselves. "Stay out after practice and work on your weakness" they are told by the coaching staff. Each player is given an improvement sheet, and we like him to use it.

If the practice is not up to the standards the coaching staff believes it should be, we will go over a 15-minute period, if necessary.

Time is just a guide for us, a working time. We do not live by it if we have not got the job done.

## TYPICAL FALL PRACTICE SCHEDULE

|  |  |
|------|----------|
| 2:45–3:00 | Specialty period |
| 3:00–3:10 | Stretching exercises |
| 3:10–3:25 | Form running, agility stations |
| 3:25–3:35 | Kicking game |
| 3:35–3:45 | Fundamental period |
| 3:45–4:15 | Technique period |
| 4:15–4:20 | Water break |
| 4:20–4:50 | Team offense |
| 4:50–5:20 | Team defense |
| 5:20 | Sprints (or perfect plays) |

## Drill

The secret of good performance at critical moments is found in drill. However, I have found drills are not as important in pro football as in college or high school. It is through drill and drill only that the coach can be reasonably sure of good performance under game pressure. There is one caution, however, that should be followed to keep player

**CHART 15-1.** *Practice schedule.*

| 1 | 2 | 3 | 4 |
|---|---|---|---|
| 8 | 7 | 6 | 5 |

#  12   Date:  5/5/75    AM _____    PM _____

Calisthenics:  Team _____  Group _____

| Per Time | Area | Time | White | Christiansen | Theder | De Sylvia |
|----------|------|------|-------|--------------|--------|-----------|
| 3:10 | X | 10 | | QUARTERBACK DRILLS | | |
| 3:20 | Stand | 15 | | CHALK TALK | Spread punt Short yardage | |
| 3:35 | 8 | 8 | | CAL & NECK | | |
| 3:43 | 8 | 5 | | AGILITY DRILLS | | |
| 3:48 | 4 | 12 | | SPREAD PUNT | | |
| 4:00 | 8 | 20 | Two QB's. to Roger | GROUP WORK | Option | 37 37 pass 34 counter |
| 4:20 | 2 | 15 | Blue vs. Orange | OFFENSE | Option | screen |
| 4:35 | 2 | 15 | | DEFENSE | | sweep |
| 4:50 | 2 | 20 | | 7-on-7 | | |
| 5:10 | 2 | 10 | | GOAL LINE TEACHING | | |
| 5:20 | 2 | 15 | | TEAM TESTING | | |
| 5:35 | | | | IN | | |

## PRACTICE FORMAT  *(90 Minutes)*

| | |
|---|---|
| Calisthenics | *5 minutes* |
| Evaluation of the individual | *10 minutes* |
| Teaching of football position | *10 minutes* |
| Agility drills | *15 minutes* |
| Position skills | *20 minutes* |
| Teaching of assignments | *10 minutes* |
| Execution teamwork | *15 minutes* |
| Conditioning relays | *5 minutes* |

interest. The individuality or initiative should not be drilled out of the players. The player should be encouraged to control the drill himself. In pro ball, we feature more team drills than in high school and college ball.

At whatever level they are used, drills should be functional. Players should be drilled in practice the way we want them to perform in a game.

### Coach's Whistle

On the whistle, every player must come "on the double!" We like them to always run when going from one area of the field to another. We tell them: "Don't be the last one!" When the coaches are talking, they must have the individual attention of the players.

Football practice might seem tiresome and monotonous at times, and a practice can be rough and tough and fatiguing, too. However, for success, it is a must. If a team is to perfect the fundamentals of the game and the execution of the plays, constant drilling must be a daily ritual. The execution of a perfect play requires the teamwork of eleven men.

There are seven check points that every practice or training program should stress:

1. Aggressiveness (mental as well as physical)
2. Conditioning or stretching
3. Alertness
4. Discipline of some form
5. Team work
6. Toughness (mental or physical)
7. Quickness improvement

### Squad Meetings

A team has to have meetings to be prepared. Players have to study off the field in order to be champions. There is not enough time to do it on the field. During the summer training program, the coaches hold nightly meetings with the players, dividing up according to position.

Personally, I am a great believer in constant meetings with players, getting a group of one to three players together and talking things over. This is the time when we can get their ideas on things and can instill in them our basic ideas on football and get them to believe in them.

We have tried to prove to our players that by following what we are telling them to do, they will improve. The coaching staff believes that if our players will follow what we have told them to do, they will win. *In 1966, when I was coaching the Rams, our major job was to get a team that had not won to believe that they could win.* In our first year there, we won eight games, followed by eleven victories in 1967 before losing out to the Packers. We were able to convince the players that by working hard and playing as a team, they can win! "The only way we can lose is to beat ourselves."

### Assigning of Specialists

On the college and professional levels, members of the coaching staff are assigned various areas of specialization. Of course, on the high school level, the head coach must

**CHART 15-2.** *Checklist for week's work schedule.*

| Sunday | Monday | Tuesday | Wednesday | Thursday | Friday | Saturday |
|---|---|---|---|---|---|---|
| Film study | Offense—test | Practice plan | Practice plan | Practice plan | QB meeting | BALL GAME |
| General | new plays | Film study of | Goal line scrim- | Finalize kicking | Signal caller | |
| evaluation | Defense—work | of opponents | mage—of- | game | meeting | |
| Coaches' game | against oppo- | Set up base | fense and | Set drills | No workout if | |
| report | nent's best | offense | defense | Two-minute | home game; | |
| Squad film study | six runs, | Play cards—key | Short yardage | offense | if away, a | |
| Staff meeting | four passes | sheet defense | Prevent | Final game | short work- | |
| Scout report to | Check kicking | Offensive | situations | plan | out | |
| staff | Practice plan | sequence | Kicking phases | Tendencies of | | |
| Discuss per- | QB review | Situation scrim- | Game auto- | opponent | | |
| sonnel | session | mage | matics | Set suit-up and | | |
| Base offense | Film study | Finalize prepa- | Film on offense | travel list and | | |
| Defense | Scout report | ration teams | and defense | post during | | |
| planning | to squad | Interchange of | Finalize defense | practice | | |
| | Set up prep- | game plans | Write up | | | |
| | aration | between of- | defenses | | | |
| | teams | fensive and | | | | |
| | | defensive | | | | |
| | | coaches | | | | |
| | | Group concen- | | | | |
| | | tration | | | | |
| | | Game plans to | | | | |
| | | squad | | | | |

handle most of the responsibilities. Since specialists will win or lose many ball games, they must not be neglected.

## Weekly Checklist

In achieving complete preparation, the head coach should compile a weekly checklist from Sunday night on up to game day.

The Sunday schedule, for example, will include the following: Film study, scout report, general evaluation, discussion of personnel.

## Typical Redskins Daily Practice Session

Wake-up call is given at 7 a.m., followed by breakfast from 7:30 to 8 a.m. Breakfast is mandatory as is the bed check at night. After breakfast, the players go to the locker rooms and start to get taped and ready for practice.

*Warm-up.* Everyone must be on the field dressed by 9:30 a.m. However, prior to this time, the quarterbacks have their regular early drill supervised by Coach Marchibroda. I like Tom Landry's warm-up program because it contains much breakdown work by positions.

*Redskins Drill.* At 9:30 a.m., we have the Redskins drill, a passing drill to warm up the quarterback's arms and get the receivers to run a little. We have two quarterbacks, one at the goal line and one at the 40, and they will throw to the receiver on their right running upfield.

*Calisthenics.* We will go directly to the

**CHART 15-3.** *Weekly offensive practice organization.*

| Area of Game | Monday | Tuesday | Wednesday | Thursday |
|---|---|---|---|---|
| Fundamental drills | | | | |
| Running offense | | | | |
| Pass offense | | | | |
| Kicking game | | | | |
| Conditioning game | | | | |

calisthenics period, which consists of about 7 minutes of warm-up exercises.

*Cadence Drill.* The offense will huddle, call a play, come out, and run 12 yards with the ball across the goal line. Each of our three offensive teams will run through this drill. I got this idea from Coach Lombardi when he was at Green Bay, and we like it as a team drill to further the warm-up.

Then, the defense will come up to the defensive spot and will call a defense in the huddle. They will come out and run a defense for those 12 yards. Again, this is a team warm-up and get-together lasting for 3 or 4 minutes.

*Agility and Fundamental Period.* Early in camp, we will start with 25 minutes of individual breakdown work. Later, we cut it down to 15 minutes, and after the season begins, we may only devote 10 minutes to this portion of our practice session. Early in camp, it

is necessary to give it considerable emphasis.

Basically, there will be five groups. However, the fifth group, consisting of the deep backs and linebackers, is often split up. I will take either the deep backs or the linebackers, and they will do different drills. The offensive backs, offensive line, receivers, and defensive line make up the other groups.

The offensive backs will work on such fundamentals as stance, where we want them spotted, hand-offs from the quarterbacks, and pass receiving.

The receivers often work in front of a net. During this session, they receive at least twenty balls in front of the big net. This is an area where they get a lot of balls thrown to them, which means considerable ball handling.

*7-on-7.* Following these warm-up drills, we go into a period we call 7-on-7. It gets its name because there are seven defensive people, four deep backs and three linebackers, against the passing game. They will defend against the offensive backs and receivers. There are no linemen in this group.

The offense will perfect its timing, its passes, and pass patterns against the defense. Both units get considerable work this way because it is up to the defense to cover the offense, and the offense is perfecting its plays. We feel this is a very good drill.

*Lineman's 7-on-7.* While the 7-on-7 is going on, the defensive and offensive lines are working against each other on another area of the field. The offensive line will be working on their blocking against the defensive line.

*Perfect Plays.* We have substituted "perfect plays" for 40-yard striders, which we used to run at the end of practice. Since the players have to sprint only 20 yards on a perfect play, by running ten or twelve of them, they can get just as much running as they did with the striders. In addition to improving their condition, they are learning plays and working together as a team.

*Separate Period.* Then, we go to the separate period where the defense will be working on new defenses put in the meeting the night before. The offense works on its new plays, too, but against no opposition. The whole offensive team and defensive team work separately.

*Redskins' Offense.* This is an area where the defense will primarily be working on plays that their opponents will run. These plays are taken from films, put on cards, and run by the offense, which emulates the team we are playing.

The offensive period consists of plays run against the type of defense that our opponent for the week is going to run. These will vary but it gives the offense a good picture of what they are going to face that week.

*Kicking.* Each day we work on one phase of our kicking game. We have it broken down into five phases: punt, punt return, kickoff, kickoff return, and the field goal, which includes the extra point team.

*Conditioning Period.* After the kicking program, we get into the conditioning portion of our daily practice session. We will run striders, interception drills for the defense, or perfect plays for the offense. All of these are designed to gain conditioning and to get some extra skill work.

## TRAINING RULES

To be successful, a football team must have discipline. Discipline cannot be enforced if punishment is varied. There cannot be a double standard. To have a well-disciplined team, training rules must apply for one and all.

"Training rules must be honored," said John McKay of the U.S.C. Trojans, "because if a player cannot make a sacrifice off the field, he is very likely to find it more difficult on the field, especially in the fourth quarter of a tight game."

While training rules may vary from coach to coach, a coach should never tolerate lying, cheating, and alibying.

If rules are broken, the football coach must take action or face a breakdown in morale and a loss of respect of his players for him and the program. Above all, when rules are broken, the same justice should be rendered the "star" as the substitute.

A "training pledge" signed by both parents and high school prospects will likely provide better results than a mere statement.

Generally, parents will cooperate quickly when telephoned about disciplinary action by the coaching staff.

The following are training rules commonly practiced by high school and college football teams:

1. Drinking and smoking are not allowed at any time. You will hurt yourself and your team.
2. Be neat around school. Dress conservatively, with clean shaves, trimmed or well-groomed hair, shirttail in, socks and shoes on.
3. Attend classes regularly and on time. Class cuts are not tolerated.
4. Use only good language on and off the field.
5. Report to practice on time and know your assignments.
6. Try to get 9 hours of sleep.
7. Do not expect favors and special treatment from your instructors.
8. Watch your weight. Your coach can recommend your best playing weight.
9. Helmets should be worn at all times on the practice field; they are not to be thrown.
10. Hustle from start to finish, whether in a game or during practice.
11. Wear ankle wraps or tape during practice and games.
12. Show respect to the managers, who have an important job to perform.
13. Cooperate in the huddle.
14. Accept the official's decisions without question.
15. Wait for the coach to call upon you to play when he sees fit. Never ask him!

## GAME PLAN

A game plan is the playbook broken down to a relatively few plays, defenses, and coverages that are expected to work against an opponent. In short, the game plan enables a team to practice what will likely be used in the next game.

As a result, a coaching staff will spend a considerable amount of time trying to determine exactly which plays and maneuvers should be used during specific situations in a particular game. They will try to determine what their opponents will employ, and then they will attempt to counteract it.

Breaking down film, setting up tendency charts, and drawing up game plans can be a tiresome chore, but not a difficult assignment.

A football team, particularly the quarterback, should be fully prepared each week against the defenses to be seen. After viewing game films and listening to scouting reports, the coaching staff on Sunday formulates the weekly game plan, which appears on a 4-×6-inch easy-to-carry card inside a transparent plastic folder.

The quarterback should master the following:

1. Defensive alignment and stunts
2. a. Zone coverage (rotation, inversion, revolve)
   b. Man coverage
   c. Semi-zone and man
   d. Free safety
2. The scheme of opponents' up-front defense
3. Strengths and weaknesses
4. Exact system of secondary coverage to be used and how to identify specific coverage
5. Individual traits of opponents
6. Expected tendencies
7. Overall plan of attack
8. Specific formations and plays available

In addition to the game plan for the offensive quarterback, the defensive captains should receive a similar tactical plan in line with the offensive strategy expected from the opponents.

### Offensive Game Plan

The offensive game plan is divided into the following sections:

scouting report. a statistical report of the opponents' operation, including diagrams and frequency charts.

*ready list.* what to employ against the opponents, i.e., six running plays, six or seven passing plays, and the basic formations that each play may originate from.

*defenses of the opponents.* diagrams of the opponents' defensive formations, including the frequency of use, against the various down and yardage situations, plus key defenses and maneuvers.

*pass coverages.* the various zones, combinations and half-zones of the opponents, all broken down into situations in which they occur.

*blitzes.* formations and variations are listed, i.e., number, situation, and who did the blitzing.

## Defensive Game Plan

Each week the head coach will prepare the defensive write-ups on the upcoming opponent. These are followed later in the week with individual position game plans.

A defensive playbook will provide the following information:

**CHART 15-4.** *Defensive game plan.*

| *Running Plays* | *Pass Plays* |
|---|---|
| 0–1 Hole | Play Action |
| | Screen Passes |
| 2–3 Hole | |
| | Draws |
| 4–5 Hole | |
| | Short Passes |
| 6–7 Hole | |
| | Medium Passes |
| 8–9 Hole | Deep Passes |
| Goal Line, Short Yardage | |
| *Defensive Signals* | |
| Audibles for the week | |
| Live color for the week | |
| *Fronts* | *Coverages* |
| Pro | Cover 1 |
| Over | Cover 2 |
| Under | Cover 3 |
| | Cover 5 |

*Continued on next page.*

**CHART 15-4.** *Defensive game plan (continued).*

| | |
|---|---|
| *Stunts* | *Blitzes* |
| Slash—Pro front | Sam Dog—Pro front |
| Tom—over front | Moe—under front |
| Ed—under front | |
| *Short Yardage* | *Prevent* |
| Pro pinch double dog | Okie cover 5 |
| Cover 1 | |

*Summary*

*The best first and 10 defense*
1.
2.

*The best second and 7 plus defense*
1.
2.

*The best second and 7 minus defense*
1.
2.

*The best third and 4 plus defense*
1.

*The best third and 4 minus defense*
1.

- Scouting reports
- The team's own defenses
- Offensive sets and plays of opponents

The coach's field chart will contain the actual defensive game plan based on the opponent's down and distance tendencies.

## FILM GRADING PLAYERS

From viewing the game films, the coaching staff is able to evaluate the progress of their players. Whatever system of evaluation is used, grading should not create a negative attitude in a player's mind. However, an effective grading system will enable the staff to examine and discuss with the players their deficiencies and thus improve their play.

A coach will enter on the grading sheet the number of plays in which the athlete participated in the game. A player will receive a check mark on plays graded satisfactory, and on plays termed nongradable.

A superplay is graded *S* and is worth +5 points. These plays involve a perfectly executed technique. On a loser play, the player receives −5 points.

**CHART 15-5.** *Player evaluation.*

*Instructions:* Rate player by circling
appropriate number:
1. Outstanding
2. Above average
3. Average
4. Below average
5. Poor

*Rate everyone:*

| | | | |
|---|---|---|---|
| Aggressiveness | 1-2-3-4-5 | Quickness | 1-2-3-4-5 |
| Agility | 1-2-3-4-5 | Reaction time | 1-2-3-4-5 |
| Balance | 1-2-3-4-5 | Size potential | 1-2-3-4-5 |
| Durability | 1-2-3-4-5 | Speed | 1-2-3-4-5 |
| Explosion | 1-2-3-4-5 | Strength | 1-2-3-4-5 |
| Intensity | 1-2-3-4-5 | | |

*If possible:*

| | | | |
|---|---|---|---|
| Character | 1-2-3-4-5 | Leadership | 1-2-3-4-5 |
| Intelligence | 1-2-3-4-5 | Pride | 1-2-3-4-5 |

## Breaking Down Game Films

The strategy employed by a team is the result of many hours of game film analysis, combined with a systematic breakdown of the films (Figure 15-8). In breaking down a game film, the staff will section off the paper according to the game period, score, down, distance to go, and field position. As an alignment is read, it is recorded in the correct

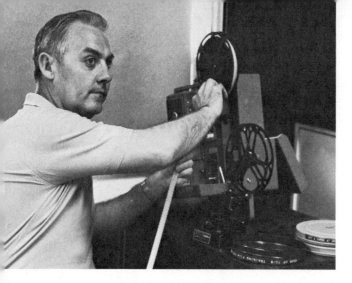

FIGURE 15-8. Film breakdown. Special assistant Bill Hickman prepares a film for showing to a group of players. Essentially, Monday is a film breakdown day in preparation for the next opponent.

area. A frequency or tendency can be determined by the end of the season. After the formations and alignments, the actual plays are recorded. Generally, the staff will work in pairs. One coach will call out the information while the other writes it down.

An offensive coach, for example, will read the defensive formations, such as: "First and 10, they are in a 4-4. . . . Second and four, 4-3," etc. Later, the staff will examine the execution of the defense more carefully.

The defensive coaches will converse in these terms: "First and 10, slot left; second and 4, flanker left," etc.

After the films are studied, they are broken down and shipped off. When the team reports on Tuesday, they will hear the game plan for the week.

## Frequencies

Most teams reveal a pattern in their offense and defense. As a result, frequencies can be determined with the prime purpose of keeping the guesswork to a minimum. As an example, a team will run off right tackle 75 percent of the time when confronted with third down and short yardage.

By having knowledge of these percentages, a team will be able to prepare more effectively for a game. It should be added, though, that frequencies do not always stand up.

## Key Sheets and Situation Charts

Key sheets and situation charts can be very effective to determine the individual efforts of each player. While many coaches are capable of teaching fundamental skills and evaluating films, they are weak in the individual teaching in group situations.

Key sheets involve a breakdown of a particular play or defense. They enable the coaches to pinpoint specific accomplishments by the players. The staff can zero in on a certain technique that needs improvement.

## PREPARING FOR A GAME

The first thing we do is to look at the films of the opponents. We try not to let anything slide by. We want to cover each and every thing as well as we possibly can, offensively and defensively.

While looking at these films, we chart the opponent's defenses, and put them into a computer system. The defenses of the opponents that week will be broken down in many categories, by down and distance, position on the field, the hash marks, and how they defense certain sets. Any set that we might want to run, we will know basically what defense they like to use from looking at the films.

Defensively, I do not use the computer

**CHART 15-6.** *Key sheet example.*

| Offense No. | Situations | Play | Defense | Comments |
|---|---|---|---|---|
| 1 | First and 10 | Option 51 | 44 | Check QB responsibilities |
| 2 | Second and 10 | 17 Draw | 40 | FB lead block |
| 3 | | | | |
| 4 | | | | |
| 5 | | | | |
| 6 | | | | |

| Defense No. | Situations | Play | Defense | Comments |
|---|---|---|---|---|
| 1 | First and 10 (Pass) | Roll-out | Even | Check contain |
| 2 | | | | |
| 3 | | | | |

at all. I have many reasons, but will not go into them now. We will chart complete offensive programs for two games, which is what our league allows. What passes do they like to throw? What do they do by down and distance? Everything is broken down by hand. It's a little slower, but we feel we can get a little more out of it ourselves breaking it down this way.

**CHART 15-7.** *Situation chart example.*

*10-yard line—coming out*

1. First and 10    37
2. Second and 7    34 Counter
3. Third and 2    41 Full

*25-yard line—coming out*

1. First and 10    92
2. Second and 10    HB Quick screen
3. Third and 7    60

*40-yard line—coming out*

1. First and 10    74
2. Second and 2    79
3. Third and 2    51 Roll

From this extensive amount of information, we will come up with a game plan, which is designed to work against this particular ball club. How should we handle this team?

### Sunday

This is the important study and strategy day for the coaching staff. Scouting reports are broken down, as the coaches analyze the strengths and weaknesses of opposing personnel. Then the game films are shown; they are studied and graded quite extensively. We run the films back and forth, back and forth, and we all make notes. This goes on until early afternoon.

Following this study, the staff starts making up the game plan. The passing patterns and strategy along with the running attack are devised according to the opposing defense.

The staff also discuss the best methods of getting the team mentally ready for the next opponent. To key the players into the

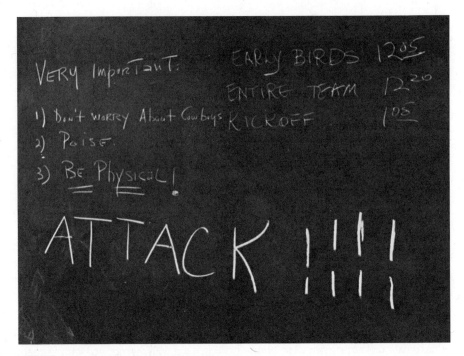

FIGURE 15-9. *The coach should get his players to think. The bulletin board, signs, and slogans can all serve as constant reminders for the team.*

game plan, the bulletin board, signs, and banners are prepared.

The players have the day off except for those who have to report to the training room for bumps and bruises. These can range from a major to a minor injury that needs treatment by the trainer.

### Monday

Before the team takes the field, a squad meeting is held, at which time the players receive a preliminary game sheet, plus a grade from the previous game.

The previous game is replayed on the screen. The offense, as a group, will look at the offensive pictures, while the defense will see the defensive pictures. Mistakes are pointed out or great plays are noted on how they did things, and what improvements they must make for the next game.

The Monday practice is an easy session, consisting of calisthenics and loosening-up drills. This session is just long enough to work out the stiffness and get everyone relaxed. After dinner, many college teams will view films of the upcoming opponent.

### Tuesday

This is the heavy work day, about 2 hours of practice at a fast pace. A thorough review is devoted to offense and defense fundamentals. An hour of offense and defense drill follows, featuring recognition exercises with the game plan in mind. The team will start to run some plays they will be using in the next game. A short scrimmage is held, matching the first and second teams. Stress is placed on the defense's ability to read tendencies and formations.

Earlier in the day, the offensive and defensive quarterbacks will have their daily meetings.

Coaching staffs on the college level will have a staff meeting each morning. Following the meeting, the staff will set up the afternoon practice schedule.

## Wednesday

An offense and defense dummy scrimmage and emphasis on the kicking game take up 1 hour of this practice session. The line spends 20 minutes in the chute for offensive takeoff, plus work on the seven-man, two-man, and one-man sleds. While the line is hard at work at their end of the field, the backs are working on offensive execution.

Later, the squad goes through all phases of pass protection, screens, and draw blocking, but with a minimum of contact. The ends and backs are given 10 minutes of work to perfect their patterns and technique.

Running plays are practiced against the various defensive formations, while the defensive players work their alignments against the opposition's known offensive patterns. Emphasis is placed on the passing game.

Defensive recognition and the defensive kicking game are carefully reviewed. Then the offensive teams run through their perfect plays, moving up and down the field, calling out the down and distance.

After most of the players go to the lockers room, the quarterbacks and ends might stay out to sharpen their passing game.

In the evening, a scout report and short film on the opponents could be presented.

## Thursday

After a good loosening-up period, the approaching game is reviewed for approximately 45 minutes. This day is a review of the plays put in the previous 2 days. The squad then works on punt returns and kickoff coverage and returns. Both the punters and the place-kickers sharpen up their skills. The major portion of this workout is devoted to warm-up, running plays, reviewing the game plan, and some jogging. However, the chief concern is that the game plan be fully understood by everyone on the team. The offensive session could end with a 10-minute "down and distance" drill, a simulated scrimmage with the defensive team giving the other team's defense. Short-yardage plays (third and 1) and the goal line offense should receive prime emphasis.

After dinner, there are more group meetings, more films, frequencies, tips on personnel, and more knowledge that can prepare a player for the game on Saturday.

## Friday

The day-before-game practice is long enough to loosen up and review short-yardage strategy. This should be a short, snappy workout in sweat clothes in which the team goes over all situations that are likely to occur (Figure 15-10). A team should cover their goal line offense and goal line defense. The special 2-minute offense should be worked on as the offense moves the ball up and down the field against the defense, attempting to stop the clock on every play. The special teams should work on kickoff coverage, kickoff and punt returns, punt protection and coverage, field goals, etc. A brief strategy session is held with the offensive and defensive quarterbacks.

College teams on the road often go to a

FIGURE 15-10. *The day-before-the-game practice should be a short, snappy workout, in sweat clothes at times, in which the team loosens up and goes over all game situations.*

movie as a group or have some other type of relaxing group activity. We try to keep the players relaxed so they will get a good night's sleep. Players should be in bed by 10:30 p.m.

## GAME DAY

Most teams, when playing Saturday afternoon, have their pre-game meal at around 10 a.m., roughly 4 hours prior to kickoff time. Following the meal, the head coach often speaks to the squad briefly before they proceed to the dressing room.

The players arrive in the dressing room, where a quiet atmosphere prevails. They are given an opportunity to think of the game coming up. The coaching staff should insist on quiet and intense mental concentration.

Several meetings are held by members of the coaching staff. The backfield coach meets with the defensive secondary and reviews coverage and various adjustments. The line coach checks his players on their blocking assignments. The defensive line players have a meeting with their coach, while the offensive and defensive signal callers go over the game plans. Before the meetings, the coaching staff should have a briefing on substitutions, what personnel will be used, the quarter, etc. During the game, the staff should not have to worry about these considerations.

As the players begin to dress, taping takes place in the training room. After observing a few moments of silent prayer, many football squads have a team prayer before they leave for the field.

FIGURE 15-11.  *Pre-game group meetings are held before the team takes the field. Here, the linebackers and defensive backs meet with Coach Allen to review coverage and various adjustments.*

FIGURE 15-12. Quarterbacks Sonny Jurgensen and Bill Kilmer review the game plan with Head Coach Allen and Offensive Coach Ted Marchibroda.

The team will take the field about 45 minutes before the game and go through a series of warm-up drills. Of course, the amount of warm-up time should depend on the day's temperature and weather conditions. Generally, the kickers and passers come out early to loosen up (Figure 15-13). Punters should kick in both directions so the receivers can field the ball looking in both directions.

After the whole team has their calisthenics, we will break into two areas. The linemen will run down to cover punts, while the punt receivers will catch the punts. The linemen will take striders downfield after the punts, while the receivers and passers will work on a passing drill, which is the same that we use in practice.

FIGURE 15-13. The kickers come out early to loosen up. The place-kickers and punters should kick in both directions.

FIGURE 15-14. *The Redskins devote 7 to 10 minutes daily to flexibility and stretching exercises. Stretching is a slow, gradual forcing of the muscle to a greater length.*

Then we will break up into individual groups of the offense, running patterns for the quarterback, the defense working on agility, and the linemen working on protection and rush. These are principally done to get loosened up. We will get together in our 7-on-7 period, throwing passes in the patterns they have worked on during the week. Then, we will go into a full group running plays, 11-on-11, for a certain segment of time. The defense will go in first, while the offense continues to end up with perfect plays, at which time everybody goes in.

FIGURE 15-15. *Taking striders down the field. The linemen will run down to cover punts, while the punt receivers will catch the punts.*

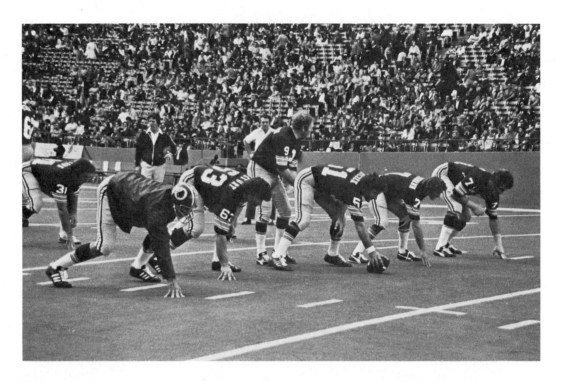

FIGURE 15-16. *After our 7-on-7 and 11-on-11 periods, the offense completes their pre-game warm-up with perfect plays, as the defense goes into the locker room.*

### Pre-game Meeting

We will discuss the basic points that we have gone over during the week, mainly repetition of those we brought up during the week at meetings (Figure 15-17). I will remind the players about how I want to kick off, what defense we want to open with, and make a few remarks before I leave them alone.

### Prior to the Kickoff

Just prior to the kickoff, the players will pair up on the sidelines and go through the fol-

lowing routine: They will pound each other three or four times with their fists on their shoulder pads, possibly a smack once on the side of the helmet. These are usually not love pats but hard blows to loosen each other up, and knock out some of the butterflies.

### During the Game

With a sufficient staff, the head coach on the college level should keep to a minimum the number of details he is responsible for. He will be far more effective if he is not bogged down with a lot of routine tasks.

Generally, the head coach is involved with the following areas:

- Making adjustments in game plan, although he should follow it whenever possible
- Encouraging the squad
- Making kicking decisions
- Evaluating the scoring combinations

His assistants are assigned these responsibilities:

- Substitutions
- Play selection (unless the head coach wishes to handle this area himself)
- Defensive calls
- Individual player adjustments
- Order on the bench

### Press Box Coaching

Press box–field cooperation is vital to football success. In this era of multiple offenses and defenses, effective communication is a must. Getting proper information from the

*FIGURE 15-17. After the warm-up period, the players return to the dressing room for a final briefing by Coach Allen.*

FIGURE 15-18. *Effective communication. Much of a team's game strategy is the result of the telephone hookup between the press box and the bench. After consulting with his assistant coach LaVern Torgeson (equipped with ear phones), Coach Allen explains a tactical adjustment to his defensive unit.*

FIGURE 15-19. *Half time must be productive. Like they did during the week in practice, the Redskins divide into groups to analyze the situation. Here, Coach Allen talks strategy with the defensive unit while offensive players are seated in the far end of the dressing room.*

press box can prove extremely valuable in making tactical decisions during a game.

The actual relay of information during a game involves two telephones (Figure 15-18). An offensive and defensive coach sit in the spotters' booth next to the main press box. The offensive coach talks to a reserve quarterback or a coach, while his offense is in the game, and to his No. 1 quarterback when the defense is in. The defensive coach does the same thing—relaying information to one of the coaches or the defensive signal caller.

### Half-Time Organization

While 15 or 20 minutes at half time can be very short, this must be a productive period of time (Figure 15-19). We will divide the team into groups, like we do during the week in practice, and discuss and analyze the situation as it involves each group. The offense is with the offensive coach, the defense with the defensive coach. They talk strategy and adjustments.

Allowing for getting off and back on the field, most teams will break up the 15-minute half time into the following three 4-minute periods:

1. *Quiet time* The players rest quietly sipping soft drinks, while members of the coaching staff meet outside the locker room to review the first half. Any necessary adjustments are made at this time.

2. *General briefing* The coaches move around the locker room answering questions, building up morale, and briefing the team on second half requirements. The coaches who view the game from the press boxes make their recommendations. Members of the staff talk to some of the players and the physician to learn about the injury situation.

FIGURE 15-20. *Coping with adverse weather conditions. While rain and other elements can be disconcerting to both players and coaches, the team that is able to disregard poor weather and play their game as best they can will likely emerge as victors. Above, Coach Allen offers encouragement to his team.*

3. *Second half plan* After reviewing the achievements and mistakes of the first half, the head coach then discusses what has to be done in the second half. If the game plan has not been satisfactory, he will tell the team what changes will be made. Finally, he must provide the motivation necessary for the team to return to the field with the proper mental attitude.

### After the Game

The first thing I do is talk to the players. Before the press is admitted, I like to have something to say to some players, something personal but general and brief.

FIGURE 15-21. *Three cheers for the Redskins! While some people might question veteran pro's cheering enthusiastically after a victory, I believe it contributes to the building of togetherness, a team feeling.*

### TYPICAL GAME DAY SCHEDULE (*High School and College*)

| | |
|---|---|
| 3:00–3:30 | Student body, pep rally |
| 3:30–4:30 | Training room: tape ankles, draw game equipment, check equipment |
| 4:45–5:30 | Suggested pre-game meal: lean beef (fish), baked potato, fruit, vegetable, dry toast, tea with sugar |
| 5:30–6:30 | At the school: movie room (30 minutes) viewing movies of tonight's opponent; gym (30 minutes): walk through various defensive adjustments |
| 6:30–6:45 | Free time, relax |
| 6:45–7:15 | Dress for game and final taping |
| 7:15–7:35 | Pre-game warm-up |
| 7:35–7:55 | Pre-game instructions |
| 7:55–8:00 | Loosening up and National Anthem |
| 8:00–10:00 | Game time |
| 10:00–10:30 | Post-game talk, showers |

When things have calmed down a bit, I check with our team physicians on the injury situation. The the coaches get together and rehash the game a little.

Another game has gone into the books, but the cycle starts all over again. It is back to work. If we lose, I have trouble sleeping, but if we win, I still have trouble sleeping.

### THE OFF-SEASON

Our off-season isn't an off-season at all for the coaching staff, contrary to what most people may think. In January at the completion of the season, I give each of our coaches a list of jobs, maybe ten or fifteen, which they must accomplish during the off-season.

Each coach must write up a report on his area of the team and submit his recommendations for improvements the next year. This goes into a booklet that the entire staff receives.

The off-season is the time when you improve. Every day, unless you make some progress you are going to get behind or someone is going to get ahead of you. We have a big sign in the weight room and it says one thing:

### *WHAT YOU DO IN THE OFF-SEASON DETERMINES WHAT YOU DO DURING THE SEASON*

Of course, high school football players, generally, participate in other sports, depending on the size of the school and the skills and talents of the players. Good track participation can be a major factor in the success of a high school football team. College players, though, usually confine their participation to just one sport.

The easiest way for a football player to cut short his gridiron career is to be lazy during the off-season and become soft and out of shape. The task of returning to tip-top condition is not always easy.

Most schools have some form of concentrated physical fitness program during the off-season (including summer months). Specific regulations, however, forbid the playing or coaching of football at any level of a school program. This does not mean that squad members cannot get together for workouts, particularly the passing and receiving combinations. Players should be told what fundamentals, skills, and patterns to work on as a group during the off-season. Footballs should be issued to quarterbacks and kicking candidates for individual use.

Strength is a prime objective in any off-season conditioning program. The program usually consists of weight lifting, rope skipping, and running. Weights and running are a great combination.

In addition to considerable running, good off-season activities are handball, basketball, badminton, paddleball, soccer, volleyball, and speedball.

A sound program of exercises could include:

1. Neck conditioning
2. Knee exercises
3. Regular push-ups
4. Mountain climber
5. Hurdler's spread position
6. Squat jump position
7. Sit-up position
8. Chin and record

Generally, a punting specialist will take a rest for several months before he resumes his kicking. He probably won't touch a football until probably May, but he will do a good deal of running. Early in the summer training season in July, he won't kick a whole lot, probably twenty-five balls in the morning and twenty-five in the afternoon. And later on during the season, he will do most of his kicking early in the week, probably Tuesday or Wednesday. On Friday he will cut way down, when he will hit maybe eight or ten punts altogether. He will try to be really fresh and crisp on Saturday.

## A Typical Conditioning Program

*December 1*  Team members are measured and tested.

*January to April*  Weight training and running; conditioning and agility program twice a week.

*April to July 15*  In addition to the January to April program, running takes place two times per week.

*July 15 to the start of season*  Conduct conditioning, agility drills, and running (five times a week.) Sprint for time (speed development): one 440-yard dash; sprint 20 yards, walk 20 yards for 100 yards (three times a week).

## Physical Fitness Test

Prior to the first practice session, a test is conducted that consists of:

1. Sit-ups
2. Push-ups
3. Pull-ups
4. 40-yard dash
5. 100-yard dash
6. 440-yard dash

All candidates are checked on their ability with the weights, and comparison is made with their efforts in March.

## Film Breakdown

The first area we get into is a comprehensive breakdown of all game films for the season just completed.

Offensively, all passes are broken down into patterns, while all runs are broken down according to holes. On the hole breakdown, the plays are categorized by 0 and 1 hole, 21 Trap, 40 Trap, etc. All plays are broken down according to the times used and the success of each.

A general overall review of our defensive films is made at the close of each season, at which time we detect the most repeated errors. We then try to correct these mistakes in order to make us a better football team. As an example, the films often show that we lose a lot of yardage by arm tackling, not getting that shoulder into the blow.

Most of the film watching is done individually because it takes a long time to do it. However, the offensive coaches do get together because they are working on the same plays.

## Manuals

During the off-season, we make up the manuals. Again, this is a coaching staff cooperation program. From the offensive standpoint, we weed out plays that have not worked well and the blocking assignments might be revised to make the play go. Of course, most NFL teams run about the same plays; the difference is in the talent they have to make the plays successful.

## Forms and Charts

Most charts and forms require constant revision if a coach is to keep up with the constant changes in offensive and defensive trends. The purpose of these charts is to assist both the coach and player before the game. The forms and charts are intended to make the players more conscious of vital statistics. In addition, they serve as a motivation to the players.

A wall chart, for example, is very useful in providing pass defenders with a visual aid to assess their performance. Pass training cards illustrate every pass pattern that the opponents could employ.

## Returning Players

The number of players returning each year should be controlled. Ideally, there should be a player coming back for each of the twenty-two positions. There should be at least eleven returning players on offense and defense. Of course, some of these players may get beat out of a job by a new player.

When a player is a junior, he should be placed in a position where he can play as a senior. Many coaches will never allow a senior to play second-string unless the first-stringer is a junior.

# 16

# Conditioning the Team

I believe that conditioning and training play a large part in the success of any football team. No one can play the game of football well unless he is in top condition. Quite often, a player is called upon to use every muscle in his body, and unless his muscles are properly conditioned, he will not be able to do an efficient job. Moreover, being in good condition reduces the risk of injury. I always tell our players that being in good condition is like taking out an extra insurance policy.

Coach John Ralston refers to the game of football as "a series of 6-second wars." "Most plays last 6 seconds," explains John, "and then a player has 25 seconds to recover and to get ready to go to war again for 6 seconds. Sell your players on going all out for these 6-second periods. If they do that, a coach will be building a base for a successful football program."

The need for daily conditioning can be emphasized when a good example is set for the players. Members of the Redskins' coaching staff run laps before and after each workout. This helps me relieve the daily tension and helps me relax. Running also gives me important strength and stamina to go through a long and rigorous season.

An off-season conditioning program should combine running, flexibility exercises, weight training, and isometric exercises. A good weight program is the best and quickest way to build strength and body size.

## TO ALL YOUNG ATHLETES

It is important for young people to develop good health habits early—plenty of rest, proper diet, exercise, and conditioning. A young athlete who has developed these

FIGURE 16-2. Breakaway speed is the result of a sound conditioning and training program. Above, wide receiver Roy Jefferson demonstrates both speed and endurance in outrunning the St. Louis Cardinals' defensive secondary.

FIGURE 16-3. Making athletes run is the best way to condition them. Coach George Allen puts his players through the Striders drill at the conclusion of practice. This is his favorite team drill.

habits as early as junior high school will be in top condition and will be able to accomplish much.

Developing healthy attitudes is important, too. Players should have self-respect and respect for the judgment of coaches, both on and off the field.

## THE REDSKINS' SUCCESS FORMULA

A football team must remain strong throughout the entire 60 minutes of play. A strong second-half performance can be attributed to the following areas:

1. *Conditioning.* If a team doesn't have conditioning, it will not be able to stay in there—blocking, running, and tackling for 60 minutes.
2. *Half-time organization.* This involves making the necessary adjustments for effective performance in the second half.
3. *Morale.* A team that has morale and enthusiasm is always going to look good the second half.
4. *The big play.* A championship team must have the ability to make the big play and take advantage of the breaks. A team usually makes its own breaks.

### Determination to Get the Job Done

When a player starts a conditioning program, he must stick with it. He shouldn't expect results in a day or two. It will take one month at least to see and feel the results. After his first workout or two, naturally, he is going to be stiff, but he must have the determination to continue. He must assign a time every day for exercise and adhere faithfully to his schedule.

FIGURE 16-4. "Being in good condition is like taking out an extra insurance policy," I continually tell my players. Above, Larry Brown and Charley Harraway engage in stretching exercises prior to taking the field.

## THE UNTAPPED 25 PERCENT

No matter how strong, how big, or how fast an athlete is, he is not going to succeed or be consistent unless he is in excellent physical condition.

A well-conditioned human body is capable of performing incredible feats of strength and endurance. Anyone who has watched long-distance runners or weight lifters will accept this without question. However, an equally accurate statement, but one which most athletes fail to wholeheartedly believe, is that this wonderful body, this great creation, can never be developed to its capacity. Persons who make their living in the field of physical development realize the truth of this statement, but they pinpoint the reluctance of athletes to accept it by citing the following figures: most persons develop their bodies to approximately 20 percent of capacity, some to 50 percent, a very few to 75 percent, and only the champions to a higher degree. If we can prove to our players

the importance of surpassing the 75 percent mark, and help them to reach that goal, we will have achieved our purpose.

The conclusion is only this. If a man takes care of himself, whether he is a high school, college, or professional player, or whether he has a weight problem or not, *he would be a much more effective football player.* I might add that coaches will some-

FIGURE 16-5. The need for daily conditioning can be emphasized when a good example is set for the players. Members of the Redskins' coaching staff run laps before and after each workout. "This helps me relieve the daily tension and helps me relax," says Coach Allen, shown here completing his daily running. "Running also gives me important strength and stamina to go through a long and rigorous season."

times assign a weight to a player without proper research. This can be dangerous. Coaches should always check first with the team physician, then the trainer.

This brings up another point: physical condition is a relative matter. It is important to be in good physical condition, but it is even more important to be in better condition than your opponent.

*In short, there are no easy ways to attain this good conditioning,* but one can take heart by recalling that only a few athletes develop the body to the 75 percent mark. There is plenty of room for an athlete to be in better physical condition than his opponent. All he has to do is *pay the price.*

### Running

Running is the greatest conditioner, so we do run a lot. If a team can run in practice more than it has to run in a game, the football game becomes easy. If a player runs only enough to go half a game, then the second half is going to seem very tough.

We urge our players to develop their endurance. To become champions, they must be stronger in the fourth quarter than their opponent. If they are not getting enough running, they should stay after practice and run on their own.

### Explosive Power

Football is a game in which explosive power plays a major role, both offensively and defensively. Explosiveness is not merely the product of strength. Speed and alertness must be applied to secure the proper explosion.

Weight training is an effective program to develop explosiveness. In lifting weights, violent body movements should be com-

bined with sheer muscle power. Making the barbells ring is a good guideline in achieving explosiveness.

## SIX QUALITIES OF A GOOD ATHLETE

There are six qualities of any good athlete in any sport. They are as follows:

1. Willingness to take coaching and study football
2. A spirit of competition in practice and in games
3. An intense desire to win and accept nothing less than victory
4. Willingness to practice hard at all times
5. Willingness to make sacrifices for the team
6. A desire for self-improvement on and off the field

## SPEED IMPROVEMENT

Many football players fail to realize their maximum running potential. While speed cannot be created beyond an athlete's potential, a highly competitive program in sprinting can be followed. The prime objective is to get the player's running muscles and wind in shape and to improve his starting and sprinting ability (Figure 16-6).

The sprinting program should start from 4 to 6 weeks before the opening practice and should continue on a three-workouts-per-week basis. The sprinting distances are 10, 20, 30, and 40 yards, with the emphasis on the 10- and 40-yard sprints. The most important distance in football is the first 10 yards, whether the athlete be a back or a lineman.

The player should practice and be tested on the ability to move from his stance to the 10-yard mark. The 40-yard sprint is felt to be the best indicator of starting and

*FIGURE 16-6. Players should practice and be tested on their ability to move from the stance to the 10-yard mark. The most important distance in football is the first 10 yards. The stopwatch and the chart combine to provide the spark of competition that is much needed in programs involving running.*

sprinting ability. A good time for a college lineman is 5.2 seconds for the 40-yard sprint, while a back with good speed should do it in 4.8 seconds. It is essential to keep a chart each day, as well as a file of the daily charts for reference use.

By adding the stopwatch to the running program, the competitive factor is added. Besides achieving good conditioning, the player will be running for the sake of "beating" the stopwatch. The competitive factor will provide the motivation to help improve speed.

The proper techniques of the sprint include four components: the stance, the start, the run, and the finish. The start is the key component for it can "make or break" the athlete. Some players lose as much as 0.2 second in the initial 10 yards because of improper starting technique.

The following rules characterize the proper uses of the hands and arms:

1. Do not clench the fists.
2. Keep the elbows in close to the body and swing them with a smooth pumping action.
3. Synchronize your arm action with that of your legs.
4. Keep relaxed.

We have continually consulted with track coaches for their advice. Jim Bush of UCLA and Payton Jordan of Stanford, also an Olympic track coach, have been helpful.

I have observed that every one of our players who participated in the sprint program has realized some degree of improvement.

The use of the stopwatch and the chart provides the spark of competition that is much needed in programs involving running.

## CALISTHENICS

The entire team goes through a 5-minute warm-up period of calisthenics. We go through about five or six stretching exercises, taking from 7 to 10 minutes, making sure they cover every vital part of the body. We try not to overdo them at first, but build up gradually.

The purpose of exercise is to condition the entire body to the highest degree possible. In this way, quickness will increase with strength.

Calisthenics can become dull and monotonous unless everyone sees that plenty of enthusiasm and pep are put into each drill. We like our players to count cadence whenever possible. A constant flow of chatter should come from the coach leading the squad. He should always change from one exercise to another without a waste of time. He must do everything possible to keep this period moving fast. Pep, enthusiasm, and spirit are the things we are looking for.

### A Strong Stomach

The focal point of any body conditioning is the stomach or abdominal area. Almost any movement involves the stomach muscles. If they are soft and flabby, the efficiency of the entire body is impaired. Good muscle tone in the stomach helps keep an athlete's internal organs in proper alignment, aids his digestion, and even helps his outlook on life.

### Developing the Legs

An athlete is only as good as his legs. This is why it is so important for him to keep his legs in top-notch condition. Running builds the legs, heart, and lungs more than any other exercise.

### Early Season Exercises

In the summer training season, our exercises are more strenuous than the loosening-up type of calisthenics engaged in after the season begins. Our exercises include:

1. Back twister
2. Crossover toe touch
3. Tail gunner
4. Quadricep exercise
5. Horizontal run
6. Prone side straddle
7. Side straddle hop
8. Alternate toe touch
9. Touch the ground
10. Arm swinging
11. Push-ups
12. Rock and roll
13. Running up and down
14. Jumping jack
15. Inguinal roll
16. The bridge

### The Redskins' Flexibility Program

We place considerable stress on giving our players vigorous and steady doses of stretching and strengthening exercises and considerable running. In fact, one of the most significant trends in athletic conditioning and training in all sports is the increased emphasis on flexibility and stretching exercises.

Before every practice or game, we want our players to stretch their muscles as much as they can and loosen them up. Our warm-up exercises are designed for the gradual stretching of the muscles, which causes the muscle fibers to become more extensible and elastic. Our stretching program takes approximately 7 to 10 minutes and involves all the major muscle groups of the body. When proper stretching is combined with daily running and weight work, maximum movement

A

B

C

FIGURE 16-7.   *The Redskins go through their pre-game flexibility program—a slow, gradual stretching of the muscles. Notice in these pictures that the players work individually on
their own stretching routines.*

*FIGURE 16-8. Head to knees, demonstrated by Chris Hanburger. From a standing position with the legs straddled, the player slowly brings his forehead to a knee. Keeping his legs straight, he can use his hands for assistance. After holding for about 3 seconds, he relaxes and repeats the exercise on the other side.*

and strength can be achieved. In addition, our stretching program has reduced significantly the incidence of all muscle injuries.

Our stretching routines are designed to lengthen the muscles so that all muscle movement will be easier. The slow stretching of muscles is accomplished by forcibly stretching the muscle beyond its resting position and stretching it gently but forcibly out to a greater length. It cannot be done too fast or too hard and has to be done on a daily basis with gradual progression.

In loosening up, the player should not "bounce" on a muscle to stretch it farther. He must not jerk or pull hard when stretching. He does it gradually, and each day he tries to stretch farther.

We will not allow our players to merely "go through the motions." The key to stretching is complete mental concentration on the area of the body being stretched. A player should concentrate particularly on tight muscles. He should think, relax, and stretch.

**A**

**B**

*FIGURE 16-9. Stretching the back and hamstring muscles. The player begins by standing with his feet spread. Keeping his legs straight, he leans over and touches the ground. Reaching back through his legs, he continues these ground-touching movements.*

A                                       B

FIGURE 16-10. Crossover toe touch. The player will make five movements downward, each moving a little farther down until he has his palms flat on the ground. He should keep his back and legs straight. This is one of the better hamstring exercises.

## Warming Up

No athlete should ever begin competition without a period of preliminary warm-up activity. Before he starts going at full speed, the player must get blood flowing into his muscles at a faster rate. We feel all our players need a minimum of 7 to 10 minutes of stretching and loosening-up exercises. We have our players warm up until the muscles in their arms and legs feel loose, and they have begun to perspire a little. Otherwise, they are asking for pulled and strained muscles.

> **FITNESS TEST**
> - A series of stamina tests
> - One mile run against time
> - 40-yard sprints
> - Chin-ups
> - Weight lifting

## WARM-UP EXERCISES

The following exercises are very effective in loosening up and stretching all muscles of

FIGURE 16-11.   Warm-up exercises. At the beginning of every practice and game, the entire squad should go through 7 to 10 minutes of stretching and loosening-up exercises. Here, Coach Don Brown provides a constant flow of chatter as the Mira Loma High School squad goes through pre-game warm-up exercises. A, Scissors. B, The rocker. C, Reaction. D, The bridge.

the body. These are some of our favorite calisthenics.

*Back Twister.* The back twister is a two-count exercise that loosens up and stretches the upper body. The player tries to throw the elbows as far as possible. On "one," he twists to the left, and on "two," he swings in a clockwise direction back to the right. He must perform this exercise as quickly as possible.

*Quadriceps Exercise.* The player starts from a kneeling position, his hands on the insteps of both shoes. Sitting back on his haunches, he extends and pushes his pelvis as far forward as possible and then bounces. This exercise stretches the groin and quadriceps.

*Horizontal Run.* This four-count exercise strengthens the belly muscles and generally loosens up the entire body. From a forward-sitting starting position with hands on helmet, the player runs in place alternately touching his elbows with his knees. On "one," he touches his left knee with his right elbow. On "two," he returns to the starting position. On "three," he touches his right knee with his left elbow. He returns to the starting position on "four."

*Tail Gunner.* Starting from the squat position, the athlete straightens both legs. He comes up on "one," down on "two," up on "three," and down on "four." This exercise is excellent for the hamstring, groin, and quadriceps muscles.

*Prone Side Straddle Hop.* This four-count exercise loosens and strengthens the groin muscles. The player begins by pointing his fingers away from him, exerting good pressure on the triceps muscle. On "one," he hops to the spread position. On "two,"

he returns to the original position, then these two moves are repeated.

## WEIGHT TRAINING

A weight training program can be of tremendous help in developing strength in the muscles used in playing football. The prime objective of a weight program is to help the athlete become larger in muscular development and body size, and a great deal stronger, while improving upon his agility.

The key areas needing muscular development are the calf and thigh muscles, the lower back for explosion, and the neck, shoulder, and triceps muscles. Our weight training program is designed to develop these areas of the body. Much loss of time and general muscular soreness could be avoided if the players devoted some of the late summer time to weight training.

The basis of weight training as a conditioner deals with the principle of overload. The use of weights during exercise speeds up the conditioning program by making the muscles do an above-normal amount of work in a short period of time. The athlete performs several repetitions with weights that can be handled with relative ease, rather than attempt to lift maximum load. By working with increasing load, he gradually builds up to heavier drills. Remember, the repetitions that hurt are the ones that build.

Prior to reporting to summer training, we encourage our players to participate in the weight program 3 days a week, and do their running 2 days a week. Regularity is a very important part of this theory. They must *never miss a workout.* We want them to be proud of their consistency.

Competition is the basic motivation for the lifter, and the athlete will generally be competing against himself. He must constantly shoot for a goal. As he achieves that goal, he can set a new and higher standard.

For every minute of weight conditioning, an equal amount of time, or even more, should be given to the development of agility. This time should be devoted to enjoyable, competitive athletic activity, such as basketball, handball, volleyball, and tennis.

Hand in hand with weight training for strength and flexibility, we stress rope jumping and short sprints for quickness of hands, eyes, and body. We feel that these two also strengthen those parts of the body most susceptible to football injury—the knees and the ankles.

After a player has worked for a long period of time, he will attain a state of peak conditioning that will give him new and greater confidence.

If, in his heart, the player knows that he has paid the price to attain top conditioning, he will be a confident and greater athlete. He will become the top man in the stretch run, in the fourth quarter, or in the final set. He will know that he is able to handle any physical challenge that might confront him.

Many football players have three different weight programs during the year: (1) off-season, (2) a much shorter program at training camp, and (3) a short program during the regular season.

During the spring months, for example, Roman Gabriel will work at least 12 hours a week. At each of the three weekly workouts, Roman will run 3 to 5 miles, followed by an hour of weight lifting. Then, he will skip rope, hit the speed bag, sprint back and forth across the field, and bunny-hop up and down the steps. He goes up twenty-five steps backwards and down frontwards, hopping all the way.

"When I change over to the in-season program at training camp, I cut back to 35 or 40 minutes with the weights," said Gabriel. "I cut it back still more in the fall, but I never

cut it out. My prime objective is to keep my lower body as strong as possible."

The athlete who needs to build up his body and strength should lift weights. However, he should combine his weight work with his schedule of calisthenics, and he must remember not to handle weights that are too heavy.

As a body-builder, weight lifting has a definite advantage over isometric exercises because the movement involved increases the size of the muscles and builds endurance in addition to strength.

For maximum results, weight lifting should be performed on alternate days, not on a daily basis.

Warm-up exercises to prepare the muscles should be done prior to the weight work. Several minutes of arm circles, side twisters, jumping jacks, and running in place will sufficiently prepare the athlete for his weight lifting.

### The Off-Season Weight Training Program

A weight training program must be highly individualized if a player is to obtain maximum results for the time he invests in the program. Many factors should be considered before a definite routine is selected. Some of these factors are the following:

1. The demands the player's position makes on him
2. The player's physical weaknesses and strengths
3. The amount of time he will invest in the program
4. The amount of energy he will invest in the program
5. The temperament of the player (will he push himself or does he have to be pushed?)

It is a simple matter to write out an elaborate program on paper. Actually carrying out the program is another matter. There is no use prescribing a program that will never be carried out. For this reason, predetermined workout programs are often a waste of time. We do know that certain exercises will develop or work certain muscles and that a certain number of repetitions will bring about certain results. Therefore, the biggest factor in a successful weight program is prescribing the best exercises for each individual.

Weight lifters and other people who have made strength and strength development their profession tell us that strength and power can best be developed by certain "big muscle group" exercises. These are called power exercises. The following routine is an excellent one for football players in the off-season. Along with the basic power exercises, the player may choose exercises for specific body parts that he might want or need to work on. The proper beginning weight can be found only through experimentation. The basic principle is to start with a weight light enough to perform the desired number of repetitions with good form. It is better to start too light than too heavy. Normal progression will soon get the lifter to the weight that will provide adequate resistance for the overload needed for strength development.

Instructions for the power routine (Table 16-1) are as follows:

1. Warm-up with flexibility and stretching exercises.
2. Do the power routine three times a week, with a day of rest between each.
3. Add weight when you can do desired number of repetitions.
4. Have a workout partner if possible.
5. Wear a belt; use spotters.

*Routines for Specific Body Parts*

1. Should be done three times a week.
2. Pick routines for individual needs.

3. *Every player should do leg work. A football player is only as good as his legs. The older you get, the more leg work you need.*
4. *Always* warm up before your workout.
5. Running and agility work should be part of your weekly workout.
6. When you are able to do the desired number of repetitions, you should progress in weight.

**TABLE 16-1.** *Power routine.*

| Exercise | No. of sets | No. of repetitions |
|---|---|---|
| Bench press | 3 | 5 |
| Squats (parallel) | 3 | 5 |
| Power clean | 3 | 5 |
| Dead lift | 3 | 5 |
| Standing press | 3 | 5 |
| Curls and dips (alternating sets) | 3 | 10 |

**TABLE 16-2.** *Leg routine.*

| Exercise | No. of sets | No. of repetitions |
|---|---|---|
| Leg press | 3 | 8 |
| Quadriceps extensions | 3 | 8 |
| Hamstring curls | 3 | 8 |
| Hip and back extension | 2 | 12 |
| Squats | 3 | 5 |

**TABLE 16-3.** *Shoulder routine.*

| Exercise | No. of sets | No. of repetitions |
|---|---|---|
| Standing press | 3 | 5 |
| Seated press | 3 | 6 |
| Behind the neck press | 3 | 6 |
| Upright rows | 3 | 6 |
| Dumbbell press | 3 | 8 |

**TABLE 16-4.** *Arm routine (alternating biceps-triceps).*

| Exercise | No. of sets | No. of repetitions |
|---|---|---|
| Strict curls | 3 | 8 |
| Dips | 3 | 8 |
| Heavy curls | 3 | 8 |
| Push-downs (Universal) | 3 | 8 |
| Strict curls (close grip) | 3 | 8 |
| Triceps extension (lying on bench) | 3 | 8 |

**TABLE 16-5.** *Upper torso routine.*

| Exercise | No. of sets | No. of repetitions |
|---|---|---|
| Bench press | 5 | 5 |
| Pull-overs | 3 | 10 |
| Pull-downs | 3 | 10 |
| Dumbbell flies | 3 | 8 |

*Basic Principles.* The following basic principles are applicable to all programs.

1. The most important ingredients in any weight program are *consistency* and *dedication.*
2. A day of rest between weight workouts usually gives the best results, with three weight workouts a week best for most athletes.

3. The "secret" ingredient of any weight program is *progression* (adding weight in the next workout after a predetermined number of repetitions have been reached in an exercise).
4. There are no shortcuts or magic formulas. You will get results from your weight program equal to the amount of *hard work* and *dedication* you put into it.
5. Basic good *health rules* must be part of any training program. These include sufficient rest and the right foods.
6. Successful weight training programs like any other worthwhile activity should be goal-oriented; in other words, know what you want and make realistic plans to achieve your goal.
7. *Always* keep in mind that weight training for an athlete is a means to an end (becoming a better athlete) and not an end in itself.
8. If possible, have a workout partner. Always use spotters in heavy exercises and follow safety rules.

### The In-Season Weight Training Program

The in-season weight program is primarily for maintenance of the strength levels reached in the off-season program. Time and energy are more in demand by the season's activities, and the in-season program must fit into a player's schedule. It is better if the workout can be done before practice, allowing the player at least 45 minutes to 1

**TABLE 16-6.** *In-season routine.*

| Exercise | No. of sets | No. of repetitions | % of maximum weight possible |
|---|---|---|---|
| Bench press | 1 set | 5 reps | 80%+ |
| Squat (parallel) | 1 set | 5 reps | 80%+ |
| Power clean | 1 set | 5 reps | 80%+ |
| Standing press | 1 set | 5 reps | 80%+ |
| Dead lift | 1 set | 2 reps | 90%+ |
| Dips | 1 set | (10–20 reps) | |

FIGURE 16-12. *The Universal gym machine is an excellent weight training machine. The "variable resistance" featured in the recent models adds a new dimension to the Universal. The upright rowing exercise, as demonstrated by Assistant Coach Jim Hilyer, who is in charge of the Redskins' weight training program, is only one of the many exercise stations on the Universal.*

hour before going on the field. The in-season program should be a low-repetition, heavy-resistance type of workout, since research has shown this to be best for maintenance of strength. Our program at Washington is set up so that twelve players can go through the workout in 15 minutes, thus allowing all of our squad to work out in 1 hour. We cut the workouts from three a week to two a week. Any 2 days that fit into the team's schedule best are satisfactory as long as: (1) at least a day's rest is allowed between workouts; and (2) the second workout is a least 2 days before a game. Like the off-season program, the in-season program can be individualized to some extent.

FIGURE 16-13. The leg press station permits football players to give the hip and thigh muscles a great workout. The calf muscles can also be worked at this station.

FIGURE 16-14. The squat. If performed correctly, the squat can be the best single exercise for football players to include in their workout. Squats are best done off a power rack. The bar should be carried "low" on the shoulders and not on the neck. After assuming a position with the feet about shoulder width apart with the toes pointing straight ahead, the lifter lowers his hips into the squat position. During the entire lift, the back should remain straight and the head up. As long as the head is held up and the back remains straight, there is no undue stress on the back. As the lifter goes into the squat position, the movements are under control. It should be a controlled movement, not a dropping into position. The thighs are lowered until they are approximately parallel to the floor. Then the lifter returns to the starting position. The thrust upward is done with the hips and thighs. The lifter should use a lifting belt and always have a spotter when doing the squat. ▶

**A**

**B**

**C**

A                B                C

*FIGURE 16-15. The dead lift is a great all-body strength builder, but is especially important in building strength in the hips, thighs, and lower back. At the end of the lift, the neck and shoulder muscles are worked by the "shrug" of pulling the shoulders beyond the perpendicular. During the entire lift, the lifter must keep his head up and his back straight. When using heavy weights, he must wear a lifting belt. In the starting position, the lifter should reverse the grip of one hand. This prevents the bar from slipping from the hands. The lifter must start from a squat position and get close "up under" the bar. He should constantly be reminded to get his hips and legs into the lift. As the bar is lifted, the hips and thighs extend, and the bar is pulled up to the level of a full-arm extension. At no time during the dead lift should the elbows bend. At the top of the lift, the head and body must be at least perpendicular with the floor, and if the "shrug" is used, they should go beyond the perpendicular.*

*FIGURE 16-16. The power clean is a great power and explosion-type exercise that builds* ▶
*strength in the shoulders, back, arms, and wrists. In the starting position, the lifter should have his back straight and head up. The legs are in the squat position. The lifter should wear a belt during this exercise. The bar is brought quickly from the floor and pulled straight up as far as possible. By snapping the elbows downward and the wrists up, the bar is carried to the chest, where it is brought under control. Then it is returned to the floor and started again. During the entire lift, the lifter should keep both feet stationary (or at least one foot).*

**A**

**B**

**C**

 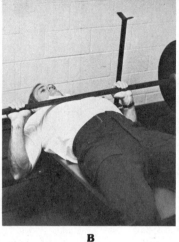 

A      B       C

FIGURE 16-17. The bench press is a good builder of shoulder, chest, and arm strength. This exercise should be done on a bench wide enough to support the hips and shoulders but narrow enough for the arms to move freely. A spotter should be used in this exercise, particularly if heavy weights are being used. The spotter should help the lifter by giving assistance in lifting the bar to the starting position, where the arms are locked straight with the bar held directly over the chest. The bar is then lowered under control to the chest and then pressed back into starting position. At no time during the lift should the hips or shoulders of the lifter leave the bench. Arching the back brings the back muscles into play and the desired effect on the chest, shoulders, and arms is not achieved. After the lifter has completed the desired number of repetitions, the spotter should help replace the bar on the rack.

A       B       C

FIGURE 16-18. The barbell, two-arm curl is the power exercise for developing the biceps muscle. The barbell is brought from a fully extended arm position to a fully contracted position. The bar should be curled to the chest (close under the chin), then lowered to the starting position. During the entire movement, the elbows should remain close to the side and the back as straight as possible.

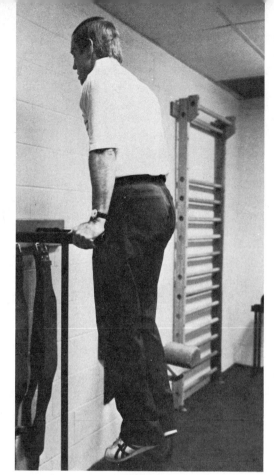
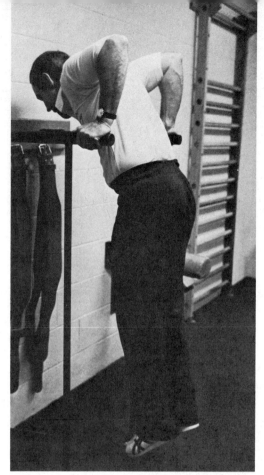

A

B

FIGURE 16-19. *Dips are probably the best single exercise for developing the triceps, which is an important muscle in football skills. If done properly, dips will also develop the shoulder and chest muscles. From an upright position on the dip bar, the elbows bend, allowing the shoulders and the chest to move toward the bars. The body should be held as straight as possible without swinging. The legs can be kept in a bent position if desired. At the lowest point in the dip, the level of the back of the arm should be below parallel with the floor. When completing each dip, be sure that the arms return to a fully extended locked position. This is called the lockout.*

### Nautilus Training Equipment*

Nautilus equipment has enjoyed considerable success in providing full-range exercise that gives the athlete strength, flexibility, and

\* For further information about Nautilus training equipment, write to: Nautilus Sports/Medical Industries, P.O. Box 1783, Deland, Florida 32720.

overall conditioning. Improved flexibility increases speed and greatly reduces the chances of injury, and improvement in flexibility is a direct result of full-range exercise.

Nautilus equipment is unique in providing all of the requirements for truly full-range exercise: (1) both stretching and pre-stretching in the starting position; (2) resistance in the fully contracted finishing position; and

FIGURE 16-20. Nautilus training equipment. With Bill Malinchak of the Redskins demonstrating the pre-stretched starting position, the Nautilus Pullover machine provides both stretching and pre-stretching of the large muscles of the torso. Stretching the muscles in the starting position of an exercise is necessary for increasing flexibility, but stretching is impossible if no resistance is available in the starting position.

(3) available resistance in proportion to the athlete's strength in every position throughout a full-range of movement.

Most of the professional football teams, including the Redskins and the Miami Dol-

phins, plus hundreds of universities and high schools, are now using Nautilus equipment, which is designed to work with the limitations of the human body.

In providing the back pressure of a force pulling against the user's muscles prior to the start of movement, the Pullover Torso machine (Figure 16-20) makes possible full-range exercise. Full-range exercise can be achieved only when there is resistance in the fully contracted position at the end of an exercise movement.

Maximum strength in the legs and lower back can be produced without imposing long and system-exhausting workouts upon the body. Thirty to forty-five minutes of proper training, repeated two or three times weekly, will quickly build maximum strength in these areas.

### The Apollo and Exer-genie Programs*

These are resistive exercise programs that the entire team can use in a short period of time. They are based on isokinetic exercise, the ability to take a muscle through a complete range of movement against a constant speed and resistance. Both programs can be maintained with relatively short workouts that will not leave the player unduly fatigued. By starting each exercise isometrically, the athlete can obtain exceptional strength benefits, and by combining it with isotonic movement, he can build much needed endurance and flexibility. This is highly important in preventing muscle pulls and strains. After the players complete the exercises, they will begin their drills.

* Printed material on the Apollo total isokinetic-aerobic program may be obtained by writing: Physical Fitness Institute, 20 Harold Avenue, Suite A, San Jose, California 95117.

Devised by Dean Miller, the new Apollo exerciser consists of an engineered cylinder and a nylon rope that can be pulled back and forth through the cylinder with equal resistance in either direction. The outer shell has been changed to a high-impact nylon, less heat conductive than the original exerciser.

*Procedure.* A team should always begin each exercise period with easy bending and stretching. A period usually takes from 10 to 30 minutes. All exercises should be done using one repetition and continued throughout the season.

There is a right way and a wrong way of using the Apollo and Exer-genie exercisers. We have our players work in pairs. By working in pairs, one player can exercise and his partner can handle the trailing rope controlling the amount of resistance needed to make him work at his full capacity. Resistance can be set at 10 pounds for high school, and 20 pounds for college and professional.

On all exercises, the trail line should be controlled with the index finger so the line will not move during the ten-second isometric contraction. It should not take more than 22 seconds to complete the exercise. The player starts each exercise with a 10-second isometric contraction and then moves through a full range of motion within 12 seconds.

Breathing is very important in performing exercises in the Apollo and Exer-genie programs. The athlete should not hold his breath, but should breathe normally.

*Apollo Football Circuit.* All exercises in the circuit are performed with a partner. The Apollo Exerciser is set on 15 pounds resistance. Each exercise begins with a 10-second isometric phase, followed by a 12-second isotonic phase in which the muscle is taken through the range of motion under constant speed and resistance.

The circuit involves the following ten stations:

1. Apollo 5 (lower back muscle groups), involving the dead lift, leg press, clean or curl, and military press
2. Lats (upper back)
3. Bench press (chest exercise)
4. Triceps (upper arm extension)
5. Repeat Apollo
6. Two-man row (upper back and arm row)
7. Sit-up (abdominals)
8. Deltoid lift (deltoid and upper arms)
9. Repeat Apollo
10. Aerobic running (endurance)

Each technique and movement can be broken down and practiced through a full range of motion using constant speed and resistance. The player uses the muscles in exactly the same position he would be using them on the field. Specific football exercises include agility, punting, passing, down lineman charge, defensive back drill, and a hamstring exercise for all players. Rather than do the bench press lying on his back, for example, specificity enables the player to assume the same position he will use to perform the skill on the field, such as delivering a hand shiver blow.

**Apollo Off-Season Program**

1. Strength—Apollo 5 exercise
2. Endurance—harness running
3. Muscle balance—isolate muscle groups and use the motion that is used specifically in your position.
4. Coach should break down skills for players, and the motion of these skills and techniques should be carried out under constant speed and resistance with the exerciser.

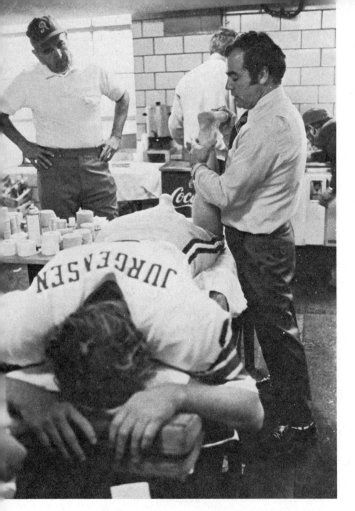

FIGURE 16-21. *The increased incidence of foot injuries today can be attributed in part to the greater use of the lighter, low-cut soccer shoes. Above, Dr. Patrick Palumbo, the Redskins' team physician, diagnoses an injury to Sonny Jurgensen's achilles tendon, one of the most serious injuries in football.*

Before an athlete is allowed to play, he must receive a complete physical checkup by a physician. (It is also recommended that a full-coverage insurance program be obtained for every athlete.) Again, the best insurance policy against injuries is a strong, well-conditioned body.

Resistance exercise should never be taken just before game time, since the re-

sulting fatigue in the exercised muscles may dull protective reflexes. The exercise should be scheduled after practice sessions or an off-day so that full recovery can take place before the next day of play or practice.

## INJURIES

Football is a hard, body contact sport in which injuries will never be eliminated, regardless of what is attempted to make the game safer. However, injuries can be sharply reduced by well-trained coaches, good equipment, better supervision and instruction, and safety-minded game officials.

Coaches and physicians must take a firm stand in demanding safer equipment. This would include requiring manufacturers to provide soft external padding of all helmets and shoulder pads to limit the injuries from blows delivered by these items.

Injuries are one of the key factors in determining a team's chances for success or failure. Through the years, teams in top physical condition have experienced a minimum of serious injuries. Indeed, a sound off-season and pre-season conditioning program can prove the difference in winning a championship.

Many football injuries can be prevented by more effective conditioning and by observing various precautionary measures. All injuries must be promptly recognized and reported, and proper treatment must follow.

Common minor injuries can be treated quite effectively by a trainer or coach. In the case of serious injuries, or when an ailment persists, the team physician should be consulted.

Injuries are often the result of inadequate face mask protection and helmets that do not fit properly. New-style helmets have been responsible for cutting down facial injuries; for example, better padding is now used on the rims.

After several years of research, there appears to be little difference in the rate of serious injuries on artificial and real turf. While artificial turf has cut the number of knee injuries, some physicians feel that more serious shoulder injuries occur on this type of playing surface.

There are more foot injuries today, which can be attributed to the more widespread use of the lighter soccer shoes. Some foot injuries can take weeks to fully heal.

### Knee Injuries

An athlete with an injured knee should begin his rehabilitation program as soon as his physician permits it. Ice or ice water should be applied immediately, and a pressure bandage should be used. Normal movements should be resumed as soon after the injury as possible.

If the knee is only sprained and swelling is not evident, the joint might be treated with rest, and cold compresses should be applied. The player can resume play as soon as symptoms allow. However, if extensive swelling or "water on the knee" occurs and the patient is unable to extend the joint, he should be examined by the physician and X-rays should be taken.

The injury might be the result of a tearing of the capsule of the joint, or ligament or cartilage damage may have occurred. Treatment may consist of traction or application of cold packs, a plaster shell, or adhesive strapping. In some cases, surgery may be necessary.

In some cases, the physician may recommend an exercise program of isometric and isotonic exercises to rehabilitate the muscles. Using both extension and flexion work, the injured athlete engages in strength-ening exercises with heavy shoes. While ultrasound and whirlpool therapy can aid in returning normal circulation to the area, the exercises really do the work.

To allow the player to keep his mobility, the knee cannot be taped too tightly.

### Hamstring Pull

As soon as a player pulls a hamstring muscle, the area should be iced down to minimize local bleeding and to eliminate pooling of the blood. An ice bag should be left on the leg for an hour. Then, the trainer will start the wrap. If the player experiences considerable pain or swelling in the area, whirlpool treatment may not begin for 48 to 72 hours.

### Sprained Ankles

A sprain is an injury to a joint causing stretching and/or tearing of ligaments or tendons and, sometimes, rupture of blood vessels with hemorrhage into the tissues. Cold applications will sedate the area, while pressure is effective in stopping the hemorrhage. Elevating the injured part allows the fluid that has leaked out to move properly.

Immediately after the accident, the ankle should be surrounded with ice packs and the injured player should be taken to a physician. In the case of a severe sprain, and when considerable swelling takes place, strapping should be applied. The foot should be elevated and surrounded by ice for a period of approximately 24 hours, followed by heat treatments.

### THE TRAINER

The team trainer is responsible for the prevention and care of injuries. In short, his

FIGURE 16-22. *The team trainer can play a vital role in the success of a football team. Injuries must be kept to a minimum. Veteran trainer Joe Kuczo, left, and his assistant, Bubba Tyer, are shown checking their supplies in preparation for a Sunday ball game.*

## THE TRAINING ROOM

Basic equipment in the training room should include:

- Training room tables (two or three)
- Whirlpool bath
- Two heat lamps
- Storage cabinet (large)
- First-aid cabinet and dressing table combination
- Dressing table
- Refrigerator
- Weight scale
- Fan for ventilation
- Hydrocollator steam pack
- Medical dictionary
- Trainer's manual

## OFF-SEASON PROGRAM

For many NFL clubs, an off-season program has reduced significantly the number of serious injuries. By making them stronger, functional strength programs enable players to better protect themselves. An off-season program generally lasts at least three months and possibly longer.

We have a big sign in our weight room that reads, "What you do in the off-season determines what you do during the season." We think that football is no longer a seasonal sport. You have to get ready for training camp in the off-season.

I tell our players that every day in the off-season you should try to do something to improve yourself. It might be working out with the weights, running, playing tennis or handball, looking at a film, or studying the playbook. But if you don't do something in the off-season, you will not be ready for training camp.

A sound physical conditioning program starts with calisthenics. These exercises tone and firm up all the major muscles of the

chief concern is to get the players ready and keep them ready. In seeing that every player is properly conditioned, he has to treat players psychologically as well as physically. The trainer is responsible for supervising the daily treatment for injured players.

Since few high schools can afford a professional trainer, an assistant coach is often assigned the major portion of the trainer's duties.

An untaped ankle, a knee bandage that becomes loose, or a missed treatment can result in problems for the player and his team. Trainers usually tape the knees last because the longer the elastic gauze is on, the looser it will become, thereby giving less support.

body. In addition, they strengthen the circulatory system, making the heart and lungs work more efficiently. They should not be discarded for isometrics and/or weight training.

We urge our players to maintain a five-days-a-week schedule. The weekly run-walk exercise can be done on Saturday.

Exercises should be done properly and thoroughly. The first month should be devoted to using lighter weights and concentrating on the correct form. The objective is not how fast the athlete can finish them. Using the schedule given earlier in the chapter, the individual should start with the minimum number of repetitions.

During the final two weeks and on up to reporting day, players are urged to bolster their workouts so they will be sharp and ready. By reporting in top shape, the team will be able to move rapidly into technical skills.

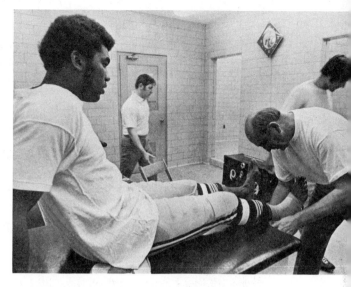

FIGURE 16-23. *Proper taping is essential in football, a game in which a pulled muscle or twisted ankle can determine victory or defeat. The Redskins are required to have their ankles wrapped or taped prior to practice. Below, trainer Joe Kuczo performs his daily taping chores.*

## PROPER DIET

A well-rounded diet plays a vital role in physical fitness. A person today has the benefit of good food, and good food supplements, and he should take advantage of them. Three meals a day, with as little eating as possible between meals (especially after the evening meal) is the best plan.

A football player in strenuous training needs a food intake that provides from 5,000 to 6,000 calories per day. The following diet will furnish the athlete with approximately 6,000 or more calories:

### BREAKFAST

| | |
|---|---|
| 1 glass of juice | 1 glass of milk |
| 2 eggs | fruit |
| 1 bowl of cereal, preferably hot | |
| 3–4 oz. portion ham, bacon, or sausage | |
| 2–3 slices toast/jelly | |

### LUNCH

Tossed salad/dressing
1 bowl soup/crackers
1 portion of meat
3–4 slices of bread/butter, jelly
2–3 oz. portions of vegetables
milk or juice
dessert

### DINNER

salad/dressing
1 portion of meat
1 portion of potatoes
2 portions of vegetables
3–4 slices of bread/butter, jelly
milk
dessert
fresh fruit

### Pre-game Meal

The last regular meal should be eaten at least 3 to 4 hours before game time. Physiologists recommend such nongreasy, non-gas-forming foods as bread, honey, broiled steak, baked potato, green peas, ice cream, and either fruit juice, vegetable juice, or tea.

However, many physiologists are now suggesting that the pre-game meal be basically a high-carbohydrate meal, such as pancakes with syrup or spaghetti.

### Weight

The common mistake a rookie makes is to come in too heavy. Most players in our league would perform better if they lost weight. Certainly, a regular check on the weight of each player should be kept. As a person grows older, this becomes even more important. Nothing destroys conditioning or causes an athlete to become ineffective faster than being overweight.

Large fluctuations in weight can also be harmful to good conditioning. A great loss of weight may be necessary for an athlete to become a champion, but this tends to reduce strength and speed until the desired weight has been reached and the body has had time to revitalize itself.

We feel so strongly about this matter of weight that we give each of our players a weight to maintain during the off-season. We ask the player to report at this weight at the beginning of each season. We also check our players periodically during the season to see if they are keeping their proper weight.

### Weight Reduction

The coaching staff should urge every overweight player to get down to his best playing weight. Excessive weight gain and laziness seem to go hand in hand.

For the player who has to lose weight, the following rules should be followed:

- Cut out or reduce breads and potatoes.
- Stay away from alcoholic beverages.
- No soft drinks between meals.
- No eating between meals, especially pies, candy, peanuts, and ice cream.
- Beverages should contain dietary, noncaloric sweetening.

### Weight Gain

To increase his weight, an athlete may use one of the many dietary supplements now on the market.* These products are available in a variety of forms—solid, liquid, and tablet; they are nutritionally balanced and provide the extra calories needed for weight gain and for meeting the increased metabolic requirements of stress. An increase in calories and protein should be accompanied by adequate exercise.

## PROPER REGIMEN

### Staleness

The common causes of staleness are overwork, monotony, and, occasionally, dietary deficiencies. Rest or change of activity and a revised diet are the surest cure for staleness. However, prevention is better than the cure.

Players shouldn't be overworked. The daily practice sessions should be made interesting and the practice routine should vary somewhat from day to day.

---

* Some of the products are Lipomul, Nutrament, and Hustle (liquids); Sigtab (tablet); and Nutri-1000. Nutri-1000 is a complete food supplement which can be purchased from Syntek Laboratories, Inc., Palo Alto, California 94304.

## Plenty of Sleep and Rest

It is best to have a regular pattern of sleep. An athlete should try to get 8 hours or more each night, not 4 tonight and 12 tomorrow. At training camp, our players are in bed by 11:00 p.m. each night. When we are on a "two-a-day" workout schedule, almost all of them spend at least 1 hour in bed following a light noontime lunch. On Saturdays (pre-game day) throughout the season, we encourage a 3-hour siesta period.

## Drinking and Smoking

Drinking alcoholic beverages is very detrimental to the physical fitness and performance of an athlete.

Rules about drinking alcoholic beverages should be stricter among young athletes. There is no question but that excessive drinking cuts down on the individual's athletic ability.

Smoking is obviously detrimental to athletic performance; furthermore, studies indicate quite conclusively that tobacco smoking is causally linked to lung cancer and cardiovascular disease. For those adult players who insist on smoking, medical authorities urge moderation.

In counseling his players not to smoke, the high school or college coach should stress the financial expense as well as the health hazard.

## Drugs

During the past decade, drugs of all kinds have been used in increasing numbers in America. Tranquilizers and barbiturates such as sleeping pills and "mood control" pills have become a concern of those in athletics. Another type, amphetamines, has the opposite effect, giving a feeling of stimulation. "Greenies" are perhaps the most widely used of the amphetamines that give an "up" or a "high" sensation. Fortunately, the percentage of players who use them is small.

Physicians of professional sports teams are unanimously opposed to the use of stimulants such as "greenies" and all other forms of pep pills. The use of amphetamines could have harmful effects on an athlete and should not be prescribed. In 1968, my Los Angeles Rams were the first team to have an expert on drugs lecture to them. Dr. Jules Rasinski, the Rams' team physician, recommended it. Today, talks of this type are quite common.

A football player is not going to perform at his best when he stimulates himself artificially. True, amphetamines can mask fatigue to varying degrees, but they will not help performance.

As for the use of "hard drugs" (heroin, opium, cocaine), the physicians feel these could be a problem if the national trend of increased usage among young people continues. But it is generally felt that hard drugs will not likely be a major problem in athletics, for the basic reason that addiction to such drugs soon destroys the ability to compete.

Statistics show that young people in rapidly increasing numbers are using marijuana. Yet, a number of physicians and psychiatrists who were in favor of legalizing marijuana before are changing their minds because of what they have observed happening to young people who habitually use this drug.

Dr. D. Harvey Powelson, director of the student psychiatric clinic at the University of California, Berkeley campus, once advocated the legalization of marijuana, but no more. Over the last 5 years, he has treated 500 students, and he now believes there is a deadly cumulative effect on the minds of those engaging in prolonged use of this drug. He has seen in those using marijuana daily for a long period (6 to 12 months), symptoms similar to those observed in organic brain disease.

Perhaps the least understood drugs used presently by athletes are androgen hormones and anabolic steroids. "While they have some effect on physique and weight gain, there is always the risk of liver damage and other health dangers," according to Dr. Thomas E. Shaffer, Ohio State University Medical School. "In young athletes who have not completed their growth, the hormones may decrease the height which the athletes would ultimately attain." In effect, these drugs are doing the exact opposite of what the athlete intended. If an athlete is to attempt hormone therapy in hopes of improving his athletic performance, he certainly should do so only under the strict care of a physician.

In 1973, eighty NFL players for sixteen NFL teams cooperated with the Drug Enforcement Administration, a federal agency, in a national poster program to combat the illegal use of drugs.

# Part Four

# MOTIVATION

# 17

# Motivating the Team

*Mental attitude and team morale are 90 percent of football.*

**George Allen**

To win a championship, a football coach and his players must have a strong will to win. I am convinced that on gridirons of all levels of play, the will to win has made the difference between mediocre athletes and outstanding performers.

Successful coaches have always been able to motivate and instill in their players a burning desire to win. While the success of coaching greats like George Halas, the late Vince Lombardi, Don Shula, Paul Brown, Ara Parseghian, and John McKay can be attributed to many factors, WINNING was their prime goal. Having different personalities, they accomplished motivation in different ways. All knew how to evaluate talent but they knew persuasion and motivation best of all.

When a team goes flat, it is usually because they go mentally and psychologically stale, not often physically. Therefore, the coaching staff must keep their players from becoming bored by employing a week-after-week routine. A team should never stay on one phase of the game for too long a time.

Still, there are practice situations when a team is not getting something, and the coach must drive his players to keep at it until they do get it.

I like emotional football players. I want them to put forth so much of themselves that after a game they are drained emotionally. No matter what the situation may be, they must have a mental attitude that never gives up. They will keep going. When we lose, I want everyone to feel miserable and disappointed. However, they should not brood, make excuses, or demonstrate a bad temper.

The past greats of professional football were driven by a burning desire to win. Winning was a way of life, a passion to them. They didn't know the meaning of "quit,"

FIGURE 17-2. *While the modern football player is much more sophisticated than the player of 20 or 30 years ago, he can still be "psyched" to greater performances. Here, Coach Allen talks to his quarterback Bill Kilmer during a time-out period.*

even when the odds seemed insurmountable. Members of the Redskins coaching staff look for men with this spirit and attitude. If players are willing to accept a season in which they win half their games, they will win half their games and they will emerge half alive.

In order to win and be prepared to win, you have to prepare yourself all week long . . . maybe for 2 weeks. You don't just show up on the day of the game.

> ### TYPES OF MOTIVATION
>
> - Individual motivation
> - Small group motivation
> - Team motivation
> - Student body
> - The community—through the news media

If you want something badly enough, you will get it. If you just stay on it and drive yourself enough, you will get it. Indeed, the mental part of the game is more difficult than the physical part. Mental preparation never ends, whereas with physical preparation, you can be out on the field for an hour and a half or 2 hours and it is over. The mental part, though, continues on and on—when you are eating, when you are sleeping, and when you are walking around.

Often, motivation is needed when positioning players to perform on defense or offense. Generally, linemen prefer to play defense than block on offense, while backs prefer to play offense. From a coaching standpoint, the coach is faced with the job of convincing each player that wherever he plays, it is in the best interest of the ball club.

> Once that whistle blows,
> You are on your own.
> Make the best of it!

*FIGURE 17-3. Football is a contact sport and players will not enjoy it unless they take real delight in playing with all the desire and intensity they can muster.*

> Win or lose,
> Keep looking ahead.
> There is no sense looking back.

## TEAM SPIRIT

We are proud of the fact that the Redskins have plenty of spirit (Figure 17-4). During a practice, it often comes out in an organized cheer by the offense or defense. Somebody will think up a yell, and suddenly a huddle full of players will burst out at the top of their voices. One day, I was standing back of the huddle when the second-string offense let loose with: "We're undefeated and we're needed!"

Following a game, the thought of veteran pro's yelling "Three cheers for the Redskins!" might seem outlandish to some people, but I firmly believe it contributes to the building of togetherness, a team feeling.

Newspaper clippings and dressing room cheers can motivate even the sophisticated professional football players of the seventies.

FIGURE 17-4. *To win a football game, each player must have the same purpose and goal. A football squad must become "one team" and forget any jealousies. The team is everything! Here, Charley Taylor and Roy Jefferson enjoy together a team accomplishment—TOUCH-DOWN, REDSKINS!!*

### Hail to the Redskins

Always a believer in cheers and fight songs, I find myself with the organization that owns professional football's oldest march, Our "rally song," by Barnee Breeskin and lyrics by Corinne Griffith, is called "Hail to the Redskins."

> HAIL TO THE RED-SKINS ——— hail vic-to-ry,
> Braves on the war-path ——— Fight for old D.C.
> Scalp 'em, swamp 'em. We will take 'em big score ———
> Read 'em, weep 'em, touchdown we want heap more ———
> Fight on. Fight on till you ——— have won.
> Sons of Wash-ing-ton (Rah! Rah! Rah!)
> HAIL TO THE RED-SKINS ——— hail vic-to-ry
> Braves on the war-path ——— Fight for old ——— D.C.

FIGURE 17-5. *A general feeling of mutual admiration and warmth is an important quality of a team. Players should respect each other and help each other, like linebacker Harold McLinton, left, congratulating running back Larry Brown.*

## A GAME OF EMOTIONS

Football is a game of emotions, a vigorous, highly competitive contact sport involving desire, discipline, and drive. It is the popping sound of pad against pad. The tenseness and nervousness of the pre-game wait in the locker room is followed by the thrill of charging out onto the field.

Victory is often highlighted by the beauty of an electrifying broken field run or the precision of a long pass. Defeat is marked by the frustration of missing the winning field goal or dropping a touchdown pass.

I'm an emotional coach and I'm proud to be that way because I put every fiber in my body into every practice and every game. I'm sometimes ill after a bad practice. I just can't help myself.

### Proper Mental Attitude

Mental attitude, therefore, plays a tremendous role in the success of a football player. An athlete can have great natural ability but will never reach his potential unless he can develop a proper mental attitude. The athlete with the right frame of mind will make his natural ability work. I would rather have a player with the proper mental attitude and less ability than a player who has more ability and a bad attitude.

When he takes the field, a football player's thoughts should be strictly football. He can groove his mind and body in performing a skill, by concentration. He must be alert and thinking every minute.

Relaxation is also highly essential in acquiring skill and perfection. Actually, concentration and relaxation go together, whether it is catching a touchdown pass or kicking a winning field goal. By concentrating on what he is doing, an athlete can remove tension and fear from the mind, and replace them with a confident mind and relaxed body.

*I try to make our players realize that one of the great things in life is to take an ordinary job and make something out of it.* We all have ordinary jobs. Whether a man be a coach or a player, a musician, or anything, he should want to do something in life and make a contribution. He should be proud of

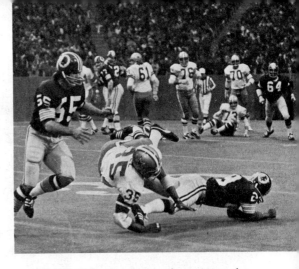

FIGURE 17-7. *Every coach enjoys the sound that echoes throughout a stadium when some player really hits someone on the field. Defensive back Ted Vactor of the Redskins has just belted running back Calvin Hill of the Cowboys.*

himself, not just go through life and eat, watch TV, sleep, drink, and drive a car.

I urge any young athlete to try to get the very best out of what they have within themselves. Not too many people do this, in any walk of life. If a player will play as well as he is capable, using all the resources that God gave him, I feel he will have done an excellent job.

We tell our Redskins that "Every play is a big play—never let down!" A player must be inspired never to let "cannot" come into his mind. Even when he may believe he is outweighed and outmanned across the line, he must have a will to win and the confidence that he can get the job done.

### Morale

After the players learn the fundamentals and plays, it is morale that makes the team. To win a football game, there must be a strong mental togetherness on the part of every player. Each player must have the same pur-

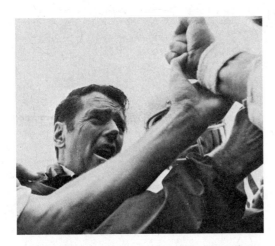

FIGURE 17-6. *A great desire to win must be a vital part of the coaches and players. Above, Coach Allen provides a brief inspirational message just before kickoff time.*

pose and goal, and it is this kind of group feeling or team spirit that wins games. We urge our squad to always have one common goal in mind—to win that next ball game. Without a burning ambition to gain victory, there would be little spirit.

We try to make everyone feel that there is no number 1 man on the Washington Redskins, no number 40 man. The team is everything! Any success we have had is the result of team play, not some individual. We can have six All-Pro's on our team, but if we don't win the championship, it doesn't mean a thing. I would rather have a team that is balanced and not have any All-Pro's and win.

Morale is a mental condition and attitude. It is characterized by a never failing ability to "come back." Time after time, our ball club had demonstrated this important quality. We have tried to create in our men a real love for the game and a spirit of work, determination, and loyalty. Convincing a whole squad of players to become "one team," to forget any jealousies or animosities, cannot be done 15 minutes before game time. The coach must start getting the team ready in the off season.

This may appear corny to many, but we want emotion and enthusiasm. To impress the team with the importance of a particular game or all-out effort and self-sacrifice on their part, we make it a practice to post various slogans on the walls of the locker room. Most young people will accept challenges, and quite often, we will challenge them with slogans and posters.

The squad meetings throughout the week, particularly the one the night before the game, provide the best times for establishing a proper mental attitude for everyone.

We try to create an atmosphere of discipline and good humor. The coaching staff tries to subscribe to the old cliche, "firm, fair, and friendly." The office doors of our staff

FIGURE 17-8. A football player has to be inspired. There must be a challenge or a goal that pulls or drives him along. Above, Coach Allen talks to two of his defensive standouts, Ron McDole and Diron Talbert.

are always open to members of the team. If a coach is genuinely interested in his boys, they will know it and believe in him.

We try to have players respect each other and help each other. In other words a general feeling of mutual admiration and warmth is an important quality of a team. We have not always succeeded in this aspect but we have tried.

Each player deserves to be treated with equality and fairness and nothing will ruin a player's morale quicker than his feeling that he is not getting a fair chance.

We do not like to hear any excuses and alibis. If we lose, we lose. We do not want to complain about the breaks of the game, the officiating, and all that.

We urge our players to be highly aggressive, with a degree of meanness in them. A player should be determined to dominate his opponent. He must hit him with reckless abandon. This is why a wise coach will withhold judgment on a promising newcomer until he gets a taste of scrimmage, some hard contact. "Let's see what he does when he gets knocked down a few times," is the feeling of most coaches.

*If you don't hustle, you will not know how good you could have been.*

### Self-discipline

If he wants to win and play his best, a football player must discipline his life—lay off smoking, drinking, overeating, or anything that keeps him from doing his best.

To be mentally tough, an athlete must show a tremendous amount of self-discipline. He must never break the discipline of his mind. There have been athletes with great physical qualities, but they couldn't control their temper.

Football demands stern self-discipline. Each player must do the things he feels are the very best for the team. He must accept responsibility and carry out his assignment to the best of his ability. This conformity to rules and regulations, personal sacrifice, and individual discipline will be of great value to the individual throughout his life.

Outstanding athletes have the mental discipline to control their moods. "I'm not happy to lose," says Johnny Unitas. "Who would be? Sure, I'm upset. It happened, so forget it and go on to something else."

### It Takes Heart

It takes a lot of heart to continue playing football in the face of defeat. Some players are front runners and excel only when they are ahead. The real mark of a champion lies in his ability to come back—to come from behind.

If a player makes an error, he should hold his head high and not get down on himself. When the breaks are going against him, he must always maintain his poise.

He must STAY IN THERE and NEVER GIVE UP!

There are always pitfalls or obstacles along the way. Many athletes are made champions by setbacks. A setback often brings out the fighting spirit in an athlete.

### Courage

Football demands courage. A player must possess the courage to throw his body around with reckless abandon on the field of play. Every football team needs a leader who can go up to his teammates and say: "We can beat them!" This is the kind of willpower that can make champions, a will to conquer and to go to the top.

There has never been a great athlete who quit when he was beaten. An athlete must have a fighting spirit that will take him through difficulty and discouragement. He refuses to go down, but can bounce back to an even greater victory. Combined with his spirit, however, is his dedication and desire to perfect his skills, spending countless hours and hours of practice, always striving for perfection.

### Extra Effort

A man must be willing to put out just a little bit more. We expect each member of the Washington Redskins to contribute just a little more than his ability indicates. That is the true test of a champion. No matter what happens, if an athlete will do his level best, his coach cannot ask anything more.

### Clutch Player

The clutch player has an overpowering team spirit and prefers team victory rather than

*FIGURE 17-9. A great catch, such as this one by Jerry Smith, is the result of extra effort by a receiver, and is often the difference between winning and losing.*

personal glory. The player who sees defeat and victory in a proper perspective is cool under fire. This is one secret of relaxation.

Clutch players are scarce only because most athletes refuse to believe the clutch player possesses a combination of qualities that they could have if they were only willing to work for them.

## Inspiration

A football player has to be inspired. There must be a challenge, a goal, a person or something that pulls or drives him along. Without this powerful inner motivation, he will always remain a mediocre ball player.

Once a player gets a vision or an idea of what he can become, he will be on the right road. With disciplined training and hard work, and a strong will to win, he will have taken a giant step toward becoming a champion.

## Confidence

The great athletes have confidence in themselves, a will or positive attitude that says, "I know I can do it!" If an offensive receiver, for example, loses his confidence in catching a touchdown pass, he will never catch the ball. The only way to really build confidence is through practice, practice, and more practice. It doesn't come any other way.

*FIGURE 17-10. A big play like Jerry's diving grab can be a tremendous morale booster for the entire team, as evidenced by the enthusiastic reception he received from his teammates.*

### Competition

A good football player welcomes competition. Most people do not compete enough—they give up too easily. They never press on. If a player is to play to his true potential, he must be willing to put out just a little more. The willingness to put out a little more often makes the difference.

### Intelligence

All football today requires a considerable amount of intelligence—smartness, the ability to learn plays well and then apply this knowledge to the proper situation. A player must study hard, not only football knowledge but in the school classrooms as well.

So, an athlete must keep up his grades. He should remember that his primary interest is education and football is secondary. Besides, a college scholarship or a lucrative professional contract might be at stake. Players who let down in their studies are usually the ones who will let down in a game.

The Redskins have many big games because we had experienced men who could quickly understand a complicated game plan and execute it without error. The ability of a

FIGURE 17-11. *Before they leave for the field, many football squads have a team prayer. A coach or player may lead the team in the Lord's Prayer or they may observe a few moments of silent prayer. Here, Tom Skinner, the Redskins' chaplain, leads the team in a post-game prayer.*

player to "read" and anticipate and make exactly the right move is so important. The well-trained, experienced players do the right thing automatically.

## Loyalty

Loyalty is essential to a winning football team. The team player never says anything bad about his teammates or his coaches behind their backs. The team player never second-guesses the quarterback, a teammate, or a coach. Regarding the clubhouse, we urge all players to "Let what you hear there, see there, and say there . . . STAY THERE!"

We try to discourage arguments and hard feelings between team members. The Redskins have a feeling of love, pride, and respect for each other.

## Discipline

The discipline the Redskins' coaching staff tries to get revolves around four basic points:

1. Making players work hard without having to scream and yell at them
2. Making them stay at a certain weight
3. Making them prepare mentally at meetings
4. Making them be proud to be part of an organization

We do not believe in chewing out and getting on the players in front of the whole squad. There are not many people who enjoy being criticized in front of fifty or sixty people. It is much better to talk to them alone. Everybody should be treated as a human being.

So, we will not criticize them for a mistake they made while trying. The only mistakes that we will criticize are mistakes of omission or let down, allowing something to happen because they did not give 100 percent to prevent it from happening.

FIGURE 17-12. *Football players can be encouraged to give greater performance. Here, Coach Allen congratulates members of the Redskins' defensive unit. If they are going to fight for him, the coach must let them know he is willing to fight for them.*

I like to be rational with them and explain to them what the problem is. I make it clear that I will apply whatever punishment is necessary. However, the matter is strictly between the player and me. If disciplinary action is taken, no one else should have to know about it.

Generally, the players will determine the type of discipline and control. Coaches will be just as nice or just or tough as their players want or need them to be.

## Encouragement

Every coach has to be himself and not try to imitate someone else. However, I firmly believe a player can be encouraged to greater performance. The more athletes are en-

FIGURE 17-13. *With strong concentration, a football player can groove his mind and body in performing a skill. Concentration and relaxation go together, whether it is kicking a winning field goal or catching a touchdown pass. Above place-kicker Curt Knight and his holder Sonny Jurgensen have their eyes strictly on the ball.*

couraged, the more a coach will get out of them and the better they will play. Then, each player will have a better relationship with his teammates.

So, we do not "browbeat" our players or chastise them for their mistakes. Basically, these things are stored for the next time we get to talk to him, when we can lay it on the line with him. However, there are corrections made on pass patterns or other plays on the field, but these are helpful corrections. They are not intended as, nor do they have the effect of "browbeating."

### Pride

The great athletes have a tremendous desire to excel, the urge to be the best. They take pride in their play. They hurt when they lose. Too many athletes are satisfied with fair or good performances, when they could do better with more effort. An athlete should always be striving for perfection. He must never be content with mediocrity.

When a coach has players who have a real pride in being champions, his team will always be tough to beat. They will never fold. Their opponents will have to kill them inch by inch.

We want our players to think in terms of winning and championships. Any player who loses and is satisfied could never play for me.

### THE PSYCHOLOGICAL PROFILE OF A CHAMPION

While in training camp, we usually outline the "Psychological Profile of a Champion" and also the profile of an "Also-Ran." When things go wrong, we sometimes call in a player and mention one of these characteristics.

*ambition.* desire for high goals. Hates to lose. Cannot stand failure. Puts goals above ability.

*coachableness.* takes advice and is easy to coach. Eager to learn. Easy to approach. Follows rules and directions.

*aggression.* a tiger! First-place-belongs-to-me type. Asserts himself.

*leadership.* shows the way and sets a good example. Respected by team members. Mixes well. Others follow his example and take his advice.

*take-charge guy.* will take over when things go wrong. Under pressure, he does something about the problem. Often a hero.

*hard worker.* one of the first to practice—the last to leave. Does extra work. Never misses practice and follows instructions.

*physical toughness.* develops toughness by hard work. In great condition. Keeps training rules and trains year around.

*mental toughness.* never gives in to his feelings. Has never-give-up attitude. Ignores heat, cold, pain.

*psychological endurance.* stays with job until the end. Will do his best against top competition. High endurance all season. Reliable.

## PSYCHOLOGICAL PROFILE OF AN ALSO-RAN

*no drive.* does not care whether he wins or loses. Goes with the tide.

*know it all.* never listens and will not accept new ideas. Rebel, griper. Works by himself.

*mouse.* never talks back. High on self-abasement. Always kicking himself. Introvert, generally.

*follower.* will go with crowd and generally behind them. Never tries to lead.

*a watcher.* Joe Milktoast. If there is an accident, he watches or runs away. Worried about what people think.

*corner cutter.* ducks practice. Cuts out tough practice. Always has excuses. Lots of absences from practice.

*hypochondriac.* a muscle grabber—always has an injury. Never works out consistently.

*complainer.* gives up easily, and is easily distracted from the job at hand. Will look good when competition is not of high caliber and will look bad in the big game.

*quitter.* cannot stick to the end. Easily distracted. Starts many jobs, finishes few. Unreliable.

## HANDLING AND UNDERSTANDING PLAYERS

People have said that I have always been able to get the most out of my football players. If I have, one reason is that I try to

*FIGURE 17-14. Approval is a great motivator. Whenever possible, a coach should try to follow any criticism with a pat on the back. He cannot antagonize and influence at the same time. Above, Coach Allen congratulates quarterback Bill Kilmer for his outstanding play.*

take time to work individually with them. I listen to their problems. When a coach has the regular workload of preparing for a game, it is difficult to give that individual attention. But I try to do it. I believe a coach should be close to his players.

If everybody is different, athletes are more so, and when you have forty of them you have got problems. You have to find out what makes your players tick so you can get the most out of them.

Each person is an individual and what works with one might fail for another. I don't try to start motivating a player right away. If I

*The true athlete should have character, not be a character.*

**John Wooden**

don't know him well, I just talk to him and get his thinking on different things—on what he hopes to achieve, what he has done in the past, why he succeeded or did not succeed.

You can learn a lot just talking to a player. After that, I see what he does on the practice field, in meetings, and off the field.

Sometimes, just the way you talk to

*FIGURE 17-15. The love of competition. A major responsibility of every coach is to develop in his players a desire for competition. Above, a keyed-up team of Washington Redskins, led by their head coach, move enthusiastically onto the playing field.*

people can motivate them. But I don't have much patience with a player who won't study and prepare himself and make a few sacrifices. That player is not going to help us win a championship.

You don't have to yell at a player. You can tell him: "This is what you did on that play." I don't believe that a coach must rant and rave at players, bring tears to their faces, and send them out like wild animals. I just want to prepare my players to play football.

While we look upon college players today as young men because of their size, they are really still boys in maturity. The coach has to bend. They have to bend. When both bend within proper bounds, you become a solid unit.

## COPING WITH PROBLEMS

If you approach problems correctly, you can solve them all. I actually feel we were put on the earth to overcome problems. I don't think there are any I can't solve or that we cannot solve together. And I do not fear them.

You cannot let problems lick you because you are going to have them. Every day I run up to 3 miles and work out with weights. I do this just to offset all the problems that come up.

It seems that the more problems I have, the more setbacks, the more things stimulate me the other way, whereas some guys get down about the least little thing.

The toughest moments of coaching are the individual conferences with players going over their problems. Not football problems. It is the other worries, the type the coach has no control over, but if he does not solve them or help solve them, then that man is not going to produce well.

If a player has a problem, I think that is my problem. I want to know every detail about it and see if we cannot alleviate it so we can win.

## TALKS TO THE TEAM

I do not believe in the frenzy type of talks to the team. True, we want our players to be in the proper frame of mind to win an aggressive and inspired brand of football. We will go over things that we must accomplish that day.

I would not classify my remarks as being a pep talk, but we do try to instill in our players a strong desire to provide 110 percent effort. As I stated earlier, football is a game of emotions, a vigorous, highly competitive contact sport. An athlete must have the right frame of mind to make his natural ability work.

Rather than encourage my players to get out on the field and throw their bodies around with reckless abandon, I prefer telling them to be alert and to think on every play.

Many coaches do not make a speech before the game. They feel that it is each man's own individual problem to get himself "up" for the game. Still, there are those athletes who find difficulty in getting keyed up for a game. These are the players who make talks of inspiration and motivation necessary.

Of course, the actual mental conditioning starts on the first day of the week. If we cannot motivate a team during the practice week, then we will have trouble on Sunday.

After a big win, the coach will try to determine "How will I ever get them up again for next week?" The problem all week is to get his players up again—all of them—for next Saturday. To do this, he has to make his team believers.

FIGURE 17-16.   *While I do not consider my pre-game message as being a pep talk, we do try to instill in our players a strong desire to provide 110 percent effort.*

The following are sample talks of what a coach might present to his team:

### TALK 1:   Day Before the Game, Following Practice

"Okay, men. Let's keep off your feet today. You need a lot of rest . Get to bed by eleven. This is a big one! They are a solid contender—a real football team you'll be facing. You must do it! Everyone is interested in tomorrow's game. They say this is the game of the year. Now, let's show them what a fine team we have."

(Before the huddle breaks, all the players shout together and slap their hands together.)

### TALK 2:   Pre-Game Talk

"Men, this is a club that can really hit! They will be out there to hit you! So, if we are going to win, we will have to take it out of them. This means you have got to be forty mean tigers out there. You will have to hit and hit 'em hard ! You're gonna have to run. Block and tackle! Explode into your man! If you do that, I have no doubt about the outcome of this game.

"But you must keep your poise. Keep your poise! There will be nothing they can show you out there that you have not seen before. Let's go get 'em ! !"

## TALK 3:   Half-Time Talk To a Team Behind

"All right, fellows. We have made some mistakes out there, but that's all over. That's out of the way and done with. Let's remember that in spite of our mistakes, we are still in this ball game. Even though they have made no mistakes, we are still right on their necks. They will make some mistakes because we are going out on that field and force them!

"Defense, you know you can stop them! You fellows on the offense. You know you can move the ball against them. You men know you are the better team but up to now, we have been stopping ourselves. That's right, we have stopped ourselves. But that's over with! Now we go, men! Let's go out and nail them down inside the 20 on the kickoff, hold them and get that ball back. Let's go!"

## TALK 4:   Post-Game Talk (*Low key, with a look to next week's game*)

"All right, fellows! Let me have your attention. That was a fine effort out there today. That's the way to play this game, but you know as I do that they were not up for this game. But the team coming in here next week will be up. They will be coming in here to knock you on your tails. Remember that! Have some fun tonight and tomorrow, but come Monday, we will have to get down to work! What do you say?"

(Players shout together and slap their hands together.)

**FIGURE 17-17.** *After reviewing the achievements and mistakes of the first half, the head coach discusses at half time what has to be done in the second half. Then, he must provide the motivation for the team to return to the field with the proper mental attitude.*

*FIGURE 17-18. Team cheer. The head coach must be capable of building togetherness, a team feeling.*

Goals should be large enough, too. They should be within reach, but not within easy grasp.

We give all of our units goals to shoot for, something we know they can attain. We set up charts in the meeting room so the players can be reminded at all times of just what they are shooting for. For example, leading the NFL in interceptions was a big achievement to come off our 1971 defensive chart. I told the defensive unit if they intercepted two passes a game, they would be winners. That meant twenty-eight for the season and we had twenty-nine. We gave them something to shoot for and they proved to themselves they could do it.

Experience over the years will help the coach know what goals to set. We have done a complete study of how teams who won got to that point. For instance, if you hold your opponents under 200 points for the season, then you should win the title.

The key to a goal system is not to allow a team to forget what it is striving to achieve. I go over it with our team all the time so they won't forget. I try to make them aware of the goals constantly so they won't let down. When they walk into the meeting room, the players see those charts on the wall. They see what they must do, what they have already done, and how it has affected the outcome of each game.

If a team is to achieve its potential, each player should be willing to subordinate his personal goals for the good of the team.

### Signs

I like signs and other constant reminders. I like to get people to think. That is why I use constant reminders. I think you have to say things over and over again because you only get through to about 40 percent the first time. It doesn't bother me that those 40 percent have to listen to it maybe seven times. It is better for them to listen to it seven times and win than not to listen to it and lose.

### SETTING GOALS

I have always been a believer in setting goals. Everyone should set goals for himself, and as a football team, we set up a list of goals each year. Without goals, where does one head?

### STANDARDS OF ACHIEVEMENT

Through the years I have had my teams strive for standards of achievement. Generally, I try to have fifteen to twenty standards, which appear on a large board on the wall.

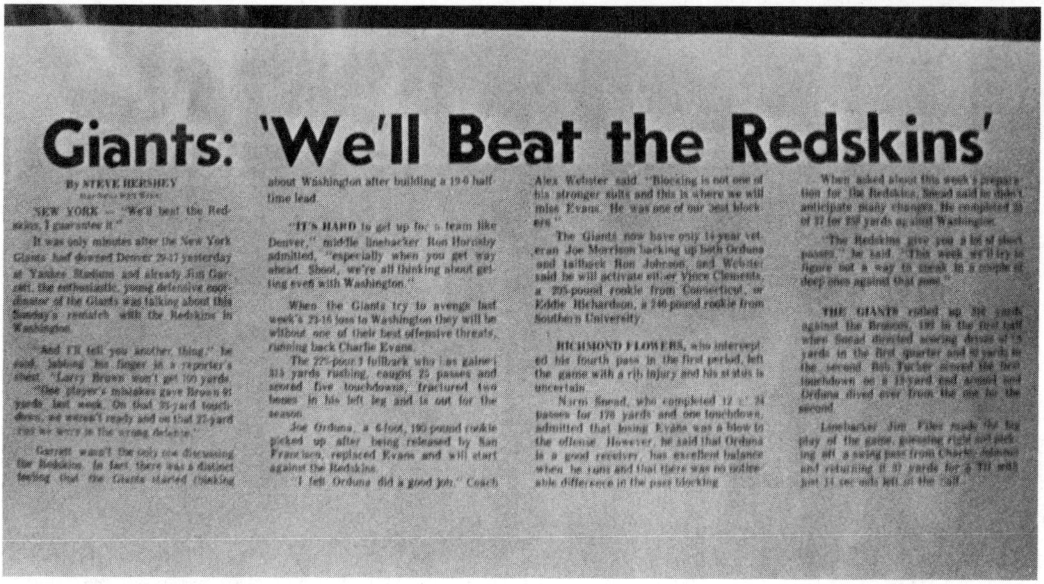

# Giants: 'We'll Beat the Redskins'

By STEVE HERSHEY

NEW YORK — "We'll beat the Redskins, I guarantee it."

It was only minutes after the New York Giants had downed Denver 29-17 yesterday at Yankee Stadium and already Jim Garrett, the enthusiastic, young defensive coordinator of the Giants was talking about this Sunday's rematch with the Redskins in Washington.

"And I'll tell you another thing," he said, jabbing his finger in a reporter's chest. "Larry Brown won't get 100 yards.

"One player's mistakes gave Brown 91 yards last week. On that 35-yard touchdown, we weren't ready and on that 27-yard [illegible] we were in the wrong defense."

Garrett wasn't the only one discussing the Redskins. In fact, there was a distinct feeling that the Giants started thinking about Washington after building a 19-0 halftime lead.

"IT'S HARD to get up for a team like Denver," middle linebacker Ron Hornsby admitted, "especially when you get way ahead. Shoot, we're all thinking about getting even with Washington."

When the Giants try to avenge last week's 23-16 loss to Washington they will be without one of their best offensive threats, running back Charlie Evans.

The 225-pound fullback who has gained 315 yards rushing, caught 25 passes and scored five touchdowns, fractured two bones in his left leg and is out for the season.

Joe Orduna, a 6-foot, 195-pound rookie picked up after being released by San Francisco, replaced Evans and will start against the Redskins.

"I felt Orduna did a good job," Coach Alex Webster said. "Blocking is not one of his stronger suits and this is where we will miss Evans. He was one of our best blockers."

The Giants now have only 14-year veteran Joe Morrison backing up both Orduna and tailback Ron Johnson, and Webster said he will activate either Vince Clements, a 205-pound rookie from Connecticut, or Eddie Richardson, a 246-pound rookie from Southern University.

RICHMOND FLOWERS, who intercepted his fourth pass in the first period, left the game with a rib injury and his status is uncertain.

Norm Snead, who completed 12 of 24 passes for 170 yards and one touchdown, admitted that losing Evans was a blow to the offense. However, he said that Orduna is a good receiver, has excellent balance when he runs and that there was no noticeable difference in the pass blocking.

When asked about this week's preparation for the Redskins, Snead said he didn't anticipate many changes. He completed 20 of 27 for 232 yards against Washington.

"The Redskins give you a lot of short passes," he said. "This week we'll try to figure out a way to sneak in a couple of deep ones against that zone."

THE GIANTS rolled up 3[illegible] yards against the Broncos, 19[illegible] in the first half when Snead directed scoring drives of [illegible] yards in the first quarter and [illegible] yards in the second. Bob Tucker scored the first touchdown on a 13-yard end around and Orduna dived over from the one for the second.

Linebacker Jim Files made the big play of the game, guessing right and picking off a swing pass from Charley Johnson and returning it 37 yards for a TD with just 31 seconds left in the half.

*FIGURE 17-19. Using newspaper clippings on a bulletin board to "psych" players can be a useful and effective psychological gimmick.*

For example, our defense will try to hold the other team to 250 or 300 total yards in a game. The offense will be challenged to complete 50 percent of their passes.

From game to game, the figures achieved are entered next to the ideal standard.

## METHODS OF MOTIVATION

There are numerous methods and techniques used by college and high school coaches to motivate players to greater performances and achievement.

Following each game, many teams choose a Blocker of the Week and post the player's picture on the bulletin board. The same accolades go to the Hitter of the Week. A hit is scored when one of the defenders records a hard enough blow with his shoulder to jolt an offensive man hard enough to show in the film. Blows delivered by the forearm or helmet are forbidden.

All teams keep a record of the number of individual and assisted tackles each player executes. In addition, players look forward to some form of grading system with emphasis on achievement.

A number of college teams like Ohio State and Michigan use the "Star" approach, in which stars are pasted on the helmet to denote outstanding achievements.

### Slogans

An effective way to motivate a football team is the use of slogans. We have found them to be of significant value in emphasizing various points in our training and organization.

FIGURE 17-20. *A little extra effort can make the difference.*

The following slogans have appeared on the Redskins' dressing room walls:

- There is no detail that is too small.
- Never take anything for granted.
- If you are not in shape, the problems will lick you.
- You will play on Saturday the way you practice during the week.
- Every day you waste is one you can never make up.
- One must accomplish to live.
- The world belongs to those who aim for 110 percent.
- Is what I am doing or about to do getting us closer to our objective—winning?
- Make things happen, instead of being forced to react to things after they happen.
- The name of the game is KNOCK!
- A winner never quits; a quitter never wins!
- If you knock the other team down more times than they do you, *you win!*

FIGURE 17-21. *To impress the team with the importance of all-out effort and self-sacrifice, slogan signs like these can be placed on the walls of the locker room.*

# 1974 REDSKINS GOAL
### ...TO BETTER LAST YEARS PERFORMANCE

| 1971 WON 9 LOST 4 TIED 1 | | | 1972 WON 11 LOST 3 TIED 0 | | | 1973 WON 10 LOST 4 TIED 0 | | | 1974 WON LOST TIED | | |
|---|---|---|---|---|---|---|---|---|---|---|---|
| 24 | CARDINALS | 17 | 24 | VIKINGS | 21 | 38 | CHARGERS | 0 | | GIANTS | |
| 30 | GIANTS | 3 | 24 | CARDINALS | 10 | 27 | CARDINALS | 34 | | CARDINALS | |
| 20 | COWBOYS | 16 | 23 | PATROITS | 24 | 28 | EAGLES | 7 | | BRONCOS | |
| 22 | OILERS | 13 | 14 | EAGLES | 0 | 14 | COWBOYS | 7 | | BENGALS | |
| 20 | CARDINALS | 0 | 33 | CARDINALS | 3 | 21 | GIANTS | 3 | | DOLPHINS | |
| 20 | CHIEFS | 27 | 24 | COWBOYS | 20 | 31 | CARDINALS | 13 | | GIANTS | |
| 24 | SAINTS | 14 | 23 | GIANTS | 16 | 3 | SAINTS | 19 | | CARDINALS | |
| 7 | EAGLES | 7 | 35 | JETS | 17 | 16 | STEELERS | 21 | | PACKERS | |
| 15 | BEARS | 16 | 27 | GIANTS | 13 | 33 | 49'ers | 9 | | EAGLES | |
| 0 | COWBOYS | 13 | 24 | FALCONS | 13 | 22 | COLTS | 14 | | COWBOYS | |
| 20 | EAGLES | 13 | 21 | PACKERS | 16 | 20 | LIONS | 0 | | EAGLES | |
| 23 | GIANTS | 7 | 23 | EAGLES | 7 | 27 | GIANTS | 24 | | COWBOYS | |
| 38 | RAMS | 24 | 24 | COWBOYS | 34 | 7 | COWBOYS | 27 | | RAMS | |
| 13 | BROWNS | 20 | 17 | BILLS | 24 | 38 | EAGLES | 20 | | BEARS | |

**1971** EASTERN DIVISION PLAYOFF
20    49'ers    24

**1972** EASTERN DIVISION PLAYOFF
16    PACKERS    3
NFC CHAMPIONSHIP GAME
26    COWBOYS    3
SUPERBOWL VII
7    DOLPHINS    14

**1973** EASTERN DIVISION PLAYOFF
20    VIKINGS    27

FIGURE 17-22. *Setting team goals is important. Aided by this visual display, which appears on the locker room wall, the Redskins strive to better last year's performance.*

- To play this game, you have to be smart, not a smart aleck.
- Be a champion on *and* off the field!
- Always pursue! Always gang tackle! Always be coming on!
- Keep your poise at all times.
- Keep your chin off your chest after you have made an error.
- What it all comes down to is how bad you want something.

## The Psychological Approach

To get the most from his players, the football coach should use the psychological approach whenever possible. He must try to get them "up," to get boys to play with emotion, heart, desire, and determination. Tradition and pride can be key factors in turning out championship football teams.

Effective techniques for psychological motivation could include the following:

1. Dedicate games to a special cause.
2. Change routine—have fun!
3. "Point" for an opponent.
4. Challenge the players.
5. Develop the art of needling.
6. Deflate the star.

# Appendix

## OVERALL ACCOMPLISHMENTS OF RAMS (1966–1970)

- Best 1-year record as Ram coach
- Best 5-year Ram record
- Best road record over 5-year period in history of NFL: 26 wins, 7 losses, 2 ties (4 losses in 1966 were in a rebuilding year).

## OVERALL ACCOMPLISHMENTS OF THE REDSKINS (1971–1974)

- Four-year record: 40 wins, 15 losses, 1 tie. Winning percentage of 0.723.
- First Redskins team in 38-year history to participate in play-offs 4 consecutive years.
- First time since 1945 the Redskins have had 4 straight winning seasons.
- Lost only 4 games in 4 years at home. Lost only 1 before play-off berth was clinched.
- Coach Allen's record of 40–15–1 is the best 4-year record of any Redskin coach.

*THE REAL MEASURE OF DEFENSE* is the number of points scored by opponents.

**CHART A.** *League standing at end of season for George Allen's teams.*

| Team | Year | Division Rank | Conference Rank |
|------|------|---------------|-----------------|
| Los Angeles | 1966 | 2 | 2 |
| Los Angeles | 1967 | 1 | 1 |
| Los Angeles | 1968 | 2 | 2 |
| Los Angeles | 1969 | 1 | 4 |
| Los Angeles | 1970 | 1 | 2 |
| Washington | 1971 | 1 | 2 |
| Washington | 1972 | 1 | 1 |
| Washington | 1973 | 1 | 3 |
| Washington | 1974 | 1 | 3 |

**CHART B.** *George Allen's pro record as head coach.*

| Team | Year | Won | Lost | Tied | Division Finish |
|------|------|-----|------|------|-----------------|
| Los Angeles | 1966 | 8 | 6 | 0 | Third |
| Los Angeles | 1967 | 11 | 1 | 2 | First |
| Los Angeles | 1968 | 10 | 3 | 1 | Second |
| Los Angeles | 1969 | 11 | 3 | 0 | First |
| Los Angeles | 1970 | 9 | 4 | 1 | Second |
| Washington | 1971 | 9 | 4 | 1 | Second |
| Washington | 1972 | 11 | 3 | 0 | First |
| Washington | 1973 | 10 | 4 | 0 | First (tie with Dallas) |
| Washington | 1974 | 10 | 4 | 0 | First (tie with St. Louis) |

**CHART C.** *Attendance totals of the Rams.*

| Year | Games | Attendance | Average Home Games (7) |
|------|-------|------------|------------------------|
| 1966 | 19 | 917,838 | 48,090 |
| 1967 | 22 | 1,230,059 | 60,173 |
| 1968 | 20 | 1,154,659 | 65,127 |
| 1969 | 22 | 1,307,883* | 71,242 |
| 1970 | 20 | 1,247,970 | 71,351* |

**CHART D.** *Attendance totals of the Redskins.*

| Year | Games | Attendance | Average Home Games (7) |
|------|-------|------------|------------------------|
| 1971 | 21 | 1,123,376 | 53,041 |
| 1972 | 23 | 1,266,847 | 53,039 |
| 1973 | 21 | 1,157,044 | 53,202 |
| 1974 | 21 | 1,064,559 | 50,693 |

* Were all-time records at that time.

# *Index*